WORDS WELL PUT

Visions of Poetic Competence in the

Chinese Tradition

Harvard-Yenching Institute Monographs Series 60

Words Well Put

Visions of Poetic Competence in the Chinese Tradition

Graham Sanders

Published by the Harvard University Asia Center
for the Harvard-Yenching Institute and
distributed by Harvard University Press
Cambridge (Massachusetts) and London, 2006

Printed in the United States of America

The Harvard-Yenching Institute, founded in 1928 and headquartered at Harvard University, is a foundation dedicated to the advancement of higher education in the humanities and social sciences in East and Southeast Asia. The Institute supports advanced research at Harvard by faculty members of certain Asian universities and doctoral studies at Harvard and other universities by junior faculty at the same universities. It also supports East Asian studies at Harvard through contributions to the Harvard-Yenching Library and publication of the *Harvard Journal of Asiatic Studies* and books on premodern East Asian history and literature.

Library of Congress Cataloging-in-Publication Data
Sanders, Graham Martin.
Words well put : visions of poetic competence in the Chinese tradition / Graham Sanders.
  p. cm. – (Harvard-Yenching Institute monograph series ; 60)
Includes bibliographical references and index.
ISBN 0-674-02140-1 (alk. paper)
1. Chinese poetry--History and criticism. I. Title. II. Series.
PL2307.S34 2006
895.1'1009--dc22

2005029569

Index by Jake Kawatski

⊗   Printed on acid-free paper

Last number below indicates year of this printing

16 15 14 13 12 11 10 09 08 07 06

For Chia Chia

for everything

Contents

	Introduction	I
1	Performing the Tradition	15
2	Baring the Soul	73
3	Playing the Game	111
4	Gleaning the Heart	157
5	Placing the Poem	203
	Conclusion	279
	Appendix	285
	Works Cited	293
	Index	301

Words Well Put

Visions of Poetic Competence in the

Chinese Tradition

Introduction

October 19, 2000. I was walking to my office at the University of Toronto on a cloudy morning. I had just turned the corner from London Street onto Bathurst Street, and there, across from the subway station, was a red mailbox that I had passed a thousand times before. The side of it was encrusted with advertisements, posters, stickers, graffiti—but one message, carefully printed in black ink on a white nametag (the kind that says, "Hello, my name is . . ."), caught my eye. It read:

You were what you said; you are what is in your head.

It struck me as significant, as somehow true. I filed it away in my memory with the thought that I might use it as the epigraph for a book someday.

I

Before I can even begin to discuss the notion of poetic competence in the Chinese tradition, I must consider the status of the surviving premodern texts that contain descriptions of poems being composed, performed, and received. When faced with thousands upon thousands of books resting silently upon shelves, it is often easy to forget that every text in those books comes from the hand of a human being. And a good number of premodern Chinese texts were transmitted with the mouth before they were set down by hand. It is not always possible to identify a point of origin for a text—a particular act of production (oral or written) by a particular person at a particular time. Many texts seem to have emerged over time, among groups of people, large and small. Some texts may have had an initial point of production, but have mutated through centuries of re-production. They come down to us by way of breath, bone, bronze, stone, bamboo, silk, and paper, jumping from one medium to an-other, evolving in their journey, spawning variants, interpolations, excisions, and paraphrases. However these texts may have ended up between the covers of books, they are certainly marked by their journey outside those covers. They are all traces of a larger realm that may be called discourse, which I define as the entire range of verbal practices through which human beings articulate themselves to others in specific contexts. A particular instance of discourse may be called an utterance. Thus a text is the trace of an oral or written utterance that endures beyond its original context, a context that, once past, can only ever be postulated rather than known. Discourse is experienced in the context of the moment; once the moment has passed, only its traces remain.

Discourse, as the etymology of the word suggests, is a "run-ning away" (*discurrere*) from the human subject. Each utterance—whether it be made in speech or writing—moves beyond the control of the person who produced it once it is received by others. It was never completely under the control of the producing subject in the first place, for he or she is always-already conditioned to produce certain types of discourse in certain situations—conditioned by the social position he or she occupies, conditioned by the web of past texts and current discourse that already defines that position. One can understand each surviving text as the trace of a speaking sub-ject's attempt to negotiate his or her position in relation to others, and in relation to the entire complex of discourse that defines those positions. Every text is the trace of a performance, an act of a dis-coursed subject discoursing.

Once a text is understood as the trace of a performance, it be-comes imperative to establish the context of that performance. Any given context is actually made up of a nested series of osmotic contexts. The immediate context of an utterance includes the cir-cumstances of its production and reception: who was present, where the parties were located, when the utterance was made, when it was received, what events recently occurred, and what possible outcomes hang in the balance. The significance of these variables is conditioned by the social context of the utterance, which defines the positions occupied by the producer and receiver and the milieu in which they move. The social context is in turn temporally shaped by a historical context; thus, positions must be understood diachronically in their development as well as synchronically in their relationships. These contexts simultaneously give rise to and are encompassed by a cultural context that determines what can and cannot be said in a given realm of discourse, depending on received ideas of what is appropriate to various positions in society.

Any attempt to delineate the immediate, social, historical, and cultural contexts of an utterance is really an attempt to arrest an instance of discourse, to keep it from "running away" long enough that it may be fully appreciated. Such an arrest is made in name only, however, because of the simple fact that every past context is itself accessible only through texts. Our understanding of premodern China is no exception—only through an understanding derived from texts do any surviving extratextual material artifacts or locations gain their significance. Objects cannot speak fully by themselves in a culture so persistently and pervasively defined by texts as China's. Witness the Chinese obsession with inscribing material objects—bones, shells, stelae, cauldrons, bells, mirrors, fans, lutes, paintings, walls, bodies, cliffs, textiles—there is scarcely a type of object that has not been inscribed, woven, carved, branded, or otherwise marked by signs. The entire realm of discourse that was premodern China—every instance of discourse that left its trace as a text, every context that now persists as a trace of discourse—appears to us as would the jewel net of Indra, with each text reflecting and being reflected by every other text. The task of the critic—one task at least—is to attempt to uncover the speaking subject implied in a given text. A careful assessment of the multivalent contexts of an utterance implied in a text—the persistent trace of a discursive performance—can reveal the desires and anxieties of the speaking/writing subject who made the utterance. But what is the status of the subject thus revealed?

In the second chapter of the *Zhuangzi* 莊子, "Discourse on Considering All Things as Equal" 齊物論, it is written:

The one who dreams of drinking wine may cry and weep when morning comes; the one who dreams of crying and weeping may set out on a hunt when morning comes. When they were dreaming, they did not know that they were dreaming. In the midst of a dream, one may even interpret a dream within the dream and only realize that it was all a dream upon waking. And so only after a Great Awakening will we know that this too is all a Great Dream. It is a fool who claims that he is already awake and is self-assured in this knowledge. He fancies himself a lord or just a shepherd? Such pigheadedness! Confucius himself is and you too are both dreaming. And when I tell you that you are dreaming—that too is a dream.

夢飲酒者。旦而哭泣。夢哭泣者。旦而田獵。方其夢也。不知其夢也。夢之中又占其夢焉。覺而後知其夢也。且有大覺而後知此其大夢也。而愚者自以爲覺。竊竊然知之。君乎。牧乎。固哉。丘也與女。皆夢也。予謂女夢。亦夢也。[1]

The speaking subject in this passage admits that his discourse, his "telling you," is just as unsubstantiated as his claim that our entire reality is unsubstantiated. His admission is a deft rhetorical move that serves to strengthen his argument by acting as its own case in point. There can be no Great Awakening for the critical project. It will always be interpreting a dream within a dream. The speaking subject of an utterance and the critic's attempt to discover that subject may be nothing more than the convergence of a mass of texts, but this should not mitigate the value of the discovery. For how people construct and portray themselves as speaking subjects—how they dream—is worth knowing.

II

Texts in the Chinese tradition are rarely lonely. On their journey to the reading present, they often pick up fellow travelers in the form of prefaces, colophons, commentaries, annotations, anecdotes, companion pieces, and a host of other texts that are in a *transtextual* relationship with the core text.[2] The poem (*shi* 詩) seems to be more

---

1. Wang Xianqian 王先謙, *Zhuangzi jijie* 莊子集解, pp. 24–25. Translations from Chinese are my own unless otherwise noted.

2. Gérard Genette defines *transtextuality* as "everything which puts the text in explicit or implicit relationship with other texts" (*Palimpsestes*, 7). He has identified

gregarious than most texts in this respect. It usually travels with a title, at the very least, and often picks up a preface and a commentary somewhere along the way. It tends to travel in packs, grouped together with other poems of the same provenance, theme, form, or some other characteristic held in common. Occasionally, a poem or a portion of a poem will hitch a ride inside another text—a speech, essay, or narrative of some kind. It is this last mode of travel—a poem being borne by a narrative—that is the subject of this book.

The act of narrating (*narration*) produces a narrative text (*récit*) that tells a story (*histoire*).[3] Thus a narrative is the textual trace of a particular act of uttering a narrative. The story told by that narrative might recount characters uttering their own utterances, including poems. The poem-bearing narrative (especially a narrative in the classical language of histories, biographies, and anecdotal collections) subordinates the poem to the narrative, relegating the production (or reproduction through citation) of the poem to the status of an event in the story.[4] In other words, the narrative is told by the voice of a narrator, who relates a story in which characters appear and in turn speak in their own voices through discourse, poetic and otherwise. Such a narrative holds out the hope of recovering, to some degree, the multivalent contexts of a poetic utterance.

---

five such relationships: (1) *intertextuality*—the presence of one text within another (citation, allusion); (2) *paratextuality*—auxiliary texts that frame a main text (*peritexts*, such as the title, preface, or footnotes, appear in the same volume, and *epitexts*, such as conversations or correspondence, appear outside the main text); (3) *metatextuality*—commentary on a text, such as literary criticism; (4) *hypertextuality*—transformation of a *hypotext* into a new form (translation, parody, versification, etc.); and (5) *architextuality*—the power of genre to determine and classify the nature of texts. A useful summary of this taxonomy is Barbara Havercroft's article in Makaryk, *Encyclopedia of Contemporary Literary Theory*, p. 335.

3. Genette develops the full ramifications of this tripartite relationship throughout *Narrative Discourse* and *Narrative Discourse Revisited*.

4. The alternative to this subordinate relationship is a coordinate one: the use of poetic discourse by the narrator rather than by characters in the story depicted by the narrative. This appears most frequently in vernacular stories and novels because of their tendency to mimic the form of oral storytelling performance, in which spoken narrative and chanted or sung poetry (often with musical accompaniment) are alternately used to relate a story to the audience.

"Poetic competence" is the term I use to designate the ability of a person to deploy poetic discourse as a means of affecting the attitude and behavior of another person in order to achieve a desired end. Such competence can only be immediately apprehended in the context of a narrative, where the conditions of a poem's production and the effects of its reception can be ascertained. The motivation for producing poem-bearing narratives, however, was to provide ideal examples of the operation of poetry, not faithful records of it. They cannot be used as a reliable basis for reconstructing how poetry *really* was performed and received in ancient China; the only historical fact that we can be sure of is that these narratives were written down at some point. The stories they narrate are surely a mixture of what happened, what might have happened, and what should have happened. The goal in this book is not to systematically establish the social conditions of poetic production and reception, but to delineate the evolving concept of what a poem is and the changing idea of what one might *plausibly* achieve through poetic performance. Such stories fulfill and deny wishes for poetry and the self—it is these wishes that merit our careful attention.

The housing of a poetic utterance within a narrative produces a nested relationship with a poem at its center, which is diagrammed in Figure 1 in the Appendix. At this point, I will beg the reader's patience while I lay down some of the theoretical groundwork needed to build a rigorous analysis of the complex relationship that arises between a poem and the narrative that houses it. The terminology and concepts I discuss explicitly in the following paragraphs inform the analysis of poetic competence in the rest of the book, where I have tried to keep them implicit as much as possible.

The text of a poem in a narrative is the enduring trace of a particular spoken or written utterance, which bears the traces of the circumstances of its being uttered.[5] The act of uttering a poem,

---

5. The distinction between the act of uttering (*énonciation*), the utterance (*énoncé*), and the traces of the former found in the latter is developed by Emile Benveniste in both volumes of his *Problèmes de linguistique générale*. Benveniste characterizes the *énoncé* as the oral utterance or written text produced by each act of *énonciation*. I prefer to reserve the term "text" to indicate the fixed pattern of words that persists in the memory or on the page after a particular act of uttering.

which may be called a performance, is in turn represented by the text of a narrative. The performance of a poem is a moment of practicing discourse—it is experienced over a brief span of time and can never be fully recuperated. The contours of a performance are implied by the utterance it produces (preserved as the poetic text) and described by the utterance that houses it (preserved as the narrative text). Clear understanding of the poetic text and its implied performance can only be derived from knowledge of the position occupied by the speaking subject and the immediate context of the performance, the kind of knowledge conveyed by the narrative text. In short, the poetic text opens up questions (who? where? when? why? how? what?); the narrative text attempts to resolve those questions with answers.

The narrative text is itself the trace of an act of uttering by a narrator, who, as a speaking subject, is the construction of an author or authors who utter the narrator into existence. Access to the circumstances of production of the narrative text—the narrating—is gained through explicit intrusion of the narratorial voice into the narrative, which frequently occurs at the point of closure in Chinese narratives. Access to the author's construction of the narrator is gained through *paratexts*, such as prefaces, colophons (peritexts), and external texts that mention the narrative text in question (epitexts). The number of paratexts that may associate themselves with a given text is open-ended, as is indicated in figure 1 by the broken line that forms the outermost boundary.

The story that is told by the narrative describes the contours of the poetic utterance depicted as an event within the story. From the story, one can gain a sense of the poetic utterance as (1) a *locutionary* act, the fashioning of an utterance to articulate something to someone; (2) an *illocutionary* act, the attempt to achieve something through an utterance; and (3) a *perlocutionary* act, which comprises the results of the utterance when it is received, which results may or

---

Such a text can then be uttered again to form a new utterance, which may or may not persist in itself as a text. There are really two types of "trace": (1) the trace that is the persistent text of a particular utterance made at a particular moment, and (2) the traces of the circumstances of the act of uttering that are found in an utterance.

may not coincide with what was intended in the illocutionary act.[6] Poetic competence can be succinctly defined as the ability to utter a poem as a locutionary act with enough illocutionary force to bring about the desired perlocutionary effects. The "acts" and the "effects" need not be tangible; they might be as ineffectual in concrete terms as venting one's frustrations to generate sympathy in a listener.

Finally, three transcontextual forces shoot through the whole complex of nested contexts that appears in figure 1. The first is *intertextuality*, which acknowledges that the boundaries between contexts are permeable, that a poetic text may call forth a certain narrative text to satisfy its urgent questions (or that a narrative may tell a story that reaches a point of such emotional intensity that a poetic utterance is inevitable), that an utterance at one level can effect the uttering at another, and that utterances can migrate and commingle. No single level of utterance is completely definitive and no single level of uttering is completely determinative. There is always another context for every context; even if one proceeds directly to the center of the diagram, to the poetic utterance itself, it too may be construed as a context—the surrounding words—of the speaking subject, which can only be known through the shape of the words that emanate from it.

The second transcontextual force is *discourse*, which simply acknowledges that all of the acts of uttering, the utterances made, and the texts produced exist in time. Any two-dimensional diagram of a practice that takes place over time immediately falls prey to the synoptic illusion that results when practices such as discourse are treated as though they can be frozen and analyzed in a state of suspended animation.[7] When dealing with a collection of narrative texts, one is dealing with the textual traces of a set of practices that are irrevocably past. The texts themselves may be static, but a con-

---

6. These three terms were developed by J. L. Austin in *How to Do Things with Words*, which took up the work of John R. Searle and galvanized the entire branch of critical theory known as speech act theory. The model of speech act theory is too limited in itself—particularly in its analysis of power—to comprise all of the facets of poetic competence that will emerge in this book, but it does provide a useful point of departure.

7. See Bourdieu, *The Logic of Practice*, pp. 10–11.

sideration of time and of space—of interval (*jian* 間)—must be re-inserted into an analysis of the practices implied by texts.

The third transcontextual force is *power*, which acknowledges that all stories are told by people who wield varying amounts of social power. It is obvious that a narrative is merely a representation of reality, but it should also be kept in mind that it is a biased representation fashioned to serve the needs and desires of the person or people who generated and transmitted the narrative.

Why is this theoretical framework necessary in order to better understand poetry? To enjoy a poem in a pristine textual state, stripped of its paratexts and narrative context, is to resurrect but a small portion of the person who uttered it—at a particular place and time, to a particular audience, under a particular set of circumstances.[8] While the poem itself may yet shine brightly in our minds, the rest of these particulars persist as a faint corona of implications to be cross-checked, verified, surmised through other sources, or simply filled in with equal parts intuition and imagination. The poem-bearing narrative provides a way to reinsert a poem into its living context, or, more accurately, into a representation of its living context. In the simulacrum of reality forged by such narratives, an ancient poem may be revivified as a vital mode of discourse with affective and suasive power, as a means of exchanging thoughts and feelings between people in the *same* place and time. The people, the world they inhabited—these are lost to us forever. But the fully rounded articulation of one person's interior to another—this can live again through the power of a narrative, through its ability to represent a world, its people, and their words.

Such a narrative carries within it the representation of the immediate context of a poetic utterance: the circumstances of its production and reception. It gives an indication of its social context: the relative status of the parties involved and the nature of the arena

---

8. There is poetry, especially poetry explicitly marked as non-occasional, that is uttered for a more general or diffuse audience, but this rules out neither a specific audience for the uttering of such a poem, nor the ability of a poet to have both a specific and general audience in mind simultaneously. There is also poetry that explicitly denies concern for an audience (certain poems by Tao Qian, Li Bai, Bai Juyi, and others), but such a denial only has force when made to an audience.

in which they discourse. When the narrative is part of a larger col-
lection of narratives that spans decades or centuries, the historical
context for the poetic utterance begins to emerge, and one can begin
to ascertain the changes that take place in attitudes toward poetic
practice over time. When that collection holds a preeminent place
in the textual legacy of a group of people, it expresses and gives
shape to the cultural context of the utterances represented within
it. Such a collection plays a role in determining what is sayable, who
may say it, and how it is said. Such culturally influential collections
are the source of the poem-bearing narratives that are the quarry of
this book.

III

This book takes four compilations of narrative texts as its case stud-
ies in poetic competence: the *Zuo Tradition* 左傳, the *Han History*
漢書, *Topical Tales: A New Edition* 世說新語, and *Storied Poems*
本事詩. Each compilation was fashioned for very different reasons,
but they all include narratives that depict poetic performance and
reception. They also share a similar composition in that each was
compiled from other sources spanning centuries, rather than being
written from beginning to end by a single author during his own
lifetime. This makes them useful cross-sections (albeit highly medi-
ated ones) of entire eras: the Eastern Zhou (770–256 B.C.E), Western
Han (206 B.C.E.–23 C.E.), Six Dynasties (265–589), and Tang (618–906),
respectively. Each of these collections was highly influential and, in
providing exemplars of poetic competence, surely shaped how sub-
sequent poetic practice was performed and depicted. The first three
books have been well studied for centuries, and I do not presume
to offer any new information on their composition; my goal is to
provide a new view of their contents pertaining to poetic perfor-
mance. The last book, *Storied Poems*, is less well known, and in ad-
dition to my analysis of its entries from the point of view of poetic
competence, I do provide an extended discussion of the history and
composition of the text, as well as copious translations (see Table 2
in the Appendix).

     Chapter 1, "Performing the Tradition," addresses the narratives
of the *Zuo Tradition*, which cover the period 722–468 B.C.E. and

were compiled by court historians from a larger body of lore (oral and written) about the conduct and speech of the different states of the Eastern Zhou era. These narratives depict the Traditionalist 儒家 advisors at the courts of these various states as refining a set of practices through which they demonstrate their mastery of the emerging canon of *Poems* 詩 as source material for performance through intoning or singing ("offering a poem" 賦詩) and quotation in speechmaking ("citing a poem" 引詩). The poetic competence they develop is part of a wider cultural competence deployed to ensure their place as advisors in the political hierarchy of the early Chinese courts. These narratives repeatedly show that a judicious use of poetic discourse can help one influence the thinking and behavior of a superior, and that the reputation of oneself and one's kingdom can be enhanced or diminished by how well one reproduces and receives the *Poems*. The primacy of the *Zuo Tradition* in China's narrative tradition establishes an enduring object lesson about poetry: words from the past, well put in the present, constitute a stake in the future.

Chapter 2, "Baring the Soul," deals with the biographical narratives found in the *Han History* compiled by Ban Gu 班固 (32–92 C.E.), many of which were derived from the *Historical Records* 史記 compiled by Sima Qian 司馬遷 (ca. 145–85 B.C.E.). In narrating the history of the Former Han dynasty (206 B.C.E.–23 C.E.), these narratives include songs that were putatively improvised by members of the Han royal house under circumstances of distress. The narratives conform to a model of literary production that Sima Qian calls "venting frustration" 發憤, in which people who are powerless to carry out their ambitions turn to literary expression as a means of compensating for their impotence. This marks a shift from the pre-Qin model found in the *Zuo Tradition* of citing the inherited words of the *Poems* in a premeditated fashion, to the production of original poetry as a result of spontaneous outbursts in song form. With this shift from the use of inherited words to the production of new words comes an attendant loss in suasive power. None of the poetic utterances in the *Han History* seems to accomplish anything of immediate value for the people who perform them. In the hands of the historians who fashioned these narratives, however, the poetic outburst becomes an effective way to capture the interior qualities of men and women who have been defeated but deserve a last word. Under this model, poetic competence shifts from adept use of old words to the heartfelt expression of new words and their subsequent insertion into biographical narratives, where they will exert an enduring power in shaping posterity.

Chapter 3, "Playing the Game," takes up the anecdotal narratives found in *Topical Tales: A New Edition*, which were compiled under the auspices of Liu Yiqing 劉義慶 (403–444), a prince of the Liu Song dynasty (420–479)—one of the Six Dynasties that followed one another during the extended time of disunion that followed the collapse of the Han dynasty. These narratives, spanning the two centuries from the fall of the Han to the time of Liu Yiqing, demonstrate a subtle combination of the two models of poetic competence outlined above. The characters depicted within are equally adept at quoting old poetry, quoting contemporary poetry, and improvising new poetry. This more sophisticated notion of poetic competence plays itself out on a much smaller stage. The conflicts between individuals depicted in *Topical Tales* concern stakes of far less moment than entire states or imperial rule, as is the case in the *Zuo Tradition* and the *Han History*. The goal of the participants in the cultural milieu depicted in *Topical Tales* is to build and maintain one's reputation for being a cultured man (or woman, or even child). The physical violence inherent in the struggle for kingdom or empire recedes into the background of these narratives (with occasional eruptions) and is replaced by a contest of wits, a significant part of which is a facility in quoting and composing poetry in an impromptu manner. Poetic competence is portrayed as a polite art, the goal of which is often nothing more than to decisively demonstrate one's competence.

Chapter 4, "Gleaning the Heart," departs in approach from the previous three chapters by examining the preface to a Tang dynasty compilation of anecdotes about poetry, known as *Storied Poems* (literally "poems based in events" 本事詩) by Meng Qi 孟棨 (fl. 841–886). The preface is dated 886, placing the compilation near the end of the Tang era, but it includes anecdotes that not only stretch back across the entire history of the dynasty but in some cases even predate it. As a paratext for the entire work, the preface explicitly discusses Meng Qi's motivations and methodology for compiling a collection of anecdotes exclusively about poetic production and reception, the first such collection of its kind. In his brief essay, Meng Qi constructs a model of poetic production and reception heavily indebted to the theory of passionate outburst and response outlined in the "Great Preface" 大序 to the *Poetry Classic* 詩經, a model demonstrated in the biographical narratives of the *Han History*. Meng Qi states that texts depicting poetic expression abound, "but instances in them of being moved to intone a poem by encountering events are what really cause one's emotions to well up. If these instances are not manifested, then who will comprehend their significance?" Meng Qi claims to be gleaning those very examples of poetic expression that show poetry in its purest form.

The preface as a genre lends itself to certain rhetorical gestures establishing a legitimate position for its accompanying text in the web of discourse that it engages. The contents of Meng Qi's collection often deviate in fascinating ways from the position of legitimacy he stakes out in his preface. A close reading of the preface teases out the influences on Meng Qi's constructed ideal of poetry and sets the stage for the more complex picture of poetic competence that emerges from the poetic practices depicted in the stories themselves.

Chapter 5, "Placing the Poem," addresses the more than 40 brief anecdotes of *Storied Poems*, which run from the fall of the Chen dynasty in the late sixth century to the late ninth century (near the end of the Tang dynasty). The collection provides an invaluable cross-section of poetic practice as it is portrayed by and among educated, literate people of the Tang—men and women, famous and obscure, in the capital and in the regions, under conditions both mundane and supernatural. The chapter comprises a translation of the bulk of this short work, with an ongoing commentary on the multivalent concept of poetic competence that emerges from its individual entries. The analysis divides the entries among three broad overlapping fields: politics, literature, and love. What results is a nuanced model of poetic competence that shows the protagonists of these narratives taking into account such variables as place, time, audience, and mode of performance in order to maximize the effect of oral and written poetic utterances. These stories indicate an explicit awareness of the affective power of heartfelt poetry as outlined in Meng Qi's preface to the collection, but they also evince an implicit awareness that the power of a poem to effect change in the world is contingent upon its deployment as a *socially engaged* form of discourse. Poetic competence means not merely that one's words be well put in a text, but that one must also put one's words well into the world of discourse that subsumes them. One must master both the utterance and the uttering to lend a poem power.

IV

What emerges in the following pages is a larger story of the development of the concept of poetic competence. It is not possible to draw a straight line of development from one source to the next. It is better to think of them as stops along the way. Poetic competence starts out as calculated performance of inherited words in the Eastern Zhou, shifts to sincere passionate outburst in the Han, then, during the Southern Dynasties, takes on the more complex form of playful facility in verbal wit, combining calculation with the *appearance* of spontaneity. All of these streams—calculation, passion, wit—converge in the Tang to produce a multivalent concept of poetic competence that designates the skill of an individual to pitch his or her poetic utterances at the right time, in the right place, and to the right person to achieve a desired outcome. By the Tang, there is no single notion of competence, but a repertoire of competencies upon which to draw as the occasion demands. The goal of this book is not to provide a stable definition of poetic competence for the entire history of pre-Tang and Tang literature, but to tell the story of the concept's evolution, to uncover its complexity, and to identify the sources and exemplars of that complexity.

Performing the Tradition

I

The royal courts of Eastern Zhou (770–256 B.C.E.) China—as with all sites of human interaction—emerged out of and were shaped by the daily practice of individuals, each with an awareness of his or her own position derived from membership in a certain group. This awareness of position led to a sense of the appropriate means of expression at a given time before a given person. Such things as "awareness" and "sense" are not easily committed to writing, how-ever, and what we are left with in texts such as the *Zuo Tradition* 左傳 are traces of how a particular group, in this case, that which we may call the Traditionalists 儒家, represented its practices to its own members and to the members of other groups.[1] The Traditionalists,

---

1. The label "Traditionalists" emerged during the period of time covered by the *Zuo Tradition* (722–468 B.C.E.) and gained a distinctly pejorative connotation of being excessively "bookish" and out of touch with pragmatic concerns. But the role filled by the Traditionalists—advisors at court who drew on their knowledge of the Tradition to guide their rulers and debate with one another—long preceded the label. The emergence of the explicit label seems to coincide with the increasing systematization and transcription of the orally transmitted bodies of knowledge and lore that constituted the cultural capital of the Traditionalists. Confucius 孔子 (ca. 551–479 B.C.E.) is the best known of these Traditionalists. Most of the advisors

as the self-designated custodians of the Western Zhou (1066–771 B.C.E.) cultural legacy, were particularly well positioned to fashion a representative account of their practices and to introduce that account into the orthodox canon of Tradition. Such an account— partial, biased, full of significant silences—can never be taken for the whole truth, even though it seeks to represent itself as such. The truth of practice can only be experienced; it cannot be represented. However, a textual account may attempt to describe, as the *Zuo Tradition* does, the various situations in which certain types of practice were carried out. This is the value of the *Zuo Tradition* in establishing the nature of poetic competence in the Chinese tradition. In it is inscribed its compilers' desire that properly deployed poetic utterances would provoke certain affects in those who heard them, with concomitant effects on their behavior. Whether these utterances really had such efficacy in any given case is beside the point. From its lofty vantage point in the canon, the *Zuo Tradition* wielded a powerful and enduring influence on later poetic practice and its representation in writing.

The power of the *Zuo Tradition* as a representative text was not originally or solely derived from its position among a growing corpus of orthodox Traditionalist texts. It was entrenched in the canon only after it was broken up and appended as a commentary to the *Spring and Autumn Annals* 春秋 traditionally attributed to Confucius. In its earliest forms, the *Zuo Tradition* seems to have emerged from a large body of orally circulated lore about the Springs and Autumns period, lore which consisted mainly of reports of speeches and rituals performed at the royal courts of various states. As such, it is in a direct line of descent from the earliest forms of historiography, such as the *Documents*, bronze inscriptions, and even oracle bone writings, which take the recording of speech in a ritual context as their main purpose.[2] The difference between the *Zuo Tradition* and these earlier texts, however, resides in its exten-

---

mentioned in the *Zuo Tradition* long preceded Confucius, and statements attributed to him would, of course, be unknown to them. However, his respect for traditional knowledge certainly reflects a wider attitude among the Traditionalists that was centuries in the making.

2. For a detailed and cogently argued discussion of recorded speech in a ritual context, see Schaberg, *Patterned Past*, pp. 21–30.

sive use of narrative to provide a framework for its represented speech. It is narrative that makes the *Zuo Tradition* a powerful text, for only narrative—as a representation of events occurring over time, emplotted with a beginning, middle, and end—can create the illusion that it carries the whole world (and its meaning) within its purview. A narrative frame for a particular instance of speech can outline the events leading up to the utterance (allowing its illocutionary motivations to be inferred), describe the variables of person, time, and place surrounding the utterance (allowing its locutionary competence to be judged), and communicate the eventual outcome of the utterance (allowing its perlocutionary effectiveness to be ascertained). And if the voice of the narrator is completely self-effacing—as is the case with the *Zuo Tradition*, which explicitly demarcates any interpretations and judgments it makes—then a narrative can create the powerful illusion that it is simply communicating the world as it is without any mediation.[3] It shows us the world as it is or was, rather than telling us how it should be, thus closing off any opportunity for rebuttal. Facts, unlike opinions and principles, are not open to disputation.

The final influential characteristic of the *Zuo Tradition* is its tendency to repeat a certain type of narrative, in two variations: salutary and minatory. In the first variation, an official in an advisory or diplomatic capacity makes an argument to a superior figure, often a ruler, who is convinced by the argument and acts or refrains from acting in such a way as to procure a positive outcome. The outcome may be immediate or delayed. In the second variation, which makes up the bulk of narratives in the *Zuo Tradition*, the superior figure does not heed the argument and meets a bad end. It is not hard to see that this type of narrative casts a favorable light on the Traditionalists, who were carving out a niche for themselves as indispensable advisors to figures of authority.

Repetition in narrative has two effects: it naturalizes the elements that are repeated, making them seem to follow the natural order of

---

3. A narrative's ability to convincingly depict an alternative version of the world can constitute an ontological challenge to versions of reality conveyed by orthodox narratives. This is a potential source of danger and explains why the Chinese tradition vigorously marginalized certain types of narrative even as it preserved them.

things (in this case indicating that superiors will inevitably stray from the proper path of morality, and that they thus require wise counsel); at the same time, it draws attention to the elements in the framework that do vary (in this case the utterances made by officials to correct deficiencies in their superiors). The point at which the official must step forward to perform continually presents itself as a moment charged with the possibility of success or failure—not only for his particular utterance but perhaps for an entire state. Again and again, the *Zuo Tradition* shows us that the man who is competent in his knowledge and deployment of Tradition will rise to the occasion and either save his superiors from misfortune or, if they prove too obtuse to heed his counsel, at least win the right to say, "I told you so." Thus the *Zuo Tradition* gradually inculcates in its readers a sense of the proper operation of hierarchy at court, namely that it behooves superiors to heed wise counsel. The narrative never has to resort to explicit descriptions of the hierarchy (other texts in the canon, such as the *Zhou Rituals*, take on this task); it wields the more subtle and thus more effective power of representing the very *process*—the specific set of practices—that constitutes and maintains the hierarchy.

The constant site for the performance and inculcation of hierarchy is, of course, the court. The ruler, whether he be called king 王 or duke 公, is the source of power and the focal point of all speech and ritual acts at court. Thus, the currency of power at court is the ability to win the ruler's attention and approval. The ruler demands a certain attitude of deference in demeanor and a certain type of language in speech if he is to let others impose themselves on his time and space (a pattern replicated in all superior-inferior interactions). It is no coincidence that the *Zuo Tradition* repeatedly portrays those officials with competence in Traditional knowledge as the ones most successful in winning the ear of the ruler, who will usually repay their efforts with an expression of appreciation such as "Excellent!" 善 and, in the best of circumstances, an attendant change in behavior that preserves or enhances the status of the state.

The encounter between official and ruler may be the major axis on which the court hierarchy is organized, but the narratives of the

Zuo Tradition make it clear that other groups are present. The business of court is transacted before an immediate audience consisting of other members of the nobility, ministers, officials, guests, musicians, and servants, as well as an extended audience including the people of the state, other courts in other states, and, ultimately, the vast readership of the narratives contained in the *Zuo Tradition*. The cultural competence of the Traditionalist is demonstrated before and judged by more than a single ruler, who may not always be up to the task of appreciating it. This is why a *Zuo Tradition* narrative will rarely close with a speech without giving at least some indication of whether the principles or predictions stated in that speech were appreciated by an extended audience and vindicated by the events of history, the ultimate impartial judge.

When an official at court succeeds in winning and maintaining power through a competent performance of Tradition before the king, his resulting position of power inside the court is reflected outside the court in his role as a delegate representing the king's interests through speech (diplomatic missions) and violence (warfare). The categories of *oratores* ("cultural" 文 scholars) and *bellatores* ("martial" 武 warriors) were not distributed evenly between two different groups of people in the Eastern Zhou. Rather, members of the elite ruling class were expected to be well versed in both disciplines. Tradition certainly encompassed both spheres. In the long view, however, the scholarly frame of mind always prevails for the simple reason that speech subsumes violence into its symbolic code: actions can only be recorded, recalled, and represented through words. Actions may speak louder than words, but words speak longer. The Traditionalist thus seeks to define and justify his position through the custodianship of words. Indeed, once his position as a repository for relevant learning is established, he can maintain his position at court (and its accompanying wealth) simply by being what he is, thereby escaping the stigma of pursuing profit directly. The *Zuo Tradition* was an important text for the Traditionalists because it demonstrated their efficacy even before they were institutionalized as a civil bureaucracy. It stakes out a place in history for the Traditionalists because its narratives constitute the very mode of legitimate history. Ultimately, the Traditionalists succeeded in transmitting a social order in which they occupy the position of transmitters of the social order.

If a custodian of words is to maintain respect and power, his charge cannot be just any group of words. Those who would seek to sway their superiors through words must carefully choose both the particular words *and* their mode of delivery. In a society such as ancient China's, whose fundamental rituals are based on continuity with and worship of human and divine ancestors, the surest way of stamping one's words with authority is to derive them from a Golden Age of antiquity. For the Traditionalists of the Eastern Zhou, the Western Zhou—as the formative stage of their own dynasty—was such a Golden Age, a source of exemplary behavior and words against which all later ages could be measured. Of course, any golden age is a retrospective construct created by cultural agents seeking a means to interpret, judge, and exercise some measure of control over events in the present. The universal impulse to compare a deficient present to a better past is rooted in anxieties over mortality coupled with the cognitive disposition of human beings to seek out a semblance of order in the chaos of daily existence. Once a segment of society has formed a fundamental set of values, the past can be construed to support those values, which are themselves shaped by the past. For the ruling class of the Eastern Zhou, the Western Zhou was golden because it was an age in which the elite knew how to be the dominant class and the people knew how to be dominated (and the members of the dominant class knew how to reproduce this scheme on a smaller scale, each person making obeisance to his superior, right up to the Zhou king). The mark of decline in this Golden Age appears when people lose their sense of the "natural" relationship between inferior and superior and must begin talking about it explicitly. Concern over the minutiae of sumptuary codes, promulgation of laws in written form, debates over proper forms of ritual and terminology: these are indications that people have forgotten how to act properly and must be compelled to do so through external strictures rather than their own sense of what is right. This is the perfect environment for the rise of the Traditionalists, who take it upon themselves to remind anyone who will listen what "right" is, based on bodies of ancient knowledge over which they claim mastery.

The irony inherent in the approach of the Traditionalists is that the very practices in which they engage to restore the values of a Golden Age are a symptom of the state of decline in their own age. If the culture of the Western Zhou can be viewed as a continuous fabric of beautiful patterning (*wen* 文), encompassing right music, poetry, ritual, and speech, then the Traditionalists of the Eastern Zhou rend that fabric and attempt to sew its luminous threads into the dull cloth of the present. This only serves to heighten the contrast between the fragments of a perfect past and a degraded present that can never be fully rectified. Mencius 孟子 (379–289 B.C.E.), who lived at the very close of the Eastern Zhou, is cited in *Mencius* as saying, "With the demise of the wooden clappers of the former Kings, the *Poems* came to an end. Only after the *Poems* had come to an end were the *Spring and Autumn Annals* composed" 王者之跡熄而詩亡。詩亡然後春秋作 (4B.21).[4] In this statement, Mencius refers to a golden age in which dedicated officials circulated among the people sounding wooden clappers to solicit and collect their songs, forming a continually changing corpus of poems with which the Kings could gauge the minds and hearts of their people and thus the quality of their rule.[5] When this practice ceased and the corpus of poems reached a stable form, it signaled a transition from an age of song to an age of history, from an age of unalloyed utterance to one in which a representation of what people said and did was purposefully fashioned. The only way to revivify proper values in this context is to internalize them and to act them out—talking about values at length, as the Traditionalists were wont to do, will not

---

4. My translation of 跡 (*ji*, "trace") as "wooden clappers" is based on a widely accepted variant reading cited by D.C. Lau in his translation of *Mencius* (p. 131) of radical 162 辶 plus 爪, meaning "wooden-tongued clappers."

5. On this matter, the *Zuo Tradition* (Xiang 14) cites a passage from the "Documents of Xia" 夏書 in the *Documents* 書. The passage is found in the section entitled "The Punitive Expedition of Yin" 胤征 and reads: "The runners circulated throughout the roadways with their wooden clappers" 遒人以木鐸徇於路. Music Master Kuang makes the citation in a speech to the Marquis of Jin, in which he describes how the ancient kings relied upon discourse flowing to them from all levels of society to maintain the quality of their rule.

bring them back and runs the risk of boring one's audience.[6] This is why competence was such an important issue for the Traditionalists: they needed to employ their words in such a way that their audience would not only pay attention, but also *act* on them.

II

It is an age of decline that engenders a need for competence. To employ the term "competence" at all is to acknowledge that there are those who are not competent, and thus to acknowledge that a Golden Age of harmony in thought and action has passed. This lesson is taught in the *Zuo Tradition* when the Duke of Song, the fiefdom of the descendants of the defeated Shang dynasty that preceded the Zhou, refuses to attack enemy forces until they have had a chance to draw up their battle lines. As a result of the duke's gallant gesture, his army is routed, his personal guards are slain, and he is wounded. The duke defends his decision by saying:

A true gentleman does not wound those who are already wounded, nor does he capture those with graying hair. When the ancients employed their armies, they did not do so by trapping the enemy in a narrow spot. Although I may be all that is left of a ruined dynasty, I refuse to strike an army in disarray. (Xi 22.8)

君子不重傷。不禽二毛。古之爲軍也。不以阻隘也。寡人雖亡國之餘。不鼓不成列。

The duke's War Chief makes the following rebuttal, which contrasts starkly with his master's nostalgia for a golden age of gentlemanly conduct in warfare:

Your lordship has never understood warfare. Should a more powerful enemy find itself in a narrow spot in a state of disarray, this is Heaven coming to our aid. Why should we not trap them there and strike them? Even in such a situation we should still be wary of them! In this battle, all the strength was with our enemies. We should have captured and taken

---

6. Confucius, after a lifetime of talking about values, seems to have reached this conclusion in his famous statement that only at the age of seventy was his mind sufficiently conditioned that he could give it free rein without fear of moral transgressions (*Analects* 2.4). Of course, few rulers in the Eastern Zhou had the will to pursue a lifetime of self-edification, and thus they tolerated the Traditionalists as a quick means to essential knowledge.

them all, right up to the elderly. Why make an exception for those with graying hair? Understanding the shame [of a potential defeat] in teaching military tactics is simply a matter of seeking to kill the enemy. If you do not inflict a mortal wound the first time, why would you not wound again? If you feel compunction over wounding again, it is as not wounding in the first place. If you feel compunction over those with graying hair, then it is as surrendering to them. Our three divisions should take every advantage. With the sounds of drums and gongs stirring our courage, we should take the advantage of trapping them in a narrow spot. With the surging sounds magnifying our resolve, we should strike them in their confusion. (Xi 22.8)[7]

君未知戰。勍敵之人。隘而不列。天贊我也。阻而鼓之。不亦可乎。猶有懼焉。且今之勍者。皆吾敵也。雖及胡耇。獲則取之。何有於二毛。明恥教戰。求殺敵也。傷未及死。如何勿重。若愛重傷。則如勿傷。愛其二毛。則如服焉。三軍以利用也。金鼓以聲氣也。利而用之。阻隘可也。聲盛致志。鼓儳可也。

The rules of the game have changed. In Golden Age warfare there were commonly accepted ground rules that resulted in consensus amidst conflict. In an age of decline, however, adherence to a common culture is not guaranteed, and one cannot simply ape ancient models of behavior and hope for the best. The goal now is to kill the enemy by "taking every advantage" 利而用之. The defeated duke lacks a *practical* sense of when it is appropriate to deploy his knowledge of the past. He is not competent in handling his cultural legacy. This is precisely the breach into which the Traditionalists thrust themselves: they claim competence in handling the Tradition (one might call this "cultural competence"). They are not passive receptacles of bodies of learning, mere human relays communicating words from the past. They are expert in *applying* knowledge of the past to present circumstances in order to produce a successful outcome. In deploying their knowledge, they must select appropriate citations and then clearly illustrate the relevance of those citations to the matter at hand.[8] The Traditionalists must reconcile

---

7. I have based my translations from the *Zuo Tradition* on the annotations of Yang Bojun (*Chun qiu Zuo zhuan zhu*) and Kamata Tadashi (*Shunju Sashi den*). For this particular passage, I also consulted Schaberg, *Patterned Past*, p. 2.

8. Once the Traditionalist canon was reified into written textual form, these two practices—selection and application—would give way to editing and annota-

ideals from the past with the less than ideal conditions of the present; their constant search for a path to a better future routes them through the muck and mire of an age of decline. This is not a grand project, for it is carried out only through the quotidian reiteration of a set of practices. The Traditionalist must engage in his practice at the appropriate moment *while* he has the attention of the appropriate person. These considerations of time and audience (which can only be conveyed in narrative form) make the Traditionalist a sort of performer, who must improvise his inherited repertoire of lines to fashion a performance powerful enough to sway his audience. The role of the Traditionalist is in a sense an implicit admission of discontinuity and loss, as he is required to be a vessel for a world that can no longer assert itself. His cultural competence is measured by how well he can reanimate that world through performing its vestiges.

A particularly important cultural vestige for the Traditionalists of the Eastern Zhou courts was the corpus of three hundred poems in tetrasyllabic meter known simply as the *Poems* 詩, which are cited in the *Zuo Tradition* far more frequently than any other text. Poetic competence—a facility for performing or quoting the right poetic lines at the right place and time—is portrayed as the primary skill in demonstrating that one has a broader sense of cultural competence. The *Poems* are treated as "deeds of words, as linguistic acts, whose significance was intimately related to the particular situation in which they were uttered."[9]

There are places in the Traditionalist canonical texts where one can find explicit discussions of cultural competence, particularly concerning the use of the *Poems*. The *Analects* 論語 is a rich source for such discussions, even though it took shape long after many of the events described in the *Zuo Tradition*. Though one must exercise caution in reading the attitudes expressed in the *Analects* back into previous centuries, the text certainly retains its relevance as the end

---

tion. This point is made by Van Zoeren in *Poetry and Personality*: "Confronted with [fixed texts] the necessary process of accommodating doctrine to new concerns and questions must be displaced from expansion and reformulation to interpretation" (p. 23).

9. Van Zoeren, *Poetry and Personality*, p. 51.

result of a long period of evolution stretching back into those centuries. In the *Analects*, Confucius is reported to have admonished his son to study the *Poems* more carefully, for "without studying the *Poems* one lacks the means to speak" 不學詩無以言 (16.13). Elsewhere, he states that the *Poems* are useless to a man who "is unable to respond independently when sent on missions abroad" 使於四方不能專對 (13.5). And he claims that to have not studied the *Poems* is akin to "standing face-to-face with a wall" 正牆面而立 (17.10). Exhorting his disciples to study the *Poems*, he lists all the benefits such cultural competence encompasses:

The Master said, "Little ones, why do you not study the *Poems*? Through the *Poems*, one may incite, one may observe, one may keep company, one may express resentment. Near at hand, one may serve one's father. At a farther remove, one may serve one's lord. And there is much to be known in them about the names of birds, beasts, plants, and trees." (17.9)

小子。何莫學夫詩。詩。可以興。可以觀。可以群。可以怨。邇之事父。遠之事君。多識於鳥獸草木之名。

But simple knowledge of the *Poems* is not enough; one must know how to apply them properly. Confucius appraises this skill in the following passage from the *Analects*:

Zigong said, "To be without obsequiousness though poor and without haughtiness though rich. What do you think of that?" The Master replied, "That is fine, but it would be better to be joyful though poor and to love propriety though rich." Zigong said, "The *Poems* say,

> As if cut, as if filed,
> as if chiseled, as if polished.[10]

Does this refer to what you are saying?" The Master replied, "Zigong, now I can finally speak of the *Poems* with you. After I told you something, you knew what it implied." (1.15)

子貢曰。貧而無諂。富而無驕。何如。子曰。可也。未若貧而樂。富而好禮者也。子貢曰。詩云。如切如磋。如琢如磨。其斯之謂與。子曰。賜也。始可與言詩已矣。告諸往而知來者。

Zigong deserves praise not for memorizing the *Poems* (acquisition of such knowledge is a bare minimum for cultural competence), but

---

10. Mao #55. After Karlgren, *Book of Odes*, p. 37.

for being able to use poetic citation to give figural expression to the crux of the matter under discussion: namely, that properly internalized moral precepts shape the person like a stone that is chiseled and polished. Confucius's statement that "I can finally speak of the *Poems* with you" implies that simply having the knowledge is not enough; one must know how to use it. In fact, speaking of the *Poems* outside their application is pointless. When Confucius tells Zigong, "After I told you something, you knew what it implied," he is praising Zigong's performance, his ability to bring his knowledge to bear on the matter at hand in a timely and appropriate fashion. He has demonstrated cultural competence. That these passages in the *Analects* are able to address matters of cultural competence explicitly is an indication that such practices were in place long before its compilation. The figure of Confucius is portrayed in the *Analects* in two roles: as an exemplar of cultural competence, who is able to handle bodies of received knowledge judiciously in his own debates; and as a teacher of cultural competence, who enjoins his disciples to do the hard work necessary to achieve fluency in certain bodies of knowledge and in a certain set of practices.[11] He is not preaching a new doctrine so much as codifying a set of existing practices that might help one to achieve distinction within the community and to succeed in the service of one's lord.

It is one thing to demonstrate cultural competence before your teacher, where praise and censure are at stake, but it is another thing in front of a ruler at court, where one's livelihood (if not life) may very well hang in the balance. The cultural competence of the ancient Chinese courtier comprises two skills similarly much prized by the Renaissance courtier in Europe: *sprezzatura*, the appearance that one is speaking off the top of one's head with wit and timing, and *mediocrità*, a solid grounding in knowledge. In fashioning a style of speech that at once appears improvised and well supported by knowledge of the past, the Traditionalists were endeavoring,

---

11. Note that Confucius never attempts to explicitly teach his disciples how to frame a good argument, or how to use a poem well; he simply does it himself or tells them what they need to achieve, tests them, and gives his evaluation of their efforts. He realizes that cultural competence is something that can only be gained by each person through practice. (See *Analects* 1.1 and 7.8.)

through daily repetition of the practice, to establish their mode of discourse as the only one acceptable at court.[12] The narratives of the *Zuo Tradition* are simply a powerful and enduring extension of that desire. The Traditionalist, through repeated citations from orthodox knowledge and insistence on proper protocol in performance of ritual, attempts to control how *and* what the world means. He does this by constantly making reference to the golden standards of the past, thus giving structure and meaning to chaotic events of the present. He either praises events and behavior for being in accord with received models, or shows exactly in what respect and by what degree they fall short, shoring up a teetering society with threads of "patterned culture" (*wen* 文). In the Traditionalist view, cultural competence becomes a matter of survival for the entire state.[13]

Cultural competence is not a set of skills that can be explicitly taught by a teacher to a student; it is inculcated in a particular environment. Much like Wheelwright Bian in the Daoist parable found in *Zhuangzi* 莊子 (chap. 13), who maintains that his skill in fashioning wheels is an innate sense derived from experience that cannot be transmitted in words, the Traditionalist develops a sense of fashioning utterances through experience. But where is a young, aspiring Traditionalist to look for guidance? In the first instance, he turns to his senior cohort, of whom Confucius eventually became the ultimate representative. But there is another place: the guidelines for competent deployment of the Tradition are already encoded within the Tradition itself. Certainly, if a Tradition is to perpetuate

---

12. The question of improvisation is vexed here. Officials often knew beforehand what sort of advice they might give or what behavior of the ruler they were attempting to rectify; so they would have had ample time to prepare their speeches. It was also in the interest of those repeating (and eventually transcribing) the narratives found in the *Zuo Tradition* to make their confreres seem as competent as possible; embellishment, polishing, and even fabrication certainly occurred after the fact. Nevertheless, the speeches were always meant to *appear* as improvised utterances, however that appearance might be achieved.

13. Haun Saussy, in *The Problem of the Chinese Aesthetic*, identifies this impulse to view the Tradition as a restorative force in the Mao prefaces to the *Poems* (or *Odes*): "the tradition reads the *Odes* as the description of a possible ethical world. It reads them in the performative mode, as narrating, in the form of history, the model actions that its own reading must second in order to make them actual" (p. 105).

itself, especially in the absence of a widespread form of durable transcription, it requires a group of people who will memorize it and utter it repeatedly. This is not enough, however—in order to justify its continuing preservation and transmission, a Tradition must be made relevant to an ever-shifting present moment at the locus of political power, the only place with the means to support a class of people with enough leisure time to study and practice traditional bodies of knowledge. In short, the Tradition needs the Traditionalist to justify its continuing existence just as much as he needs it to do the same. Knowledge and person are bound in an inextricable symbiotic relationship.[14]

It should come as no surprise, then, that the bodies of knowledge inherited from the Western Zhou were not transparent to their recipients in the Eastern Zhou and subsequent eras. They exhibit the very lacunae, inconsistencies, and ambivalences needed to provide space for a class of people to interpret them and to allow those people the latitude to apply them to a wide variety of circumstances. In addition to providing this space, they bear encoded guidelines for their use. For example, the *Changes* is a divination manual for interpreting the operations of the cosmos that takes the form of a series of interpretations nested one within the other; the *Documents* is largely a collection of important speeches that is used as a rhetorical resource in speeches; the *Poems* contain a variety of encoded guidelines, including how to deduce an interior state of mind from ambiguous external evidence (Mao #65, 76), how to fashion a song of praise for your superior (Mao #235, 240, 260), how to use metaphorical language to veil satirical intent (Mao #113, 155), how words may be used to enact and preserve ritual (Mao #245, 272, 282, 283), and a host of other skills necessary for a Traditionalist to demon-

---

14. This symbiosis is akin to the one between human beings and genes. Do our genes encode the pattern of life necessary to perpetuate our existence, or are we simply the means by which genes perpetuate their own existence, as Dawkins argues in *The Selfish Gene*? The answer, of course, is "both." Remove one element and the other perishes; attempts at separating them only lead to paradox. Certainly, the First Emperor of the Qin dynasty 秦始皇帝 realized the nature of this relationship when, in 213 B.C.E., he ordered both books *and* scholars to be destroyed during the "Burning of the Books and Burying of the Traditionalists" 焚書坑儒.

strate his cultural competence.[15] The Chinese Tradition is perpetu-
ated through the very sorts of practices (namely, interpretation and
application) for which it stands as a model. Even this overarching
principle is encoded within it. One of the *Poems* tells us: "Hew
an axe-handle, hew an axe-handle, / The model is not far off" 伐柯
伐柯/其則不遠.[16] This recursive quality means that the Tradition
constantly expands to include all later acts of interpretation and
application, even as it preserves a kernel of originary knowledge at
its core.

The Eastern Zhou, as it is depicted in the *Zuo Tradition*, is an era
of transition from a time in which the core bodies of knowledge in
the Tradition were accessed through ritual reenactment to a time in
which they were treated as a rhetorical resource for speechmaking.
In either case, Traditional knowledge in the Eastern Zhou is still
something to be *performed* with a measure of cultural competence.[17]
The two modes of performance—reenactment and speechmaking—
are clearly manifested in two types of practice common at court:
"offering poems" 賦詩 and "citing poems" 引詩.[18] Both practices
embody what might be called poetic competence, a specific and es-
sential component of cultural competence in general.

The difference between offering a poem as a form of ritual re-
enactment and citing a poem in a speech is a difference in the mode

---

15. Arthur Waley in *The Book of Songs* organizes his translation of the *Poems*
along such lines.

16. Mao #158. After Karlgren, *Book of Odes*, p. 103.

17. With the imperially sanctioned transcription of the Traditionalist canon in
the Han dynasty, the stage was set for cultural competence to move into the arena
of written composition. Advancements in writing technologies, territorial expan-
sion of the empire, and the increasing complexity of its bureaucracy (and eventually
the advent of the imperial examinations) placed a premium on interpreting and
applying Traditional knowledge as writing *in* writing.

18. Both Yang Xiangshi (*Zuo zhuan fushi yinshi kao*) and Zeng Qinliang (*Zuo
zhuan yinshi fushi zhi shijiao yanjiu*) collect and annotate all instances of offering and
citing found in the *Zuo Tradition*. Schaberg (*Patterned Past*, pp. 72–80, 234–43)
discusses both practices, while Tam's dissertation ("Use of Poetry in *Tso Chuan*") is
on offering, which he terms "chanting." Lewis (*Writing and Authority*, pp. 155–63)
also briefly addresses the practice. In what follows, I will discuss only a few salient
examples of each practice as they relate to the notion of poetic competence.

of discourse during performance. Each mode has its appropriate context and demands a certain type of response from its audience.

To cite a poem—as is suggested by the Chinese character *yin* 引 "to draw a bowstring"—means to "draw in" or to "intromit" the marked language of the *Poems* into one's own discourse, usually a formal speech made before a peer or a superior at court. The *Poems* are but one rhetorical resource to be exploited during the performance of a speech; other bodies of Traditional knowledge, such as the *Documents* and *Changes*, are also cited, though not with the same frequency as the *Poems*. It is the performance of the speech as a whole that commands the attention of its audience, and, if properly deployed, wins the heart and mind of the listener.[19] The citation of poetry is just one rhetorical practice that goes into fashioning a successful speech, but it has a profound influence on the evolving concept of poetic competence, for it is through such practice that the *Poems* are continuously applied and interpreted in an explicit fashion.

To offer a poem—as suggested by the Chinese character *fu* 賦 ("to remit, to give over"), cognate with *fu* 敷 ("to spread")—means to "display" a selection from the *Poems* through performance, usually as part of ritual protocol at a banquet. As a form of reenactment, it revivifies the poem in its primordial role as a form of marked discourse (that is, singing, chanting, or intoning) distinct from every-

---

19. The *Zuo Tradition* tells of a Zheng official, named Zichan, who protests against the cramped conditions in the lodgings that the state of Jin provides for visiting dignitaries. He makes a finely crafted speech that shames Jin into correcting the problem. In appraising this speech, a Jin minister, Yangshe Shuxiang, says, "The impossibility of doing away with words (*ci* 辭) is surely exemplified here. Because Zichan had a capacity for words, the feudal lords benefited by him. So how could we ever dispense with words? The *Poems* say:

> The harmony of the words
> is the concord of the people;
> the kindness of the words
> is the tranquility of the people.   (Mao #254.
> After Karlgren, *Book of Odes*, p. 214)

Zichan surely knew this." (Xiang 31.6) 辭之不可以已也如是夫。子產有辭。諸侯賴之。若之何其釋辭也。詩曰。辭之輯矣。民之協矣。辭之繹矣。民之莫矣。其知之矣。

day speech articulating what is on the mind of the performer.[20] Such a use of the *Poems* demonstrates the power of the Tradition to assert its continuity through reenactment: "we do this as it has always been done."[21] The audience in this case is required to participate in the ritual by making the appropriate obeisance in acceptance of the poem and possibly by offering another in response. The application of the poem is in its moment of performance; its interpretation is left unspoken, but may be inferred from the response of the audience. As the timeline of the *Zuo Tradition* progresses, descriptions of the practice of offering poems become increasingly scarce until they dwindle away altogether in later texts, suggesting a gradual transition in attitude toward the Tradition from ritual reenactment to rhetorical resource. This is a clear mark of decline: from a time in which the efficacy of Traditional knowledge was manifest in its unalloyed performance into a time when such efficacy must be bolstered by subordinating it to the practice of speechmaking. It is a shift from the *implicit*, with its assumption of stable and uniform understanding, to the *explicit*, with its assumption of a lack of understanding. As it is written in *Mencius*, "Only after the *Poems* had come to an end were the *Spring and Autumn Annals* composed" (4B.21).

III

Many cases of offering poetry depicted in the *Zuo Tradition* are what might be called "protocol offerings" 例賦.[22] At the formal banquets convened to receive diplomats from other states or to host

---

20. The explicit formulation of this "primordial" role of poetry is found in the "Canon of Shun" 舜典 in the *Documents* 書: "The poems should articulate intent, singing should intone the words, notes should correspond with the intonement, and modes should harmonize the notes" (Ruan Yuan, *Shisan jing*, vol. 1, p. 45).

21. Note that this principle too is encoded within the Tradition. "She Bore Our People" 生民 (Mao #245) is a liturgical text detailing the origins of agricultural practices and rituals with the ancestor of the Zhou people, Lord Millet (Hou Ji 后稷); its closing lines read "Hou Ji initiated the sacrifice / and the multitude has given no offence nor cause for regret / unto the present day" (Karlgren, *Book of Odes*, p. 202). Performing the same poem in the same way as the ancestors did is its own assertion of continuity in the Tradition.

22. This is a term used by Yang Xianshi, *Zuo zhuan fushi yinshi kao*, p. 11.

meetings between rulers, either the host himself or the court musi-
cians at his behest would perform certain selections from the *Poems*
to convey the joy of the host in receiving his guest.[23] The guest
would then request the musicians to perform (or would himself
perform) a selection to convey his gratitude to the host. Clues as to
the origin of this practice may be found in traditional texts on ritual,
particularly the *Ceremonies and Rituals* 儀禮, which discusses the
role of music as an integral part of the formal (and less formal) rituals
conducted between host and guest at court.[24] In numerous early
texts, there is a recurring theme of music evoking and demonstrating
harmony of thought and feeling between various participants who
may feel separated from one another by the strictures of ritual.[25]
Certainly, the *Poems* were treated as a musical repertoire in the
Eastern Zhou,[26] but the narratives of the *Zuo Tradition* indicate that
more often than not a selection from the *Poems* is not offered solely
for its music, but just as much for the import of its *words*. Some of
the protocol offerings do "double duty" as banquet songs and as
subtle indicators of the state of mind of participants at the banquet.
Members of court routinely offer poems and respond in kind to one
another outside the context of welcoming guests at banquets.[27] The
narrative will specify by title which poem is being offered, some-
times indicating which particular stanza is being performed, or
even quoting the exact words. There is a wide range of modes of
performance (singing, chanting, and intoning among them) included
under the rubric "offering." All of these things argue against
identifying the practice of offering a poem exclusively with

---

23. The most common selection for welcoming a guest to a banquet was "The
Deer Cry" 鹿鳴 (Mao #161), which includes the following apposite lines: "I have
a fine guest, we play the lute and blow the reed-organ" (Karlgren, *Book of Odes*,
p. 104).

24. For an extended discussion, see Tam, "Use of Poetry in *Tso Chuan*," p. 40.

25. The "Record of Music" 樂記 of the *Classic of Rites* 禮記 states this baldly as
"Music unifies; rites set things apart" (Owen, *Anthology*, p. 69); *Xunzi* 荀子 says
"Ritual is in respect of culture, while music sets its sights on harmony" 禮之敬文
也。樂之中和也 (chap. 1).

26. The most salient example of this is the grand concert for Jizha (Xiang 29).

27. Tam calculates that 55 percent of the poem offerings in the *Zuo Tradition* are
conducted between officials ("Use of Poetry in *Tso Chuan*," p. 154).

music. It is important to keep in mind, however, that even as the practice slips away from its musical context, it still carries with it the connotation of being a vehicle for expressing harmony of thought and feeling. With the passing of a Golden Age, however, such harmony must be won through poetic competence (in performer and audience) and can no longer be assumed. This becomes exceedingly clear in those narratives of the *Zuo Tradition* concerned with a lack of poetic competence in offering.

In the *Analects*, Confucius is quoted as spelling out the results of poetic incompetence:

> If one can chant the three hundred *Poems* yet does not succeed when entrusted with governmental duties and is unable to respond independently when sent on missions abroad, then what use are the *Poems* even though one knows so many?

誦詩三百。授之以政。不達。使於四方。不能專對。雖多亦奚以爲。(13.5)

Note that the failure does not lie in a lack of knowledge of the *Poems*, but in a lack of competence in deploying them. The phrase "unable to respond independently when sent on missions abroad" is likely a direct reference to the practice of offering poems in the context of a diplomatic banquet, a practice well established before the time of Confucius. The term *zhuandui* 專對 is glossed by traditional commentators as "to respond by oneself," the implication being that a diplomat sent to a foreign state must have the judgment and wherewithal to deal with situations on his own as they arise. In this case, the diplomat must have the necessary poetic competence to respond appropriately when he is called upon to offer a poem or respond to a poem offered to him.[28] Poems are routinely offered and responded to in the narratives of the *Zuo Tradition* with little or no comment. It is only when poetic competence is called into question, as it is in the following account, that it is addressed explicitly.

---

28. One minister of Jin, Zhao Meng 趙孟, is depicted in the *Zuo Tradition* as being highly competent in poetic offering. At a banquet given in his honor by the Earl of Zheng, Zhao asks for all seven of the officials in attendance on the earl to offer poems to him so that he may "thereby observe the intent of the seven gentlemen" 以觀七子之志 (Xiang 27.5). He then engages in a tour de force critique of the (im)propriety of each of their performances.

The following passage is an episode from one of the most engaging stories narrated in the *Zuo Tradition*, which relates the travels of Prince Chong'er 重耳, who must flee his own state of Jin when he falls under suspicion of rebellion due to the slander of his father's new wife (Xi 4). The prince spends twelve years among the Di "barbarians," a non-Chinese people in the north, where he takes a wife and fathers children. He then departs and spends the remainder of his twenty years in exile wandering from state to state, encountering varying levels of hospitality from their respective rulers before returning to take, by military force, his rightful place as the Duke of Jin. In his travels, he is accompanied by a retinue of advisors, two of whom stand out as being particularly adept: Hu Yan 狐偃 and Zhao Cui 趙衰. Members of the various courts they visit repeatedly describe them as worthy gentlemen.[29] Hu Yan emerges as a gifted military strategist dedicated to seeing his master return to strengthen the state of Jin.[30] Zhao Cui is portrayed as a

---

29. The wife of a minister in the state of Cao tells her husband, "I have observed the Prince of Jin's followers, and they are all capable of administering an entire state. If he makes use of their aid, that man will certainly regain his state" (Xi 23). When the Duke of Zheng treats Chong'er impolitely, his own minister points out that this is a dangerous course of action because the prince is destined to become a ruler. One of the proofs is that "he has three gentlemen (*shi* 士) that are worthy of being ranked superior men and yet they follow him" (Xi 23). Hu Yan and Zhao Cui are traditionally counted among these three.

30. When the prince is given a clump of dirt to eat by a peasant of Wei, Hu Yan explains to the indignant prince that it is a favorable omen sent by Heaven; when the prince meets with great hospitality in Qi and decides to stay, it is Hu Yan who devises a plan to get him drunk and whisk him away (Xi 23). When the prince returns to Jin, Hu Yan considers his goal accomplished and tenders his resignation, which Chong'er refuses. This turns out to be a wise decision as it is Hu Yan who negotiates an agreement between Qin and Jin that allows the prince to take his place as undisputed ruler of Jin even though it was Qin's military might that placed him there (Xi 24). Once the prince assumes his position as the new Duke of Jin, Hu Yan helps him to build up his army and to devise military strategies that eventually see Jin establish hegemony over the other states (Xi 27). Hu Yan then advises his lord in a conflict with the state of Chu, correctly interpreting his master's disturbing dream—of the Chu ruler bending over him and sucking out his brains—as a good omen, since the Duke of Jin was facing up to Heaven (Xi 28). After the death of the Duke of Jin in 628 B.C.E., Hu Yan is not mentioned again until 597 B.C.E. when a military advisor at the Jin court argues against doing battle with Chu by quoting the advice that Hu Yan once gave his own lord in a similar situation. The

man with impeccable cultural competence, able to deploy Traditional knowledge on behalf of the prince and to select worthy men by judging their mastery of such knowledge. There is a division of labor between Hu Yan, who is the epitome of the pragmatic advisor on military (*wu* 武) matters, and Zhao Cui, who is the epitome of the Traditionalist, an advisor that aids his lord with his cultural (*wen* 文) competence. The division is clearly shown in the following excerpt from Duke Xi 23rd Year (637 B.C.E.), the year before Chong'er returns to Jin. Prince Chong'er has just been escorted from the state of Chu to the state of Qin:[31]

The Duke of Qin provided him with five of his daughters, including Huai Ying.[32] She held up a basin for him as he washed up, but when he was through he just shook the water off his hands [onto her rather than waiting for a towel]. She became angry and said, "The states of Qin and Jin are equals; how could you treat me so poorly?" This alarmed the prince so he immediately bared his upper body and assumed the repentant posture of a prisoner.

On a day thereafter, the duke invited the prince to a banquet. Hu Yan said to the prince, "I do not measure up to Zhao Cui's skill in cultural matters; I would ask that you have him go with you instead." [At the banquet] the prince offered the poem "River Waters." The duke offered "Sixth Month" in response. Zhao Cui said, "Chong'er bows in acceptance of this!" The prince stepped down [from the platform], bowed, and then touched his head to the ground. The duke then descended one step to decline this gesture. Zhao Cui said, "Your lordship referred to Chong'er as a means 'to help the Son of Heaven' in giving him your command. How could he dare *not* to bow down?" (Xi 23.6)

秦伯納女五人。懷嬴與焉。奉匜沃盥。既而揮之。怒曰。秦晉匹也。何
以卑我。公子懼。降服而囚。他日。公享之。子犯曰。吾不如衰之文也。
請使衰從。公子賦河水。公賦六月。趙衰曰。重耳拜賜。公子降拜稽首。
公降一級。而辭焉。衰曰。君稱所以佐天子者命重耳。重耳敢不拜。

---

words of Hu Yan are thus converted into a kind of local traditional knowledge, to be cited as a rhetorical resource by later generations of Jin advisors.

31. The original text uses a variety of different names to refer to a single person. To avoid confusion, I consistently use one name in my translations.

32. Huai Ying was the wife of Chong'er's own nephew, who was being held as a Jin hostage in Qin.

The prince is a guest at the Qin court and is Duke Mu's social infe-
rior, but because of his noble lineage, and because Duke Mu believes
that Chong'er is destined to be a duke himself one day, he is ac-
corded the special honor of being served by the duke's own
daughters. Through the water-spattering incident, the narrative
implies that the prince's courtly manners are rough around the
edges, perhaps because of his years among the barbarians. The seem-
ingly minor offense demonstrates the significance of even the most
trivial matters of etiquette at court, for Huai Ying construes the
prince's carelessness as a slight against her entire state. The prince
atones for his inadvertent rudeness by baring his upper body and
crouching down, a ritual act of self-deprecation mimicking the
posture of a prisoner, which seems excessive and somewhat vulgar
in this context. The narratives of the *Zuo Tradition* are exceedingly
terse and no detail is superfluous. This vignette establishes the
prince as a man of physical action: both his offense and his apology
are wordless and both are carried out in a somewhat clumsy fashion.
It also charges his impending audience before Duke Mu with a
heightened degree of anxiety: his political future is at stake and he is
already off on the wrong foot. He will need a man with verbal fa-
cility to salvage the situation.

The narrative skips directly to the day of the meeting, with the
phrase "On a day thereafter" 他日. The *Zuo Tradition* is careful to
note exact dates when they matter. In this case, however, the nar-
rative is less concerned with an incremental chronology of events as
it is with a juxtaposition of two incidents: the first, an example of
cultural incompetence, and the second, an example of consummate
competence. Any extraneous events that took place between these
incidents are elided from the account.

Duke Mu invites Chong'er to be the guest of honor at a banquet.
Hu Yan, being a strategic thinker, realizes that the prince will need
someone with a high degree of cultural competence to successfully
negotiate a diplomatic banquet with the duke. And, being a wise
advisor, Hu Yan also realizes that Zhao Cui is better suited for the
job than he is. This is an astonishing admission. First, it implies that
the prince, a man born and raised as a member of the Jin nobility,
lacks the cultural competence needed to attend a banquet at a royal

court. Second, it acknowledges that only a certain type of man possesses the necessary competence. Hu Yan's exact words are: "I do not measure up to Zhao Cui's culture" 吾不如衰之文也. Cultural competence is now something that can be measured by degrees; indeed, it can only be measured against incompetence. The Eastern Zhou—as it is conveyed in the narratives of the *Zuo Tradition*—is a dangerous world that only makes sense to those people whose cultural competence makes it sensible. That ability increasingly devolves upon a certain class of "professionals": the Traditionalists. The rise in power of the advisor with competence in Traditional knowledge necessarily entails an evacuation of power from its usual seat: the ruler. The ruler becomes a sort of passive "placeholder" in the political hierarchy. He is theoretically the source of power in the state, but that power is heavily mediated by the Traditionalist advisor, who seeks to delimit the ruler's actions and words using parameters derived from received wisdom. The *Zuo Tradition* "wins" its argument by repeatedly showing that part of being a successful ruler is to heed the advice of a competent advisor.

The passing of agency from the hands of the ruler into those of the advisors is clearly shown in the cycle of narratives regarding Prince Chong'er. The passivity of the prince is most apparent when he decides to stay and enjoy the hospitality of Qi (Xi 23). Hu Yan, realizing that the prince is squandering his opportunity to become Duke of Jin, hatches a plot with Chong'er's wife to get him drunk and smuggle him out of the state. Upon sobering up, the prince repays Hu Yan for his trouble by chasing him with a spear! The entire cycle of narratives suggests that the prince's ascent to the throne of Duke of Jin and his subsequent success there are not achieved because of his personal motivation, but because he had the good fortune of being surrounded with competent advisors.

Zhao Cui's competence comes to the fore in the banquet with Duke Mu. After Hu Yan asks the prince to bring Zhao Cui along, the narrative jumps immediately to a poetic offering conducted by the prince. No account of the formal welcoming and response protocol that opens most diplomatic banquets is given, which suggests that its routine nature renders it irrelevant here. Chong'er's choice of poem, "River Water" 河水, is likely made on the advice of

Zhao Cui, as this would be one of his functions as an advisor with cultural competence. Most commentators gloss "River Water" as a variant title for a piece found in the *Poems* called "Swelling Water" 沔水, which reads as follows:

> Swelling is that flowing river,
> it goes to pay court to the sea.
> Swift is that flying hawk,
> now it flies up, now it settles down.
> Oh, you brothers of mine,
> oh, you friends among the people of the kingdom!
> There is nobody who wants to heed the disorder,
> yet who has no father and mother!
>
> Swelling is the flowing river,
> its flow is voluminous.
> Swift is that flying hawk,
> now it flies up, now it soars.
> I think of those lawless men,
> now they rise, now they set out.
> Oh, the grief of the heart,
> it cannot be stopped or forgotten.
>
> Swift is that flying hawk,
> it goes along that middle hill.
> The people's false speeches,
> how is it that nobody stops them?
> Oh, you friends of mine, be careful,
> slanderous words are rising.[33]

Duke Mu responds by offering "Sixth Month" 六月, the first three stanzas of which read as follows:

> In quiet rest of the sixth month,
> the war chariots were equipped;
> the four stallions were strong;
> we loaded the uniforms;
> the Xianyun were greatly ablaze,
> we were thereby pressed;

---

33. Mao #183. Karlgren, *Book of Odes*, pp. 126–27. The "Lesser Preface" 小序 states, "'Swelling Water' is meant to regulate King Xuan (r. 827–782 B.C.E.)" 沔水。規宣王也.

the king sent out a war expedition,
in order to set aright the kingdom.

We matched according to quality the four black horses,
we trained them according to the rules;
in this sixth month,
we prepared our clothes;
our clothes were prepared
in our thirty league homesteads;
the king sent out a war expedition,
it was to help the Son of Heaven.

The four stallions were long and broad,
they were large and bulky;
we attacked the Xianyun,
and achieved fine deeds;
we were grave and reverent,
we provided the war clothes;
we provided the war clothes,
in order to settle the kingdom.[34]

In this apparently simple poetic exchange there lurks the complex issue of what cognitive scientists call "theory of mind"—the ability of a sentient creature to form an impression of what another is thinking. Theory of mind is measured in degrees that can be expressed through a series of nested statements such as, "I know X_0; you know (I know X)$_1$; I know (you know (I know X))$_2$; you know (I know (you know (I know X)))$_3$"; and so on.[35] In this case, Prince

---

34. Mao #177. After Karlgren, *Book of Odes*, p. 120. Of this song, the "Lesser Preface" states, "'Sixth Month' is about King Xuan's northern campaigns" 六月。宣王北伐也. These campaigns were waged against the Xianyun "barbarian" tribes.

35. Such a nested series in negative form is at the heart of the famous anecdote found in the "Autumn Floods" 秋水 chapter of *Zhuangzi* (chap. 17):

Zhuangzi and Huizi were strolling across the bridge over the Hao River. Zhuangzi said, "Those minnows are darting about so freely—this is the happiness of fish!" Huizi said, "You are not a fish, so how can you know the happiness of fish?" Zhuangzi said, "You are not me, so how can you know that I do not know the happiness of fish?" Huizi said, "I am not you, so I certainly do not know if you know; but you are certainly not a fish, so your not knowing the happiness of fish is completely proven!" Zhuangzi said, "Let's return to the root of this argument. Your asking me something such as *how* do I know the

Chong'er is thinking that he wants help from Duke Mu when he goes to the banquet.₀ The duke knows the prince wants help.₁ The prince knows the duke knows the prince wants help.₂ The duke knows the prince knows the duke knows the prince wants help.₃ It is only at this third degree that the poetic exchange can effectively take place. When Prince Chong'er offers a poem as a plea for help, it is under the assumption that the duke knows why he is there, in other words he knows that the duke knows what he wants. Likewise, the duke's poem offered in response is read as a product of a state of mind that includes an impression of the state of mind of the prince (which includes an impression of the duke's state of mind); both the prince's and the duke's states of mind *precede and coexist with* the offering of their poems. The poems cannot be read as simple vessels of zero-degree states of mind. Without mutual and *preexisting* impressions of each party's state of mind at the time of offering, the poems would pass each other as ships in the night, accomplishing nothing.

To attack it from a different angle, imagine that the prince simply arrived at the banquet, walked straight up to the duke, and said, "I need your help"—and that the duke replied, "You shall have it." There is no subtext here. The plain discourse simply articulates the state of mind of each party: pleading and agreement. The exchange of poetry, however, is a much more nuanced interaction and is thus more diplomatically useful. The very form of poetic offering—as a ritual exchange of specially marked discourse within the context of sharing food and drink—is an assertion of commonality and respect. The respect is derived from the form of the ritual offering itself: the language of the *Poems* and the mode of its offering (chanting, singing) are appropriate in this context. They signal an adherence to

---

happiness of fish means you already knew that I knew it when you asked me. I know it as I stand over this river." (Wang Xianqian, *Zhuangzi jijie*, p. 148)

Huizi attempts to adhere to a logical argument, while Zhuangzi exploits the inadequacy of language to frame such arguments. Theory of mind is not about knowing for certain what another is thinking—as Huizi points out, this is impossible without complete identity—it is about forming an impression of what another is thinking, which underlies the way we use language to communicate with others (just as it does Huizi's original question).

protocol, which is an explicit form of submission to the hierarchy of power supported by that protocol.

Respect is also implied in the obliquity of the special language of the *Poems*. The text of "Swelling Water" is not a direct plea for aid, but a description of a lamentable state of affairs that is traditionally attributed to the reign of King Xuan 宣 (r. 827–782 B.C.E.) of the Western Zhou. Its key "inciting image" (*xing* 興), meant to arouse sympathetic thoughts and feelings in those who hear it, is found in the first couplet: "Swelling is that flowing river, / it goes to pay court to the sea." The image figures Prince Chong'er as a flowing river that seeks help by paying court to the powerful state of Qin, figured as the sea. It can only be understood as such if the flowing water is taken as an analogy for lesser states paying homage to greater ones.[36] The figure only crystallizes, making the urgency of the inherited words relevant to the present, if Duke Mu chooses to take Prince Chong'er's state of mind into account in listening to the poem. The duke must also have prior knowledge of many things, including the state of affairs in Jin, how they have affected Prince Chong'er, the preeminent role Qin has among the feudal states, and its relationship to Jin. Based on this knowledge, the duke can form a reasonably accurate impression of what the prince must be thinking when he offers the poem: "He comes to me for military aid to invade Jin because he has been cheated out of his rightful place on the throne, and because I am the ruler of a powerful state that is no friend of the current Jin ruler."[37] In his poetic offering, the prince is counting on the ability of the duke to form an accurate impression of the prince's state of mind *prior* to the actual performance of the poem. Based on such an impression, the duke can form an accurate

---

36. I refer to the figure as an analogy rather than a metaphor because the image of lesser waters flowing into greater is not an absent, abstract verbal construct (vehicle) standing in for a specific notion (tenor) of lesser states paying homage to the greater; both waters and states are concrete and present phenomena similar in their adherence to the overarching principle of the lesser tending towards the greater.

37. The entry for Duke Xi 15th Year (645 B.C.E.) tells of a battle in which Duke Mu of Qin defeated and captured Duke Hui of Jin. Duke Mu was eventually forced to repatriate his prisoner because of the entreaties of his own wife, who happened to be Duke Hui's elder sister.

"reading" of the prince's poetic offering by measuring the words of the poem against his impression of the sentiment that the prince must be trying to express. If the words are too far out of alignment with the supposed sentiment, it may mean one of several things: (1) his impression of the prince's motivations is erroneous, (2) his reading of the poem is incompetent, or (3) the prince's choice of poem is incompetent. The prince, for his part, does not know if the duke was successful in forming an accurate reading of the offered poem until the duke responds in kind. The prince (in this case, through his proxy, Zhao Cui) "reads" the response based on the assumption that the duke knows what the prince is thinking. The duke's response, therefore, is based on the assumption that the prince knows that the duke knows what the prince is thinking. The whole interaction is a house of cards that will stand or fall depending on whether the choice of poems bears out the assumptions.

The proof is in the poem, so to speak. In his poetic response the duke has three choices: (1) he can offer a poem that indicates his understanding of, and favorable disposition toward, the prince's request, (2) he can offer a poem that indicates his understanding and unfavorable disposition, or (3) he can simply offer a poem that does not indicate his state of mind with any degree of clarity. Thus, the duke is not placed in the uncomfortable position of having to explicitly turn down a direct request, which would be his prerogative, but which would also run the risk of making him lose face as a ruler lacking in munificence.

In the ritual form of offering a poem, respect is shown through adherence to the demands of protocol in making the utterance. The obliquity of language in poetic offering also shows respect, in surrendering some measure of control to the interlocutor in his reception of the utterance. In this context, poetic competence becomes a matter of maintaining as much control as possible over one's poetic utterance while not overstepping the bounds of decorum. This is achieved by correctly gauging the state of mind of one's interlocutor so that one may make the most efficacious choice of poem and the most adept timing of its delivery. When Hu Yan advises the prince to take Zhao Cui with him to the banquet, it is because he has recognized that the banquet is the best time and venue for the prince to make his plea. The offering of a poem at a banquet is demanded by protocol, but Hu Yan realizes that it can also be seized as an opportunity to advance his master's cause. He shows sensitivity to the variables of poetic competence (time, place, person) even if he does not possess the actual Traditional knowledge that Zhao Cui has. The ritual exchange of poetry becomes a double-edged sword for those in a position of power. The prince is beholden to speak to the duke in a certain fashion with certain words, but, provided he does so competently, the duke is then beholden to make a response. If the prince were to make a direct request of the duke in plain language, the duke could obviate the embarrassment of refusing him by ignoring the request altogether as a violation of protocol. Once the prince has agreed to play by the rules of the game, the duke must abide by them as well. To refuse to play would be to erode the very underpinnings of his symbolic power. It is the ritual context of the utterance that demands attention, more than the words themselves, which are heeded *because* of the ritual context. The eventual transition of the *Poems* from a corpus for ritual reenactment to a rhetorical resource entails a shift in potency from ritual context to the words themselves, as will be seen later in this chapter.

When Zhao Cui makes the choice of "Swelling Waters" for the prince, it is a choice informed by a sophisticated theory of mind. He knows that the duke knows that they are there to enlist Qin's superior military might in the campaign to take the throne of Jin. Zhao Cui chooses a poem that flatters the duke in its opening image by figuring him as the great sea to which all the lesser powers, including Prince Chong'er himself, flow. The rest of the poem laments that no one will come to the aid of a party wronged by slander: "There is nobody who wants to heed the disorder, / yet who has no father and mother!" and "The people's false speeches, / how is it that nobody stops them?" The offered language of the poem casts Duke Mu as a powerful and great ruler, while subordinating Prince Chong'er to a position of humility combined with righteous indignation. The audience at the banquet—other officials, court musicians, attendants—will have taken the point. The language of the *Poems* may be oblique, but Zhao Cui manages to pitch it so that Duke Mu would appear culturally incompetent if he were not to acknowledge the implicit request and ungracious if he were not to grant it. Poetic competence thus goes far beyond simply knowing the *Poems*, and includes a practical sense of where, when, and before whom they are best deployed for a desired effect.

The Duke of Qin may have been willing to grant Prince Chong'er's request all along, but the cultural competence of Hu Yan and Zhao Cui have made it very difficult for him to do otherwise. The narrative indicates that the duke responds immediately by offering the poem "Sixth Month" without any intervening actions or words. The prince's performance is so pointed as to create a tension that demands immediate resolution. The duke's ability to respond instantly without deferring to his own advisors or musicians reflects well on his cultural competence. The positive nature of his response—"The king sent out a war expedition / in order to set aright the kingdom"—reflects well on his sense of righteousness. It seems that the prince, with the aid of his advisors, was successful in the timing of his offering, thus extracting the desired reading and response from his audience.

The ball then returns to Prince Chong'er's court, for he must demonstrate that he has successfully read the duke's poetic offering in response. The prince is clearly not up to the job, remaining silent and motionless until Zhao Cui prompts him by saying, "Chong'er bows in acceptance of this!" 重耳拜賜.[38] The prince takes the cue but, just as with his excessive apology for the water-splattering incident, he clumsily overdoes the obeisance by "stepping down, bowing, and touching his head to the ground" 公子降拜稽首. This surfeit of humility causes the duke to redress the imbalance immediately by "descending one step to decline the gesture" 公降一級而辭焉. Zhao Cui, being culturally competent, realizes that he must explain the reason behind the prince's excessive display of gratitude—that it is warranted and not simply a result of overstepping the bounds of decorum. It is in this explanation that Zhao Cui's reading of the duke's poetic response is made public. Ideally, the exchange of poetry should have been transparent, taking place

---

38. The term *bai* 拜 indicates "kneeling, then bending until the head is level with the waist and the fingers touch the ground" (*Hanyu da cidian*, s.v. "bai"). It does not normally entail touching one's head to the ground.

without commentary. It is only when things start to break down that the need to discuss them explicitly arises.[39]

In explaining the prince's extraordinary show of humility, Zhao Cui says, "Your lordship referred to Chong'er as a means 'to help the Son of Heaven' in giving him your command. How could he dare not to bow down" 君稱所以佐天子者命重耳。重耳敢不拜? On the surface this statement simply explains ritual action (bowing) as a response to a poetic offering, but on closer reading it reveals itself to be a way of controlling meaning in reception—a shrewd demonstration of poetic competence. First, Zhao Cui characterizes Duke Mu's entire poetic offering as a "command" 命 to Chong'er, taking the poem not simply as a call to arms, but as a commitment by Duke Mu to be the figure of authority behind Chong'er's campaign. The traditional reading of this poem, amply supported by the poem's internal evidence, is that it is an ode in praise of Jifu, who was sent on a military expedition by King Xuan (r. 827–782 B.C.E.) to do battle against the northern Xianyun tribe, which was making incursions into Zhou territory. Zhao Cui casts Duke Mu in the role of the Zhou king and Prince Chong'er in the role of Jifu. Just as King Xuan outfitted Jifu with a military force and commanded him to rid the kingdom of its enemies, so too will Duke Mu outfit Prince Chong'er and command him to expel the slanderers from the state of Jin. Zhao Cui clearly indicates this relationship when he quotes directly from the duke's poetic offering, saying that it refers to the prince "as a means 'to help the Son of Heaven.'" Duke Mu, as the implied referent for the term "Son of Heaven," deserves the profound show of respect that the prince has given him. And thus Zhao Cui is able to explain why Prince Chong'er felt it necessary to touch his head to the ground in accepting the poem.[40]

---

39. Ironically, it is the need to explain things that are no longer self-evident in a context of decline that constitutes the raison d'être of the Traditionalists, even as they endeavor to halt that decline. If the Traditionalists were ever to be truly successful, they would put themselves out of a job. However, as Confucius, and later, Mencius, found, telling someone what is right and getting them to act on it are entirely different matters.

40. A conservative Traditionalist advisor by the name of Meng Wubo 孟武伯 is quoted in the *Zuo Tradition* as stating that only the Zhou King can properly receive

This small rupture in ritual, and the attempt to repair it with words, opens up a window through which to view the essence of poetic offering as ritual reenactment. Poetic offering functions as an effective diplomatic tool for negotiating the tension between commonality and difference. The commonality underlying the offering of poetry is found in its ritual context (most often the banquet) and in the corpus of words on offer—the *Poems*. Offering a poem is a way of reenacting a ritual that has been reenacted countless times before, thus signaling adherence to the ground rules of a diplomatic encounter. In many cases, and particularly in the formulaic welcome of the host and the response by the guest, offering a poem is a sort of phatic communication, the content of the words being secondary to the practice of their utterance as means of establishing an air of sociability.

Where difference arises is not in the form of ritual offering, nor in the words on offer, but between individual instances of application and interpretation of an offered poem. The room for difference arises out of the status of the *Poems* as words inherited from the past. There is a gap between then and now, between that place and this place. An educated man of the Eastern Zhou manifests his poetic competence in how his utterance and understanding of the *Poems* bridges that gap. Some Traditionalists assume the position that ritualistic poetic offering can only be legitimately reenacted by people who are in direct lineage with the "originating" parties, the ones who participated in the initial poetic exchange that produced a given poem. Poetic competence in this case means the ability to recognize and respond appropriately to the propriety or impropriety of a particular poetic offering. In practice, this means that the pieces in the *Poems* directed to the Zhou king during the Western Zhou should only be directed to the Zhou king in the Eastern Zhou.[41] And poems originating in a particular state are properly

---

a kowtow (Ai 17.6). Zhao Cui is obviously more expedient in his interpretation of ritual, which may indicate a more flexible attitude among the early Traditionalists.

41. An envoy from Wei, by the name of Ning Wuzi 甯武子, refuses to respond to poems offered to him at a banquet by the Duke of Lu. When asked the reason for his behavior, he says that it would constitute a crime to accept the "grand honors" 大禮 reserved for Zhou kings and princes (Wen 4). Another fastidious Tradition-

sung only by people from that state.[42] These strictures seek to stabilize interpretation by narrowing the field of application. They are an attempt to halt the disintegration of an old order of the world by tying it to an old order of words.

The more agile among the Traditionalists realize that though the old world order may be irrecoverable, the old words still have potency as means of effecting a better new world order *along the lines of* the old world order. This again is analogous thinking. The *Poems* may be perceived as having specific points of origin, but this does not preclude them from being used outside the parameters of those origins if they are taken as examples of general principles that still apply (or at least should apply) to the present situation. In this case, poetic competence in utterance means choosing the right poem and pitching it to the right person at the right time and place, so that its relevance is so apparent that its cogency cannot be easily denied. Poetic competence in understanding means being able to recognize that relevance and to incorporate it as a factor in one's own utterance in response. Differences can arise in *how* relevance is measured. Two people could have different interpretations of the same poetic offering because each of them has applied the poem to the situation at hand in slightly different ways. This is a matter of interiority, which does not find its way to the surface of *Zuo Tradition* narratives. Such differences amidst commonality can only be inferred by subsequent behavior and words.

When Prince Chong'er makes his deep obeisance to Duke Mu, it implies a certain understanding of the poem offered by the duke. The duke's explicit rejection of the prince's obeisance is an implicit rejection of the prince's reading, which the duke has inferred from the prince's behavior. There is a difference between how the duke intended his poem to be applied to the situation at hand and how the prince (via Zhao Cui) chooses to apply it. Prince Chong'er's initial poetic offering to the duke was less problematic because it lacks the specificity of the poem given by the duke in response. The

---

alist, Zhao Meng, refuses to accept various poetic offerings from the officials of Zheng because they should be directed to rulers instead (Xiang 27).

42. Xuanzi 宣子 asks the ministers of Zheng to perform songs of Zheng for him at a parting banquet so that he can ascertain "the mind of Zheng" (Zhao 16).

prince's poem lacks internal evidence tying it to a particular person, place, or audience. The "Lesser Preface" 小序 tells us that it was originally composed "to regulate King Xuan" 規宣王也 of the late Western Zhou era, but the poem itself can easily be generalized as a blanket complaint against the absence of a political will to quell the rise of petty men and slander. A strict Traditionalist might object to the offering of this poem to the Duke of Qin rather than the King of Zhou, but the general principle articulated in it is readily apparent and obviously related to Prince Chong'er's own situation. The role set out for Duke Mu as the "brother" and "friend" who should come to the aid of the victim is also plain. Duke Mu would have to be quite obtuse to miss these points. It is the very specificity of Duke Mu's response with "Sixth Month," however, that facilitates a difference in application and interpretation. It is possible, even probable, that Duke Mu meant the poem to be interpreted as synecdoche: "King Xuan is an example of a ruler who was concerned with quelling disorder, as a good ruler should be. I am such a ruler as well, and so I will help you." Zhao Cui, however, understands the poem analogically: "Prince Chong'er is to Jifu as you, Duke Mu, are to King Xuan, the Son of Heaven. You order him to lead your forces against the enemy." In the end, it is Zhao Cui's reading that stands because it is the only one made public by the *Zuo Tradition* narrative. If the prince's initial poetic offering is encompassed under this analogical reading, the entire poetic exchange effectively recasts the state of Qin as the center of power, deserving of words meant originally for Zhou and possessing authority originally reserved by Zhou. Such flexibility in interpretation is what drives the staunchest Traditionalists toward restricting the range of application to the "original" set of parameters. But it is only through the willingness of Traditionalists such as Zhao Cui to step outside these parameters that the Tradition can remain relevant to a changing world, one that may no longer have Zhou at its center.

It is no accident that, in this brief narrative surrounding a poetic exchange at a banquet, the *Zuo Tradition* gives all of the directly quoted words before the banquet to Hu Yan and those at the banquet to Zhao Cui. The principal partners in the exchange—the prince and duke—simply perform their set pieces and step aside. It is the secondary players, the advisors, who are given all of the lines and even some of the stage directions. They are the ones who facilitate the ritual and attach meaning to it. They are the ones who have the first and last word, converting practice into object lesson. What is to be learned here is that the highest level of poetic competence consists of more than knowing the *Poems* and ritual protocols. Mastery of the practice of poetic offering requires being able to win some measure of control over how others are disposed to interpret your utterance and how you choose to interpret theirs. The ritual form of offering and the restricted repertoire of poems that may be offered do place limitations on such control, but the truly competent are able to turn such limitations to their advantage by mastering them. They can win control by exploiting the variables of the ritual, taking the time, place, and recipient of their offerings into account. They may also exploit gaps in the repertoire, bridging the distance between the "then" of the *Poems* and the "now" of their application according to their own agenda. It is no accident that it is Traditionalist advisors who are most often heard in the narratives of the *Zuo Tradition* explicitly discussing the proprieties surrounding the offering of poetry. It is they who have been inculcated with the lessons encoded in the Tradition, and it is they who are the custodians of ritual modes of performance. In other words, it is they who have intimate knowledge of what should be said (*lexis*) and how it should be said (*hexis*). This guarantees them the highest degree of success in controlling interpretation, which is the ultimate goal of every scholar-exegete.

The competence that allows a smooth performance of Tradition through poetic offering must efface itself to be effective. It remains submerged, hidden to *both* parties in the exchange, even as it guides the exchange. To overtly signal the presence of ulterior motives in a poetic performance would be to remove the semblance of spontaneity and sincerity that give the performance its suasive power. This explains why the only occasions in which the *Zuo Tradition* can depict explicit discussions of poetic competence is when that competence is partially or completely absent.[43] In these cases, the failure

---

43. Confucius's own discussions of poetic competence in the *Analects* are always framed in the negative. For a practice that is best carried out when its principles are

is framed and made discernible by a larger discussion of it. If a performance goes off smoothly, it is signaled by a *lack* of explicit comment. When the performance breaks down because one party is not holding up his end and thus is impeding the satisfactory completion of the exchange, then comment about the performance may intrude. This is a result of the performance taking place over time. The offering of a poem immediately sets up a tension that requires response for closure. If closure is not provided through appropriate response, then the tension must be resolved through other means, namely by subordinating the aborted performance to the status of object of discourse.

Stand-up comedy provides an apt analogy. If a comedian tells a joke and the audience laughs, then an appropriate exchange has taken place, and he quickly moves on to the next joke without comment. He builds upon the measure of approval he has won from the audience and parlays it into a favorable disposition for his next joke. Each successful exchange augments his authority to be standing before the audience as a comedian. To stop and say, "You must have really enjoyed that joke—let me tell you why," would kill his momentum, unless it was a segue to another joke. However, if he tells his joke and it "hangs there" without the expected laughter in response, a palpable tension results. It must be resolved or he will lose his authority to continue. He cannot simply move on to his next joke and pretend nothing happened. If he is thinking quickly, he will turn the failure of his joke into the object of his next joke, which (if successful) will reestablish his authority. If his audience is thinking quickly, they will leap into the breach and heckle the comedian, turning his failed joke into fodder for their own joke. This is highly damaging to the comedian's authority unless he can turn the tables and make the heckler the object of his next joke. The *Zuo Tradition* has a wonderful account of poetic heckling when Qing Feng 慶封 of Qi visits the court of Lu and repeatedly fails to observe diplomatic protocol.[44] The members of the Lu court offer

---

fully internalized, it is always easier to address the reasons for failure—which "stick out" as signals of inadequate internalization—than it is to analyze the elements of success, which necessarily efface themselves as a precondition of their efficacy.

44. Xiang 27.

him the poem "Look at the Rat" 相鼠, which reads in part, "Look at the rat, it has its skin; a man without manners—a man without manners, why does he not die?"[45] This is a doubly devastating critique for it uses the Tradition to mock a lack of facility in traditional knowledge. Qin Feng fails to understand even this pointed insult.

Thus competence can be demonstrated in how one handles instances of incompetence in oneself or others. This is really a matter of nesting one level of (in)competence inside another level. In order to operate effectively, the highest level of competence will efface itself even as it makes the second level explicit, which it must do to establish its own authority. This is the fundamental relationship between the offering of poetry and the citation of poetry in speechmaking. The application and interpretation of the *Poems* that remained implicit in the ritual of offering are rendered explicit when a citation from them is framed in a speech. What was once a performance of poetry through ritual reenactment is "flattened out" into a rhetorical resource for a different type of performance: speechmaking.

IV

Cultural competence in offering a poem is very similar to the competence required for successful speechmaking. Indeed, the offering of a poem can be thought of as a very specialized form of speechmaking. In either case, the speaker takes the variables of time, place, and audience into account, adjusting his discourse according to his impressions of what his audience must be thinking. Officials make most of the speeches depicted in the *Zuo Tradition* to rulers or other officials, for these are the very class of people who must justify their existence through the skillful handling of discourse. The prime function of *Zuo Tradition* narratives is to demonstrate the competence of Traditionalists in this practice. Rulers are not required to make extended speeches because, as the focal point of the court, they naturally occupy the position of audience. In speaking at court, an official must impose his body upon the privileged space defined by the presence of the ruler and impose his speech upon the ruler's

---

45. Mao #52. Karlgren, *Book of Odes*, p. 33.

time. Even when officials are speaking to one another at court, the ruler is the tacit audience for these public exchanges of discourse. Such impositions require a mode of performance—involving particular postures and types of speech—that implicitly acknowledges and maintains the hierarchy atop which the ruler sits. Adopting this mode of performance allows an official to "take the floor," but it does not guarantee his success. The speaker must demonstrate competence if he is to continue speaking, if he is to be persuasive, and if he is to be allowed to speak again. It should come as no surprise that in the narratives of the *Zuo Tradition* such competence is demonstrated by building speeches around citations of Traditional knowledge, the *Poems* being the most frequently cited rhetorical resource. Many of the speeches depicted in the *Zuo Tradition* can be read as object lessons, acting as testaments to the power of poetic competence in fashioning truthful and persuasive speeches.[46]

The phrase "to cite a poem" (*yinshi* 引詩) suggests "drawing" or "intromitting" words from the Traditional body of knowledge called the *Poems* into the discourse of a speech. Because the *Poems* were a relatively stable and widely disseminated body of knowledge during the Eastern Zhou, and because they are invariably intoned in a tetrasyllabic meter, the provenance of their language is readily apparent upon utterance. Even so, a citation from the *Poems* is almost always explicitly marked in a speech, usually with the phrase "The *Poems* say . . ." 詩曰. This indicates that the authority of the *Poems* is derived just as much from their status as an explicitly labeled body of knowledge as it is from being a special form of language. The announcement that the speaker is about to cite a Traditional body of knowledge prepares the listener for the archaic sounds of the old words, which may not even be fully understood by the audience unless they too are well versed in Traditional knowledge. The intromission of words that sound "mysterious" helps to elevate and legitimate the mundane sounds of ordinary speech just as liturgical Latin does in a Catholic mass. It is actually

---

46. Schaberg (*Patterned Past*, pp. 72–80), Yang Xiangshi (*Zuo zhuan fushi yinshi kao*), and Zeng Qinliang (*Zuo zhuan yinshi fushi zhi shijiao yanjiu*) all address poetic citation, the latter two collecting and annotating every instance of it found in the *Zuo Tradition*.

desirable to the Traditionalist advisor that his citation from the *Poems* not be immediately transparent, for he displays his competence in applying and interpreting the citation with regard to the matter at hand in his speech.

A citation from the *Poems* may be integrated into a speech in a variety of ways, but it always involves application and interpretation.[47] In *offering* a poem as a form of ritual reenactment, application is a matter of choosing the appropriate poem for the given time, place, and audience; interpretation is a matter of construing the relationship between the poem and the current situation, an activity that occurs tacitly on *both* sides of the exchange. The competence required to interpret an offered poem is assumed for both parties—its absence is a remarkable occasion. It is desirable that the applicability of the offered poem (and hence its intended interpretation) be self-evident, for the necessity of further comment would signal the exchange's failure. In the context of poetic offering, the human participants are to some extent subordinated to the poem, the vehicle to which they entrust their sentiments. However, as was evident in the exchange between Prince Chong'er and Duke Mu, there is always "wiggle room," an exploitable difference in commonality.

With poetic *citation*, however, the human being reasserts his dominance over discourse. It is he who fashions his speech, and the poem is put in service of it. Application is no longer a matter of

---

47. Yang Xiangshi (*Zuo zhuan fushi yinshi kao*, pp. 65–67) establishes eight classifications of poetic citation in speeches. The first and last items in the list below are more general principles of citation rather than specific usages.

斷章取義 breaking off a stanza to seize upon a meaning (at odds with the one suggested by the original context)

摭句證言 choosing a line to prove what one is saying (often treated as historical evidence)

先引以發其下 opening the argument with a citation (often through application)

後引以承其上 closing the argument with a citation (often as a general case)

意解以申其義 explaining the meaning (of a citation) to extend its meaning (to the argument)

合引以貫其義 combining two citations to link their meanings

分句釋旨 explaining/applying the parts of a stanza separately

同文異事 the same text is applied to different situations

choosing the appropriate poem for the time, place, and audience (consideration of these variables has shifted to the speech as a whole), but is a matter of selecting the right *lines* from a poem and inserting them at the appropriate time and place in the speech for maximum effect. Interpretation is no longer a matter of tacit construing, but of articulated explication. The poem is no longer revivified through ritual reenactment as a performative utterance forming a self-evident "organic" link to the world. It is now a rhetorical resource, a group of words, a form of discourse that links to another form of discourse (the speech), which in turn links to the world.

The speech belongs to the speaker and thus the interpretation of the poem cited in his speech belongs to him as well. In fashioning a speech, the competent Traditionalist builds a frame in which he can capture only those lines from the *Poems* of immediate use to him, "flatten" them out by stripping them of the multiple dimensions derived from a ritual context, and put them in service of his larger argument. This is a powerful move, for it places him in the role of dominant exegete, dictating meaning within the hermeneutically sealed environment of his speech. Such a move is predicated on a certain measure of ignorance in the audience, which requires the guidance of a competent Traditionalist to properly understand the relevance of Traditional knowledge. The Traditionalists can only consolidate their role as transmitters of the Tradition in a context of decline, for they count upon the incompetence of others to define their own competence. They usher in a world in which it is no longer sufficient to manifest the relevance of old instances of discourse by reenacting them; one must explain their relevance by subsuming them into a mode of discourse that is created anew on each occasion: the speech.

The most common type of speech contained in *Zuo Tradition* narratives is the remonstration (*jian* 諫). The act of remonstrating with his "king" (or duke, or marquis) provides the Traditionalist with the perfect opportunity to demonstrate the continuing relevance of the Tradition, thereby providing the justification for its (and his) preservation. The king, by virtue of occupying the position of King, has the right to demand certain forms of action and discourse from his inferiors. However, the position makes certain demands of those who would fill it, and it seems that very few people, once the Golden Age of the Western Zhou had passed, could meet those demands without constant advice and aid from their subordinates. Indeed, acknowledging one's own limits and being open to remonstration were the signs of a good king, of one that was striving to live up to the Kingly ideal. Thus, when a Traditionalist attempts to hold the ear and win the mind of the king, he does so by appealing to a Tradition of knowledge derived from an age of Kings (notably King Wen). Remonstrating with citations of traditional knowledge is a powerful strategy because the king himself occupies a position defined by the Tradition. Thus, the remonstrating official is quoting the Body of Kingly Knowledge before the body of the king, fashioning a collision of essence and corporeality.

Such a collision can prove dangerous at times. The following passage from Duke Xuan 2nd Year (607 B.C.E.) narrates an instance of remonstration with a duke who verges on being a caricature of a ruling reprobate. The likely prospect of the remonstration failing makes the parameters of its performance the subject of explicit discussion, both by the personages within the narrative *and* by the narrator, making this a particularly informative illustration of the practice of citing poetry in remonstration.

Duke Ling of Jin did not live up to the role of ruler. He took in heavy taxes in order to decorate the walls of his palace. He would shoot at people with a slingshot from his terrace just to watch them dodge the pellets. Once his chef boiled a bear's paw for him, but it was underdone. The duke killed him and stuffed his body in a grain hamper. He then had his ladies carry the hamper out past the court. Zhao Dun and Shi Ji saw a hand [protruding from the hamper], and when they asked what had happened, they were horrified by it. They were about to remonstrate with the duke, when Shi Ji said, "If we both remonstrate and he does not accept it, then there will be no one left to continue in our place. Let me be first and if he does not accept what I say, then you may carry on after me."

Shi Ji made three advances towards the duke and only when he had reached the eaves over the dais did the duke turn to look at him. "I realize that I have my faults," said the duke. "I am going to correct them." Shi Ji touched his head to the ground and responded, "Is there anyone among us without faults? But to have faults and be able to correct them: there is no good greater than that! The *Poems* say,

> There is nobody who has not a beginning,
> but few can have a normal end.[48]

This being so, there are truly few who are able to amend their faults. If your lordship is able to bring things to 'a normal end,' then our altars of earth and grain will be secure. How could it be the officials alone who rely upon them? The *Poems* also say,

> When the embroidered fabric of the royal robe has a hole,
> Zhong Shanfu alone can mend it.[49]

So one is able to amend faults. If your lordship is able to amend his faults, then the royal robe need not be thrown away."

But the duke still did not correct his behavior.

Then it was Zhao Dun who remonstrated with him repeatedly until the duke grew sick of him and dispatched Chu Mei to destroy him. Chu Mei went at dawn but found the door to Zhao Dun's bedroom already open and Zhao himself fully dressed and ready to attend court. It was early yet and he was just sitting there, dozing. Chu Mei withdrew and sighed to himself, "He is so mindful of his duties; this man is a mainstay of the people. To destroy the mainstay of the people is to be disloyal to them, but to ignore the command of one's lord is to be unfaithful to him. If I must choose between these two, I would prefer death." So he smashed his head against a locust tree in the courtyard and died. (Xuan 2.3)

晉靈公不君。厚斂以彫牆。從臺上彈人。而觀其辟丸也。宰夫胹熊
蹯不熟。殺之。寘諸畚。使婦人載以過朝。趙盾。士季。見其手。問
其故。而患之。將諫。士季曰。諫而不入。則莫之繼也。會請先。不
入。則子繼之。

　三進及溜。而後視之。曰。吾知所過矣。將改之。稽首
而對曰。人誰無過。過而能改。善莫大焉。詩曰。

　　靡不有初
　　鮮克有終

夫如是。則能補過者鮮矣。君能有終。則社稷之固也。豈惟群臣賴之。
又曰。

　　袞職有闕
　　惟仲山甫補

能補過也。君能補過。袞不廢矣。
　猶不改。

宣子驟諫。公患之。使鉏麑賊之。晨往。寢門闢矣。盛服將朝。尚
早。坐而假寐。麑退。歎而言曰。不忘恭敬。民之主也。賊民之主。不
忠。棄君之命。不信。有一於此。不如死也。觸槐而死。

The narrative begins by explicitly labeling Duke Ling as a ruler unfit
for the role designated by that name (*jun* 君). Because part of being a
true ruler is heeding remonstration, the opening sentence sets up the
narrative inevitability that the remonstration will fail (knowledge
shared by reader, narrator, and narratees alike). This is a paradox
faced by all Traditionalist advisors: the very people most in need of
their advice are the least likely to heed it. The narrative provides key
instances of Duke Ling's "unrulerness." He fails in his public duties
by exacting taxes to gratify his own appetites rather than to improve
his state as a whole. He fails in his personal impulses by tormenting
his people for his own amusement rather than pursuing the proper
pleasures of a king. He is "unkingly" without and within. The last
egregious instance—the murder of an incompetent chef—provides a
bloody transition from a general list of Duke Ling's failings to the
particulars of this anecdote. That Duke Ling realizes the difference
between right and wrong is shown in his clumsy attempt to conceal
the cook's murder from the attendants at court by stuffing the
corpse in a basket. Having his ladies lug the basket through the au-
dience chamber, however, was not the most inconspicuous means of
disposing of the body. When the two advisors, Zhao Dun and Shi
Ji, spot the dead man's hand protruding from the basket, their keen
faculties tell them that something is amiss. This act of "interpreta-
tion" seems a macabre parody of a process reiterated in the Tradi-
tion itself: surmising the state of the interior from external evidence.
The advisors, fully aware of the duke's recalcitrance and violent
temper, hatch a plan to remonstrate with him in succession. What is
never stated explicitly by Shi Ji, but is surely implied in his proposal,
is that remonstrating with such a ruler poses a grave risk. The duke
may do more than ignore the message; he may kill the messenger.
A good Traditionalist must be willing to die in defense of his
Tradition. When Shi Ji tells Zhao Dun, "If he does not accept what I
say, then you may carry on after me" 不入則子繼之, he is
acknowledging that just as there is a position of Ruler that will be

filled by a succession of rulers, so too is there a position of Advisor that will be filled by a succession of advisors.

Shi Ji is aware of the proper way to approach the duke: advancing in stages until he is noticed. This tactic—aside from building suspense in the narrative, for we surely know what is in store for this hapless advisor—simultaneously signifies both Shi Ji's respect for the duke's authority and his determination to remonstrate with him. Duke Ling correctly interprets the signal and, much as a child would do to avoid a spanking, attempts to head off the remonstration by immediately avowing his guilt and declaring that he will change. The reader senses that the duke has made this promise many times before. Shi Ji is a skillful advisor, though, and will not be preempted. He seizes the duke's avowal as an opportunity to remonstrate with him on his recidivist nature. Shi Ji bows his head to the ground as he does so, placing his body in a posture of humble deference even as he utters words calculated to place the duke in a state of discomfiture.

Shi Ji opens his speech in a conciliatory tone, acknowledging that everyone makes mistakes but that the important thing is to change one's behavior to avoid repeating them. He seems to hold out hope for his reprobate ruler. Then he cites the following lines from "Grand" 蕩 (Mao #255): "There is nobody who has not a beginning / but few can have a normal end" 靡不有初。鮮克有終. Shi Ji explicitly announces that he is citing this source of Traditional knowledge; in addition, the meter in which they are uttered (two lines of four characters each), their parallel grammatical structure, and the characteristic usage of some of the words (*mi* 靡, *xian* 鮮, and *ke* 克) all endow this utterance with the authority of the *Poems*. In case Duke Ling has missed the import of these lines (as seems likely), Shi Ji provides an explicit interpretation—"there are truly few who are able to amend their faults"—in which he forms an explicit linguistic link between the duke's own statement regarding "faults" (*guo* 過) and the citation's assertion that "few" (*xian* 鮮) people can see themselves through to a proper ending. Shi Ji began by applauding the duke's promise to reform his ways, but his citation from and ensuing interpretation of the *Poems* immediately juxtapose the duke's declaration with the Tradition, which casts serious doubt upon the ability of the duke to live up to his own words. It is inconceivable for Shi Ji to simply say to the duke, "You are lying," or even, "You may believe you can change, but you will not." The Tradition *can* say this for him. It says this and even more.

When Shi Ji cites and interprets the lines from "Grand," he forms more than an explicit intertextual link between the citation and the duke's own words; he also evokes an implicit link between the citation and the rest of the poem from which it is drawn. The practice of poetic citation as it is depicted in the *Zuo Tradition* is often characterized using the term "breaking off a stanza to seize upon a meaning" 斷章取義, with the connotation that lines from the *Poems* are quoted out of context in order to articulate sentiments that are not necessarily compatible with the poem as a whole. While this exact phrase is not found in the *Zuo Tradition* itself,[50] an early variation of it is found in Duke Xiang 28th Year (545 B.C.E.), which tells of Lupu Gui 盧蒲癸, who married a woman with whom he shared a common surname, thus violating the incest taboo. He defended his action by saying, "It is just like breaking off a stanza when offering a poem: I take from it whatever I am seeking" 辟之賦詩斷章。余取所求焉 (Xiang 28.9). It is important to note that Lupu uses the term "offering" here rather than "citing." He explicitly acknowledges a degree of manipulation in poetic offering, in the selection of which stanza is actually performed. Only those stanzas that serve the interests of the performer are uttered. When the *Poems* shifts from words for performance through ritual offering to words for citation in a speech, this manipulation becomes overt and

---

50. It is found in the Six Dynasties work of literary criticism called *Wenxin diaolong* 文心雕龍 by Liu Xie 劉勰 (ca. 465–522), in the chapter entitled "Stanza and Line" 章句: "If we consider the way in which the poets of the *Book of Songs* made metaphorical references, even though they may sometimes have made their point in detached stanzas [斷章取義], still the stanzas (*zhang*) and lines (*ju*) in a piece are like silk drawn from a cocoon, starting from the beginning and carrying it through to the end, the form always in layered succession [as with fish scales]. The periods that begin the journey anticipate the concepts (*yi*) in the middle of the composition; the words used at the close go back to carry through the significance of the previous lines" (Owen, *Readings*, p. 254). Liu is using an organic metaphor to illustrate the unity of a literary composition. This has a bearing on intertextuality for it suggests that even a partial citation will always carry implicit within it the connotation of the whole piece from which it is drawn.

is often reduced to the level of couplet rather than stanza. It is also important to note, however, that although Lupu may be willfully ignoring the context of his bride (that is, that she and he are of the same clan) in his actions, he is still acutely aware of it in his perceptions. He asks, "How can I recognize her ancestry?" 惡識宗, suggesting that he has already done so in his mind, but has simply refused to let his behavior be guided by that knowledge. Similarly, an advisor such as Shi Ji may cite particular lines from the *Poems* out of context, bending them to the situation at hand, but this does not remove the weight of their context. This weight may be provisionally ignored, but it is present nonetheless. In this case, Shi Ji seems to be counting on it to make a point that he would dare not articulate explicitly.

The entire text of "Grand," from which Shi Ji draws his citation, is a diatribe by the founder of the Zhou dynasty against the last ruler of the preceding Shang-Yin dynasty:

> Grand is God on High.
> he is the ruler of the people below;
> terrible is God on High,
> his charge has many rules;
> Heaven gives birth to the multitudinous people,
> but its charge is not to be relied on;
> there is nobody who has not a beginning,
> but few can have a normal end.
>
> King Wen said: Alas!
> Alas, you Yin-Shang!
> Those men are refractory,
> they are crushing and subduing,
> but they are in official positions,
> they are in the services;
> Heaven sent down in them a reckless disposition,
> but you raised them and give them power.
>
> King Wen said: Alas!
> Alas, you Yin-Shang!
> You should hold on to what is right and good;
> the refractory have much ill-will,
> with false words they answer you;
> robbers and thieves are used within,

they stand up and imprecate evil,
without limit, without end.

King Wen said: Alas!
Alas, you Yin-Shang!
You shout and brawl in this central kingdom;
you make it a virtue to heap ill-will upon yourself;
you do not make bright your virtue,
and so you do not distinguish the disloyal and perverse;
your virtue is not bright,
and so you do not distinguish the supporters, the
    true ministers.

King Wen said, Alas!
Alas, you Yin-Shang!
It is not Heaven that steeps you in wine;
it is not right that you are bent on it and use it;
you have erred in your demeanor;
you make no distinction between light and darkness,
you shout and clamor,
you turn day into night.

King Wen said, Alas!
Alas, you Yin-Shang!
You are noisy like cicadas, like grasshoppers
    you chatter,
like bubbling water, like boiling soup;
small and great are approaching to ruin,
but people still pursue this course;
here you are overbearing in the central kingdom,
and it extends even to Guifang.

King Wen said, Alas!
Alas, you Yin-Shang!
It is not that God on High is not good;
Yin does not use the old ways;
but though there are no old and perfected men,
there still are the statutes and the laws;
you have not listened to them;
the great appointment is therefore tumbling down.

King Wen said, Alas!
Alas, you Yin-Shang!

> The people have a saying:
> When a tree fallen down and uprooted is lifted,
> the branches and leaves are yet uninjured;
> the root is then first disposed of;[51]
> the mirror for Yin is not far off,
> it is in the age of the lords of Xia.[52]

With cognizance of the entire poem from which Shi Ji has cited one couplet—cognizance that Shi Ji certainly had and that even Duke Ling might have had in some debased form—it is impossible to escape the conclusion that Shi Ji's citation is meant to communicate more than the difficulty of amending one's faults. As a wholesale condemnation of the dissolute last rulers of the Shang dynasty by the founding father of the Zhou, this poem is an early articulation of the principle that a dynastic house engaged in immoral behavior forfeits the charge to rule granted to it by Heaven. Through his citation from the Tradition, Shi Ji attaches significance to the random violent acts and irrational brutality of the "refractory" Duke Ling: they lead to the demise of his own person and the ruling house; they imperil the very existence of the Jin state. The Tradition has a place for the likes of Duke Ling, and there is little he can do to escape it. In the end, Shi Ji's citation is less for the edification of an incorrigible ruler in a particular historical moment than it is for the extended audience of his speech, who will see for themselves the continuing power of traditional knowledge to bring order to a chaotic world.

There are really three intermingled voices in Shi Ji's speech: one speaking his own words, one speaking his citation from the *Poems*, and one murmuring darkly of the fate of those who refuse to listen. The first voice belongs to Shi Ji, the third to Tradition, and the second, the intermediary, is shared between these two entities. Shi Ji's poetic competence is manifested in how he manages the intersection of his own voice and that of the Tradition in his citation

---

51. Karlgren notes: "So 'the root' of the state, the royal house, is disposed of, without the branches and leaves, i.e. the people, coming to any harm" (*Book of Odes*, p. 261 note d).

52. After Karlgren, *Book of Odes*, pp. 214–16. Xia was the dynastic house preceding Shang-Yin.

from the *Poems*. In this case, he can hold out the possibility that the duke may change, while qualifying that possibility with a citation from the *Poems*, which in turn smuggles in a latent threat that will be realized in the likely event that the duke fails to change.

Perhaps feeling that he has tilted too much toward the negative in his citation, Shi Ji resumes his speech by imagining the positive outcome of a successful change in the duke's behavior. His conditional premise, "If your lordship is able to bring things to 'a normal end'" 君能有終則, which commingles the language of the citation with his own, places the responsibility for a happy conclusion squarely on the shoulders of the duke. How will Duke Ling be able to live up to this responsibility? The answer to that question is to be found in the Tradition; Shi Ji cites the following lines from "Multitudes" 烝民: "When the embroidered fabric of the royal robe has a hole / Zhong Shanfu alone can mend it."[53] Every ruler needs a loyal and competent official to help him in his administration of the land and to remind him of proper behavior. Zhong Shanfu is the paradigm of such a coadjutant, and the explicit mention of his name here evokes the entire poem about him, which reads as follows:

> Heaven gave birth to the multitude of people,
> they have bodies, they have rules;
> that the people hold onto norms
> is because they love beautiful virtue;
> Heaven looked down upon the domain of Zhou,
> and brightly approached the world below;
> it protected this Son of Heaven,
> and gave birth to Zhong Shanfu.
>
> The virtue of Zhong Shanfu
> is mild and kind and just;
> he has a good deportment, a good appearance,
> he is careful and reverent,
> he has the ancient precepts as his norm;
> he is strenuous about his fine deportment,
> and obedient to the Son of Heaven;
> he causes the bright decrees to be promulgated.

---

53. Mao #260. After Karlgren, *Book of Odes*, p. 229.

The king charged Zhong Shanfu:
"Be a model to those many rulers,
continue the service of your ancestors,
protect the king's person,
give out and bring in reports about the king's decrees;
be the king's throat and tongue;
promulgate the government abroad;
in the states of the four quarters it will then be set
      in function."

Solemn is the king's charge,
Zhong Shanfu handles it;
whether the states are obedient or not,
Zhong Shanfu brightly discerns it;
he is enlightened and wise,
and so he protects his person;
morning and evening he does not slacken,
in the service of the One Man.

The people have a saying:
"If soft, then eat it,
if hard, then spit it out";
but Zhong Shanfu
neither eats the soft,
nor spits out the hard;
he does not oppress the solitary and the widows,
he does not fear the strong and the refractory.

The people have a saying:
"Virtue is light as a hair,
but among the people few can lift it";
we only estimate and consider it,
but Zhong Shanfu alone can lift it;
we love him, but nobody can help him;
when the embroidered fabric of the royal robe has a hole,
Zhong Shanfu alone can mend it.

Zhong Shanfu went out and sacrificed to the Spirit of
      the Road;
the four stallions were robust;
the soldiers were brisk,
each of them afraid of lagging behind;
the four stallions went *bang-bang*

the eight bit-bells tinkled;
the king charged Zhong Shanfu to fortify that
   eastern region.

The four stallions were strong;
the eight bit-bells tinkled in unison;
Zhong Shanfu marched to Qi,
and quick was his returning home;
Jifu has made this song,
stately is the pure-sounding air;
Zhong Shanfu has constant anxieties;
by this song I comfort his heart.[54]

In his citation, Shi Ji evokes an ancient and extremely powerful model of the proper relationship between the ruler—the Son of Heaven—and his officials. The officials serve to protect the ruler, to stand as examples of proper deportment for him, to promulgate his decrees, to remonstrate with him fearlessly, to deal with his people fairly, and to lead his military forces in ensuring the security of his state. In practice, of course, these various duties are distributed among a large group of officials, but they are concentrated here in the figure of one über-official. With his citation, Shi Ji is "seizing upon a meaning" among all of the various duties listed in the entire poem, namely the official's difficult and lonely duty to remonstrate with his superior in an attempt to repair any damage that the mantle of leadership may have suffered through the ruler's misbehavior. In making this poetic citation, Shi Ji engages in the very activity— remonstration—called for in the citation, thereby casting himself in the role of the ideal official, Zhong Shanfu. This rhetorical move implicates Duke Ling in the role of Son of Heaven, the poem's King Xuan 宣 (r. 827-782 B.C.E.) of the Western Zhou. If King Xuan required and heeded remonstration from his official, then surely Duke Ling must do the same if he wishes to be a true ruler. Shi Ji's poetic citation from the Tradition casts a template over the present, staking out a place for himself and for Duke Ling. Shi Ji is already occupying his assigned position; it is time for Duke Ling to move into his. "So one is able to amend faults," says Shi Ji, holding out the possibility for Duke Ling's redemption. If the duke is willing to

---

54. Mao #260. After Karlgren, *Book of Odes*, pp. 228-30.

accept Shi Ji's help in mending his faults, "then the royal robe need not be thrown away." This is a brazen statement for someone in Shi Ji's position to be making. It is tantamount to saying, "Listen to me or you will lose your throne." He is motivated to make it because of the extremity of Duke Ling's offenses. He is able to make it because he has the force of Tradition behind him.

Duke Ling is too obtuse or too refractory (or both) to heed Shi Ji, who suddenly drops from view in the narrative, never to reappear. He is immediately replaced by Zhao Dun. The narrative realizes in its form what Shi Ji proposed at the outset: "if he does not accept what I say, then you may carry on after me." The duke soon grows tired of Zhao Dun's remonstrations and tries to have him killed, which the reader presumes was also the fate of the absent Shi Ji. When the man sent to kill Zhao Dun witnesses the noble deportment of his target, he has a crisis of conscience and commits suicide rather than carrying out his mission. The assassin, Chu Mei, is placed in an impossible position. According to Tradition, he is supposed to be loyal to his ruler. But what if one's ruler is not living up to the role prescribed to him by Tradition, and one's potential victim is? Chu Mei is unable to choose between what he is *supposed* to do, according to the pragmatic considerations of the here-and-now, and what he *should* do, according to the precepts of a Tradition that precedes the present and will outlast it. His solution is to remove himself from the here-and-now, and in doing so he becomes another victim of the rapacious Duke Ling even as his death serves to affirm the Tradition.

The halo of authority that surrounds Zhao Dun as he dozes—the aura that protects him from the assassin's blade—is derived from his communion with Tradition. He knows his proper place and he occupies it to the best of his ability. And it is the *place* that is permanent. This is why Duke Ling is unable to stop the remonstrations by killing the remonstrators. He can kill as many corporeal beings as he likes, but he cannot destroy the place that is defined for them.[55] If he only had the virtue to occupy the place that has been defined for

---

55. Another moral reprobate, an official who assassinated his own ruler, finds this out when he kills the historian who dared to record his crime, only to find a succession of four brothers taking his place (Xiang 25).

him, he could come to a "normal end." But—as the reader knew all along—Duke Ling "did not live up to the role of ruler," and he ends up being murdered in his peach garden. In the final analysis, he occupies the only place Tradition holds ever ready for those who would dare to ignore its precepts: the minatory example.

What of poetic competence in this case? If Shi Ji truly were, as he certainly seemed to be, a wise official in command of his traditional bodies of knowledge, then why did his poetic citations fail to achieve their intended effect? This apparent failure of the Tradition to reassert itself through the efforts of a competent official is why the *Zuo Tradition* must narrate the eventual violent demise of Duke Ling. The failure was not in the citation, nor in the one who made it, but in the one who received it; poetic competence applies to reception as well as utterance. In essence, the *Zuo Tradition* is implying that being a bad listener can be fatal, thus underscoring the importance of a class of advisors who are not only adept in citing traditional knowledge but also in appreciating the full import of such citations. Shi Ji made every attempt to render the import of his poetic citations clear to Duke Ling, but to the duke they remained just some "old poems" with no immediate bearing upon him. He may have understood what was being said, but he failed to understand *who* was saying it. When Shi Ji stepped forward and employed his cultural competence to pitch the right poetic citations in the right place at the right time, he ceased to speak with the voice of a lone man and began to speak with the voice of an entire Golden Age. The voice of a single man may be ignored with little consequence; the voice of a legion of ghosts is ignored at one's peril.

Ghosts may speak, but they may not live again. The practice of offering selections from the *Poems* is an attempt to emulate the ghosts. When the occasion is routine (such as welcoming a guest to a banquet), or when the poem is sufficiently general in its referents (such as in Mao #161, 175, 182, 278, or 284), the emulation can be transparent and complete. When there is more at stake (such as a military pact), or when the poem is marked by previous usage (referring to specific names, places, or events of the past), the emulation becomes clouded by motive and fractured by separation. Cultural competence is required to apply and interpret the poem, to clarify the motive, to bridge the separation between past and present. With poetic citation, the motive and separation are brought to the surface and dealt with in the surrounding speech. The ghosts are no longer emulated in action, but their voices are invoked in a highly controlled form. This is the move from words for ritual re-enactment to words as a rhetorical resource. In either case, the need for poetic competence arises out of the possibility (often probability) of misapprehension by one's audience. The inevitable paradox is that while the words of the *Poems* derive their authority from their antiquity, their mode of preservation and transmission is contingent upon their continuing application to a present that always falls short of the precepts encoded within them.

It is as though the Zhou dynasty begins as a wonderful play—in the West End of course. All of the players inhabit their roles completely (heroes, villains, and bit parts alike), deliver their lines exquisitely, and hit their marks flawlessly. The critics love it and the play receives rave reviews for its fine performances and uplifting moral message. Then the play is moved to a venue in the east, actors come and go, and things begin to go awry. The players start missing their cues, overstepping their marks, fumbling over their lines. The worst among them appear on stage in the wrong costume or even speak someone else's part. The critics are appalled and begin shouting at the players from their seats. Eventually they get up on the stage themselves. They show the players how to deliver their lines and even resort to explaining the meaning of the play to them. "They used to do this so well in the West End!" they cry. "Why can't you be like that?" In desperation, they begin rewriting the play themselves, weaving in what they can salvage from the original production, always hampered by the knowledge that the principal actors are just not up to their roles anymore. The audience and the players soon realize that the critics have now become the authors and supporting cast of the play and are threatening to steal the show. One of the more ambitious actors, playing the role of the King of Qin, decides to draw the curtain on the shambles of this once great play and to open his own one-man show as Emperor of Qin. He burns the old script and buries its authors. His show promises to be a grand spectacle, but the critics are not invited.

V

Over the course of the many narratives contained within the *Zuo Tradition*, it becomes clear that the *Poems* are never uttered or received apart from a moment of application (and its attendant interpretation), which requires competence in order to be handled effectively. Even the few mentions of moments of composition rather than quotation show that poems are produced in order to be applied to a situation at hand.[56] When the *Poems* are performed as a musical repertoire, it is as a form of display—the concert given for Jizha being the most extensive example (Xiang 29.13)—and they are invariably subject to moral interpretation. In the world described by the *Zuo Tradition* narratives, an original matrix of meanings may be posited as the source of the *Poems*' authority, but it is beyond recuperation. The *Poems* are not so much knowledge *of* the past *in* the present, as they are *past* knowledge *for* the present. This sort of knowledge is not an object of knowing, but a means of performing. It is a repertoire of possibilities. Conceived as such, the *Poems* cannot be tied to particular authors in particular circumstances. In the words of Lao Xiaoyu, "People have no stable poems and the poems have no stable referents" 人無定詩。詩無定指.[57] They can be used by anyone who knows them in any situation for which they are appropriate. And, as with any tool, some people are better at using them than others.

If the "original" meanings of the *Poems* are lost with their original circumstances, then what do they mean? Rather than a stable meaning, each has a history of moments of application, some earlier and some later, in different contexts governed by different motives and practices. To look for the "original" meaning is really just an-

---

56. See Min 2, Yin 3, and Wen 6. The one instance of poetic production that does not seem to have an immediate application is the strange pair of couplets exchanged by Duke Zhuang of Zheng and his mother upon their being reunited (Yin 1). While these lines do not appear in the *Poems* and do not constitute entire poems in and of themselves, their impromptu production under the stress of deep emotion prefigures the theory of literary production as a spontaneous outburst, which became dominant in the Han dynasty.

57. *Remarks on Poetry of the Spring and Autumn Era* 春秋詩話. Cited in Tam, "Use of Poetry in *Tso Chuan*," p. 33.

other application and interpretation in this long history. It is an attempt to find stable ground on which to base judgments of all other applications and interpretations by the degree to which they diverge from a contrived "original" meaning.

What, then, does *shi yan zhi* 詩言志 mean in the context of *Zuo Tradition* narratives? The *locus classicus* for the phrase is found in the following passage from the "Canon of Shun" 舜典 in the *Documents* 書:

Emperor Shun said, "Kui, I command you to regularize the music to instruct my sons. It should be upright yet mild, magnanimous but stern, tough but not injurious, concise but not supercilious. The poems should articulate intent, singing should intone the words, notes should correspond with the intonement, and modes should harmonize the notes. The sounds of the eight instruments should be in concert and not clash with one another. Then the spirits and people will thereby achieve harmony." Kui said, "Yea! I will strike my stone chimes and I will tap my stone chimes. And the many beasts will be led to dance."

帝曰。夔。命汝典樂。教冑子。直而溫。寬而栗。剛而無虐。簡而無傲。詩言志。歌永言。聲依永。律和聲。八音克諧。無相奪倫。神人以和。夔曰。於。予擊石拊石。百獸率舞。[58]

Emperor Shun commands Kui to produce a canon of exemplary music with which to inculcate a proper sense of morals and decorum in his sons. The emphasis throughout the passage is on the *performance* of the music. It consists of words that will articulate the mind's intent, a style of singing to intone these words, musical notes corresponding to the intonement, and tonal modes that will organize the notes into a harmonious melody that can then be played on instruments to bring human beings and spirits into a state of concord. Kui responds to this charge by claiming that his musical performance is so powerfully suasive that it induces the very beasts to dance in response.[59] There is no explicit mention of where the words and their accompanying music come from or whose intent will be expressed through them. In fact, the emperor's initial

---

58. Ruan Yuan, *Shisan jing,* vol. 1, p. 45.

59. Guo Shaoyu suggests that the phrase *bai shou shuai wu* 百獸率舞 might also refer to a primitive totemic dance employing the images of various animals (*Zhongguo lidai wen lun xuan,* vol. 1, p. 1).

command that Kui "regularize the music" 典樂 implies that there is a previously extant body of music from which Kui can form a canon. In this context, the term "music" encompasses words, singing, melody, tonal modes, and dance. The passage taken as a whole does not rule out the possibility that Kui or others might compose new music and words, but that is certainly not its primary denotation. If music is to be the means of inculcating certain moral qualities in the sons of the clan, then Kui's role seems to consist primarily of selecting, regularizing, and performing pieces of music from the past suited for this task.

This reading of the passage leaves open the question of exactly whose "intent" is being articulated through a poem as a verbal element of a piece of music. If the music is from the past, then the "intent" articulated in its verbal component may be from the past as well; in this case, the performance is not for immediate expressive purposes so much as for illustrative purposes. Or, perhaps the melody is from the past, but the words are composed anew to articulate the "intent" of whoever is uttering them. A third possibility is that the melody and words are both from the past, but they are being used as a suitable vehicle to articulate the "intent" of the performer in the present. The passage does not force us to choose between these options. The question of production of new words versus quotation of old words is not at stake here. It is the proper *performance* of words and melody (whatever their origin) that matters. Poetic competence is not about producing good words; it is about using words well.

This passage from the *Documents*—as is the case with so many passages from the Classics—quite generously accommodates different interpretations. The three-character phrase *shi yan zhi* 詩言志, in particular, has often been "broken off" in order to "seize upon a meaning"—one that varies depending on who is doing the "breaking."[60] It appears in the *Zuo Tradition* itself, with one telling emendation. In Duke Xiang 27th Year (546 B.C.E.), the Earl of Zheng convenes a banquet in honor of the Jin minister, Zhao Meng, who asks seven of the officials in attendance on the earl to offer poems to him so that he may "thereby observe the intent of the seven gen-

---

60. See a history of the use of this phrase in Zhu Ziqing, *Shi yan zhi bian*.

tlemen" 以觀七子之志. After the banquet is over, he turns to one of
his fellow Jin ministers and says of one of the performers, "Boyou
will soon be executed. We use poetry to articulate intent, and he is
intent upon maligning his master, who resents him for it" 伯有將爲
戮矣。詩以言志。志誣其上。而公怨之 (Xiang 27.5). In the context
of this passage, the statement that "we use poetry to articulate in-
tent" refers to a preexisting poem—a selection from the received
corpus of *Poems*—to be used as an instrument to articulate an im-
mediate intent. This formulation is certainly borne out by poetic
praxis as it is depicted in the *Zuo Tradition* narratives, which can be
characterized as repeated illustrations of the "use" (*yi* 以) of the
Poems to express what is on the mind of those who utter them, ei-
ther through ritual offering or through citation in speeches. What
the narratives also show is that such "use" is neither transparent nor
easily mastered. Later reformulations of the maxim "the poem ar-
ticulates intent" 詩言志, beginning with the "Great Preface" 大序 to
the *Poems*, attempt to "cleanse" the concept of poetry of the political
taint occasioned by its somewhat disingenuous use in the *Zuo
Tradition*, which casts poetic competence as part of the Tradition-
alists' larger concern with a cultural competence aimed at political
success.

The Traditionalists depicted in the *Zuo Tradition* are not so much
seeking distinction through cultural competence as *creating* dis-
tinction by defining what it means to be culturally competent. The
preservation and transmission of the *Zuo Tradition* is ostensibly
justified because of its status as a "commentary" on the *Springs and
Autumns*, but its true power lies in staking out and monopolizing a
field of cultural capital, one that is predicated on explicitly labeled
bodies of traditional knowledge and their associated practices. Its
narratives then demonstrate the efficacy of that capital as well as the
danger of ignoring those who monopolize it. The lessons taught in
the *Zuo Tradition* become all the more powerful as it assumes the
status of *the* authoritative account of its age, thus allowing its de-
piction of past practices—including poetic practice—to influence
later practices. Ultimately, the Tradition and the Traditionalist are
both governed by the same insight: words from the past, well put in
the present, constitute a stake in the future.

CR TWO SD

Baring the Soul

I

The *Han History*, compiled by Ban Gu 班固 (32–92 C.E.) and others,[1] depicts two famous song performances at critical turning points in the founding of the Han dynasty. The songs are by Xiang Yu 項羽 (232–202 B.C.E.) and Liu Bang 劉邦 (256–195 B.C.E.), who set out as brothers-in-arms in the rebellion against the despotic Qin dynasty, but ended up locked in a battle for supremacy once Qin was defeated. The first song, "Song of Gaixia" 垓下歌, was performed by Xiang Yu as he faced Liu Bang's overwhelming forces in 202 B.C.E.:

Xiang Yu was camped at Gaixia with only a few soldiers and at the end of his food supplies. The Han commander, with the Imperial Marquises and their soldiers, surrounded him in several files. In the night, Xiang Yu heard the Han forces on all sides singing the songs of Chu. He was astonished by

---

1. Ban Gu is the principal compiler of the *Han History*, but the project was initiated by his father, Ban Biao 班彪 (3–54 C.E.), and completed by his sister, Ban Zhao 班昭 (d. 116 C.E.). A large portion of it seems to be derived from the *Historical Records* 史記 by Sima Qian 司馬遷 (ca. 145–86? B.C.E.), although I only cite *Han History* (Ban Gu, *Han shu*) here as it deals exclusively with the Western Han dynasty.

this and asked, "Have the Han already taken Chu? How many men of Chu there are!" He got up to take drink within his shelter. He had a beautiful consort, named Lady Yu, whom he had always favored for accompanying him, and a fine steed named Dapple Gray, which he always rode. And so he was moved to sing mournfully with passionate feeling, composing a song verse himself that said,[2]

> My strength could uproot mountains   my vigor
>   overshadowed the age,
> but the times are against me   and now Dapple Gray
>   will not escape.[3]
> Dapple Gray will not escape   what can I do?
> and Yu, oh my Yu   what can be done for you?

He sang it through several times and his beautiful consort sang in unison with him.[4] Several lines of tears ran down Xiang Yu's face. Everyone in attendance wept, and none could raise his head to look upon them.[5]

---

2. The original poem is four lines in the basic Chusheng 處聲 meter of two trisyllabic hemistiches divided by the caesura particle *xi* 兮 as in XXX 兮 XXX. In my translation, I separate the hemistiches with spaces. The *Chusheng* meter is flexible in that the hemistiches can be expanded and collapsed and the *xi* particle may sometimes be omitted or appear at the end of a line rather than the middle.

3. Yoshikawa Kōjirō ("Kō Yu no 'Gaikako' ni tsuite") and Suzuki Shūji (*Kan Gi shi no kenkyū*) both cite a recension of *Historical Records* preserved in Japan that provides seven extra characters in the middle of this line (威勢廢威勢廢兮), effectively pulling line 2 apart and making an extra line from it thus:

> But the times are against me   my prestige and power fail me.
> My prestige and power fail me   Dapple Gray will not escape.

Suzuki notes that the interpolation fits the meter of the rest of the poem. I would add that it also preserves (and even enhances) the symmetry of the poem's argument by introducing a pair of repeated hemistiches marking the transition from a general statement regarding Xiang Yu's failing power to his particular inability to save his horse and concubine. The presence of this variant indicates the "elasticity" of the orally uttered poems in *Historical Records* and *Han History* when compared to the relatively stable narrative prose.

4. Zhang Shoujie 張守節 in *Shiji zhengyi* 史記正義 (preface dated 737) quotes Lady Yu's pentasyllabic song in response. It is cited in Suzuki (*Kan Gi shi no kenkyū*, p. 31), who casts doubt on the authenticity of this song and its reliability as evidence for the use of pentasyllabic meter early in the Han dynasty. The character *he* 和 (falling tone) can be translated either as "join in" or "in response."

5. Ban, *Han shu, juan* 31, p. 1817.

羽壁垓下。軍少食盡。漢帥諸侯兵圍之數重。羽夜聞漢軍四面皆楚歌。
乃驚曰。漢皆已得楚乎。是何楚人多也。起飲帳中。有美人姓虞氏。常
幸從。駿馬名騅。常騎。乃悲歌慷慨。自爲歌詩曰。

> 力拔山兮氣蓋世
> 時不利兮騅不逝
> 騅不逝兮可奈何
> 虞兮虞兮奈若何

歌數曲。美人和之。羽泣下數行。左右皆泣。莫能仰視。

Xiang Yu manages to escape alone from the encirclement to live another day, but when Liu Bang's forces eventually hunt him down, he decides to take his own life, offering up his body to a former friend who might claim the reward for it.

The second song, "The Great Wind" 大風, is performed by Liu Bang six years after his victory over Xiang Yu. Liu Bang, now the undisputed emperor, makes a return visit to his hometown of Pei in 196 B.C.E.:

When the emperor was making his way back to the capital, he passed through Pei and stayed for a while. He arranged for a banquet in the Pei Palace to which he invited all of his old friends, the village elders, and the young men to join him in drinking. He summoned 120 boys from the village and taught them a song. When everyone was well in their cups, the emperor struck the lute and sang the song himself:[6]

> A great wind arises and the clouds are swept away,
> my majesty weighs upon the realm as I return to
> my homeland.
> Where will I find brave warriors to keep this vast land?

He ordered the boys to repeat it in unison with him. Then the emperor rose to dance to his song and was struck with such passionate feeling that tears streamed down his face. He said to the elders of Pei, "The wanderer grows homesick and while I may have established my capital within the Pass, even in death my soul will still long for Pei."[7]

上還。過沛。留。置酒沛宮。悉召故人父老子弟佐酒。發沛中兒得百二
十人。教之。酒酣。上擊筑。自歌曰。

---

6. This song is also in *Chusheng* meter, with the first hemistich varying between three and four characters.

7. Ban, *Han shu, juan* 1b, p. 74.

大風起兮雲飛揚
威加海內兮歸故鄉
安得猛士兮守四方

令兒皆和習之。上乃起舞慷慨傷懷。泣數行下。謂沛父兄曰。游子悲故
鄉。吾雖都關中。萬歲之後吾魂魄猶思沛。

These songs perfectly capture the different personalities that gradually emerge in the chronicles of the struggles between these two men.[8] The construction of these personalities may have more to do with the imperatives of historical narrative than with the realities of historical persons, but they stand as the enduring record of the two. Just as the narrative accounts were constructed and likely embellished to serve the agendas of the historians who recorded them, so too were the songs fashioned (and perhaps even fabricated) to serve the demands of the story told in the narratives. In his song, Xiang Yu produces an elegiac valediction for a fallen kingdom in which the cosmos itself turns against him; the loss of those dearest to him becomes synecdoche for an entire world now beyond recovery. Liu Bang produces an ambivalent salutation for an infant empire. He does not envision a world lost, but the lifting of a cloudy veil from a new age rife with the challenges of a grand rule. The first man casts himself as a tragic hero, whose ambition is spited by Heaven; the second man casts himself as the reluctant victor, who might hold the empire in the palm of his hand but is all too aware of its weight. The hand of the historian(s) is behind these castings—the type of song that each man produces is put forward as a transparent indicator of his interior nature.

The way in which these two men are depicted in the performance of their songs also suggests their differences in personality. Xiang Yu is more spontaneous, more personal, with his impromptu midnight libation in his battle tent. The narrative reports that he is moved with "passionate feeling," and the song seems to come to him naturally as a result of his emotions in response to "the Han forces on all sides singing the songs of Chu." The depth of his passion is

---

8. Durrant summarizes their personalities as follows: "Xiang Yu, for all his action, is plainly moving forward toward the past. . . . Liu Bang, however, represents the newly emergent bureaucratic state" (*Cloudy Mirror*, p. 135).

magnified in the response of his beloved concubine and overflows with the tears of the onlookers, who cannot bear to look upon such deep sorrow.

By comparison, Liu Bang's song performance is completely staged. He invites an entire village to a formal banquet in the town hall, in preparation for which he conscripts and trains a choir of 120 boys. At the banquet, Liu Bang personally plays the music and sings a song of his own composition, commanding the choir to join in with him. Once the choir is singing the song, he then rises to dance and is moved to tears with "passionate feeling" in listening to his own composition. The locus of emotion in Xiang Yu's performance is in the passionate feeling that produces his song; in Liu Bang's it is the passionate feeling he feels in response to his own song. Liu Bang is staging the act of reception by usurping the role of the immediate audience for himself. The attendees at the banquet (who do not weep as they do for Xiang Yu's song) are not so much witnesses to Liu Bang's personal expression of his feelings as to his own response to a choral performance of that expression.[9] The difference in performance styles of the two songs is striking: Xiang Yu's is the spontaneous performance of one man that affects many; Liu Bang's is the staged performance of many that affects one man, himself. This is the difference between a lone tragic figure who has lost a kingdom and is rendered impotent, and a man who has won an empire and knows how to behave as an emperor should.

The narrative frames provided in these prose passages give the reader an idea of the immediate circumstances that occasioned the songs, a description of how the songs were composed and performed, and a mention of the reaction of those who heard them.[10] Each song is then further enriched by the larger context found in

---

9. "The Great Wind" became a song of remembrance for Liu Bang and was performed annually in the imperial ancestral temple by the youth of Pei, thus allowing him to persist as the audience of his song even in death. The text of the song was carved into a stone stele there.

10. The shape of a narrative often bears the imprint of a poem; note how the narrative frame for Xiang Yu's song must make a slight digression to explain the identity of Lady Yu and Dapple Gray before the poetic performance can be depicted.

the *Han History*'s accounts of Xiang Yu and Liu Bang's rebellion against Qin, their own subsequent power struggle, and the eventual founding of the Han dynasty by Liu Bang. A reciprocal relationship emerges: the song lends the narrative an emotional vividness, while the narrative increases the depth of appreciation for the song. But there is more than enriched reading here—the narrative frame for a song can lead to a better understanding of contemporary concepts of what a song was and what one could plausibly do with it. The very different representations of song performance in these two passages suggest that concepts of the song form in the Han were multivalent and require greater attention. Fortunately, the *Han History* has preserved accounts of a number of song performances, most of which are by members of the Han royal family (the Liu clan and their wives and concubines). From these accounts it is possible to gain a sense of the expectations surrounding song performance during the Former Han dynasty (206 B.C.E.–23 C.E.).

II

Every historical narration of song performance is mediation between "how it was" and "how it should be." The compilers of the *Han History* were fully aware of "how it should be" and took great pains to explicitly spell out canonical principles of poetic production and song performance. The "Treatise on Literature" 藝文志 found in the *Han History* quotes from the *Documents* 書 in providing the following brief exposition on the *Poems*:

The *Documents* say, "The poems should articulate intent, singing should intone the words." Thus, when a mind is moved in a state of sorrow or joy, the notes of singing and intoning will issue forth. If one recites the words, then it is called a poem; if one intones the notes, then it is called a song. Thus, in ancient times there were officials who gathered poems; through them the rulers could observe the customs of their people to know their own successes and failures so that they might examine and rectify themselves.[11]

---

11. Ban, *Han shu, juan* 30, p. 1708.

書曰。詩言志。歌詠言。故哀樂之心感。而歌詠之聲發。誦其言謂之詩。
詠其聲謂之歌。故古有采詩之官。王者所以觀風俗。知得失。自考正也。

This gloss on the canonical definitions of poetry and song makes
two important points. First, poetry and song are two forms of the
same thing—an articulation of the mind in a state of excited emo-
tion—and differ only in their performative aspect. When feelings are
stirred in the mind, the notes of song naturally issue forth; emphasis
on reciting the words is a poem, while emphasis on singing the notes
is a song.[12] Simply put, a poem comprises the words to a song,
which can stand alone without musical accompaniment. The gloss
implies, however, that singing is the most natural, spontaneous way
to produce and perform a poem.[13] Judging by accounts in the *Han
History*, singing was the most common way of uttering a poem at
the Han court.

The second point states that rulers collected poems (that is, verbal
remnants of songs, which would later be set to music at court) by
their people as a gauge of the quality of their rule. Thus, a poem is a
reliable means of finding out what people are thinking and feeling.
Just as the rulers would collect poems as a window into the minds of
their subjects, so too do the historians of the *Han History* collect
poems to provide windows into the minds of *their* subjects, who
often include rulers.

The reliability of the poem as a transparent medium for reflecting
the interior derives from its being an involuntary production, an
"issuing forth" (*fa* 發). This canonical concept of the "poem/song"
(*shi ge* 詩歌)—as words/sounds spontaneously issuing forth in re-
sponse to an emotional reaction—can be called the "outburst song."
Its most explicit formulation is found in the "Great Preface" 大序 to
the *Poems*:[14]

---

12. For the sake of clarity, I will reserve the term "poem" to refer to the text or
verse of a song and the term "song" to refer to the musical performance of a poem.

13. The clauses in the sentence, "Thus, when a mind is moved in a state of sorrow
or joy, the notes of singing and intoning will issue forth," are explicitly joined by
the particle *er* 而, indicating that the mind being moved is the necessary and per-
sistent condition under which the sounds of song will naturally issue forth.

14. The "Great Preface" is the opening section of the "Preface to the Mao
Poems" 毛詩序, which also contains over three hundred "Lesser Prefaces" 小序,

When feelings are stirred within, they take on outward form in spoken words. When speaking them is not enough, then one sighs them. When sighing them is not enough, then one intones and sings them. When intoning and singing them is not enough, then, unconsciously, the hands dance them and the feet tap them.[15]

情動於中而形於言。言之不足。故嗟歎之。嗟歎之不足。故永歌之。永歌之不足。不知手之舞之。足之踏之也。

What the "Great Preface" promises with its model of spontaneous poetic production through the "outburst song" can be summarized in three unities: (1) unity of person, which holds that a person is uttering a poem of his or her own composition;[16] (2) unity of time, which holds that a person's performance of a song is simultaneous with its production (that the composition is spontaneous and the performance is not deferred); and (3) unity of voice, which holds that the voice that speaks in a poem is the voice of the person who performs the song. As with the three dramatic unities in Aristotelean literary theory—of time, place, and action—these three unities of the outburst song are often violated in practice, but it is upon this template that the *Han History* builds its representations of poetic production and performance.

There is another influence shaping the template of the outburst song and that is the template for the *Han History* itself, namely the *Historical Records* 史記 by Sima Qian 司馬遷 (ca. 145–86? B.C.E.). In his "Letter in Reply to Ren An" 報任安書 and his "Grand Historian's Account of Himself" 太史公自序, Sima Qian outlines his theory that literary production stems from feelings of overwhelm-

---

one for each of the entries in the *Poems*. The "Preface" likely reached its present form in the first century of the Common Era, but is putatively based on ideas passed down from one of Confucius's disciples and is certainly a synthesis of ideas that predated the Eastern Han.

15. Ruan Yuan, *Shisan jing*, vol. 2, p. 270.

16. The "Great Preface" does not explicitly state that a poem must be a new composition, and it is possible to concede that these principles could also apply to the performance of poetry through quotation. It is interesting to note, however, that every *song* performance depicted in the *Han History* is of a new composition, although other people then perform some of the poems subsequent to the initial moment of production.

ing frustration, a theory that is quoted at length in his biography in the *Han History*. Sima Qian lists a series of canonical literary works and argues that each work was produced by an author suffering profound frustration caused by a sense of impotence. He ends his list with the *Poems* and then sums up the general principle:

The three hundred *Poems* were largely composed as a result of worthy men and sages venting their outrage. These people all had something pent up inside their thoughts but were unable to find a way to put it into action. Thus, they related what had happened to them in the past in consideration of those to come in the future.[17]

詩三百篇。大氐賢聖發憤之所爲作也。此人皆意有所鬱結。不得通其道。故述往事。思來者。

Sima Qian's own thoughts on literary production were surely shaped by the suffering he underwent as a result of being castrated for gainsaying Emperor Wu. Again and again in his accounts of pre-Han figures—Boyi and Shu Qi, Confucius, Qu Yuan, and Jing Ke, among others—people caught in trying circumstances reach a crisis point and then burst forth into song. Sima Qian seems to have had a particular affinity for those figures in history whose noble intentions were frustrated by circumstances. The song form, to him, becomes the most potent way for historical writing to capture those intentions, or at least the frustration that resulted from failing to achieve them. This model of poetic production—a song arises from suffering frustration in extreme situations—was surely the other main influence on the template of the outburst song found in the *Han History*. For while the canonical gloss in the "Treatise on Literature" explains that a song arises when "a mind is moved in a state of sorrow or joy," there is not a single joyful song in the entire *Han History*, only the venting of frustration and outrage.

III

Proceeding chronologically, the next song by a member of the Han royal family to appear in the *Han History* is also by Liu Bang

---

17. Ban, *Han shu, juan* 62, p. 2735.

(Emperor Gaozu 高祖, or Gaodi 高帝) and was performed by him at court just six months after he performed "The Great Wind" in Pei Palace. The *Han History* records that Liu Bang took a favorite concubine, known as Lady Qi 戚夫人, by whom he had a son. Liu Bang felt that this son was more akin to him than was the "kind but weak" heir apparent he had by Empress Lü 呂后. Lady Qi was aware of the emperor's feelings and requested that her son be installed as heir apparent instead. Liu Bang would have indulged her if not for four venerable advisors who pledged their allegiance to the son of Empress Lü as a result of her machinations on the advice of the Marquis Zhang Liang 張良. Liu Bang realized that he could not, in good conscience, depose an heir apparent who was able to gain the loyalty of four such men. In the following passage, he informs Lady Qi of his decision at a court banquet:

The four men finished wishing the emperor long life and scuttled off. The emperor looked after them as they left, summoning Lady Qi to his side. Pointing them out to her, he said: "I want to replace the heir apparent, but those four men have come to his aid. Now that he has gained these wings it will be difficult to move him from his position. Empress Lü truly is in charge now." Lady Qi wept and the emperor said to her, "Perform a Chu dance for me, and I will perform a Chu song for you." He sang,

> The wild swan soars on high,
> with one beat he covers a thousand leagues.
> He goes on his wings,
> and can cross the four seas.
> He can cross the four seas,
> so what more can I do?
> Though I may have a snare arrow,
> still, how could I use it?

He sang the song through several times until Lady Qi began to sob and weep. Then the emperor rose to leave, bringing an end to the meal. In the end, his not replacing the heir apparent was because of the influence of these four men, who had been originally summoned by Zhang Liang.[18]

---

18. Ban, *Han shu, juan* 40, p. 2036.

四人爲壽已畢。趨去。上目送之。召戚夫人指視曰。我欲易之。彼四人
爲之輔。羽翼已成。難動矣。呂氏眞乃主矣。戚夫人泣涕。上曰。爲我
楚舞。吾爲若楚歌。歌曰。

> 鴻鵠高飛
> 一舉千里
> 羽翼以就
> 橫絕四海
> 橫絕四海
> 又可奈何
> 雖有矰繳
> 尚安所施

歌數闋。戚夫人歔欷流涕。上起去。罷酒。竟不易太子者。良本招此四
人之力也。

This song is also in *Chusheng* meter, which was favored by Han
royalty in their songs because, under the influence of *Li sao* 離騷, it
came to be seen as the proper mode for making a lament.[19] The *Chu-
sheng* meter must have also come readily to southerners such as the
Liu clan in their personal compositions because it was the native
song meter of the south; it was clearly marked as such in com-
parison to the tetrasyllabic form found in the *Poems* from the
north.[20] The song contained in this passage, which came to be
known as "The Wild Swan" after the first line, appears to be in
tetrasyllabic meter despite being explicitly labeled as a "Chu song."
Suzuki explains this by saying that there are examples of tetra-
syllabic songs in the *Lyrics of Chu* 楚辭 (notably the "Heavenly
Questions" 天問) and that if one inserts a *xi* 兮 character at the line
breaks, the song resembles those found in the "Nine Sections" 九章
of the *Lyrics of Chu*.[21] These explanations may be superfluous. In

---

19. Suzuki Shūji makes this observation and refers to *Chusheng* poetry as the
"whining genre" of the Han court (*Kan Gi shi no kenkyū*, p. 15).

20. Elsewhere in the *Han History* the long tetrasyllabic *poem* (rather than song)
is still submitted in written form as a formal mode of remonstration by officials at
court. See Ban, *Han shu, juan* 73, pp. 3101, 3105, 3110.

21. There are numerous examples in which the *xi* character was dropped from
Chu songs in the process of transmission. This happened to "The Great Wind,"
which was converted to a heptasyllabic song without the *xi* by the time it found its

light of the *Han History*'s definition of song as "intoning the notes" and considering the name of the *Chusheng* meter itself, which may be literally translated as "Chu notes," the essence of a Chu song seems not to lie so much in the textual residue recorded in the pages of history as in the very thing that cannot be captured in writing: the musical performance. What distinguishes a Chu song from other sorts of songs and poems is not simply the presence of a *xi* character, but a whole mode of performance predicated on singing, which often includes instrumental accompaniment and dancing. The texts of these songs are never simply chanted or written down for reading; they are produced and received as songs first and foremost. This is why it is crucial to read them in situ, for while a narrative can never hope to capture a musical performance, it can at least describe it.

Liu Bang's performance of "The Wild Swan" adheres to the principle that an outburst song is produced out of feelings of frustration, but the notion of spontaneity is complicated here, as it is in the case of "The Great Wind." Liu Bang is certainly frustrated as he finds himself backed into a corner, unable to make his favorite son the heir apparent because of the machinations of the empress. His statement to Lady Qi that "Empress Lü truly is in charge now" is a startling admission of his political impotence in the face of his wife and hints at the absolute power she will soon enjoy after his death. Liu Bang was more comfortable seeking advantage on the open battlefield, where one's enemies can be clearly seen, rather than in the shadowy court, where cunning counts for more than military prowess.

This difference in setting between battlefield and court is what complicates the idea of "spontaneity" that is at the core of the outburst song. In a sense, the battlefield is the perfect ground for spontaneity: there is a time and place for premeditated strategy, but in the heat of hand-to-hand combat between individuals one must act immediately and produce immediate results. The battlefield setting for Xiang Yu's "Song of Gaixia" contributes in large part to its sense of immediacy. The idea of sitting down to compose a poem

---

way into the *Chronicles of the Three Kingdoms* 三國志 (Suzuki, *Kan Gi shi no kenkyū*, p. 12).

for performance does not agree with the picture of Xiang Yu as an impulsive man of action and is at odds with the urgency of the battlefield. The sense of drama produced in the scene comes from its narration, not the premeditated actions of Xiang Yu himself, who is simply doing what occurs to him at the moment.

However, when Liu Bang sings "The Great Wind" in the Pei Palace, or sings "The Wild Swan" to accompany Lady Qi's dance, he is the stage director. He had the time to assemble a choir, to play the music, and to train the singers or request a dance before he "took the stage" to perform his song. Premeditated military strategy for the battlefield is converted into premeditated self-presentation before an audience in court. Simply put, Xiang Yu is too busy on the battlefield to worry about how his song might be received by an audience (during the singing of his song he may well have been formulating his escape); Liu Bang, on the other hand, must worry about how he strategizes his performance; he *is* thinking about his audience. The question of spontaneity becomes vexed under these circumstances.

Many Chinese critics refer to Liu Bang's songs as "spontaneous" 即興 compositions, but it is hard to see how this is tenable given their narrative frames. The actual words for the song (the "poem") may have been spontaneously produced. Perhaps Liu Bang had no idea what he was going to say until he said it, although this possibility seems remote given his foreknowledge of the subject of his songs in both cases. What is not spontaneous is the song performance itself—he trains a choir for "The Great Wind" and provides stage directions for his performance of "The Wild Swan." The lack of spontaneity in performance leaves its traces in the content of the songs; both of them employ figurative language, which suggests some measure of reflection went into choosing apposite figures (the wind for Liu Bang's military might and the swan for the ascending heir apparent). The occasion for Xiang Yu's performance, by contrast, takes him completely by surprise (the narrator says that he was "astonished"), and his impromptu performance seems to result directly from his "passionate feeling." The content of his song centers on the concrete images of his favorite horse and concubine, the immediate objects of his cares.

Strategy is also a matter of when, where, how, and by whom a song is performed, in addition to what is actually said through it. Formulation of strategy in performance requires time: Xiang Yu had little on the battlefield, while Liu Bang had much at court. If the effort that goes into staging the variables of song performance is a form of strategy, then the natural question is "what is to be gained by that strategy?" In "The Great Wind," Liu Bang specifically asks, "Where will I find brave warriors to keep this vast land?" He won the empire against great odds with the help of advisors who died soon afterward, and worries that his "kind but weak" son will be unable to maintain it without sound military advice. Liu Bang does not seriously ask his question of the old men and children gathered in Pei to hear his performance (he bestows upon them the honor of maintaining his "bath town" and exempts them from taxes). The question is a rhetorical one, posed to give an indication of the worries that come to his mind now that he has achieved his goals and returned to the place from which he started. The strategy here is not so much to achieve a concrete goal but simply to give public expression to his private concerns, to vent his feelings.

Who exactly is employing this venting strategy? Perhaps a combination of lore and precedent led Liu Bang to believe that the performance of an outburst song was simply what one was expected to do in these circumstances and thus he staged it for maximum effect. Or, it could be the historian who felt that such a performance appropriately provided a glimpse of Liu Bang's state of mind at this crucial point in the narrative. Both narrator and narratee are conditioned by canonical principles and precedent—it is impossible at this remove in time and place to extricate one from the other. This story—stretched as it is between the poles of fact and fiction, between principle and practice—in turn persists as a model for later protagonists who find themselves in similar situations.

If Liu Bang is venting publicly at Pei, then what is Liu Bang doing at court in "The Wild Swan"? He tells Lady Qi in plain language that the heir apparent's position is unassailable and that she had best resign herself to Empress Lü's superior position. So why the song and dance? When Liu Bang says to his weeping concubine, "Perform a Chu dance for me and I will perform a Chu song for you," he is proposing a form of shared venting. His song and her dance work together to articulate the frustration that they both feel. In performing it several times through, they have a chance to savor their pain, which reduces the concubine to pathetic sobs. When the performance is done, the emperor rises and departs, drawing the curtain on their defeat and providing them with some sense of closure. The inclusion of the song at this point in the narrative allows the narrator to show that Liu Bang is sympathetic to Lady Qi even if he is powerless to help her. If there is any strategy employed by Liu Bang here beyond venting, it may reside in the knowledge that Empress Lü will hear of this performance, although it is hard to see how she could be anything but encouraged by its tone of resignation.

And encouraged she was. When Liu Bang died later that year (195 B.C.E.), Empress Lü saw her own son take the throne as Emperor Hui 惠帝 and moved swiftly to consolidate her power as the empress dowager. One of her first acts was to have Lady Qi imprisoned. Lady Qi made the mistake of complaining through song, leading to dire consequences for her son and herself.

When Gaozu died, Emperor Hui took the throne and Empress Lü became the empress dowager. Thereupon, she ordered the palace discipline service to imprison Lady Qi, shave her head, chain her neck, dress her in the scarlet robes of a convict, and have her pound rice husks. Lady Qi pounded while she sang:

> The son is a prince,
> the mother a prisoner.
> All day I pound until dusk,
> I serve as a constant companion of death.[22]
> Separated by three thousand *li*,
> whom shall I send to tell you?

---

22. Yan Shigu interprets this line to mean that she is the companion of criminals sentenced to death (see his commentary interpolated in Ban, *Han shu*). Yang Shuda disagrees, saying it means she could die at any time and that this usage of the character *si* 死 is closer to the abstract idea of a "spirit of death" (*Han shu kuiguan*, *juan* 2, p. 767). Yang's reading seems preferable because there are no parallel usages of *si* by itself referring to criminals that have been sentenced to death.

The empress dowager heard of this and was greatly enraged, saying, "So, you still look to your son, do you?" She then summoned the son, the Prince of Zhao, in order to execute him. The envoys made three trips, but the administrator of Zhao, Zhou Chang, refused to dispatch him. The empress dowager then summoned the administrator of Zhao himself, who arrived in Chang'an in compliance with the summons. Then she sent people to summon the prince once again and he came.

Emperor Hui was a kind and gentle person who knew that the empress dowager was furious, so he went personally to greet the Prince of Zhao at Bashang[23] and brought him into his own palace where he accompanied him in waking and sleeping, drinking and eating. A few months later, Emperor Hui went out one morning to hunt, but the Prince of Zhao was unable to get up that early. The empress dowager was secretly informed that he was at home alone and sent someone with poisoned wine for him to drink. When Emperor Hui returned, the Prince of Zhao was dead.

The empress dowager proceeded to cut off Lady Qi's hands and feet, gouge out her eyes, cauterize her ears, render her mute with poison, and have her placed in a cellar, calling her the "human swine." After she had been there for a few months, the empress dowager summoned Emperor Hui to see the "human swine." He looked at her and had to ask before he realized that it was Lady Qi, whereupon he cried out bitterly, fell ill as a result, and was unable to rise from his bed for more than a year. He sent someone to beg leave from the empress dowager, saying, "This was not the act of a human being. As I am the son of the empress dowager, I shall never be fit to rule the empire again!" And so he took to drinking everyday and indulged in wanton pleasures, refusing to listen to administrative affairs. Seven years later, he died [in 188 B.C.E.].[24]

高祖崩。惠帝立。呂后為皇太后。乃令永巷囚戚夫人。髡鉗衣赭衣。令舂。戚夫人舂且歌曰。

> 子為王
> 母為虜
> 終日舂薄暮
> 常與死為伍
> 相離三千里
> 當誰使告女

---

23. An eastern suburb of Chang'an.
24. Ban, *Han shu*, *juan* 97a, p. 3937–38.

太后聞之大怒。曰。乃欲倚女子邪。乃召趙王誅之。使者三反。趙相周
昌不遣。太后召趙相。相微至長安。使人復召趙王。王來。惠帝慈仁。
知太后怒。自迎趙王霸上。入宮。挾與起居飲食。數月。帝晨出射。趙
王不能蚤起。太后伺其獨居。使人持鴆飲之。遲帝還。趙王死。太后遂
斷戚夫人手足。去眼熏耳。飲瘖藥。使居鞠域中。名曰。人彘。居數月。
乃召惠帝視人彘。帝視而問知其戚夫人。乃大哭。因病。歲餘不能起。
使人請太后曰。此非人所爲。臣爲太后子。終不能復治天下。以此日飲
爲淫樂。不聽政。七年而崩。

This song certainly qualifies as an outburst song; Lady Qi vents her
frustration at meeting with such precipitous injustice, but her
closing line—"Whom shall I send to tell you?"—suggests that there is
a measure of strategy at play in her performance.[25] The implication
is that Lady Qi harbors some hope that her song will be a vehicle for
making her mistreatment known to her son, Prince Ruyi of Zhao,
who had been Liu Bang's own choice for succession to the throne.
Unfortunately for Lady Qi, the song makes its way to the ears of
Empress Lü instead, who seizes on the final line of the song, saying,
"So, you look to your son, do you?" and does away with the song's
intended audience by killing him. Her violent reaction to this song
is easily the most severe "reader response" one is likely to encounter,
and constitutes a deep perversion of the canonical model of poetic
production and reception. The proper response to hearing a song is
sympathy—usually expressed through tears or a matching song, as
can be seen in other passages—not intense antipathy. This whole
narrative has a gruesome circularity to it. It is Empress Lü who is
the author of Lady Qi's woes, prompting her to burst forth in song.
She then becomes the audience for Lady Qi's performance and in-
scribes her own outraged response upon Lady Qi's very body.
Empress Lü literally strips away the external attributes—limbs,
sensory organs, voice—that make Lady Qi a human being in an at-
tempt to erase the interior revealed in her song. It is not enough
simply to kill her, for that would allow memory of her as a human

---

25. The text of Lady Qi's song does not appear in the *Historical Records*; it seems
to have been interpolated in the *Han History*'s account of the incident, suggesting
that the song might have been composed by a third party in the interim between
the compilation of the two histories.

being to remain pristine; it is far more effective to convert her into a "human swine," a base animal incapable of poetic expression. Ironically, it is the empress herself who is deemed inhuman by her own son, who says to her, "This was not the act of a human being." It is the act of a savage animal, not a civilized person, to respond to a poetic text with such brute physicality.

Over the subsequent course of the *Han History*, Empress Lü emerges as a sort of monstrous muse, single-handedly creating the frustrating circumstances that lead her victims to vent their outrage through outburst songs. When Prince You 友王 is sent to rule over Zhao after Ruyi's untimely demise, he too meets with the wrath of Empress Lü.

"Captive" Prince You of Zhao was established as the prince of Huaiyang in 196 B.C.E. "Reclusive" Prince Ruyi of Zhao died, so during the first year of Emperor Hui's reign (194 B.C.E.), You was transferred to rule over Zhao, where he held the throne for a total of fourteen years.

You took a woman from the Lü clan to be his princess, but he did not love her, loving another concubine instead. The Lü woman left in a rage and slandered him to the empress dowager, claiming, "The prince said, 'Why should the Lü clan get [Liu] princes? After the empress dowager dies, we will certainly strike them down.'" The empress dowager was furious and summoned the Prince of Zhao on a pretext. When he arrived, she had him placed under house arrest without even granting him an audience, posted guards around him, and did not permit him any food. When some of his officers managed to smuggle him some food, they were immediately arrested and sentenced. The Prince of Zhao was starving, so he sang the following song:

> The Lüs are in power,
>   the Lius are feeble;
> They oppress the princes and marquises,
>   and force a wife upon me.
> My wife was jealous and so
>   she maligned me with malice;
> Slanderous women disrupt the kingdom,
>   but the emperor never wakes up to it.
> I may be without my loyal ministers,
>   but what reason is that to abandon my kingdom?

If I had finished myself off in the wilds,[26]
    gray heaven would have admitted my rectitude.
Alas! I cannot regret it now,
    I should have killed myself early on.
For a prince who starves to death,
    who shall feel pity?
The Lüs transgress all principles,
    I trust in heaven to avenge me!

Then, he died alone in captivity. He was accorded the funeral rites of a commoner and buried as such in Chang'an.[27]

趙幽王友。十一年立爲淮陽王。趙隱王如意死。孝惠元年。徙友王趙。
凡立十四年。友以諸呂女爲后。不愛。愛它姬。諸呂女怒去。讒之於太
后曰。王曰。呂氏安得王。太后百歲後。吾必擊之。太后怒。以故召趙
王。趙王至。置邸不見。令衛圍守之。不得食。其群臣或竊饋之。輒捕
論之。趙王餓。乃歌曰。

> 諸呂用事兮劉氏微
> 迫脅王侯兮彊授我妃
> 我妃既妒兮誣我以惡
> 讒女亂國兮上曾不寤
> 我無忠臣兮何故棄國
> 自快中野兮蒼天與直
> 于嗟不可悔兮寧早自賊
> 爲王餓死兮誰者憐之
> 呂氏絕理兮託天報仇

遂幽死。以民禮葬之長安。

Prince You's "Captivity Song" seems to be a true outburst song, performed on the verge of death and in isolation, without any expectation of an audience, save for that of "gray heaven." And yet the words of the song somehow managed to be preserved in the *Han History*. This passage more than any other strains the claim of veracity implied in official histories. Prince You was kept under close guard and forbidden any visitors; so there should not have been anyone present to hear this song. Certainly no one in the Lü faction would want to see this song preserved or transmitted, so how did it

---

26. I have followed Yang Shuda (*juan* 2, p. 303), who suspects *kuai* 快 to be a scribal error for *jue* 絕, which is the variant found in *Shi ji*.

27. Ban, *Han shu, juan* 38, p. 1989.

end up here? The song itself provides an answer. While it may be read as an expression of the prince's immediate feelings, it can also be read as a bald piece of propaganda directed against the Lü clan. History—written and transmitted by men loyal to the Liu clan—was not kind to Empress Lü, who is invariably portrayed as a grasping, unprincipled woman rising above her station by ruthlessly usurping power from young, weak emperors. The historian cannot deny the basic facts: Empress Lü did manage to wrest power away from weak Liu princes and rule in their stead. The "good guys" lost in the world of cold, hard externals. The only recourse the historian has to recuperate the reputation of the losers is to make them victors in the more pliable (and enduring) world of the represented interior. The text of a song may be preserved and transmitted in the crucible of historical narrative, persisting for centuries after the disintegration of Empress Lü's bones. She may have briefly enjoyed her absolute power, but song gives her victims the last word. Thus, the performance of an outburst song acts as a release valve for two parties: the frustrated historical figure who needs to get something off of his or her chest at the time, and the frustrated historian who may not rewrite the main plot of his narrative, but who may use songs to show the "goodness" of his characters even if they were powerless to act on their intentions. The historian takes the place of the "gray heaven" upon whom Prince You called, endowing the memories of those who have been wronged with a measure of justice and revenge.

Empress Lü, as the *Han History* tells it, was unrelenting in her persecution of the Liu princes. Prince You's successor in Zhao, Prince Hui 恢, was the next in line to suffer at her hands, in 181 B.C.E.:

When the "Captive" Prince of Zhao died, Empress Lü transferred Prince Hui to rule over the kingdom of Zhao and he grew despondent in his heart. The empress dowager sent a daughter of Lü Chan to be his wife.[28] All of her attendant officials were also members of the Lü clan; they appropriated power within the palace and spied on the prince until he no longer had a life of his own. The prince had a concubine whom he doted upon, but his

---

28. Lü Chan 呂產, a relative of Empress Lü, was enfeoffed as the Prince of Liang and served as prime minister.

wife sent someone to assassinate her with poison. The prince then composed four stanzas of song verse and bid the musicians sing them. He was grieved with longing and took his own life in the sixth month [of 181 B.C.E.]. When the Empress Dowager heard of this, she disposed of his heirs, because the prince had killed himself on account of this woman without regard for the proper rites of the royal ancestral shrine.[29]

趙幽王死。呂后徙恢王趙。恢心不樂。太后以呂產女爲趙王后。王后從官皆諸呂也。內擅權。微司趙王。王不得自恣。王有愛姬。王后鴆殺之。王乃爲歌詩四章。令樂人歌之。王悲思。六月自殺。太后聞之。以爲用婦人故自殺。無思奉宗廟禮。廢其嗣。

This passage is notable for its depiction of song composition prior to performance. In every other case of an outburst song, the composition or production of the song is portrayed as simultaneous with its initial performance, even if that performance has a contrived quality to it. Here, the narrator explicitly states, "The prince then composed four stanzas of song verse and bid the musicians sing them." An interval between composition and performance has been introduced, and one might suspect that the song verses were first *written down* by the prince, then forwarded to the court musicians to be set to music and performed.[30] The lack of an initial composition/performance outburst may help to explain why the narrator does not choose to quote the text of the song at the time of its composition. Prince Hui seems to be imitating the example of Liu Bang and "The Great Wind" in casting himself as the audience for his own song. The sequence of events in the narrative suggests that listening to the song contributed to the prince's grief and eventual suicide, through a sort of "feedback loop" in which both the sympathetic audience and the creative source of the expressed sorrow were one and the same person.

The disjunction introduced here between composition and performance is significant. Liu Bang may have opened the door with

---

29. Ban, *Han shu*, j. 38, p. 1990.

30. A similar case is found in the famous "Biography of Lady Li" 李夫人傳, in which Emperor Wu 武帝 is so moved by a ghostly vision of his deceased lover that he pens a poem about her, then bids the court musicians to set it to music (Ban, *Han shu*, j. 67a, p. 3952).

"The Great Wind," but his composition of the song is still depicted as being simultaneous with its *initial* performance; only after his own performance does he bid the choir sing it back to him. In this passage, Prince Hui seems to compose his song specifically for an initial performance by others at a later time. There are really two types of disjunction at play here, both of which violate the canonical unities of an outburst song: the first separates the time of composition from the time of performance, the second divides the person who produces the song from the person who performs it. These discrepancies in time and person open up intervals that accommodate the possibility of strategy in performance, although Prince Hui does not seem interested in exploiting them, preferring to wallow in self-pity instead.

There is one unity left to be violated in the canonical model, and that is the unity of voice, which holds that the voice that speaks in a song is the voice of the person who produced that song. If one were to compose a song to express the sorrow of another person and then have that very person perform the song, a bizarre ventriloquism would violate all three unities of the canonical model. The *Han History* contains just such a bizarre case: the story, set in 144 B.C.E., of Prince Qu 去王 of Guangchuan, his jealous wife Zhaoxin 昭信, and his unfortunate concubines:

Later, Prince Qu established Zhaoxin as his principal wife and appointed his favored concubine, Tao Wangqing, as Lady Xiumi in charge of textiles, and appointed his favored concubine, Cui Xiucheng, as Lady Mingzhen in charge of the palace discipline service. Zhaoxin repeatedly slandered Wangqing, saying, "She is very discourteous to me, her clothes are always flashier than mine, and she hoards all of the best silks to make the palace women beg for them." Qu replied, "You may malign Wangqing repeatedly, but you cannot diminish my love for her. Now, if I were to hear that she had been wanton, then I would boil her alive."

After that Zhaoxin told Qu, "Earlier, when the painters were painting Wangqing's quarters, she bared her back and shoulders and powdered herself right beside them. She also went in and out of the south gate several times to sneak glances at the attendants and clerks, and I suspect there may have been some illicit affairs." Qu replied, "Keep a close eye on her." Because of this, he grew to love Wangqing less and less.

Later, when he was drinking with Zhaoxin and the others, and all the concubines were in attendance, he composed a song for Wangqing:

You have turned your back on your parents-in-law,
have been careless in your wantonness.
You have plotted perversities,
given rise to your own end.
You have gadded about,
produced your own woes.
There is no hope for trust,
now, who shall you blame?

He had his beauties sing it in concert. Qu said: "One of you should recognize yourself in this."

Zhaoxin knew that Qu was already angry and accused Wangqing of repeatedly pointing out the sleeping quarters of the attendants and clerks and knowing all those in charge. She also said that one attendant had ordered a brocade quilt from Wangqing and that she suspected there had been an illicit affair. Qu then went with Zhaoxin and the other concubines to Wangqing's rooms, where they stripped her naked and took turns beating her. Then he ordered the concubines to each take a branding iron and brand Wangqing together. Wangqing ran away and threw herself into a well where she died. Zhaoxin took her body out, pounded a wooden stake into her vagina, sliced off her nose and lips, and cut out her tongue. Then she told Qu, "Earlier, when I killed Zhaoping,[31] she came back to haunt me, so now I want to pulverize Wangqing, making it impossible for her to turn into a spirit." She and Qu dismembered the body, placed it in a huge cauldron, stewed it with peach lime and poison, and called all the concubines to watch over it day and night until it had completely dissolved. They also killed Wangqing's younger sister, Du.

Afterwards, Qu called for concubine Rong Ai several times and drank with her, so Zhaoxin slandered her, saying: "Concubine Rong looks smug and has a base manner; I suspect she may be having a secret affair." Qu took a shirt, the collar of which Ai had been embroidering at the time, and burned it. Ai was terrified and threw herself into a well. When they pulled her out she was still alive, so they whipped her and interrogated her until she admitted falsely that she had had an illicit affair with the physician. Qu bound her up and tied her to a pillar, burned her eyes out with a hot knife,

---

31. Zhaoping was another one of Zhaoxin's unfortunate victims, who appeared to Zhaoxin in her dreams after she had been murdered.

cut her legs off at the thigh while she was still alive, and poured molten lead into her mouth. Ai died and they dismembered her, burying her under a pile of thorny brambles. Of all the concubines who were in Qu's favor, Zhaoxin managed to kill every one of them with her slander. A total of fourteen people were buried under Longevity Palace, the dwelling of the prince's mother. The palace women dreaded Zhaoxin and none dared to cross her.

Zhaoxin wanted to monopolize favor for herself, and said: "Your majesty put Lady Mingzhen in charge of the concubines, but she was unable to check the unruly lewdness. I ask that you lock up the doors to all the concubines' quarters and not let them out to take their leisure." She made her senior maidservant the acting supervisor in charge of the palace discipline service, who then locked up all their quarters and gave the key to Zhaoxin. Except for when they were summoned to large banquets, the concubines were not to be seen. Qu pitied them and composed a song which said,

> No sorrow is more sorrowful,
> than to live in such despair.
> My heart is in knots,
> my feelings strangled.
> Inside I am choking,
> my grief and sadness pile up.
> I cannot see the sky above,
> what good is living anymore?
> The day is lost,
> the time will not come again.
> I long to cast off my body,
> and to die without regret.

He ordered Zhaoxin to sound the drums for the rhythm and instructed all of the concubines in singing it. When the song was over, each one of them returned forthwith to the long halls and sealed their doors. Only Zhaoxin's niece, Chu, Lady Chenghua, was permitted an audience day or night. Zhaoxin gave over ten slaves to Qu to accompany him in playing games, drinking, and relaxing.[32]

後去立昭信爲后。幸姬陶望卿爲脩靡夫人。主繒帛。崔脩成爲明貞夫人。主永巷。昭信復譖望卿曰。與我無禮。衣服常鮮於我。取善繒諸宮人。去日。若數惡望卿。不能減我愛。設聞其淫。我亨之矣。後昭信謂

---

32. Ban, *Han shu, juan* 53, pp. 2429-31.

去曰。前畫工畫望卿舍。望卿袒裼傅粉其傍。又數出入南戶窺郎吏。疑有姦。去曰。善司之。以故益不愛望卿。後與昭信等飲。諸姬皆侍。去爲望卿作歌曰。

背尊章
嫖以忽
謀屈奇
起自絕
行周流
自生患
諒非望
今誰怨

使美人相和歌之。去曰。是中當有自知者。昭信知去已怒。即誣言望卿歷指郎吏臥處。具知其主名。又言郎中令錦被。疑有姦。去即與昭信從諸姬至望卿所。嬴其身。更擊之。令諸姬各持燒鐵共灼望卿。望卿走。自投井死。昭信出之。椓杙其陰中。割其鼻脣。斷其舌。謂去曰。前殺昭平。反來畏我。今欲靡爛望卿。使不能神。與去共支解。置大鑊中。取桃灰毒藥弁煮之。召諸姬皆臨觀。連日夜靡盡。復共殺其女弟都。

後去數召姬榮愛與飲。昭信復譖之。曰。榮姬視瞻。意態不善。疑有私。時愛爲去剌方領繡。去取燒之。愛恐。自投井。出之未死。笞問愛。自誣與醫姦。去縛繫柱。燒刀灼潰兩目。生割兩股。銷鈆灌其口中。愛死。支解以棘埋之。諸幸於去者。昭信輒譖殺之。凡十四人。皆埋太后所居長壽宮中。宮人畏之。莫敢復迕。

昭信欲擅愛。曰。王使明貞夫人主諸姬。淫亂難禁。請閉諸姬舍門。無令出教。使其大婢爲僕射。主永巷。盡封閉諸舍。上籥於后。非大置酒召。不得見。去憐之。爲作歌曰。

愁莫愁
居無聊
心重結
意不舒
內茀鬱
憂哀積
上不見天
生何益
日崔隤
時不再
願棄軀
死無悔

令昭信聲鼓爲節。以教諸姬歌之。歌罷輒歸永巷。封門。獨昭信兄子初爲乘華夫人。得朝夕見。昭信與去從十餘奴博飲游敖。

Zhaoxin seems to have taken a page from Empress Lü's book in her treatment of her husband's concubines, as she systematically destroys them through slander and murder. When she succeeds in turning the prince against the hapless Wangqing, he chooses to make his feelings known through a song performance at a drinking party. After composing his song of accusation, he then has the concubines themselves perform it, telling them that "one of you should recognize yourself in this." The accused are placed in the uncomfortable position of accusing themselves; and Zhaoxin takes her cue from this song to intensify her campaign against Wangqing.

The situation becomes even more bizarre with the final song performance. The concubines have been placed under house arrest and are only allowed out to attend banquets. This causes Prince Qu to pity them and, in classic outburst fashion, he vents his emotions through composing a song. But the song does not speak of his emotions; it is written in the voice of the imprisoned concubines. The prince himself is responsible for the suffering that he now presumes to vent on behalf of the concubines. To add insult to injury, he then has Zhaoxin—the direct author of the concubines' woes—provide the musical accompaniment; the imprisoned women are released just long enough to perform a song written by another person purporting to convey their own feelings. The outline of the outburst song—spontaneous poetic production occasioned by frustration—is still visible here, but in a strangely twisted form. None of the unity of time, person, and voice is preserved in this ventriloquist's act. When Prince Qu commands his concubines to sing a song that he wrote for them in their own voice, he is *simulating* an outburst song. He becomes the narrator of their story, placing himself in the role of the historian who provides the text for what his protagonists must be feeling at a given point in time. The narrators of the *Han History* seem benevolent in their motives, using songs to recuperate their subjects' noble intentions by giving them a voice that may not have been heard otherwise. Prince Qu's motives, however, are more suspect. His composition appropriates the genuine voice of his concubines, converting it into an aesthetic object for his consumption at a drinking party.[33] His command that they perform his song to musical accompaniment further objectifies the concubines as mere vehicles for an expression of emotion that does not originate in them. Prince Qu has perverted the idea of a genuine outburst song, reducing his concubines from expressive human beings to singing automatons.

What is the strategy in all of this? Is Prince Qu exploiting discrepancies in time, person, and voice for a particular end? The narrator mentions that he "pitied" the concubines, but there is never any intimation that he feels responsible for their suffering; he brutally tortured and murdered Rong Ai himself. If any of the concubines were to complain directly, retribution would be swift and severe. In composing the song himself and commanding Zhaoxin to perform the musical accompaniment, Prince Qu's aestheticization of his concubines' suffering effectively destroys any promise that poetry can be a powerful means used by inferiors to criticize their superiors.

After reading multiple narratives containing poetry in the *Han History*, one gradually forms the impression that venting feelings through a *Chusheng* outburst song is simply the expected way for a member of the royal family to complain. The habit is followed even when there is no expectation that one's audience will understand the song. Between 110 and 105 B.C.E., the imperial princess Xijun was sent to be the bride of the elderly leader of the Wusun nomadic tribe in the northwest.

When the princess arrived in their domain she took up residence in a palace under her own management. She met with the chieftain repeatedly throughout the year, putting on banquets and bestowing coins and silks upon his favored attendants. The chieftain was old and she could not communicate with him in his language. The princess was struck with sorrow and she composed the following song for herself:

---

33. The difference is that the historians of the *Han History* are dealing with dead people, who survive only through their textual traces. Prince Qu is confronting the living, who *could* speak for themselves if they were allowed to do so. Even worse than silencing them, Prince Qu is putting words into their mouths, saying that they wish to die because of suffering that he himself has inflicted.

My own family married me off to this distant corner
    of the earth,
sent afar to this foreign land and its barbarian chieftain.
A yurt for my chamber banners for walls,
only meat for my meals kumiss for drink.
I brood in homesickness my heart aches within,
oh, that I were a yellow crane winging its way homeward.

When the emperor heard of this, he pitied the princess and dispatched couriers at yearly intervals bearing gifts of fine tents and brocades for her.[34]

公主至其國。自治宮室居。歲時一再與昆莫會。置酒飲食。以幣帛賜王
左右貴人。昆莫年老。語言不通。公主悲愁。自爲作歌曰。

吾家嫁我兮天一方
遠託異國兮烏孫王
穹廬爲室兮旃爲牆
以肉爲食兮酪爲漿
居常土思兮心內傷
願爲黃鵠兮歸故鄉

天子聞而憐之。間歲遣使者持帷帳錦繡給遺焉。

All the requisite elements of the outburst song are here: it takes place at a banquet, during which the princess is "struck with sorrow" over her lamentable situation. "She composed the following song for herself," the narrator reports, suggesting the striking spontaneity of the princess's action at an event for which there would have been designated performers. The text of her song tells how she came to this foreign land, describes her particular rustic circumstances (which evoke within her painful thoughts of home), and then closes with the figure of a "yellow crane" returning to its native land. Not only does her performance adhere to the form of general outburst song practice, but the song's content also reiterates a familiar pattern in these sorts of songs. The opening couplet describes the general situation of the performer, the middle couplet depicts immediate and painful particulars, and the closing couplet articulates an emotional reaction to those particulars. Precisely this tripartite form typifies the earlier outburst songs contained in the *Han*

---

34. Ban, *Han shu, juan* 96b, p. 3903.

History, including Xiang Yu's "Song of Gaixia," Lady Qi's "Husking Song," and Prince You's "Captivity Song." The pattern does not really obtain in Liu Bang's songs at Pei and at court, nor in Prince Qu's songs for his concubines. Regarding this admittedly small sample of songs, one should note that the former group is presented as being more spontaneous, with less consideration of audience, while the latter group is portrayed as being more contrived or staged. This may have something to do with differences in setting: Xiang Yu is on the battlefield, Lady Qi and Prince You are imprisoned, and Princess Xijun is on the frontier. They are confronting and reacting to the immediate cause of their suffering; the shape of their emotional response becomes the shape of the song. Liu Bang and Prince Qu, however, find themselves in more contrived circumstances at Pei and in court, where they summon the audience and direct the variables of performance. They are not confronting immediate and urgent situations so much as making strategic moves in ongoing power plays. The more diffuse quality of their songs may be a reflection of this difference in setting and agenda. Prince Qu's second song, in the voice of the concubines, does retain more of the tripartite structure of a spontaneous song (especially in the immediacy of its middle line, "I cannot see the sky above"), but the sheer contrivance of its composition and performance shows it for what it is: a simulation.

The composition and performance of Princess Xijun's song seems all the more spontaneous because her immediate audience, her Wusun husband, is not even able to understand it. Indeed, his inability to understand it is what allows the princess to so frankly express her regret and sorrow. But after the narrator finishes quoting the song, he immediately reports, "the emperor heard of it and pitied her." At the time of Xijun's performance, her song may have fallen upon deaf ears, but in the narrative the emperor becomes her immediate audience. The proximity of words on the page is able to erase the intervals of time and space that separated Princess Xijun's performance on the remote frontier and the emperor's exposure to it in the capital. The emperor responds to the song by sending gifts of "fine tents and brocades" to replace the "yurt" in which she must live. His response shows that he is a sympathetic audience, but his material gifts will never compensate her adequately for the debt of sorrow owed her.

This narrative arouses suspicions in the reader that Princess Xijun may not have been acting so spontaneously after all. Perhaps she intended all along for her song to reach the ears of the emperor. This ambivalence in reading is predicated on the song's narrative context, which raises the possibility that a poem may be shaped by two "states of mind." The first is the state of mind articulated in the poem itself; the second is the state of mind manifested in the performance of the poem. The first is what is promised by principles: a direct and transparent sublimation from one state (mind) to another (word). The second is what is possible in practice: a circuitous and murky exploitation of intervals in person, voice, time, and place to fashion a strategy of poetic performance. Thus it is in narrative that the innocence of poetry is lost.

By the time one comes to the latest examples of song performance in the *Han History*—songs performed by two princes on the verge of death—the performances produce a palpable sense of banal routine, despite the urgency of the circumstances.

In 80 B.C.E., Prince Dan 旦王 of Yan is plotting to usurp the emperor's throne, but his plans are exposed:

When Prince Dan heard of it, he summoned his Minister Ping and said, "Our plot has been ruined; should we send out our troops?" Ping replied, "The Senior General is already dead, the people all know about it—we cannot send them out." The prince was filled with dread so he arranged for a banquet in the Palace of Longevity and gathered together guests, officers, wives, and concubines to take part in the drinking. The prince himself sang,

> Returning to an empty city:
>   the dogs do not bark,
>   nor do the cocks crow.
> How barren and empty are the avenues:
>   one surely knows the kingdom is deserted.

Lady Huarong rose to dance, and sang,

> Hair lies strewn clogging the ditches,
>   bones pile up without a proper resting place.
> Mothers look for dead sons,

wives look for dead husbands.
Lingering between the ditches,
    how can the lord abide in peace?

Everyone seated there wept.

An order of amnesty arrived and the prince read it, saying, "Alas! This only pardons the officers and the people, but does not pardon me!" Then he received his principal wife, concubines, and ladies into the Hall of Shining Light, where he told them, "That bunch of decrepit slaves is striking against my entire clan because of this." He was about to commit suicide, but his attendants said, "With any luck you may be stripped of your kingdom, but you will escape death." His wife, concubines, and ladies, all sobbing and weeping, stopped the prince from proceeding.[35]

旦聞之。召相平曰。事敗。遂發兵乎。平曰。左將軍已死。百姓皆知之。
不可發也。王憂懣。置酒萬載宮。會賓客群臣妃妾坐飲。王自歌曰。

> 歸空城兮
> 狗不吠
> 雞不鳴
> 橫術何廣廣兮
> 固知國中之無人

華容夫人起舞曰。

> 髮紛紛兮寘渠
> 骨籍籍兮亡居
> 母求死子兮
> 妻求死夫
> 裴回兩渠間兮
> 君子獨安居
> 坐者皆泣。

有赦令到。王讀之。曰。嗟乎。獨赦吏民。不赦我。因迎后姬諸夫人
之明光殿。王曰。老虜曹爲事當族。欲自殺。左右曰。黨得削國。幸不
死。后姬夫人共啼泣止王。

This narrative is striking for its similarity with the narrative containing "Song of Gaixia." In both cases, the protagonists reach an impasse, which produces an emotional reaction in them; they set the stage with drinking; they sings songs of despair; their concubines sing songs in response; then all those in attendance weep. The dif-

---

35. Ban, *Han shu, juan* 63, p. 2757–58.

ference here is that the scene is set in the palace of a prince, not on a darkened battlefield. The epic proportions of tragedy have all but vanished and the dramatic elements seem all too contrived, much like the prince's ensuing suicide attempt. The genuine quality found in Xiang Yu's outburst song is compromised here by the impression that the prince is simply following accepted practice for the expression of sorrow at court.

While Prince Dan's performance may be unremarkable, the content of his and Huarong's songs is noteworthy. Both provide bleak but powerful images of desolation and death, followed by a single line expressing the singer's despair. The states of mind captured in these songs are not reactions to immediate circumstances, but imaginative depictions of circumstances that will emerge only after the deaths of the singers.[36] The narrative frame provides a time of composition and performance that can be compared with the time frame suggested in the poem itself; only within such a narrative frame does this sophisticated handling of time become apparent. This may be an "outburst" in reaction to present circumstances, but it is cast as a bleak vision of the future.

A similar story unfolds in 54 B.C.E. when Prince Xu 胥王 of Guangling is exposed in his plot to place a curse upon the emperor. The emperor sends officers to investigate, and Prince Xu admits his crime to them. He then busies himself with setting the stage for his farewell song and suicide.

Once Prince Xu saw the emissaries had returned, he arranged for wine in the Hall of Brilliance. He summoned the heir apparent Ba, his daughters Dongzi and Husheng, and others for a night of drinking. He bid his favorites, Consort Guo Zhaojun, Woman of the Household Zhao Zuojun, and others to play the zither and sing and dance. The prince himself sang,

> We all want life to go on without ceasing,
> but this eternal unhappiness will it ever end?
> I received my Heaven-allotted span not an instant more,
> the superior steed halts and waits in the road.

---

36. Suzuki notes that both of these songs, in their envisioning of a scene after death, prefigure the "pall bearer's song" 挽歌 in which the poet describes a posthumous scene (*Kan Gi shi no kenkyū*, p. 35).

In the Yellow Springs below in the dark depths,
  is where all human life must end,
  so why should one worry over it so?
How does one find happiness but in what delights the heart?
Yet I come and go in this joyless state with only a glimpse
  of happiness.
We are summoned to the Mountain of Death inspected
  at the gates,
the dead cannot send substitutes in their place,
  it is we ourselves who must go.

One after another, all those in attendance toasted him with tears in their eyes. The banquet lasted until cockcrow. Then Xu told the heir apparent Ba, "The emperor treated me with generosity, but now I have betrayed him deeply. When I die it is only fitting that my bones be left unburied, but if I am fortunate enough to be granted a funeral, you should make it spare without extravagance." He then hanged himself with his seal cord and died. Then Consort Guo Zhaojun and the other woman both killed themselves. The emperor showed extraordinary mercy and granted amnesty to the prince's sons, allowing them to live as commoners. He then bestowed the posthumous title of Cruel Prince upon Prince Xu. He had held his position for sixty-four years before he was sentenced to death and his kingdom was abrogated.[37]

胥既見使者還。置酒顯陽殿。召太子霸及子女董訾胡生等夜飲。使所幸八子郭昭君家人子趙左君等鼓瑟歌舞。王自歌曰。

欲久生兮無終
長不樂兮安窮
奉天期兮不得須臾
千里馬兮駐待路
黃泉下兮幽深
人生要死
何爲苦心
何用爲樂心所喜
出入無悰爲樂亟
萬里召兮郭門閱
死不得取代庸
身自逝

---

37. Ban, *Han shu*, juan 63, p. 2762.

左右悉更涕泣奏酒。至雞鳴時罷。胥謂太子霸曰。上遇我厚。今負之甚。
我死。骸骨當暴。幸而得葬。薄之。無厚也。即以綬自絞死。及八子郭
昭君等二人皆自殺。天子加恩。赦王諸子皆爲庶人。賜諡曰厲王。立六
十四年而誅。國除。

The sorrow expressed in the song seems genuine enough, but after
the performance is over and the audience has shed the requisite tears,
the wine continues to flow and the banquet does not break up until
dawn. The song itself, rather than an outburst on the verge of death,
becomes merely another item on the agenda of the last feast.[38] A far
cry from spontaneity, a sense of rote ritual pervades the song per-
formance, just as it does the suicide that follows it. Prince Xu's final
words to the heir apparent suggest that his song performance and
suicide are all part of a strategy of expressing contrition, whereby
the prince hopes to shape his treatment and remembrance after his
death. His strategy seems successful, as his sons are spared death and
the prince himself is granted a posthumous title.

IV

Several passages discussed above indicate that the poetry appearing
in the *Han History* is of questionable historical veracity. Poems seem
to fall into the same camp as the dramatic dialogues frequently
employed by Sima Qian and Ban Gu: these are the historian's
re-creation of what these people probably said (or *should* have said)
in given circumstances. The inclusion of poetry among the putative
words of famous figures in history is perfectly compatible with Han
conceptions of biographical writing, for the biography is meant to
construct a coherent narrative of historical events along the thread
of an individual's life, thereby highlighting, preserving, and trans-
mitting that person's historical significance to later ages. When
strong emotion threatens to invade the coherency of that narrative,
the historian channels it through song, the natural mode of expres-

---

38. Note the absence of the ubiquitous emotional tag phrase ("with sorrow,"
"with passion," and the like) prior to the performance.

sion for such feelings.[39] As a verbal form that "puts a state of mind into words," a poem is able to encapsulate the emotional impact felt by a certain person at a certain point in history, thus providing a window into that person's inner nature, and, by extension, into the entire age—poetry is the interior of history, allowing the historian to write a comprehensive biography, recording not only actions and words of his subjects, but their thoughts and feelings as well. Because judgments of moral character are based on intention, rather than action, a poem allows the reader to judge the quality of a person's character even if that person has failed to act.[40] A poem is the perfect vehicle to show that though historical figures may not always have been able to carry out their intentions, their hearts were in the right place.

A narrative frame around a poem creates a space in which the variables of poetic performance (and their exploitation) can be displayed. Many of the individuals in these narratives are depicted as approaching the production of poetry in a very purposeful and self-conscious way—as though they are aware of earlier exemplars and know that this is the way one is *supposed* to have a poetic outburst. The frequency with which poetic utterance is staged and contrived in these accounts suggests that either the subjects of the biographies or the historians (most likely a combination of both) have been conditioned by an ideal vision of the composition of poetry as spontaneous reaction to particular circumstances. The historical biography provides the perfect ground on which to work out such a vision—the particular circumstances are already at hand in the account, and if tradition is kind enough to provide a song, then a perfect match can be made. Of course, once a person recognizes that he or she is meant to be spontaneous in a particular

---

39. There is a remarkably consistent division of labor across all genres of poem-bearing narratives in premodern Chinese literature: narrative describes the exterior; poetry inscribes the interior. The direct depiction of an interior psychological state in narrative prose is exceedingly rare; the use of free indirect discourse, in which the voice of the narrator takes on the characteristics of a character's interior monologue, is unknown.

40. See Sima Qian's "Grand Historian's Self-Explication" 太史公自序 (*Shi ji*, *juan* 130, p. 3290).

situation, that possibility is precluded. The opportunity to strate-
gize poetic performance then creeps into these narratives, which
themselves become potent exemplars for later generations.

The *Zuo Tradition* and other pre-Qin texts show quotations from
the *Poems* readily pressed into service to make a persuasive argu-
ment or an oblique proposition, becoming the cornerstone of rhe-
torical and diplomatic strategies. Pre-Qin texts do not seek to ex-
plain the production of the *Poems* in the past as much as they do to
demonstrate the apt quotation of them in the present. The emphasis
during the Han dynasty shifted from quotation to production: the
"Great Preface" and the "Lesser Prefaces" reframe the *Poems* not as a
rhetorical resource, but as the result of spontaneous and genuine
outbursts by "the people" and various figures in Zhou history.
Under this model, the suasive power of poetry stems less from
skilful deployment than from genuine feeling guaranteed by spon-
taneity. In fact, the pre-Qin practices of offering and citing the
Poems and the Han depiction of poetic production are all supported
by the canonical definition found in the *Documents*: "poems ar-
ticulate intent." In the pre-Qin case, an extant poem is quoted to
communicate a particular intent, usually to persuade one's inter-
locutor of a certain point of view, to bolster an argument, or to
make a proposition. In the Han case, a *new* poem is spontaneously
produced to give verbal form to the mind's emotional state.[41] The
first case involves premeditated articulation through quotation to
achieve a certain goal; the second emphasizes spontaneous articula-
tion through production to vent one's feelings.

What these narratives from the *Han History* show, however, is
that a residue of purposefulness left over from the pre-Qin use of
poetry still clings to song performance in the Han. The production
of a poem may be a spontaneous matter, but the variables of song
performance can still be controlled. It is possible to produce *and* use
a poem for suasive effect. However, even though performance of
poetry in these Han narratives is frequently staged, the suasive effect
is usually incidental, often minimal, and in some cases, even horri-

---

41. The "Great Preface" explicitly introduces the sentimental element with its
use of the term "feelings" (*qing* 情).

bly counterproductive. These narratives are largely free of any ex-
pectation that a poem will actually accomplish anything—it is more
a venting mechanism than a persuasive tool. This lack of efficacy
may be explained in part by the "cult of impotence" started by Sima
Qian, which holds that noble intentions, when thwarted in the
present, will find their way into literary expression and thus be
preserved for later ages. Writing well—or, in these cases drawn from
the *Han History*, singing well and then having someone write about
it in a book destined to be read for centuries—is the best revenge
from the standpoint of posterity.

In the *Han History*, the individual is subsumed into the larger
sweep of history by the placement of his or her biography within
the context of the larger historical work. The poem within the biog-
raphy is the product of an individual reacting to specific circum-
stances: a window into the heart of one person and thus into the
entire age that he or she inhabits.[42] This ultimately explains the lack
of efficacy in these poetic performances. These protagonists are not
displaying poetic "talent" 才 for a particular end;[43] they are in-
variably on a political stage, and thus are inextricably "bound" 繫 to
the picture of the age being painted by the historian. Their poems
cannot be portrayed as effective because they themselves were in-
effective political agents. They were trapped by larger forces, against
which their poems rail in vain. Only with the collapse of a stable
political stage in the four centuries of disunion following the Han
dynasty was it possible to sever this bond and to portray individuals
using poetic performance for personal ends, disassociated from a
larger political picture.

The net result of these narratives in the *Han History* is to show
the *possibility* of strategizing personal poetic production and per-
formance, even if such strategies prove ineffective. The canonical

---

42. This principle is found in the "Great Preface" in its explanation of the "Airs
of the Kingdoms" 國風: "Thus, when the affairs of an entire kingdom are bound to
the root of one person's [experience], then it is called an 'Air'" 是以一國之事。繫
一人之本。謂之風.

43. Western Han literary figures, Sima Xiangru 司馬相如 (179–117 B.C.E.) being
the most notable, usually chose to display their poetic talent through composing
long, ornate pieces of rhyming prose known as "poetic expositions" (*fu* 賦).

model cannot address this possibility, since, as an attempt to pre-scribe the theory of poetic production, it fails to take into account the variables of time, person, and voice that are opened up in the reality of poetic practice. A narrative frame for a poem says the unsayable. It shows, rather than tells, an abiding truth: no human utterance, not even a poem, is innocent.

CR THREE SO

Playing the Game

I

In broad terms, the *Zuo Tradition* deals with individuals as instruments of competition between states, while the *Han History* deals with competition between individual members of the nobility to consolidate and maintain imperial power on behalf of their clans. Both forms of competition are closely tied to violence or the threat of violence. The utterance of poetry complements or results from these violent struggles—the competent performance of poetry is not an end in itself.

In the case of the *Zuo Tradition*, it is the working out of the relationships between the vying states of the Eastern Zhou that is paramount. Performance and citation of selections from the *Poems* are only one tool used by the culturally competent to establish, maintain, and evaluate these relationships and to advise superiors on how to manage them. The poetic performance is used diplomatically to avoid violence; but when violence cannot be avoided and states go to war, the *Poems* are used to strike alliances, declare aggression, and offer strategic advice. The *Poems* are even used to negotiate the terms of victory and defeat after a battle has concluded.

In the *Han History*, the struggle between states gives way to struggle between clan-based political factions. Once Liu Bang decisively defeats Xiang Yu and establishes imperial rule—both events marked by songs—an interminable competition for power begins between positions occupied by the emperor, the empress and her clan (the Lüs being the most notorious), and the enfeoffed princes of the empire. This competition often culminates in the ruthless use of force, and thus the outburst songs found in the *Han History* are invariably occasioned by either the threat or the experience of violence.

The Six Dynasties era (220–589 C.E.) that followed the dissolution of the Han dynasty was marked by the violent disintegration of a vast and long-lived empire, but was shaped even more profoundly by the *memory* of that empire: a memory that certainly persisted in the ambitions of the successive ruling houses of the Wei (220–265), Jin (265–420), and Southern Dynasties (420–589).[1] The rulers of these miniature empires were acutely aware that their influence now extended over a much smaller region than that of the once glorious Han dynasty, the culture of which they sought to preserve and emulate. The political stage shrank drastically, producing liberating effects on cultural expression in general and poetic competence in particular. Simply put: the stakes were smaller, which allowed the individual to loom larger. States still engaged in war, and clans still vied for imperial power, but the records of the age also tell stories of individuals competing for nothing more than elevated status in the eyes of fellow members of the elite ruling classes. Struggle through cultural means is portrayed as a viable, and often more effective, alternative to physical violence.

The one compilation of records that most insistently depicts the power of cultural competence is *Topical Tales: A New Edition* 世説新語, a work commissioned by the Liu Song prince, Liu Y-qing 劉義慶 (403–444), containing an extensive commentary, drawing upon contemporary works, by Liu Jun 劉峻 (462–

---

1. For an extensive study on this topic, see Holcombe, *In the Shadow of the Han: Literati Thought and Society at the Beginning of the Southern Dynasties.*

521).[2] The catholicity of its source materials makes classifying *Topical Tales* difficult; many have argued that it is a *sui generis* work with character appraisal as its unifying theme.[3] It certainly cannot be accepted as a reliable historical source. The depictions of poetic performance and reception in its pages range from the patently apocryphal to the possible to the probable. These are visions of poetic competence rather than faithful records. In its attempts to appraise its subjects, *Topical Tales* includes demonstrations of poetic competence that *should* have happened, that are *in character* for those people as they were perceived by their peers: other members of the émigré aristocracy that made up the ruling class of the era. If the *Zuo Tradition* casts individuals as agents of the state and the *Han History* casts them as members of imperial clans, then *Topical Tales* casts them as representatives of their class and lineage. In their struggle for distinction and power, members of the elite of this era eschew the coarse tool of physical violence in favor of the subtler instrument of symbolic violence.[4] At least, this is how they are *depicted* in the pages of *Topical Tales*, which says something about those who compiled these anecdotes and those who enjoyed them.

The pages of *Topical Tales* still contain many depictions of violence, but the relationship between violence and poetic utterance has changed from that depicted in the *Zuo Tradition* and the *Han History*. A familiar case in point is the following famous, and surely apocryphal, anecdote about an encounter between the talented Cao Zhi 曹植 (192–232), Prince of Dong'e, and his jealous older brother, Cao Pi 曹丕 (187–226), Emperor Wen of Wei (r. 200–226):

---

2. The term *shi* 世 has both a temporal denotation ("era") and a spatial one ("world"), which is why I choose to translate it as "topical," a word that spans spatial and temporal denotations in English. The book was first known simply as *Shishuo* (*Topical Tales*), then as *Shishuo xinshu* 世説新書 (*Topical Tales: A New Edition*) to differentiate it from an earlier work of the same name by Liu Xiang 劉向 (ca. 77–6 B.C.E.). This then became *Shishuo xinyu*, where *xinyu* 新語 might be translated along the lines of "fresh topics for conversation" 新的話題. It is likely in this case that *xinyu* continues to denote a "new edition."

3. See chapters 1 and 3 of Qian's *Spirit and Self in Medieval China*.

4. Pierre Bourdieu, in *Language & Symbolic Power*, provides an extended analysis of the use of language as a means of accruing and wielding power.

Emperor Wen once commanded the Prince of Dong'e to compose a poem within the time it takes to walk seven steps, or face the ultimate punishment should it not be completed in time. The prince immediately shot back with the following poem:

> Boil beans to make some soup,
> Strain them to get the broth.
> The stalks are burning 'neath the pot,
> The beans are weeping up on top:
> "We are from the same root born,
> So why the hurry to cook me up?"

The emperor's face flushed deeply with shame. (4.66)[5]

文帝嘗令東阿王七步中作詩。不成者行大法。應聲便爲詩曰。

> 煮豆持作羹
> 漉菽以爲汁
> 萁在釜下然
> 豆在釜中泣
> 本自同根生
> 相煎何太急

帝深有慚色。

The contrast drawn here between the two brothers is a stark one. Cao Pi, as the emperor of Wei, has a monopoly on sanctioned physical violence, the full weight of which he brings to bear in threatening his talented younger brother with the "ultimate punishment" of death. Cao Pi's ruthlessness does not mean that he lacks culture or an understanding of literature. He was a poet in his own right and is the author of an early work of literary theory known as the *Authoritative Discourses* 典論.[6] In a chapter of that work entitled "Discourse on Literature" 論文, Cao Pi calls literary works "the supreme achievement in the business of state" 經國之大業, divulging his fervent hope that it would be in the production of literature, not in the force of arms, that his most enduring legacy

---

5. My translations are based on Liu Yiqing's *Shishuo xinyu* and Todo's *Sesetsu shingo*. I have also consulted Mather's eminent translation, *A New Account of Tales of the World* and Qian's *Spirit and Self in Medieval China*.

6. Over forty poems are attributed to him in Lu Qinli, *Xian Qin Han Wei Jin Nanbei chao shi*, vol. 1, pp. 389–406.

would survive.[7] How galling it must have been for him that his younger brother, Cao Zhi, was universally acclaimed as a "literary genius" 才子 and was consequently favored by their father. The anecdote about the "Seven Steps Poem" *can* be read simply as a piece of pro–Cao Zhi propaganda, casting Cao Pi as a jealous, paranoid older brother foiled in his attempt to humiliate and destroy his upstart younger brother. It is certainly apocryphal and was fashioned and transmitted purely as a means to embellish Cao Zhi's reputation as a literary genius.[8] But it is about more than that; it is about an encounter between two men who have very different attitudes toward literary production. Furthermore, it is an encounter that takes place in time—a sense of which gives one man an advantage over the other.

In essence, the "Seven Steps Poem" is a command performance with very high stakes. As emperor, Cao Pi has the power to summon Cao Zhi and to set the parameters for his poetic performance, which establish death as the substitute for the more genteel penalty of having to drink a flagon of wine to pay for poetic failure. Cao Pi also demarcates the time limit in spatial terms as being "within seven steps" 七步中. These parameters put Cao Zhi in a highly charged position, contrived to strain to the utmost his lauded talent for improvisation. The whole scenario has a dramatic quality to it; one can almost feel those in attendance holding their breath as they watch Cao Zhi take each step and hear him chant each line.

Cao Pi is playing a risky game in attacking Cao Zhi on the very grounds he finds most comfortable: improvised literary production. He obviously hopes that his brother's talents will fail him and that he will either produce a piece of doggerel (thus damaging his reputation as a literary genius) or produce nothing at all (thus damaging his reputation and person). Should Cao Zhi fail, Cao Pi would be in

---

7. Translated in Owen, *Readings*, pp. 57–72.

8. As emperor, Cao Pi would surely have had more direct means at his disposal of dealing with his brother than this showy trap. The hero must survive for the narrative to continue, of course, but the familiar scenario is also an opportunity for the hero to demonstrate his ingenuity and to gain the moral imperative to destroy the man who would destroy him.

a position to augment his own reputation by magnanimously commuting the death penalty. This would avoid turning his younger brother into a martyr, and instead let him live on under a cloud of literary failure, indebted to Cao Pi for his life.

Cao Zhi does not fail, of course, or the tale would not be worth the telling. Instead, he deftly turns the tables against his brother, rebounding the full force of his attack. His poem not only satisfies his older brother's stringent criteria, it also acts as a vehicle of criticism, taking Cao Pi to task for being so cruel. There is a delicious recursion at work, in that the poem constitutes an improvised complaint about having to perform such a poem in the first place. It is an occasional poem about the injustice of the occasion. The ingenious central figure of the poem—beans being boiled on a fire stoked with beanstalks—is so pointed and the performance so perfectly pitched that Cao Pi is given no room to maneuver in his response to it. He is left speechless, the only indication of his interior state being the unmistakable color of shame rising in his face, surely witnessed by all those in attendance. At the beginning of the anecdote, Cao Pi set out to harm the person of his younger brother by pushing his literary faculties to the breaking point. By the end of the anecdote, it is Cao Pi's own dignity that suffers harm, as he realizes that he has sorely underestimated his brother's talent, and has made himself appear malicious and petty in the eyes of his people.

There is an exquisite alchemy at work in this anecdote, which transforms the threat of physical violence at the hands of the emperor into symbolic violence at the hands of the prince. Yet the emperor's ability to threaten physical violence in the first place is contingent upon a symbolic mode of expressing imperial power, which sanctions the use of violence by the emperor in dealing with his inferiors. Cao Pi occupies the position of emperor, with all of the material trappings and symbolic connotations that manifest and maintain the permanence of that position. He perceives Cao Zhi as rising above the position of prince on the strength of symbolic power derived not from the external trappings of the position (which Cao Zhi actively eschewed), but from innate literary talent. This was an anxiety planted in Cao Pi's heart when the brothers were still boys, according to a source cited in *Topical Tales*:

Cao Zhi was the younger full-brother of Emperor Wen [Cao Pi]. When he was still a teenager, he was able to recite from memory countless poems, essays, and pieces of rhyming prose, and was highly skilled at writing. His father [Cao Cao], upon reading one of his son's works, once said to him, "Someone else wrote this for you!"

Cao Zhi fell to his knees and said, "My words come forth as essays, my brushstrokes turn into chapters. Test me yourself and see whether I need anyone else to write for me!"

At that time the Bronze Sparrow Terrace at Ye had just been finished, so Cao Cao gathered all of his sons and took them up to it. He had each one of them compose a piece of rhyming prose. Cao Zhi took up his brush and finished immediately with impressive results.

He had an easygoing manner and did not affect a regal air; nor did he care for ostentatious trappings in chariots and clothing. Whenever faced with a difficult question, he could always respond without hesitation. Cao Cao doted on him and almost made him the Crown Prince on several occasions. (4.66n)[9]

陳思王植字子建。文帝同母弟也。年十餘歲誦詩論及辭賦數萬言。善屬文。太祖嘗視其文曰。汝倩人邪。植跪曰。出言爲論。下筆成章。顧當面試。奈何倩人。時鄴銅雀臺新成。太祖悉將諸子登之。使各爲賦。植援筆立成。可觀。性簡易。不治威儀。輿馬服飾。不尚華麗。每見難問。應聲而答。太祖寵愛之。幾爲太子者數矣。

In the end, however, it was the older son, Cao Pi, who ascended the throne according to the rules of primogeniture. Perhaps the father, Cao Cao, who himself came to power through the astute use of violence, realized that the world was not yet ready for a man to ascend the throne on the basis of literary talent alone.

When the two brothers encounter one another as grown men in the anecdote of the "Seven Steps Poem," Cao Pi is willing to risk that Cao Zhi may succeed at his impossible task because it is the only way to deflate the source of symbolic power that he enjoys as a literary genius. If Cao Zhi's literary reputation is compromised, Cao Pi could retreat from physical violence and return to the means of symbolic violence at his disposal for containing Cao Zhi's ambitions, mainly transferring him from fiefdom to fiefdom and re-

---

9. Liu Jun cites the "Account of Wei" 魏志 section (of *Account of the Three Kingdoms* 三國志 by Chen Shou 陳壽) for this anecdote.

quiring frequent expensive trips to the capital. Ironically, it is poetic complaints against this form of mistreatment that help build Cao Zhi's literary reputation, the source of his competing symbolic power.[10]

For Cao Pi, Cao Zhi represents a symptom of the way imperial power seeks to assert and perpetuate itself.[11] The emperor, once in power, is concerned with maintaining the longevity and continuity of that power. He is forced to look to a more distant horizon, constantly seeking to manifest the stability and permanence of his position.[12] The outside challenger does not have access to the emperor's superior symbolic capital. He is forced to live in the present moment, constantly improvising ways to subvert the power that marginalizes him.[13] Cao Pi's outrageous demands are an attempt to break Cao Zhi's ability to improvise, to flatten out the forms of his brother's talent, and thus to deprive him of his destabilizing effect on Cao Pi's grand vision of empire. Cao Pi pits the power of his position against the talent of a single man. When the single man

---

10. "Given to Prince Biao of Baima" 贈白馬王彪 and "Brown Sparrow" 黃雀 are the most famous examples.

11. By the term "symptom" I am referring to Slavoj Žižek's definition of it as "a particular element which subverts its own universal foundation" (*Sublime Object*, p. 22).

12. This anxiety over stability and longevity is expressed in Cao Pi's own poetry. In the second stanza of his feast poem, "Grand," he writes,

> All is hushed in the high halls,
> and cool winds enter my chamber.
> Hold it at fullness, without spilling over,
> one with virtue can bring things to happy ends;
> yet a good man's heart is full of worries,
> his cares are not just one alone;
> he comes decently down from his plain rooms,
> bolting his food so as to miss naught.
> The guests are full now and go home,
> yet the host's cares never are done. (Owen,
> *Anthology*, pp. 281–82)

13. These are the contours of the main conflict between Xiang Yu and Liu Bang, as seen in their song performances in the *Han History*: between a man of action who refuses to be subsumed into a new imperial order and a man of vision who sets the stage for that new order and is anxious to stabilize it.

wins, it becomes painfully clear that the power of the emperor's position is also contingent—at least in part—upon the talent and judgment of the man who occupies it. When Cao Pi's face colors with the hot blood of shame, it is a vivid reminder of the limits of corporeality in the man who would be emperor forever.

What does Cao Zhi's victory mean, beyond his escape with person intact and reputation enhanced? It signals a shift in attitude during the aftermath of the Han dynasty's collapse toward literary production or utterance instead of political violence. In the *Zuo Tradition*, poetic competence in deploying selections from the *Poems* was a tool for framing, interpreting, and navigating treacherous political struggles. The narratives of the *Han History* concerning outburst songs show poetic production not as means of avoiding or negotiating violent confrontations, but as a result of them. The emphasis in depiction shifts away from calculated quotation to spontaneous production, with the result that the notion of competence shifts away from the one who utters the poem (a supposedly involuntary act) to the one who records that utterance at a place in the narrative providing maximum vindicatory effect for those who felt they were wronged by the violent events of history.

Moral worth is closely entwined with poetic utterance in both cases. In the *Zuo Tradition*, one's moral worth is repeatedly and explicitly linked to the level of one's cultural competence. Poetic competence in particular is shown to be a reliable barometer of the morality of individuals and states. It is not so much the content of the poems that matters—it is already determined in the corpus of the *Poems*—as the propriety with which they are offered or cited. In the *Han History*, the recording of a poetic utterance serves to manifest the interior moral worth of a historical figure prevented by external circumstances from putting that moral worth into practice. It is a way for the historians to provide a window into the hearts and minds of the subjects of history, although what is seen there is usually a picture of frustrated impotence.

The "Seven Steps Poem," purportedly uttered just after the fall of the Han, is a new type of performance. It is reminiscent of the *Han History*'s spontaneous outbursts of frustration, but it has also regained the suasive power of poetic utterance so prominent in the

Zuo Tradition. In this anecdote, and throughout *Topical Tales*, poetic competence emerges as the ability to deploy poetic utterances from a wide variety of sources—the *Poems*, noncanonical poetry, spontaneous production—in order to decisively demonstrate one's talent. The lessons learned, on the one hand, about poetry's efficacy in the *Zuo Tradition*, and, on the other hand, about its particular expressive power in the *Han History*, have been brought to bear, in the narratives of *Topical Tales*, upon the dramatically shrunken stage of competition between individuals.

This "shrunken stage" results from the obsession in *Topical Tales* with the qualities of individual people: their talents, their moral character, their verbal acuity, and even their physical attributes and modes of attire. The anecdote of the "Seven Steps Poem" does not seek, as the *Zuo Tradition* does, to illustrate the utility of cultural competence in Traditional knowledge in the struggles between states. It is not part of a larger narrative arc about the establishment and continuation of imperial power, as found in the *Han History*. The anecdote is included in the fourth chapter, "Letters and Scholarship" 文學, simply as a particularly engaging account of talent in literary production.[14] That the two men in the encounter are brothers with a troubled relationship—who also happen to be emperor and prince—certainly informs the parameters and content of the performance; but it is the quality of the performance in and of itself that justifies its inclusion in the collection. The pages of *Topical Tales* show that the highly elastic concepts of cultural competence in general, and poetic competence in particular, were redefined and expanded during the period of disunion following the Han. But what appears to be a truly innovative notion—one attested to by the very existence of the *Topical Tales* collection—is that the political ramifications of cultural competence could be subordinated to the quality of the performance. The demonstration of cultural competence through performance becomes a legitimate source of power in and of *itself*, a source of symbolic power favorably portrayed against the backdrop of more brutish forms of power con-

---

14. Although the translations from *Topical Tales* are my own, I have adopted Mather's renditions of the chapter titles used in his translation, *Tales of the World*.

tingent upon physical violence.[15] The account of the "Seven Steps Poem" is important as a demonstration of the triumph of poetic competence over violence. The victory is likely apocryphal and we are told that Cao Zhi "became frustrated and unhappy, dying in his forty-first year." But even if the victory never occurred historically, it finds a life of great moment in the realm of the symbol, on the pages of the inscribed narrative.

II

Poetic competence of the more ancient variety—namely, the apt citation of lines from the *Poems*—is still demonstrated in *Topical Tales*, but in often surprising places.[16] Women and children now step forward in these narratives to demonstrate their poetic competence. Following is a typical example:

Sun Sheng, who was secretarial aide to the Honorable Yu Liang, accompanied Yu on a hunt, bringing his two young sons along with him. Yu was not aware of this until, there on the hunting grounds, he suddenly spotted Sun Fang,[17] who was only seven or eight years old at the time. Yu hailed him by saying, "Have you also come, kind sir?" The boy shot back in reply, "It's a case of:

> Without distinction between small and great,
> All follow the prince in his going."[18] (2.49)

孫盛爲庾公記室參軍。從獵。將其二兒俱行。庾公不知。忽於獵場見齊莊。時年七八歲。庾謂曰。君亦復來邪。應聲答曰。所謂。

> 無小無大
> 從公于邁

---

15. Rouzer notes that in *Topical Tales* the "the strain or even violence of competition is always near the surface" (*Articulated Ladies*, p. 86) and provides an extended discussion of "Competition and Violence" in the collection (pp. 85–110).

16. There are at least seventeen quotations from or allusions to the *Poems* scattered across the 36 chapters. Five of these are in the second chapter, "Speech and Conversation" 言語, under the following entry numbers: 1, 11, 36, 49, and 80.

17. The original text calls Fang by his courtesy name, Qizhuang 齊莊 or "Rivaling Zhuangzi." I consistently use given names in the translations to avoid confusion.

18. The poem quoted is "Semicircular Water" 泮水 (Mao #299). My translation is after Karlgren, *Book of Odes*, p. 256.

This anecdote was surely included in *Topical Tales* because of the tender age of the boy who cites the *Poems* with such pointed alacrity. It is evidence that the Traditionalist canon of texts was already firmly entrenched as part of the educational curriculum for the children of the elite classes.[19] Simply *knowing* the poems, however, is not a noteworthy accomplishment in itself; one must demonstrate competence, as Sun Fang does in this anecdote.

The encounter takes place on the "hunting grounds" 獵場, the proper arena for men to demonstrate their strength and martial skills. Yu Liang 庾亮 (289–340) was appointed General Chastizing the West 征西將軍; staging hunting expeditions was a way to hone the skills he needed to keep the "barbarians" at bay.[20] The abrupt appearance (marked explicitly in the text with the phrase "suddenly spotted") of a young boy in this arena of men prompts the general to verbally challenge the interloper. He addresses the boy in tones of mock politeness, asking him to explain his presence.[21] Speed is of the essence in this exchange. All parties are on horseback and the quarry is at hand; there is no time for drawn out justifications or apologies. Yu Liang, the ranking superior on the field, has made a verbal thrust in the direction of Sun Fang, the lowest inferior. The boy parries with consummate skill by immediately responding (the text literally says "echoes" 應聲) with an apt citation from the *Poems*, demonstrating a quickness of mind that justifies his presence on the hunting grounds, as well as a facility in the Tradition that indicates his status as a nascent man of culture. Once again, against a backdrop of violence, poetic competence is shown as a means of winning, of meeting a challenge and silencing the challenger.

Sun Fang's citation is appropriate on two levels. The words themselves are appropriate because of their reference to the "prince"

---

19. In the *Analects* (16.13), Confucius tells his own son, "Without studying the *Poems*, one lacks the means to speak" 不學詩無以言.

20. Yu Liang's appointment in 334 and his attendant responsibilities are noted in Sima Guang, *Zizhi tongjian, juan* 95, p. 2996.

21. Yu Liang uses the polite pronoun *jun* 君 ("sir/master") to address the child in tones of ironic formality, a strategy of condescension used by superiors in addressing inferiors. Yu Liang's use of the final interrogative particle *ye* 邪 implies that he expects Sun Fang to justify his presence at the hunt.

公 (the same character is used in Yu's courtesy title, "Honorable Yu" 庾公) and to those who join him on an expedition being "small and great" 小大 (in this case, carrying the double entendre of status and physical size). But the citation is also appropriate when its context in the whole poem is considered. The poem "Semicircular Waters" 泮水 is in lavish praise of the Marquis of Lu 魯侯, or Duke Xi 僖公, and his military officers, for their pacification of the barbarian tribes of Huai 淮夷.[22] The citation thus casts Yu Liang in the role of an illustrious Eastern Zhou ruler establishing peace in his state. The exalted status of Duke Xi and the fulsome praise in the poem evoked by Sun Fang's citation could be read as a strategy of reverse condescension. Just as Yu Liang addressed the boy in inflated terms, Sun Fang turns the tables and casts the general in a grandiose role. The discrepancy between the original referents of the poem (a Zhou era ruler campaigning against barbarians) and the implied referents of its application in the present moment (a Jin general on a hunt) has grown so large that the only way to bridge the gap is through an ironic reading. The men and women (and children) of *Topical Tales* know full well that they live in a smaller world, far removed from the grand concerns of the Zhou era and its vying states. Competition between individuals is now worthy of record, but the symbolic capital inherited from the Zhou still persists and takes on a new status in the realm of erudite banter.

Ironic or flippant citations of the *Poems* occur frequently in *Topical Tales*, indicating a more casual attitude toward the received "texts" of the Tradition than is found in the staid examples of the *Zuo Tradition*.[23] Traditional knowledge can even be applied to interior decorating, as in the following anecdote about Xie Lingyun's

---

22. The "Lesser Preface" identifies the Marquis of Lu as Duke Xi 僖公 (r. 659–627 B.C.E.), who conducted campaigns against the "barbarian tribes" living to the southeast in the Huai river basin.

23. This "relaxation" of the strictures of application—admitting irony—can already be discerned in the Han dynasty work *Supplementary Commentary on the Han School Poems* 韓詩外傳, which includes many joking citations from the *Poems*, playing on the dissonance between the original context of the words and their present application.

cousin, Xie Zhong, which appears in chapter 25, "Taunting and Teasing" 排調:

The reception hall of the Eastern Palace was a wood-paneled chamber. Xie Zhong went to visit the Grand Mentor [Sima Daozi] once when the room was filled with guests. From the outset, Xie Zhong would not exchange a word with any of them; he just looked straight up and said, "I see the prince has made himself a Western-barbarian chamber." (25.58)

東府客館是版屋。謝景重詣太傅。時賓客滿中。初不交言。直仰視云。
王乃復西戎其屋。

Xie Zhong was known for his facility with words, which he often put to use as an administrator in service of Sima Daozi, a member of the Jin royal family renowned for his intemperate and ruthless nature.[24] This narrative sets the stage for Xie Zhong's carefully pitched barb about Sima's extravagant tastes. The wood-paneled room is "filled with guests," the requisite audience for the exchange. Xie refuses to engage anyone in idle chitchat, holding himself silent and aloof so that when he does speak his words will carry more weight. His quip about Sima's "Western-barbarian" room is recondite to the point of opacity for modern and premodern readers alike, as evidenced by Liu Jun's notation on it made in the sixth century. Understanding the reference hinges on knowledge of a selection from the *Poems* entitled "Small Carriages" 小戎, which contains the lines:

> I am thinking of my lord;
> how refined he will look, like jade
> in those plank huts;
> it disturbs the innermost recesses of my heart.[25]

Even this knowledge alone is not sufficient to unravel the allusion. One must also be aware of the "Lesser Preface," which states that this poem is in praise of Duke Xiang of Qin 秦襄公 (r. 777–766 B.C.E.) in his campaigns against the Western Rong 西戎 tribes, and of

---

24. See *Topical Tales*, 2.100–101. Sima Daozi headed up a powerful faction at court, which was challenged by a man named Wang Gong. In retaliation, Sima had Wang Gong, his brother, and his five sons all put to death in 398.

25. Mao #128. After Karlgren, *Book of Odes*, p. 82.

the Mao commentary, which notes that the "plank hut" was the style of residence among these "barbarian" tribes. Xie Zhong's densely packed allusion is evidence that the whole exegetical apparatus known as *Zheng's Annotation of the Mao Poems* 毛詩鄭箋, compiled by Zheng Xuan 鄭玄 (127-200 C.E.) during the Eastern Han, is now part of the curriculum of Traditional knowledge required for cultural competence. Xie deploys his knowledge in natural speech, without chanting, singing, or specifically identifying its source. His joke would only register for those who had an ear properly trained to pick out the allusion.

It is not clear how many people in the crowded room would have actually "gotten" Xie Zhong's joke; his refusal to speak to any of them indicates he doubted their ability to appreciate his quip.[26] In fact, Xie was probably counting on the ignorance of his audience. Tweaking a royal family member's nose before a gathering of his lessers is a dangerous game to play, one that could have violent ramifications when a man of Sima's choler is concerned. If Xie Zhong were to simply blurt out loud to those around him that the prince was overly lavish in his tastes—even though this fact is plain to everyone—the prince would perceive him as seeking solidarity among the other non-royals in common derision of their host. He would incur the ire of the man upon whom he depends for his livelihood and likely acquire a reputation for being uncouth. By turning the mild insult into a subtle private joke—perhaps enjoyed by Xie Zhong alone—he diverts attention from the prince as a target of derision and toward his own performance of poetic competence, an outward sign of his membership in a select group with facility in elite knowledge. Xie Zhong's allusion depends on knowledge of the *Poems* and two of its commentaries, combined with an ironic tone in its comparison of a princely residence to the "plank huts" of barbarians. It could even be read as a backhanded compliment in that it implicitly links the prince to the figure of Duke Xiang of Qin,

---

26. Yu Jiaxi, in his 1993 annotation of *Topical Tales*, offers the following opinion: "There were certainly people among those present who would fail to understand the meaning, which is why he refused to speak with them and derided him [Sima Daozi] instead with this veiled barb" (*Shishuo xinyu jianshu*, p. 819).

who was seen as a civilizing force in the face of a barbarian threat. If Sima Daozi understood the full import of Xie Zhong's remark (the narrative gives no indication either way), the quip, far from alienating his affections, would instead have formed a bond of implicit understanding between two men of similar cultural competence. They could both chuckle conspiratorially in sharing their private joke, as the ignorant guests looked on with blank gazes. If Sima Daozi did not fully understand the remark, he would have remained blissfully unaware that he had been insulted at all, much like poor Qing Feng in the *Zuo Tradition*, who did not even realize he was being told to drop dead through a poetic offering from the *Poems*.

The anecdote is not about making Sima look bad so much as making Xie look good. The actual content of the allusion and its moral implications are not at stake here; it is the gesture itself that is being held up for admiration. By demonstrating his command of Traditional knowledge and his ability to deploy it artfully, Xie stands out as a man worthy of serving the prince, and, even more important in terms of posterity, as a man worthy of notation in the pages of *Topical Tales*. Later generations of readers (with the help of Liu Jun whispering in their ear) can share in the joke and admire Xie's wit. The dividing line is not drawn between the one who fashions the barb and the one who is (wittingly) pierced by it—they are playing in the same game, after all—but between those who understand the rules of the game and those who do not. This sense of play when it comes to demonstrating competence in Traditional knowledge is the hallmark of *Topical Tales* and is even read back into the points of origin of such knowledge.

As was noted above, Xie Zhong's allusion relies upon knowledge derived from two commentaries on the Mao edition of the *Poems* that were included in an Eastern Han work by Zheng Xuan, called *Zheng's Annotation of the Mao Poems*, indicating that the commentaries had become an integral part of the Traditional knowledge surrounding the *Poems*. By the end of the Han, Zheng Xuan had been canonized as a custodian and transmitter of Traditional knowledge. The following apocryphal anecdote about Zheng Xuan's household appears in chapter 4, "Letters and Scholarship," of *Topical Tales*:

Even the slaves of Zheng Xuan's household all read books. One time he set a task for a female slave, but she did not meet his expectations. He was about to beat her, when she started trying to explain herself. Zheng Xuan became furious and had someone drag her through the mire. Shortly after, another female slave came by and asked her,

"Why are you out here in the mire?" [27]

She replied,

"When I went and complained,
I met with his anger." [28] (4.3)

鄭玄家奴婢皆讀書。嘗使一婢。不稱旨。將撻之。方自陳説。玄怒。使
人曳箸泥中。須臾。復有一婢來。問曰。

胡爲乎泥中

答曰。

薄言往愬
逢彼之怒

This anecdote, surely invented long after Zheng Xuan's time, reads like a joke: "Zheng Xuan's household was *so* literate that even the slaves chanted poetry!" Here again is the juxtaposition of humor, violence, and poetic competence—somewhat jarring to modern sensibilities—that appears so frequently in the pages of *Topical Tales*. The unfortunate female slave was threatened with a beating and dragged through a bog, and yet maintains the aplomb to respond appropriately with an apt citation from the *Poems* when teased by another slave. The humor in the anecdote derives from the ironic portrayal of society's basest and least educated members as highly proficient in elite practices—a more sophisticated form of dressing up chimpanzees in suits and teaching them to ride bicycles. [29] The danger of exploiting the dominated for the amusement of the dominant, however, is that it can reflect poorly on the dominant.

---

27. A line from "No Use" 式微 (Mao #36).

28. A quotation from "Cypress-wood Boat" 柏舟 (Mao #26).

29. There is also a story, cited by Bai Juyi 白居易 in his annotation of his poem "A Pair of Parrots" 雙鸚鵡, about one of Zheng Xuan's oxen being able to scratch out Chinese characters on the wall with its horns. (Cited by Yu Jiaxi in his annotations of this entry in *Shishuo xinyu*.)

In this anecdote, Zheng Xuan—a scholar-exegete who naturally wields symbolic power—is the sole source of brutal physical violence, while his slaves—instruments of physical labor—appear highly proficient in the very sorts of knowledge that he produces. The lines they chant are chosen because the words fit the situation at hand, but their context in the *Poems* also evokes a subtext (or extratext) that speaks pointedly to the unequal power relations between the female slaves and their male master.

When the first slave comes along and sees the second slave lying in the bog, she quotes the final line of a selection from the *Poems* entitled "No Use" 式微:

> It's no use, it's no use,
> why not return;
> if it were not for the lord's sake,
> why be out here in the dew.
>
> It's no use, it's no use,
> why not return;
> if it were not for the lord's person,
> why be out here in the mire?[30]

The "Lesser Preface" to this song explains it thus: " 'No Use' is about the Marquis of Li staying in Wei and his officers exhorting him to return home" 式微。黎侯寓于衛。其臣勸以歸也. The Marquis of Li took refuge in the state of Wei after being driven from his own state by the Di 狄 barbarians. Zheng Xuan, in his own annotation of the poem's second couplet, paraphrases it as "If we were without a ruler, then why would we stay in this place?" 我若無君。何爲處 此乎. He glosses it as "The officers' repeated and urgent remonstration of their ruler" 臣又極諫之辭.[31] In essence, the poem comprises the words of inferiors speaking against being in an undesirable place because of their superior. The first slave's citation of this poem hardly poses an innocent question; it implies that the second slave must be in the mud because of her master and that she would rather be back home but for his wishes. In asking her question through this

---

30. Karlgren, *Book of Odes*, p. 23.
31. Ruan Yuan, *Shisan jing*, vol. 2, p. 305.

citation, the first slave is expressing her solidarity with the second by speaking in language already loaded with connotations critical of actions taken by a superior.

The second slave's response is even more pointed, as she quotes from the second stanza of "Cypress-wood Boat" 柏舟:

> Drifting is that cypress-wood boat,
> drifting is its floating;
> I am wide awake and do not sleep,
> as if I had a painful grief;
> but it is not that I have no wine,
> to amuse and divert myself.
>
> My heart is not a mirror,
> you cannot scrutinize it;
> true, I have elder and younger brothers,
> but I cannot rely on them;
> when I go and complain,
> I meet with their anger.
>
> My heart is not a stone,
> you cannot turn it;
> my heart is not a mat,
> you cannot roll it;
> my dignified demeanor has been perfect,
> you cannot measure it.
>
> My grieved heart is pained,
> I am hated by all the petty ones;
> I have met with suffering in plenty,
> I have received insults not a little;
> in the quietude I brood over it,
> awake I knock and beat my breast.
>
> Oh sun, oh moon,
> why are you eclipsed from time to time?
> The grief of the heart is like an unwashed dress;
> in the quietude I brood over it,
> but I cannot rush up and fly away.[32]

---

32. Mao #26. Karlgren, *Book of Odes*, pp. 15–16.

The "Lesser Preface" starts out by stating, "'Cypress-wood Boat' is about a humane person being mistreated," and goes on to read the piece in more explicitly political terms: "During the reign of Duke Qing of Wei, humane men were mistreated while petty men were at his side." Zheng Xuan concurs with this political interpretation, reading the poem as the plaint of a worthy officer who is unappreciated by his ruler (figured as "brothers" in the poem) and maligned by jealous rivals ("all the petty ones"). This political interpretation is just one of many possible interpretations. Later scholars and modern readers are more likely to read this poem as the plaint of a woman being forced by her brothers into a marriage she detests. Read thusly, the poem becomes a perfect vehicle for a woman to lament her inability to determine her own destiny when faced with unfair treatment at the hands of male superiors.[33] Thus, the slave shows herself to be poetically competent on two levels. First, she knows the *Poems* well enough to be able to choose an apt impromptu citation. Second, her application of the citation to her own circumstances ends up generating a "reading" that fits the text more naturally and seems less forced than her master's own annotations.

The first couplet of the stanza from which the slave quotes reads "My heart is not a mirror,/you cannot scrutinize it." It is a celebrated line from the *Poems*, and while the slave did not quote it directly, it is certainly heard in the background of any citation from this poem. As with so many lines in the *Poems*, this couplet is open to interpretation. On the face of it, it seems to be saying, "I do not lay bare my feelings for anybody to scrutinize."[34] The tacit presence of this couplet asserts the slave's own interiority, independent of her master's wishes. The narrative of the anecdote relates that Zheng Xuan threatened to beat the slave because "she did not meet his expectations" and that when she attempted to "explain herself," to give an indication of what she was thinking, he had her dragged through the mire. The slave is meant to be a physical extension of

---

33. In one entry of *Topical Tales* (19.18), a daughter successfully wins the right not to remarry when she refers to her household as "ruined and in trouble" 殄瘁, a compound found in the fifth stanza of Mao #264.

34. Karlgren, *Book of Odes*, p. 16, note b.

the master, animated by his wishes. The master will not tolerate the slave having a mind of her own—to do so would acknowledge the barbarity of enslaving the body *and* mind of another. He must forcibly quash her expression of interiority, but in the end it will make itself known through the conduit sanctioned by Tradition: the *Poems*.

Zheng Xuan, in his commentary on the poem, glosses the line "My heart is not a mirror" as follows:

When a mirror is used to observe the outward form of something, one can only discern its shape and color but is unable to ascertain its truth or falsity. The phrase "My heart is not like this mirror" means when it comes to good and evil, that is, the *inner* and outer qualities of other men, my heart is able to discern and ascertain them.[35]

鑒之察形但知方圓白黑。不能度其真偽。我心非如是鑒。我於眾人之善惡外內。心度知之。

This reading posits the heart not merely as the passive residence of one's interior qualities, but as an active instrument used to judge the interior qualities of others. The heart/mind, properly used, allows one to "read" external evidence critically rather than simply reflecting it, to ascertain the moral quality of another based on their words and behavior. This gloss on the nature of the heart takes on deeply ironic undertones when considered in conjunction with this anecdote about Zheng Xuan's mistreatment of his slave, for it is precisely Zheng Xuan's refusal to use his mental faculties critically that leads to his rage and the slave's violent punishment. He did not take the time to hear the slave's explanation or to ascertain the quality of her character. Her subsequent citation of "Cypress-wood Boat"—a witty application of felicitous words on the face of it—*can* be read as a tacit indictment of her master's moral deficiencies. The originator(s) of this narrative may not have explicitly intended such an indictment, but it is there nonetheless. The potential for envisioning—even in ironic terms—the use of Traditional knowledge against the very people who would act as its custodians teaches an

---

35. Ruan Yuan, *Shisan jing*, vol. 2, p. 296.

important lesson about cultural competence: a monopoly on it is never secure because it belongs to whoever practices it.

The narratives of *Topical Tales* are constantly attempting to show that the symbolic power derived from cultural competence can compete with, and even be victorious over, the crude forms of power derived from violence. In the anecdotes cited so far, there has always been one party who appears more brutish—Cao Pi, General Yu, Prince Sima and his audience—and one party who appears more cultured—Cao Zhi, Sun Fang, Xie Zhong—with the latter always coming off better than the former. In this anecdote about Zheng Xuan's household it is the man of culture who acts like a brute and the lowly slaves who appear cultured. The punished slave may not have been able to avoid or forestall the violence she suffered by dint of her poetic competence, but this is not because of a deficiency in her competence so much as an inability to plead her case properly due to her low station. To even attempt to speak to her master directly provoked such rage in him that she was summarily dragged off for punishment. However, the narrator gives her the last laugh by recording her apt citation from the *Poems*. Though unable to gain control of the confrontation with her master's violence, she did manage to control the way it would be perceived and remembered after the fact. For the duration of the narrative, at least, the reader is on her side. Her handling of the aftermath of her punishment did not change her status as a slave during her lifetime, but it did ensure that her experience would be recorded and transmitted (albeit without reference to her name) in the pages of *Topical Tales*.

In all likelihood it did not happen, this poetic encounter between master and slave. But someone *wished* it had happened. The ironic inversion of the brutish scholar and his cultured slave infuses the anecdote with its humor, but it teaches another lesson: namely, that the symbolic power derived from cultural competence can be wielded by *anyone* to negotiate the unequal power relations that determine their place in the social hierarchy. The Traditionalist courtier of the Eastern Zhou may be executed by his king for his remonstration, but he is remembered for the competence with which he made it, and is vindicated by the events of history. The slave may be punished by a Traditionalist scholar, but she is remembered for the competence with which she uses the scholar's own tools to respond to his violence. It does not matter who occupies the position of superior—benighted ruler or enraged scholar. It does not matter who occupies the position of inferior—learned courtier or slave. What matters is the form of the encounter: inferior comes out ahead (in the eyes of posterity at least) because of his or her cultural competence. Over the course of the narratives in *Topical Tales*, control over cultural competence appears to slip the grasp of the Traditionalists who helped constitute it, and the *form* of cultural competence assumes content that is decidedly non-Traditional.

The practice of quoting poetic lines rhetorically in *Topical Tales* is not restricted to the *Poems* alone. It extends to the body of secular poetry that had emerged since the Han dynasty. In one passage, Huan Xuan 桓玄 (369–404), who seeks to overthrow the Eastern Jin, hears that the Prince of Liang, Sima Zhenzhi 司馬梁王珍之 (d. ca. 420), has fled. Standing in his ship, Huan chants the following lines from a Ruan Ji 阮籍 (219–263) poem at the top of his voice:

> The sounds of flutes and pipes still linger,
> But the King of Liang, where could he be? (13.13)

簫管有遺音
梁王安在哉

The original context of these lines (cited from one of Ruan Ji's "Poems of My Heart" 詠懷詩) makes it clear that the "King of Liang" refers to King Hui of Liang 梁惠王 (r. 370–319 B.C.E.), who appears in the first chapter of *Mencius*. Huan's rather forced application of these lines—based on a coincidence in name only—is typical of the "breaking off a stanza to seize a meaning" usage previously confined to the *Poems*. The cryptic nature of Ruan Ji's poems makes them a natural vehicle for this sort of usage because they are able to support multiple interpretations.

Secular poems in *Topical Tales* are also performed in their entirety as an expression of one's intent, just as the *Poems* are offered in the *Zuo Tradition*. In the following passage, Wang Dun harbors a motive in choosing a particular drinking song, a *yuefu* by Cao Cao 曹操 (155–220) called "I May Be Old" 龜雖壽:

Every time Wang Dun had a few drinks, he would always chant,

> The old charger lies in his stable,
> but his will still runs the long course.
> The fierce warrior is late in years,
> but his valiant heart will never fade.

He would keep time by striking the spittoon with his backscratcher until the rim of the spittoon was completely smashed. (13.4)

王處仲每酒後輒詠。

> 老驥伏櫪
> 志在千里
> 烈士暮年
> 壯心不已

以如意打唾壺。壺口盡缺。

Mather points out that the context for this passage, given in the *Jin History* 晉書, "implies that the song and the accompanying spittoon-smashing were expressions of Wang's resentment at not getting a post at court in 320."[36] In choosing "I May Be Old" as his performance piece, Wang Dun is "cashing in" on the legacy of Cao Cao—who was posthumously known as "The Martial Emperor" 武帝—casting himself as the cultivated warrior, a man with a heroic heart and literary sensibilities who still longs to serve even though he is past his prime. This poetic intervention thus has a pedigree that serves to elevate and ennoble what might be construed as a selfish concern for position and power.

The preceding two examples of poetic competence are manifested as *citation* from the *Poems* and secular poetry; the performances serve to comment on events without seeking to affect their outcome. Any prestige garnered from such a performance results from the aptness of the citation. When poetic competence is demonstrated through the *composition* of poetry—as in the case of Cao Zhi's "Seven Steps Poem"—it is usually in response to a challenge. The resulting prestige is derived from the finesse with which one meets that challenge. Cao Zhi's very life was at stake during his performance, but many other performances depicted in *Topical Tales*

---

36. Mather, *Tales of the World*, p. 302.

lack such drastic stakes, and feature a strong element of play in po-
etic composition.[37] General Huan Wen 桓溫 (312–373) challenges his
attendants to describe some walls he had rebuilt. When the
painter-poet Gu Kaizhi 顧凱之 (345?–406) captures their beauty in a
poetic couplet, Huan Wen rewards him with two female slaves,
converting Gu's symbolic capital into economic capital in human
form (2.85). Elsewhere, two friends compete by boasting about their
respective homelands, reflecting the quality of the landscape in their
style of poetry (2.24). A monk captures in words a picture of a
snowy journey for the benefit of his fellow monks (2.93). A courtier
rebuffs a jealous rival with a pointed poem alluding to the *Poems*
(2.94). All of these instances occur in the second chapter of *Topical
Tales*, entitled "Speech and Conversation" 言語, and exemplify the
crucial role poetic competence plays in constituting a form of cul-
tural competence known as the "art of conversation." Being a re-
spected member of elite society meant having a sense of *sprezzatura*,
an ability to demonstrate verbal facility and erudition under the
temporal constraints of improvisation. The prestige derived from
impromptu composition is derived just as much from its extempo-
raneous quality as it is from the content of the composition itself.
When fine language and nimble performance can be wedded, it is an
undeniable mark of innate skill and good breeding.

It should thus come as no surprise that a society prizing aptitude
in rapid poetic composition would come up with a way to test and
hone that skill. There are two examples in *Topical Tales* of a popular
game, known as "word chain" (*yuci* 語次), in which the host offers a
line of poetry using a certain rhyme scheme and topic and each
participant must improvise a line of poetry to match the host's
choice. The game can accommodate any number of players, who
must continue improvising suitable lines—often taking their cue
from other players—in order to stay in the game. The first example

---

37. There is an element of play to be found even in Cao Zhi's "Seven Steps"
performance. Although Cao Pi, in placing his brother's life at stake, converts what
is meant to be a lighthearted occasion into something with grave consequences, Cao
Zhi, in the language of his poem and in his performance, still manages to maintain a
playful, nonchalant air, thereby augmenting the prestige he receives from meeting
the challenge with such finesse.

of the game is also found in the second chapter on "Speech and Conversation":

Grand Mentor Xie An was gathered with his family indoors on a cold, snowy day. He was expounding on the meaning of literary texts to the boys and girls when there was a sudden blast of snow. Master Xie was delighted by this and said,

"The white snow in wild flurries, how does it appear?"

His nephew, Xie Lang, said,

"Scatter some salt in the air and you're almost there."

His niece said,

"That can't compare to willow catkins rising on air."

Master Xie laughed out loud with glee.

His niece was the daughter of his eldest brother, Xie Yi, and the wife of General-of-the-Left Wang Ningzhi. (2.71)

謝太傅寒雪日內集。與兒女講論文義。俄而雪驟。公欣然曰。

白雪紛紛何所似

兄子胡兒曰。

撒鹽空中差可擬

兄女曰。

未若柳絮因風起

公大笑樂。即公大兄無奕女。左將軍王凝之妻也。

This anecdote opens with a domestic scene of Xie An 謝安 (320–385), a prominent figure in an influential noble family, gathering the younger members of his family indoors on a wintry day to discuss literature, or more precisely, "the meaning of literary texts" 文義. This is a brief glimpse into the site of inculcation of hermeneutic skills in juvenile members of the elite class. Being able to recognize what constitutes a literary work in the first place and then being able to interpret and understand it are key skills for developing cultural competence. Not only are these skills valued in and of themselves, but they are prerequisites to developing the aesthetic sense and knowledge base required for competence in citation and composition. This is why Xie An is "delighted" when a sudden snow flurry interrupts their deliberate explications of literature. It provides the perfect opportunity to test his young charges' skill at impromptu composition. Xie An demonstrates his own poetic competence by asking them to describe the snow with the very sort of line they are meant to emulate—a seven-character line ending with a (*-i*) rhyme. He even isolates the particular quality of snow—"wild flurries"—that they are meant to describe through an explicit simile. His nephew comes back with the image of salt scattered in the air, which might capture the visual quality of the snow as specks of white, but fails to convey its sense of fluid motion when it is blown into flurries. His niece comes up with a more fitting image—willow catkins caught on the wind—and even squeezes in a jab at the nephew by saying his image "can't compare" to her own in capturing the quality of the snow. Xie An is so delighted with his niece's line that he laughs out loud, giving the senior literary arbiter's stamp of approval to her contribution. Xie seems particularly delighted that in this case it is a girl, traditionally among the least educated members of elite society, who has bested a boy.[38] The narrative immediately indicates the girl's pedigree—daughter of Xie An's eldest brother and wife of Wang Ningzhi 王凝之 (d. 399)—providing a familial and conjugal context for the poetic competence that she has just demonstrated. She already belongs to elite society by virtue of her lineage and marriage; she has just proved that she is well on her way to developing the skills necessary to excel in that society.[39]

The anecdote about Xie An's niece and nephew is yet another example of the playful attitude toward literary production that permeates the pages of *Topical Tales*. The ancient form of poetic competence—demonstrating skill in citation or performance for the approval of others—endures, but becomes more lighthearted in the domestic context. Play has its own set of ground rules, and, as long

---

38. This is yet another example of the fascination shown by the compilers of *Topical Tales* for salient examples of cultural competence found among juveniles and females. Skills considered de rigueur among educated adult males become remarkable when demonstrated by women and children.

39. The Liu Jun commentary to *Topical Tales* cites a source named *The Women's Collection* 婦人集, which identifies the niece as Daoyun 道蘊 and says that she had "literary talent" 文才 and that her "poems, poetic expositions, eulogies, and odes were passed down to later ages."

as these are adhered to, one might get away with saying things that would not be appropriate in other circumstances. Even in the company of friends, however, the bounds of propriety can be crossed. Chapter 25 of *Topical Tales*, "Taunting and Teasing" 排調, includes an anecdote about Huan Xuan, Yin Zhongkan 殷仲堪, and Gu Kaizhi gathered together to play a few rounds of "word chain" (25.61). They set the word "peril" 危 (*ngjwie*) as the topic and rhyme for one of the rounds. The three men each come up with a fanciful image of a precarious situation, then Yin Zhongkan's aide dares to intervene with a couplet: "A blind man riding a purblind horse / in the dead of night nears a deep pool" 池 (*d'ie*). This provokes Yin to shout, "Look here! That's a bit pointed!" for he himself is partially blind in one eye from a mishap suffered in preparing medicine for his ailing father. The aide's line is not particularly insulting—just a bit overdone, perhaps, with its image of a blind man on a blind horse at night—but it does seem to be spoken out of turn and among men who are above his station. Yin could have just as easily ignored the line, as it does not refer explicitly to him. His choice to interpret it as pointed reflects genuine pique less than it does his desire to verbally "slap down" the presumptuous aide. The whole exchange is made in good humor, but the lines of social division are drawn nonetheless.

The tables are turned in another anecdote from the "Taunting and Teasing" chapter, when it is a social superior who is making fun of his inferior's appearance and poetry is used as a form of self-defense.

Kang Sengyuan had deep-set eyes and a tall nose. Counselor-in-Chief Wang Dao was always teasing him about it. Once Sengyuan said,

> The nose is a mountain on the face,
> The eyes are pools in the face.
> A mountain that is not tall lacks majesty,
> A pool that is not deep lacks clarity. (25.21)

康僧淵目深而鼻高。王丞相每調之。僧淵曰。

> 鼻者面之山
> 目者面之淵
> 山不高則不靈
> 淵不深則不清

Kang, a renowned Buddhist monk, was probably of Sogdian descent and bore the appearance of a foreigner. Wang Dao, who was a major figure at the Eastern Jin court, held a number of prominent posts, including prime minister, governor, and president of the Imperial Secretariat. The encounter between these two men is an intersection between the epitomes of the "religious man" and the "man of politics." Although this anecdote is found in a chapter called "Taunting and Teasing," the narrative does not transcribe the actual taunts used by Wang to tease the monk, and one might assume they were rather pedestrian; it is Kang's response that bears recording. The poem's first line is derived from a physiognomic principle based on the *Changes*, which holds that the nose on the face is akin to a mountain in the middle of the heavens. The second line contains a reference to pools (*yuan* 淵)—a pun on the second character in Kang's monastic name, Sengyuan 僧淵 (literally, "Monk's Pool"). After Kang uses his first couplet to recast the features of his face in a philosophical and religious context, he uses his second couplet to imply that the prominence of his features indicates his vigor and clarity of mind. The poem deftly converts a perceived physical deficiency into an intellectual asset and puts Wang Dao, the would-be mocker, in a bad light. For not only do Wang Dao's flat nose and shallow-set eyes suggest a comparative lack of profundity, his failure to "read" Kang's features properly indicates a lack of perspicacity. Wang Dao's temporal power is derived from his political position and attendant economic capital, but it does him no good when he attempts to match wits in the verbal arena with a monk possessed of poetic competence.

The display of poetic talent in these cases is largely bound up with improvisation. The ability to instantly produce an apt poetic utterance allows one to take control of a situation: to win an argument, receive a reward, deflect an insult, avoid a severe punishment, or simply to get through a turn in a game. In many of these anecdotes, the last person to speak in the narrative is the one who has just uttered a poem, literally giving him or her the "last word" in a story of poetic competence. Such stories depict people who excel in what Bourdieu calls "the 'art' of the *necessary improvisation* which defines excellence"—or, more colloquially, "a feel for the game."[40] People negotiate their way through life with practices that have been inculcated in them by virtue of growing up and participating in a particular habitus. These practices happen in time and it is a "practical sense" or "practical logic" that allows one to improvise with them in order to be socially competent. In the rarefied world of *Topical Tales*, having a "feel" for poetic quotation and composition is necessary to successfully navigate the often unpredictable waters of elite society.

III

The ability to utter poetry—either as citation or as production—is only one half of poetic competence. The other half consists of the ability to judge and appreciate the poetry and poetic performance of others. This skill is so important that it is explicitly taught to children at a young age. Once again, it is Xie An who is depicted inculcating literary appreciation in the younger generation:

When all the younger members of his family were gathered together, Master Xie An asked them what they thought were the most exquisite lines in the Mao version of the *Poems*. Xie Xuan put forward,

> Long ago, when we marched,
> the willows were luxuriant;
> now when we come back,
> the falling snow is thick.[41]

Master Xie said,

> With great schemes he stabilizes his heavenly appointment,
> with far-reaching plans he makes timely announcements.[42]

He declared that these lines especially capture the profound expression of the cultured man. (4.52)

---

40. Discussed by Bourdieu in *Outline of a Theory of Practice* (p. 8) and *Other Words* (p. 61).

41. Quoted from "Gather the Wei" 采薇 (Mao #167). Karlgren, *Book of Odes*, p. 112.

42. Quoted from "Dignified" 抑 (Mao #256). Karlgren, *Book of Odes*, p. 217.

謝公因子弟集聚。問毛詩何句最佳。遏稱曰。

　　昔我往矣
　　楊柳依依
　　今我來思
　　雨雪霏霏

公曰。

　　訏謨定命
　　遠猷辰告

謂此句偏有雅人深致。

When Xie poses his question to the "younger members" of his family, he already assumes that they have the entire corpus of the *Poems* memorized. Intimate knowledge of canonical texts is a necessary condition for poetic competence, but insufficient in and of itself. What one *does* with such knowledge is the means of constituting competence. Xie's question presupposes that the children are not passive receptacles of the *Poems*, but have thought about them long enough to exercise their judgment in choosing what they feel to be the "exquisite lines." The term "exquisite" (*jia* 佳), as in "exquisite couplet" (*jiaju* 佳句), usually connotes the brilliance or splendor of a finely wrought image, a judgment made on purely aesthetic grounds. Xie An's nephew Xuan seems to make his choice accordingly, picking out a pair of couplets that use the transition from an image of luxuriant willows to thickly falling snow in order to indicate the passage of time spent by troops guarding the frontiers against barbarian threats in the time of King Wen. The imagery is arresting, with its contrast between the inherent qualities of green leaves and white snow, captured by binomes peculiar to the *Poems*. These naturally occurring phenomena take on a human poignancy when they are juxtaposed in the context of soldiers marking the time spent away from home.

However, such a finely wrought image, even with its sentimental overtones, is apparently not what Xie An was looking for when he posed his question to the youngsters. He vetoes his nephew's choice, replacing it with his own: "With great schemes he stabilizes his heavenly appointment, / with far-reaching plans he makes timely announcements." This is a very different type of passage; not an image at all, it is a declaration couched in high-flown rhetoric regarding the qualities demanded of a great ruler. According to the Mao preface, it is part of a speech made by Duke Wu of Wei to the wayward King Li of Zhou, entreating him to see the error of his ways and to live up to the ideal of a good king. Xie An declares that these lines "especially capture the profound thoughts of the cultured man," his superlatives leaving no room for dispute as to the quality of the passage.

It is obvious that Xie An and his nephew are employing different criteria in determining what they feel to be the "finest" passage from the *Poems*. The nephew has chosen his passage on the grounds of its aesthetic (and perhaps sentimental) appeal, while the uncle has made his choice on what may be called moral rather than aesthetic grounds. For Xie An, the who, where, when, and why of the passage—that is, the social context of its putative point of origin—matter just as much as what the passage says or how it says it. His nephew's choice may be aesthetically appealing, but, as it articulates the words of soldiers on a campaign, it is morally incompatible with the "profound thoughts of the cultured man." The "cultured man" will recognize and appreciate the poetry of other cultivated men; the lofty words of a morally upright duke qualify as "exquisite" in Xie An's book, while the plaint of a lowly soldier—however gracefully put—does not.[43]

It does matter who is right in this difference of opinion between uncle and nephew—we are surely meant to agree with Xie An's trumping of his nephew's naïve choice with a morally superior selection. What matters even more, however, is that there is room for such a debate at all, which indicates an increasing flexibility in the notion of poetic competence during the period of disunion following the Han. This flexibility emerges from a recognition that a poem may be appreciated for the beauty and power of its language

---

43. There is a pun in Xie An's declaration: the phrase "cultured man" (*yaren* 雅人) contains the same word used to designate the section of the *Poems* from which Xie's selection is drawn—the "Greater Odes," sometimes translated as the "Greater Elegantiae" (Daya 大雅).

without constant recourse to moral didacticism.[44] It may be significant here that a younger member of Xie's family is able to admit this more readily than Xie An himself, who occupies the position of "master" interpreter.

There are numerous other examples of such aesthetic appreciation to be found in *Topical Tales*. In one anecdote, a guest at Xie An's house—always a popular spot for literary appreciation, it seems—volunteers his favorite lines from the *Lyrics of Chu*:

Wang Huzhi was seated among Master Xie An's guests, when he chanted the following:

> Without a word he came in to me   without a word he left me:
> He rode off on the whirlwind   with cloud-banners flying.[45]

He said to everyone else, "At that point I feel as though I am seated all alone with no one else around." (13.12)

王司州在謝公坐。詠。

入不言兮出不辭
乘回風兮載雲旗

語人云。當爾時。覺一坐無人。

The focus of this narrative—found in Chapter 22, "Virile Vigor" 豪爽—is on the emotional reaction Wang Huzhi has to a particular passage in the *Lyrics of Chu*. He does not discuss any religious, philosophical, or political content to be found in "The Lesser Master of Fate." The only reason Wang brings up the passage at all is to tell others how its language makes him *feel*, not what it makes him think. His statement that it makes him "feel as though I am seated all alone with no one else around" suggests that the *Lyrics of Chu* is a text normally chanted in the company of others—for collective appreciation of both the text itself and the quality with

---

44. Later traditional readers side with the nephew, Xie Xuan, over Xie An. The most famous is Wang Shizhen 王士禛 (1634–1711) who, in his *Random Notes by an Antiquated Man in his Pavilion* 古夫于亭雜錄 (*juan.* 2), says, "I think that what Xie Xuan and Yan Zhitui said is right. As for Grand Mentor Xie An's 'profound thoughts of the cultured man,' I just do not understand what he means by that in the end." (Cited by Yu Jiaxi in his comments on this entry.)

45. From "Lesser Master of Fate" 少司命, one of the "Nine Songs" 九歌 of the *Lyrics of Chu*. See Hawkes, *Songs of the South*, p. 111.

which it is chanted. Wang's assertion that the affective quality of the text makes him forget that he is performing it for others evokes a moment of transcendent ecstasy. His appreciation—felt physically rather than explained verbally—comes closer to recuperating the text's putative origins in shamanistic trance ritual than any discursive commentary. Of course, while Wang may feel alone in his moment of appreciation, he immediately emerges from it and remarks on it "to everyone else." At some level, Wang must remain conscious of the members of his audience if he is to tell them that he has forgotten about them. In effect, what he is performing for the judgment of others is not a poem so much as the act of appreciating a poem, of becoming lost in a poem.

Acts of appreciating cultural competence in others are deemed just as valuable by the *Topical Tales* as are demonstrations of such competence. The fourth chapter alone, "Letters and Scholarship," records no fewer than twenty acts of appreciation of the different skills that constitute cultural competence. Kang Sengyuan, the monk who used a poem to rebut insults regarding his facial features, is praised for his facility in the recondite form of "pure conversation" 清談 (4.47). A religious debate is admired for the verbal pyrotechnics displayed by its participants; the audience "without exception clapped and danced" in appreciation and "each and every one sighed over the eloquence of the two men's arguments, not even discerning whether there was any logic to them" 眾不莫不抃舞。但嗟詠二家之美。不辯其理之所在 (4.40). Men of culture are often classified as competent in either oral or written discourse, scoring victories in the arena that suits their skill the best (4.70, 73). In one anecdote an impressive display of impromptu composition is held up as having some compensatory value for a defeat in the arena of politics because it "won a verbal advantage" (literally, "won advantage through the teeth and tongue" 齒舌間得利) (4.96). The judgment of a man with an established literary reputation is deemed worthy of preservation in itself: Sun Chuo's opinions on the writings of Pan Yue, Lu Ji, and Cao Pi are carefully noted (4.84, 93), just as his own works are held up for praise (4.78). *Topical Tales* even addresses how a literary reputation can be manufactured by asking the right person to publicly appreciate your work (4.68, 79).

The role of collections such as *Topical Tales* in illustrating cultural competence for an extended audience is mirrored in a discussion of a popular collection of the day, *Forest of Conversations* 語林, which "spread far and near to such a great extent that every single young person current with such things had made his own copy and passed it along" 大為遠近所傳。時流年少。無不傳寫。各有一通 (4.90). There are repeated examples of praise for a person's ability to rapidly produce or emend a literary work "off the cuff" (4.92, 95, 103). A poem can be appreciated under a variety of circumstances: Wang Ji is so moved by a mourning poem by a recently widowed friend that he says, "I cannot tell whether the text is born of the emotions or the emotions of the text, but when I read it over it leaves me in sorrow as it enhances the gravity of the marriage bond" 未知文生於情。情生於文。覽之悽然。增伉儷之重 (4.72); Huan Yin shows his admiration for Yang Fu's "Ode to Snow" 雪贊 by inscribing it on his fan (4.100); Wang Gong picks his favorite line from the "Nineteen Old Poems" 古詩十九首 while under the influence of drugs (4.101). There is even an acknowledgment that one can appreciate the literary work of a man one might find distasteful in other ways. Ruan Fu praises a poem by Guo Pu, saying, "It has a deep majesty and chilly desolation that I truly cannot put it into words. Every time I read these words I always feel my spirit soaring and my body transcendent" 泓崢蕭瑟。 實不可言。 每讀此文。輒覺神超形越 (4.76). In Liu Jun's commentary on this entry, he quotes *An Independent Account of Guo Pu* 郭璞別傳, which states that Guo Pu

had a speech impediment and rushed his intonation so that ordinary people thought nothing special of him. Moreover, he did not hold to the rules of etiquette, his frame was wracked; he was wanton, insulting, and shiftless. From time to time he would lapse into bouts of drunkenness and gluttony. (4.76n)

訥於言。造次詠語。常人無異。又不持儀檢。形質糟索。縱情嫚惰。時有醉飽之失。

This is an important acknowledgment that the link between the quality of the work and the quality of the man may be more complicated than is suggested in pre-Qin and Han thought, that it may require a refined sensibility to distinguish fine work from what, on the face of it, appears to be a questionable source.

In some cases the literary work or performance that is being appreciated is not even quoted or depicted—the anecdote exists solely to record the appreciation. In the many anecdotes that narrate both a performance of cultural competence and an appreciation of it, however, it becomes difficult to determine whether it is the performance or its appreciation that is the raison d'être for the narrative. The answer is that both are essential. Appreciation is the flip side of performance. People perform for the appreciation of others; the judgment encoded in an appreciation is what measures and thereby establishes the competence of the performer. But the judge must be competent too, if his or her appreciation is to carry any weight. There is room for a difference of opinion, but some people's opinions matter more than others. The note regarding Guo Pu quoted above indicates that "ordinary people thought nothing special of him," implying that only those with an extraordinary sagacity could appreciate his work. The anecdote regarding the reception of *Poetic Expositions on the Three Capitals* 三都賦 by Zuo Si 左思 (ca. 253–ca. 307) states that when Zuo first completed them (after a reputed ten years of gestation), "his contemporaries all mocked and criticized them together" 時人互有譏訾, but that Zhang Hua recognized their true value and suggested that Zuo "should put them under the auspices of a gentleman with a lofty reputation" 宜以經高名之士. Zuo Si enlisted the aid of Huangfu Mi, who wrote a preface for them, after which "every single one of those people who had denigrated them previously all drew their lapels together to salute them and passed them along" 於是先相非貳者。漠不斂衽讚述焉 (4.68). Both Zhang Hua 張華 (232–300), author of the encyclopedic *Records of Extensive Matters* 博物志, and Huangfu Mi 皇甫彌 (215–82), author of several collections of biographies, enjoyed reputations for erudition and literary skill. When these influential individuals are associated with Zuo Si's work, collective opinion is forced to change. This anecdote is surely meant as a condemnation of "popular" taste as opposed to the superior judgment of individuals competent enough to appreciate the true value of a work. It also admits the more troubling possibility, however, that a literary reputation may be built on an undeserving work simply through the recommendation of influential people, who may or may not be competent to render aesthetic judgments.[46]

Zuo Si's *Poetic Expositions on the Three Capitals* was eventually established in the canon alongside Ban Gu's *Poetic Expositions on the Two Capitals* 兩都賦. This can be seen already in an anecdote in *Topical Tales* that relates the reception of yet another poetic exposition on a capital:

When Yu Chan had finished composing his *Poetic Exposition on the Yang Capital*, he presented it to Yu Liang. Considering their family ties, Yu Liang did much for estimation of the work by saying, "It may be a third along with the *Two Capitals* and a fourth with the *Three Capitals*." After this, everyone vied with one another to write out their own copies until paper in the capital became very dear as a result. Grand Mentor Xie An was reported to have said, "It is a failure. It is just a case of 'constructing a house under an existing house'; every element is a matter of imitation through study, so it cannot avoid being base and narrow." (4.79)

庾仲初作揚都賦成。以呈庾亮。亮以親族之懷。大爲其名價云。可三二京。四三都。於此人人競寫。都下紙爲之貴。謝太傅云。不得爾。此是屋下架屋耳。事事擬學。而不免儉狹。

The key relative clause in this passage is "considering their family ties" 以親族之懷, which identifies an ulterior motive for Yu Liang's high praise of his relative's literary work. He is not basing his judgment upon aesthetic or even moral criteria, but upon the obligations of kinship. Yu Liang is often depicted in *Topical Tales* as being the foil or "straight man" who allows others to display their cultural competence.[47] He did not enjoy the reputation for scholarly erudition that Zhang Hua and Huangfu Mi did. The influence of his opinion stems from his political power. He was the brother of Empress Mu and rose to become president of the Central Secretariat at court, and then General Chastizing the West and governor of a

---

46. There is also the possibility that such judgments could be fabricated. Liu Jun quotes the *Unofficial Biography of Zuo Si* 左思別傳, which claims, "All the comments and annotations were actually fashioned by Zuo Si himself. Out of a desire to amplify his own writings, he availed himself of the names of his contemporaries" 凡諸注解。皆思自爲。欲重其文。故假時人名姓也 (4.68).

47. See 2.30, 49, 50, 52; 4.75, 77. It was Yu Liang who challenged Sun Fang on a hunt and was put in his place by the precocious boy (2.49).

region comprising three provinces. Everyone in the capital heeds his opinion because he is a powerful person, not because he is eminently suited to make aesthetic judgments. The narrative notes that people were so eager to copy Yu Chan's poetic exposition that "paper in the capital became very dear as a result," measuring the influence of Yu Liang's opinion in the crass monetary terms of an economic market. By contrast, when Huangfu Mi praises Zuo Si's poetic expositions, the narrative says that people "drew their lapels together to salute them," measuring the influence of his opinion in gestures of deference and sympathetic response rather than material consumption.

At this point in the narrative, the voice of an exasperated Xie An suddenly intrudes (without any physical context) to provide a corrective opinion. The narrator uses the term *yun* 云, which explicitly marks an indirect quotation and is rendered as "was reported to have said" in my translation. The term suggests that everything narrated up to this point was simply to fill in the background for Xie's remarks. Unlike Yu Liang's opinion, which is based on "consideration of family ties," Xie's is based on a carefully articulated aesthetic principle denigrating a literary work that is simply a pastiche of former works: "constructing a house under an existing house." Xie's judgment is the kernel of the anecdote and so it is given pride of place at the point of closure in the narrative; his is the final word. The narrative does not state whether Xie's characterization of Yu Chan's poetic exposition as "base and narrow" deflated the price of paper in the capital. Neither he nor the compilers of *Topical Tales* seem to place much stock in the uninformed opinion of an ephemeral and undifferentiated readership made up of "everyone" in the capital. It is more telling that, despite its contemporary popularity, hardly any of Yu Chan's literary output survives; Zuo Si's works, on the other hand, are firmly entrenched in the canon.

In both anecdotes regarding the manufacture of literary reputation, the opinion of the many responds to the judgment of one influential man. In the first case, the unguided collective opinion is mistaken at first but is then brought into alignment with proper dictates of taste by Huangfu Mi's preface, which constitutes a public act of appreciation by a "gentleman of lofty reputation." In the second case, the collective opinion is guided from the outset by the judgment of Yu Liang, a man wielding great political power. But his judgment is made in "bad faith"—it is based on "consideration of family ties"—and so it must be corrected by Xie An, who articulates the pertinent critical standards and renders his contrary judgment. Both anecdotes devalue the opinion of the many as too easily swayed either toward or away from the proper. The "many" lack the feel for literature that can only be found in the highly educated individual, who can wield the power to shape collective opinion. In the first anecdote, it is Zhang Hua who alerts Zuo Si to the existence of such power, and Huangfu Mi who exercises it on his behalf. The depiction of these literary men, colluding in private to put the proper "spin" on a work of literature so that it receives the public accolades it deserves, esteems the power of the few just as it disparages the passivity of the many. The "few" and the "many" in this case are all members of the elite, of the dominant ruling class, but the few are connoisseurs while the many are merely consumers. This opposition is even more apparent in the second anecdote, with its picture of "everyone" in the capital scurrying around to buy up as much paper as they can. The voice of the connoisseur in this case, Xie An, is oddly impotent. His judgments are made after Yu Chan's reputation has been made, and they are not given a particular context, addressee, or result in the narrative. Xie An is not a party in manufacturing (or destroying) a reputation; he simply comments on it. In stripping Xie An's utterance of its context and addressee, the narrative attempts to efface Xie An's lack of immediate efficacy by moving his judgment into the realm of the universal. He is saying what every good connoisseur knows, summed up in the adage "constructing a house under an existing house." The intended addressee for Xie An's comment as it is narrated in this anecdote is the implied reader of the anecdote: a person who thinks of himself or herself as a connoisseur, or aspires to become one.

In all of these cases, the poetic works in question are no longer being treated as modes of discourse, but as objects of discourse. They are proof that literature has emerged as a distinct entity that can be appreciated on its own terms without constant recourse to political or moral didacticism. In the shift from offering to citation in the *Zuo Tradition*, the *Poems* are converted from modes of discourse into objects of speech discourse; such discourse still retains its didactic purpose. Here, the poems are objects of the discourse of appreciation, which justifies itself solely on the grounds of invidiously demonstrating one's cultural competence in appreciating these objects.

The traditional mode of appreciating a Chinese poem is to chant it aloud to savor its euphony. Thus, the act of appreciating a poem becomes a physical performance that can be appreciated by another. The parameters of this sort of interaction are never more clearly delineated than in their parodic form.

Gu Kaizhi aggrandized his own abilities shamelessly, so all of the young men would tease him by singing his praises. When he was Cavalier Attendant-in-Ordinary, his compound adjoined that of Xie Zhan (387–421). He was chanting poems beneath the moon one night—he said of himself that he captured the air and control of the old worthies—when Zhan began applauding him from a distance. Kaizhi was inspired by this to exert himself to the utmost with no thought of growing tired. Zhan was getting sleepy, so he told someone else who had been tapping his toe nearby to take his place. Kaizhi did not detect the difference and went on almost the entire night before stopping. (4.98n)[48]

愷之矜伐過實。諸年少因相稱譽。以爲戲弄。爲散騎常侍。與謝瞻連省。夜於月下長詠。自云得先賢風制。瞻每遙贊之。愷之得此。彌自力忘倦。瞻將眠。語捶腳人令代。愷之不覺有異。遂幾申旦而後止。

The humor in this anecdote is derived from the inversion of proper values. The connoisseur is meant to chant his poem out of a sincere love for the literature and those who appreciate his appreciation are meant to do so sincerely. Here vanity is rewarded with flippancy and the connoisseur is hoist with his own petard.

The purest connoisseur does not seek to display his competence. He appreciates a work for itself, not for the accolades of others.

One night while Wang Huizhi was living in Shanyin, there was a heavy snowfall. He woke up, opened his shutters wide, and ordered some wine to be poured so that he might survey the glowing whiteness all around him.

---

48. Liu Jun cites this from *Xu Jin yangqiu* 續晉陽秋.

Then he got to his feet and paced about the room, chanting Zuo Si's poem, "Summoning the Recluse." He suddenly thought of his friend, Dai Kui, who was staying in Shan at the time and set out at once in a small boat to see him. He traveled the whole night through to get there, but when he arrived at his friend's gate he turned around and went back without going in. When someone asked his reason for doing this, Wang said, "I started out for there on an impulse, but when that impulse subsided I turned back. What need was there to see Dai?" (23.47)

王子猷居山陰。夜大雪。眠覺。開室。命酌酒。四望皎然。因起仿偟。
詠左思招隱詩。忽憶戴安道。時戴在剡。即便夜乘小船就之。經宿方至。
造門不前而返。人問其故。王曰。吾本乘興而行。興盡而返。何必見戴。

Wang's poetic performance, though an example of quotation rather than production, recalls the many performances of "outburst" songs depicted in the *Han History* in which the singer first takes the time to order wine, then rises to perform a song occasioned by immediate circumstances. The differences here are that Wang's outburst is not occasioned by a sense of frustration and that he is alone for his performance, constituting his own audience. The poem then gives rise to an impulse (*xing* 興) in him to seek out his friend, Dai Kui, a "recluse." It is the quality of this impulse—how it is generated, transferred, preserved, and dissipated—that is at the core of this anecdote. It is an intensely private process, but one that must inevitably become public to find its way into the pages of *Topical Tales*.

In the *Analects*, Confucius exhorts his disciples to study the *Poems* for a variety of reasons:

The Master said, "Little ones, why do you not study the *Poems*? Through the *Poems*, one may incite, one may observe, one may keep company, one may express resentment. Near at hand, one may serve one's father. At a farther remove, one may serve one's lord. And there is much to be known in them about the names of birds, beasts, plants, and trees." (17.9)

子曰。小子。何莫學夫詩。詩。可以興。可以觀。可以群。可以怨。邇
之事父。遠之事君。多識於鳥獸草木之名。

Exactly what Confucius means by each of the items in his catalogue of poetic utility is subject to debate. There is, however, an underlying common theme: the *Poems* are envisioned as public property for matters of public discourse. Confucius's list readily inventories

many of the uses toward which the *Poems* are put in the narratives
of the *Zuo Tradition*—certainly the ways in which the *Poems* are
used to gauge the morality of individuals and states, to express so-
ciability at banquets, to remonstrate with superiors, to serve on
diplomatic missions, and to demonstrate one's command of Tradi-
tional knowledge. And the observation that one may use poetry to
"express resentment" covers virtually all of the outburst songs de-
picted in the *Han History*. The first use listed by Confucius—that
"one may incite" or "give rise to an impulse [興]"—is the most dif-
ficult to define, but in the context of the *Analects* and other pre-Qin
texts it can be read as referring to the ability of the *Poems* to provoke
those who hear them to emulate proper behavior or to curb im-
proper behavior. This concept of the morally suasive power of the
Poems underpins poetic practice as it is depicted in much of the *Zuo
Tradition* and as it is codified in the "Great Preface."

The *Topical Tales* anecdote about Wang Huizhi 王徽之 (d. 388)
clearly depicts a different concept of poetic performance stemming
from impulses. In the first place, the initial impulse to perform the
poem does not arise from a need to praise, to blame, or to vent
frustration; it is simply generated by Wang's aesthetic appreciation
of the snowfall. The narrative carefully sets up the parameters of
Wang's appreciation. Wang wakes from sleep to find his villa sur-
rounded by newly fallen snow: the moment is unexpected and
ephemeral. The reason for his waking is not given; it is simply a
fortuitous gift. Wang proves himself a man of sufficient sensibility
to appreciate the gift, opening the shutters of his room to frame the
scene in his window and ordering wine to enjoy "the glowing
whiteness all around him." The impulse generated by his apprecia-
tion animates him physically as he gets up and begins pacing back
and forth. He starts humming and finally the impulse bursts forth in
verbal form as a performance of Zuo Si's "Summoning the Recluse"
招隱士.[49] Wang's choice of poem is decidedly noncanonical and

---

49. The physical aspect of Wang's verbal performance recalls the "Great Pref-
ace": "When the emotions are stirred within, they take on outward form in spoken
words. When speaking them is not enough, then one sighs them. When sighing
them is not enough, then one intones and sings them. When intoning and singing

contemporary. He is not motivated in his choice by a received interpretation of the poem, nor is he motivated by a need to communicate a certain "message" to another party. Just as the impulse to sing a poem was generated by aesthetic appreciation, his choice of poem is guided by an aesthetic appreciation of an apt image found in one of its lines. "Summoning the Recluse" is quoted by Liu Jun in his annotations and opens as follows:

> Leaning on my staff, I summon the recluse,
> The overgrown path cuts across past and present.
> In the mountain caves nothing is constructed,
> In the hills there is the sound of a singing zither.
> White snow lingers on the shady ridge,
> Scarlet blossoms shine in the sunny grove.

> 杖策招隱士
> 荒塗橫古今
> 巖穴無結構
> 丘中有鳴琴
> 白雪停陰岡
> 丹葩曜陽林

The only mention of snow in the poem is found in the first line of the third couplet, which, with its mention of "shady ridge" and "sunny grove," does not apply very well to Wang's nocturnal surroundings. And this seems to be the point. There is no anxiety on Wang's part (nor should there be on the part of the reader) about making his performance suit the occasion. There is no need to bridge the gap between the conditions of the poem's origination and its current application. It is simply enough that snow lies on the ground outside and that snow is mentioned in the poem—a happy coincidence that requires no further justification. Yet out of this happy coincidence another impulse is generated that moves Wang to action. As the speaker of the poem, he decides to emulate the speaker in the poem by going to "summon the recluse": his friend Dai Kui. The narrative underscores the spontaneity of this impulse by stating that Wang's friend "suddenly came to mind" and that "he

---

them is not enough then, unconsciously, the hands dance them and the feet tap them."

set out at once" on a small boat to visit him. Wang spends the entire night acting on this poetically inspired impulse, but just prior to achieving its end he turns back and goes home. The reader would be left to his or her own devices for interpreting Wang's enigmatic actions were it not for the intervention of a commentator, who happens to be Wang himself.

The anecdote could have simply ended with Wang turning back, completing a self-contained episode reported by an unknown narrator who came by his knowledge through undisclosed means. However, it is an enduring feature of Chinese narratives to identify their own provenance. There is usually some indication of how the narrative became public knowledge. When the story involves figures at the center of power on the political stage (as in the *Zuo Tradition*, the *Han History*, and some of the anecdotes already cited from *Topical Tales*), it is assumed that an account of events will become part of the public record. When the action involves more marginal characters, the narrator will often identify his source, a practice that first gained currency with Sima Qian and the *Historical Records* and that is a ubiquitous feature of Tang dynasty tales. In this anecdote, the line "When someone asked his reason for doing this, Wang said . . ." suggests that it is Wang Huizhi himself who is responsible for initially transmitting this narrative. He has left an unanswered question at the center of his narrative about himself: why would he turn back after traveling all night? The only possible reason for denying a satisfying sense of closure at the end of a narrative is because one knows there will be an audience demanding that closure. One can imagine Wang telling this story to his friends, then sitting back with an enigmatic smile on his face, waiting to see who will be the first to yield to his curiosity and ask him why he turned back.

When this narrative was first transmitted in oral form, the question asked of Wang and his answer in reply were not part of the narrative itself but part of the social context of its transmission and reception. It is only when the narrative is transcribed onto the written page that the miniature metanarrative must be appended. For we—the readers of the narrative at the present moment—fill the role of that "someone" asking about his reason; and Wang's answer to our inevitable question must be duly inscribed for he is long since dead, survived only by the narratives about him. The appended metanarrative effectively converts the anecdote that supports it into a secondary narrative. The primary narrative tells a frame story, one about the telling of the anecdote and its explication.[50] The intersection of these two narratives allows Wang to control every role involved in storytelling: he is a character *in* the story, the narrator and transmitter *of* the story, and commentator *on* the story. This whole process has then been transcribed and preserved on the pages of *Topical Tales*. Whence this desire to control every variable, and the concomitant desire to depict every variable being controlled? Wang plays a fascinating but ultimately self-defeating game: he demonstrates his cultural competence by framing an example of his indifference toward cultural competence. What the audience is being asked to judge here is Wang's apparent lack of concern for the judgment of an audience, which is why the project is ultimately self-defeating as long as it is Wang who is doing the telling.

Something of significance does emerge from this "defeat," however. The portrayal of this unobserved performance in a private home is a portrayal of the liberation of poetic discourse from the pressures of public performance on the political stage. The very poem that provides the text for Wang's performance, Zuo Si's "Summoning the Recluse," is traditionally read as an exhortation made to a talented man who has chosen reclusion over service to an unworthy government. Wang chooses the poem for its aesthetic dimension, pointedly ignoring its "original" meaning and application. Both Wang and Dai are already in service; they adopt the label "recluse" provisionally, with a knowing wink, to describe their leisure time spent in natural surroundings. The impulse to chant the poem, the choice of poem, and the resulting impulse to visit a friend: all are marked by a sense of play. In the end, none of it really matters except as a means of defining a place where poetry does not have to

---

50. The first half of the frame—describing the gathering of friends at which Wang tells his anecdote—is missing, but is certainly implied by the second half. It may have been considered superfluous since the anecdote was surely circulated at such social gatherings even after its transcription.

matter. It is a place of individual freedom, where the minutest variables of poetic performance can be controlled, and where the individual can own the resulting performance. Ownership makes display possible. Wang Huizhi's true cultural competence in this narrative is not manifested in his poetic competence, but in his ability to frame, own, and display an example of his poetic competence to others.

In the end, this is what most of the interactions through poetic discourse depicted in *Topical Tales* seem to be about: ownership and display as a means of establishing one's reputation for poetic and cultural competence. *Topical Tales* can be read as a sort of handbook of examples of competence in the production and reception of utterances, poetic and otherwise. In recording these examples, it carves out and gives shape to the space in which these activities take place. Any place where the members of the educated elite meet, individuals seek distinction by demonstrating their competence in producing and appreciating language marked by wit, beauty, and polish.

CR FOUR ℘

Gleaning the Heart

I

The Southern Dynasties allowed poetic performance to be owned by the individual in a space that constituted itself as separate from, and often in opposition to, the political stage. The nearly three centuries of the Tang dynasty (618–906) saw the gradual integration of this individualized space of poetry within the larger political sphere. The consolidation of the imperial examination system as the primary route to employment as a government official and the decision to test the ability to compose poetry on the most prestigious examinations produced an explosion in the number of people who wished to learn how to compose, perform, and evaluate poetry with an acceptable level of competence. Poetry continued to be a means of improving one's standing in social circles, but it also became a means of literally winning and advancing one's career in officialdom. The spectrum of poetic competence was broadened to include goals as petty as winning a friendly game over drinks and as lofty as attaining a post in high officialdom or even evaluating the cultural worthiness of the emperor himself.

The records of poetic performance from the Tang—which include official and unofficial histories, biographical materials, poetry anthologies, prefaces, anecdotes, and letters—show that poetic competence mattered in almost every facet of life for the newly expanded educated elite of the Tang. One particularly rich source of narratives depicting poetic production and reception during this era is *Vast Gleanings of the Taiping Era* 太平廣記, which contains over 360 poem-bearing anecdotes drawn from 108 Tang collections. By far the highest concentration of these anecdotes is drawn from a collection called *Storied Poems* 本事詩, which continued to circulate independently with its own preface even after it was incorporated into *Vast Gleanings*.

Storied Poems (literally, "poems based in events" 本事詩) is an ideal source for examining accounts of poetic practice that are less beholden to upholding the canonical principles of poetry articulated in the "Great Preface," the "Lesser Prefaces," and the attendant commentaries on the Mao *Poems*. As the ensuing analysis of the provenance and prefaces of *Storied Poems* and related collections shows, their accounts of Tang poetic practice seem more proper to the anecdote-swapping raconteur than to the orthodox exegete. It is through these depictions that one can gain a sense of the freely expressed wishes that accompanied poetry: that its production, performance, and reception might effect real change in the lives of those who would practice it.

II

An annotated bibliography called *A Record of Books Read in the Prefect Studio* 郡齋讀書志 by the great Southern Song bibliophile Chao Gongwu 晁公武 (d. 1171) records the existence of a book called *Storied Poems* 本事詩 in one *juan*, attributes it to Meng Qi 孟棨 (fl. 841–886) of the Late Tang, and describes it as follows: "It gathers together lyrical poems of poets through the ages who were moved by events around them and narrates the stories behind them. It includes a total of seven categories" 纂歷代詞人緣情感事之詩。敘其本事。凡七類也.[1]

---

1. Chao, *Junzhai dushu zhi*, *juan* 20, p. 4a.

This accurate description of the contents of the *Storied Poems* is extant in a variety of texts today and provides the earliest independent corroboration that it was divided into seven categories.[2] The settings of the anecdotes contained in *Storied Poems* range from the fifth century, in the Liu Song dynasty, to as late as the ninth century, in the Late Tang. As with any anthology, *Storied Poems* reflects the biases of its compiler, the limitations of its sources, and the myriad subtractions, additions, and corruptions that are the consequence of centuries of transmission. It cannot be taken as representative of the entire Tang age—no single work can—but the collection is a valuable repository of narratives from a broad cross section of hundreds of years of Tang elite society. Despite its brevity, *Storied Poems* was an influential collection, spawning such imitators as the famous Song collection *Recording the Events of Tang Poems* 唐詩紀事, and is credited as the progenitor of the entire "Remarks on Poetry" (*shihua* 詩話) genre that was so popular during the Song dynasty.[3] Its relatively few pages contain a great variety of manifestations of poetic competence, indicating an increasing sophistication during the Tang in imagining of what a poem is and does.

Over the centuries of its transmission, *Storied Poems* has received numerous classifications, which indicate the different emphases of those who have classified its contents. To the compilers of the *New Tang History* 新唐書 working under Ouyang Xiu 歐陽修 (1007–1072), it was the poetry;[4] to Hu Yinglin 胡應麟 (1551–1602), it was

---

2. It is also listed as a work in one *juan* in a later Southern Song private bibliography called *An Annotated Register of the Books of Upright Studio* 直齋書錄解題 by Chen Zhensun 陳振孫 (fl. 1236). Chen, in his short note on the book, mentions that Meng Qi held the post of Director of the Bureau of Merit Titles 司勳郎中 during the Tang. Since the only place that this information can now be found is in Meng Qi's own preface to certain extant editions of *Storied Poems*, this is a good indication that the preface was still circulating with the work in the Southern Song (1127–1279).

3. The *Annotated Full List of the Complete Library of Four Branches of Books* 四庫全書總目提要 identifies *Storied Poems* as the exemplar of no fewer than six other works (Ji, *juan* 195).

4. See "Bibliographic Treatise" 藝文志 in *juan* 60 of the *New Tang History*, where it is classified as a "general collection" 總集 of poetry.

the anecdotes;[5] to Ji Yun 紀昀 (1724–1805) and his team of compilers, it was how the anecdotes could be used to illuminate the poetry.[6] Whether it is called an anthology of poems, a collection of *xiaoshuo* materials, or a work of literary criticism, the work itself remains, stubbornly refusing a consistent classification; the different classifications in which it has been placed say less about *Storied Poems* than about the interests of those who would classify it. This is a result of the heterogeneous nature of its contents. It is not a single, coherent piece written from beginning to end by one author. It is cobbled together from different types of sources and is, ultimately, placed in a bibliographical classification that does not house any one of those sources: a testament to its innovation in drawing on the familiar to make something new.[7] *Storied Poems* is best characterized as a specific impulse to collect, projected onto a variety of different materials. The bibliographer is at a loss to classify impulses; he must choose one aspect of the material that he feels is paramount and place the work accordingly. These classifications, however, all result from a retrospective gaze.

There are extant documents that indicate how Meng Qi and his contemporaries viewed their own compilation activities. In his preface to *Storied Poems*, Meng Qi claims, "In the passages drawn from strange tales and bizarre records I have omitted anything of doubtful veracity," a statement that raises more doubts than it assuages regarding his source material. Do the anecdotes of a collection such as *Storied Poems* have any basis in fact? How did the compilers view their materials? There are at least eleven anecdotal

---

5. See *Collected Notes from the 'Humble Abode' Mountain Retreat* 少室山房筆叢, where Hu Yinglin claims that *Storied Poems* does not really belong to the classification of "remarks on poetry" 詩話 or of "literary criticism" 文評, but to *xiaoshuo* 小說—a term with a long and complicated history that may be rendered as "trivial stories," and which had a distinct connotation of "fictional stories" by Hu's time. For a translation and analysis of the relevant passages, see Laura Hua Wu's "From *Xiaoshuo* to Fiction," pp. 339–71.

6. See preface to *juan* 195 on "criticism of poetry and prose" 詩文評 of the *Annotated Full List of the Complete Library of Four Branches of Books*, which states that *Storied Poems* "ranges widely to collect background details" 旁採故實.

7. See Figure 2 in the Appendix for a diagram reconstructing the compilation and transmission of *Storied Poems*.

collections that *Storied Poems* has demonstrably drawn upon for its anecdotes (see Table 1 in the Appendix). By using this data in conjunction with a critical reading of extant prefaces to these collections, it is possible to shed some light on the narrative practice behind the production of anecdotal collections in the Tang.

From the data in Table 1 we can see that compilers of these anecdotal collections spanned the range of official posts, from the powerful military commissioner 節度使 and prefect 刺史 to the lowly retainer 從事官, and that Fan Shu 范攄 remained outside of officialdom altogether as a "recluse" 處士. Both Liu Su 劉肅 and Li Kang 李伉 compiled their collections after withdrawing from official duties, as was the case with Meng Qi. There is no discernible pattern in location either, with postings both in the capital and in outlying regions, and frequent transfers between the two—hardly surprising given the mobility of officials during this time. There does seem to be a preponderance of officials who managed documents of one kind or another, whether as editors in the palace library 校書郎, right rectifiers of omissions 右補闕 involved in compiling history (修國史/史館), or scholars of the Hanlin Academy 翰林學士.

There are many interesting links between the collections themselves. At least four (and probably more) quote other collections on the list, with Liu Su's 劉餗 *Amusing Stories of the Sui and Tang* 隋唐嘉話 being a favorite source. Many of these works also quote collections that do not appear on this list (and we should keep in mind that all of these works were used as sources for *Storied Poems*). As with *Storied Poems*, at least five collections were used as sources for orthodox histories such as the *Old* and *New Tang History* and Sima Guang's 司馬光 (1019–1086) *Comprehensive Mirror for Aid in Government* 資治通鑒.

The men who compiled the collections have interesting connections as well. Liu Su was the son of the famed historiographer Liu Zhiji (and, incidentally, was highly commended in his duties by Han Huang 韓滉, who appears in entry 1.7 of *Storied Poems*). The administration of Li Deyu 李德裕 (787–849), a principal in the notorious Niu-Li factional struggles, once included Duan Chengshi 段成式 and Wei Xuan 韋絢, who compiled *Miscellaneous Offerings from Youyang* 酉陽雜俎 and *A Record of Fine Conversations with Adviser to the Heir Apparent Liu* 劉賓客嘉話錄, respectively. Li was also a friend and mentor of Lu Zhao 盧肇, compiler of *Remnants of History* 逸史. Li Deyu seems to be associated with much storytelling; even his nemesis, Niu Sengru 牛僧孺 (779–847), is credited with a collection of classical tales called *Record of the Mysterious and Weird* 玄怪錄. Finally, we might note that Li Jun 李濬, compiler of *Miscellaneous Records of Pine View Studio* 松窗雜錄, was the son of Li Shen 李紳, who appears in entries 1.9a and 1.10 of *Storied Poems*.

All of these intertextual and interpersonal links between various anecdotal collections and their respective compilers (who were particularly active in the ninth century, judging from this list), attest to a loose but energetic network of officials often associated with historiography and other forms of document production who enjoyed collecting and swapping stories with one another, either by word of mouth or through textual citation.

Certainly gossip and casual storytelling among groups of people are constants across cultures. But why did members of the Tang official class compile these sorts of anecdotes so assiduously? Robert Campany provides a model of the motivations behind these collections, summing up the nature of Six Dynasties and Tang "anomaly accounts" (*zhiguai* 志怪) as "a casting of familiar nets of historical, geographical, and biographical writing over an ever more demarcated, isolated, and articulated domain of objects that shared the fundamental taxonomic marker of being anomalous."[8] In the collections I am discussing here, the "fundamental taxonomic marker" seems to be, in the words of Li Jun, the "particularly extraordinary" 特異 things that happen to or are done by members of the official class or the royalty they serve.

The casual context in which these anecdotes were told, heard, retold, written down, and read frees them somewhat from the burden carried by more orthodox forms of writing, which are expected to convey messages of moral significance. Often it appears that simply being a "good story" is enough to warrant preservation

---

8. Campany, "Chinese Accounts of the Strange," vol. 1, p. 158.

in an anecdotal collection. At the end of entry 1.8 in *Storied Poems*, Meng Qi tells us how he came to hear the story he has related:

I had just finished my assignment in Wuzhou, where there was an "old general" from Daliang named Zhao Wei who was serving as a prefect in Lingwai. He was almost ninety years old, but his hearing and eyesight were still good. When he was passing through Wuzhou, he talked [with me] about past events in Daliang and recounted them in an engaging manner. He said that he had witnessed the entire story with his own eyes, and so I have recorded it here.

余罷梧州。有大梁凤將趙唯。爲嶺外刺史。年將九十矣。耳目不衰。過梧州。言大梁往事。述之可聽。云此皆目擊之故。因錄於此也。

Meng relates the story to us simply because he finds it "engaging" 可聽. There is no high-minded appeal to patterns of morality inherent in human behavior, such as we find in official historiography (and as is so evident in Sima Qian's closing judgments). What does remain is historiography's concern for the truth: Meng is careful to tell us that Zhao Wei's sensory faculties are reliable and that he was an eyewitness to the events in the account.

Insistence on the "truth" 實 is echoed in the prefaces of many anecdotal collections in the Tang. We have already seen that Meng Qi claims to have omitted anything of "doubtful veracity" 疑非是實 in his anecdotes. Li Jun claims to be giving us accounts that "must be true" 必實. Li Deyu, in a wonderful example of blatant hypocrisy, quotes the following assertion about one of his sources: "He witnessed it all firsthand, and it is not derived from hearsay; it is credible and proven by evidence, and so it may constitute a veritable record" 彼皆目睹。非出傳聞。信而有徵。可爲實錄.[9] This is the same man who, for the bulk of his collection, claims to have drawn upon hearsay—passed through no fewer than three intermediaries—about Xuanzong's reign. The dissonance between Li's two statements may provide us with a clue about attitudes toward the veracity of these accounts.

---

9. See the preface to *Collecting Mr. Liu's Stories of the Past*, in Huang, *Zhongguo lidai xiaoshuo*, p. 115.

When Li Deyu, Meng Qi, Li Jun, and others make claims for veracity in their collections, they do so in their prefaces: the very arena in which one draws upon canonical precepts in order to bolster the "acceptability" of one's work. They *must* say that their narratives are true accounts of the world—to do otherwise would disqualify their texts from being considered worthy of preservation or transmission, and would brand the compilers as frivolous men for attempting to transmit them. Whether anyone really believes these stories to be true is irrelevant; they are to be *taken* as true.

The pleasure of reading (or hearing) stories about other people like oneself lies in believing that they are entirely true despite *knowing* that the account is likely a mixture of truth, half truth, and outright fiction. It is precisely this quality of verisimilitude that makes the story "engaging." In this way, the anecdotes of a collection such as *Storied Poems* are very much like gossip and urban myth. The line between truth and fiction is never easily drawn in these cases (for that would destroy the pleasure of the story). This might explain why five of these collections appear as "unclassified biographies and history" 雜傳記/雜史 in the *New Tang History*, while the other six find their way into the *xiaoshuo* category reserved for accounts of questionable veracity. The anecdotal collection resides in a liminal zone of belief, bleeding over the border between fact and fiction.

Thus the narratives of *Storied Poems* cannot serve as reliable accounts of poetic praxis in the Tang. Yet, we should proceed in reading these stories, for they can tell us about something more than historical fact. Just as gossip expresses a desire to erode the status of the person being maligned, just as urban myth expresses an anxiety about wilderness invading civilization, so too do these stories have something to teach about the desires and anxieties surrounding poetry in Tang China. Conceptions of poetic competence in the Tang are more complex and varied than those found in the texts of preceding ages—a broad cross section of those conceptions is played out in the anecdotes of *Storied Poems*. Meng Qi's preface to the collection, completed in 886, is a fascinating discursive attempt to organize these anecdotes and to find them a proper place in the tradition from which they emerge.

III

The preface to *Storied Poems* is important not only as a statement of Meng Qi's motives and methods in compiling his collection, but also as a form of literary criticism that influenced the compilation of later collections. In reading it, one can gain a sense of how he regarded the interaction between poetic utterance, the written text that records it, and the world inhabited by both. By means of his preface, Meng Qi positions his collection in a discursive field defined by canonical statements on poetry and narrative as well as by received poems and narratives themselves, including those found in the *Zuo Tradition*, official histories, and *Topical Tales*. In what follows, I quote a short passage from the preface and then compare it with the critical tradition upon which it draws and with other prefaces from anecdotal collections in the Tang, in an attempt to delineate the position Meng Qi seeks for his collection.

詩者。情動於中而形於言

A poem results when feelings are stirred within and
they take on outward form in spoken words.

In quoting the "Great Preface" to open his preface, Meng Qi implicitly aligns his work with the most orthodox of statements regarding classical *shi* poetry and seeks protection from accusations of frivolity by donning the mantle of the Confucian canon. The practice of appealing to canonical sources is de rigueur in prefaces. In his preface to *Topical Tales: A New Edition for the Great Tang Dynasty* 大唐世說新語,[10] Liu Su 劉肅 (fl. 820) refers to the invention of writing itself by the legendary founder of Chinese civilization, Bao Xi 庖犧 (also known as Fu Xi 伏羲), as well as to the canonical works the *Classic of Documents* 書經 and the *Spring and Autumn Annals* 春秋 (Huang, p. 105). Fan Shu 范攄 (fl. 870), in his colophon

---

10. This book is also known by its shorter title, *Novel Discussions of the Great Tang Dynasty* 大唐新語.

to *Friendly Debates at Misty Brook* 雲溪友議, invokes the canon by saying that "Confucius collected the airs and ditties of the myriad states [in the *Poems*] in order to complete his *Spring and Autumn Annals*" 孔子聚萬國風謠。以成其春秋也. He follows this with a citation from the "Call to Learning" 勸學 chapter of *Xunzi* to justify his inclusion of noncanonical materials: "The rivers and oceans do not turn back the tiny rivulets and so are able to grow great by them" 江海不卻細流。故能爲之大.[11] Duan Chengshi 段成式 (d. 863) tries to deflect criticism of his unorthodox *Miscellaneous Offerings from Yuyang* 酉陽雜俎 by claiming that the *Classic of Changes* 易經 "approaches matters of the strange" 近於怪也, and that the use of the "affective image of the Southern Sieve constellation by the poets [of the *Poems* to suggest slander] approaches jesting" 詩人南箕之興。近乎戲也, so that the strange matters and jesting in his humble collection should prove "no threat to the Tradition."[12] Some compilers justify the frivolousness of their collections by citing a statement attributed to Confucius's disciple Zixia: "Even in lesser pursuits, there is always something worthy of regard" 雖小道。必有可觀者焉.[13] Ban Gu quotes this passage (erroneously attributing it to Confucius) in the "Bibliographic Treatise" of the *Han History* to justify his inclusion of a *xiaoshuo* category; so it is only natural that it should continue to appear in connection with unorthodox narratives.

Meng Qi does not adopt the apologetic tone of the compilers mentioned above, who attempt to justify their swerve away from tradition by quoting the tradition itself. He is collecting instances of classical poetry (*shi* 詩), which, unlike the casual narratives collected

---

11. Huang, *Zhongguo lidai xiaoshuo*, p. 141.

12. Huang, *Zhongguo lidai xiaoshuo*, p. 121. The Southern Sieve constellation (which contains four stars in Sagittarius) has a narrow "heel" and a wide "mouth," making it an appropriate figure for slander.

13. This passage (*Analects* 19.4) is paraphrased by Liu Su, both in his preface mentioned above and in the anonymous preface to *Hearsay Noted from the Great Tang Dynasty* 大唐傳載 (Huang, *Zhongguo lidai xiaoshuo*, p. 132). They both omit the conclusion to the passage: "but one risks getting bogged down if they are carried too far; so the superior man does not engage in them" 致遠恐泥。是以君子不爲也.

by the other compilers, belong squarely in the orthodox tradition of literary expression. The very title of Meng's collection, *Storied Poems* 本事詩, with the word "poem" placed after the modifiers, indicates that he is compiling poems that have stories attached to them rather than stories that happen to have poems in them.[14] Thus, Meng is able to open his preface by simply quoting from the "Great Preface" as his definition of poetry. But a closer examination of his source shows that he has quoted it selectively for his own ends. The opening lines of the "Great Preface" read:

A poem is what intent goes to. In the mind it is intent; issuing forth in words it is a poem. When feelings are stirred within, they take on outward form in spoken words. When speaking them is not enough, then one sighs them. When sighing them is not enough, then one intones and sings them. When intoning and singing them is not enough, then, unconsciously, the hands dance them and the feet tap them.

詩者。志之所之也。在心爲志。發言爲詩。情動於中而形於言。言之不足。故嗟歎之。嗟歎之不足。故永歌之。永歌之不足。不知手之舞之。足之踏之也。[15]

In his abridged citation of this passage, Meng Qi elides the preceding mention of the concept of "intent" 志 and the ensuing discussion of the musical quality of poetic utterance.[16] He reduces the equation to three terms—poem, feelings, and words—and draws a one-to-one correspondence between the poem and the expression of internal feelings in external words.

The reduction of the poetic process to these simple terms can be found in Kong Yingda's 孔穎達 (574–648) *Standard Meaning of the Mao Poems* 毛詩正義, part of the *Standard Meaning of the Five*

---

14. We might recall that *Storied Poems* is classified as a "general collection" of poetry in the bibliographical treatise of the *New Tang History*.

15. Ruan Yuan, *Shisan jing*, vol. 1, pp. 269c–70a.

16. By "intent" I do not mean a fully formed plan to act, but the legal usage referring to an overall state of mind when it is "firmly fixed" or "concentrated" upon something—a meaning derived "from Latin, an extending, from *intentus*, attentive to, strained, from past participle of *intendere*, to direct attention" (*The American Heritage Dictionary of the English Language*, 3rd ed., s.v. "intent"). This etymology happily coincides with the traditional Chinese etymology of *zhi* 志 as "that to which the mind goes" 心之所之.

Classics 五經正義, which was the curriculum for the civil service examinations during the Tang. Meng Qi certainly became intimately familiar with this commentary during his decades of preparation for the examinations. In Kong's comment on this passage from the "Great Preface," he states:

The "feelings are stirred within" is still "in the mind it is intent"; "and take on outward form in spoken words" is still "issuing forth in words it is a poem." The first part [of the passage] delineates how a poem follows from the manifestation of intent. This part describes how a poem is inevitably sung, and therefore it emphasizes the patterned language. . . . The "Bibliographic Treatise" [of the *Han History*] says, "If one recites the words, then it is called a poem; if one intones the notes, then it is called a song." Therefore, in the mind it is intent and issuing from the mouth it is words. Recited words are a poem, and intoned notes are a song. When the notes are distributed among the eight tones [of different instruments], it is called making music. All of these are simply different names for a single process extended over time.

情動於中。還是在心爲志。而形於言。還是發言爲詩。上辨詩從志出。此言爲詩必歌。故重其文也。 . . . 藝文志云。誦其言謂之詩。詠其聲謂之歌。然則。在心爲志。出口爲言。誦言爲詩。詠聲爲歌。播於八音。謂之爲樂。皆始末之異名耳。[17]

To Kong, intent issuing forth in words as a poem is equivalent to feelings stirred within taking on outward form in words. This equation is based on a premise of the identity between intent and feelings, which he asserts explicitly in his annotation of the nature of intent in the entry for Duke Zhao 25 of the *Zuo Tradition*: "Within the self it is feelings, but when feelings are stirred it forms intent. Feelings and intent are one and the same; the difference only arises from the word used" 在己爲情。情動爲志。情志一也。所從言之異耳。[18] In claiming they are the same, Kong has actually made a subtle distinction: only when the feelings are stirred and given direction do they constitute intent. The equation in the "Great Preface" becomes clear: feelings stirred = intent; therefore, feelings stirred expressed in words = intent expressed in words = a poem.

---

17. Ruan Yuan, *Shisan jing*, vol. 1, p. 270a.
18. Ruan Yuan, *Shisan jing*, vol. 2, p. 2108b.

The poem remains in its "pure" state when its words are simply recited, granting a primacy to the text of the poem. When the "patterned language" 文 of the poem is emphasized—that is, when the notes are intoned or sung—it becomes a song, which can then be set to music. Kong is careful to maintain, however, that this is not a transformative process; the singing and music are merely the performative aspect of the poem's irreducible text.

Meng Qi's emphasis on feelings and words is not novel. The practice of "reciting a poem" 賦詩 to express a political or diplomatic "intention," depicted so often in the *Zuo Tradition*, gradually eclipsed the denotation of *zhi* 志 as pure "intent." As Stephen Owen puts it, "Ultimately the ethical and political dimensions of *Zhi* [志] became so strong in the tradition that most writers on literature preferred to substitute other terms as the source of the poem in the psyche, especially *qing* [情], 'the affections.'"[19] One such writer, Lu Ji 陸機 (261-303), in his *Poetic Exposition on Literature* 文賦, coined the phrase, "a poem follows from the feelings" 詩緣情, which became the dominant concept of poetry into the Tang.[20]

The preface to the *Anthology of Literature* 文選 by Xiao Tong 蕭統 (501-31) quotes the very same abridged passage from the "Great Preface" as Meng Qi does, with no mention of intent or music. Another Tang preface, by Li Deyu, for *Notes on Traveling in Zhou and Qin* 周秦行紀, drops the element of poetry altogether and works in the opposite direction as Meng Qi. Li's preface discusses how one penetrates to the state of mind through words, not how feelings produce words: "By examining the words, one will know the interior. By savoring the phrases, one will discern the state of mind" 故察其言而知其內。玩其辭而見其意矣.[21] Li Deyu is interested in reception, in knowing the interior through words. This concept was discussed at length as early as *Mencius* 孟子 (2A.2, 4A.15, 5A.4, 5B.8). Meng Qi is interested in both production and reception, but both he and Li Deyu make a strong link between feelings and words.

---

19. Owen, *Readings*, p. 28.
20. Lu Ji, *Wen fu*, p. 104.
21. Huang, *Zhongguo lidai xiaoshuo*, p. 113.

By opening his preface with a selective quotation from the "Great Preface," Meng invokes an ancient tradition while simultaneously staking out his own position in relation to it. He focuses on the feelings as the source of poetic production—a tendency inherited from changes in the tradition outlined above. He makes the words—the text—his primary objective and dispenses with the musical aspect of poetry, which is to be expected in a collection consisting of a patchwork of excerpts from written sources. Finally, by engaging the "Great Preface," Meng signals that he is using this canonical work as a metatext, not only in constructing his own preface, but in selecting and editing his entries as well. The explicit relationship invoked with the "Great Preface" continues in Meng's own preface.

故怨思悲愁。常多感慨。

And thus resentment and melancholy always
result in many passionate outbursts.

The use of the connective "thus" 故 sets up a strong logical link: this sentence is a specific example (though not necessarily the only one) of the general principle stated in the previous sentence. In this case, the "feelings stirred within" are "resentment" 怨思 and "melancholy" 悲愁, and the "outward form in words" is a "passionate outburst" 感慨. All of these terms have a significant history, which may help to explain why Meng Qi chooses to use them here.

The term for "resentment" (or, more precisely, "resentful thoughts") appears in the "Lesser Preface" to one of the *Poems*, "Scattered Waters" 揚之水, which is read as a criticism of King Ping of Zhou (r. 770–720 B.C.E.):

"Scattered Waters" criticizes King Ping.

He did not care for his people, but garrisoned them afar in his mother's homeland. The people of Zhou harbored resentful thoughts over this.

揚之水。刺平王也。不撫其民。而遠屯戍于母家。周人怨思焉。[22]

---

22. Mao #68. Ruan Yuan, *Shisan jing*, vol. 1, p. 331b.

These "resentful thoughts" supposedly led to the composition of a poem about "scattered waters" that "cannot even bear a bundle of firewood away" 不流束薪—a metaphorical image for the shallow feelings that King Ping had for his people.

The feeling of resentment was associated with the *Poems* long before the "Lesser Prefaces." In the *Analects*, Confucius is portrayed as urging his disciples to study the *Poems* for their many practical uses, including that "one may express resentment" 可以怨 through them (17.9). Sima Qian, in his "Grand Historian's Account of Himself," says, "On the whole, the three hundred *Poems* were composed as a means for the worthies and sages to vent their frustration" 詩三百篇。大抵賢聖發憤之所爲作也.[23] The "Great Preface" also comments on this topic in its description of how a poem reflects the circumstances that produce it: "The tones of a chaotic age are resentful and angry" 亂世之音怨以怒.[24] Immediately prior to this, the "Great Preface" does allow that the "tones of a well-governed age are peaceful and joyous" 治世之音安以樂, but the dominant view came to regard poetry as a vehicle for dissatisfaction. As we shall see, the "wronged" official is a recurrent protagonist in the anecdotes collected by Meng Qi; so it is not surprising that he would emphasize this aspect of poetry.

Meng continues this gloomy but traditional view in his second example of an emotion that stimulates poetic production: melancholy. This term finds an early usage in the *Lyrics of Chu* (in the third of the "Nine Arguments" 九辯): "Far from the prime of my fragrant lushness, I am decrepit and melancholy" 離芳藹之方壯兮。余萎約而悲愁.[25] There is a definite connotation of sadness due to separation (temporal or spatial) that well suits the thematics of many entries of *Storied Poems*.

After specifying the types of emotions in which he is interested, Meng Qi turns to the nature of the poetic utterance itself. What I translate as "passionate outburst" 感慨 literally means to be "moved by passion" and carries connotations of righteousness, often to the

---

23. Sima Qian, *Shi ji*, vol. 10, *juan* 130, p. 3300.
24. Ruan Yuan, *Shisan jing*, vol. 1, p. 270b.
25. Qu et al., *Chu ci*, p. 11.

point of moral indignation. The idea of a *verbal* outburst suits the context in which Meng Qi uses this term because a sense of "passion" 慨 (or 慷慨) is frequently associated in the tradition with poetic production. It is the most common tag phrase to appear before outburst songs in the *Han History*, the "passionate outburst" in song being the stock response to trying circumstances.

By referring to the "passionate outburst," Meng Qi integrates spontaneity into his model of poetic production. While this may be his intention, it is already clear from pre-Tang narratives containing poetry (as it is in the entries of *Storied Poems* itself) that the act of uttering a poem is often carefully staged, involving an awareness of time, place, and audience. Passion may serve as the poem's impetus and can also characterize the impression that its performance creates, but the deployment of the verbal "outburst" itself can be highly controlled by an agent with a degree of poetic competence. While Meng Qi is not free to acknowledge this within the restrictive parameters of rhetoric appropriate for a preface, the anecdotes themselves bear out a sophisticated awareness of the multivalent qualities of poetic competence, as I will show in the next chapter.

抒懷佳作。諷刺雅言著於群書雖盈廚溢閣。其間
觸事興詠。尤所鍾情。不有發揮。孰明厥義。

Exquisite compositions of lyricism and elegant words of admonition may be recorded in myriad books filling up shelves and overflowing cabinets, but instances in them of being moved to intone a poem by encountering events are what really cause one's feelings to well up. If these instances are not manifested, then who will comprehend their significance?

Here Meng Qi moves from his model of poetic production to the issue of the inscription of poetic utterance in writing. The term "exquisite composition" 佳作 suggests a work of literature worthy of preservation. Using a parallel construction—a common practice in prefaces—Meng pairs this term with "elegant words" 雅言. This term appears in the *Analects* (7.17) to describe the orthodox language in which Confucius recited the classics, but here it seems simply to denote "elegant language."

The way in which Meng Qi chooses to qualify these two terms is significant. The phrase I translate as "lyricism" 抒懷 literally means to "pour forth what you hold in your heart." Meng coined this term based on a similar phrase meaning "to pour out your feelings" 抒情, which appears in the *Lyrics of Chu* (in the first of the "Nine Pieces" 九章): "Sorrowfully I plead my case and summon my cares; I unleash my ire and pour out my feelings" 惜誦以致愍兮。發憤以抒情.[26] What at first glance may have seemed a fairly neutral term is tinged with the familiar pattern of highly personal dissatisfaction, the expression of which involves the baring of one's soul. The entries of *Storied Poems* contain many examples of such personal expression, but usually with an awareness of the reaction of the audience to which one "pleads a case."

The second qualifying phrase employed by Meng, "admonition" 諷刺, has an overtly political character. It means something like "to jab with gentle language" and is drawn from the following passage in the "Great Preface":

Superiors use the *feng* to transform inferiors. Inferiors use the *feng* to criticize superiors. When patterned language is paramount in making a veiled admonition, then he who speaks it is without culpability and he who hears it will take sufficient warning. Therefore, it is called *feng*.

上以風化下。下以風刺上。主文而譎諫。言之者無罪。聞之者足以戒。故曰風。[27]

I have left the word *feng* 風 untranslated because of its multiple denotations in this passage.[28] Its primary meaning is as an abbreviation for the "Airs of the States" 國風, the first section of the *Classic of Poetry* that includes short folk songs purportedly from the different states of ancient China. These pieces are usually referred to collectively as a synecdoche for the entire *Classic of Poetry* although they are not entirely representative of the work's other sections.

----

26. Qu et al., *Chu ci*, p. 92.

27. Ruan Yuan, *Shisan jing*, vol. 1, p. 271b.

28. For a brief discussion of the semantic range of *feng*, see Owen, *Readings*, pp. 586–87.

Any statement about the *feng* adheres to the *Classic of Poetry* and, by extension, to poetry as a whole. Playing on the literal sense of *feng* as "wind"—and its ability to bend the reeds against which it blows (see *Analects* 12.19)—the "Great Preface" tells us that the *feng* can be used to transform behavior in the people and correct it in their rulers.

Kong Yingda's comment on this passage in the "Great Preface" deemphasizes the top-down use of *feng* to transform the people:

The *Poems* were all composed by ministers to remonstrate with their rulers. Only afterward did the rulers use them to transform their inferiors. The reason this passage first says, "superiors use the *feng* to transform inferiors," is because the didactic [nature of *feng*] stems from the ruler. Superiors and inferiors all use [the *feng*], but while the former is respected, the latter is disparaged.

詩皆人臣作之以諫君。然後人君用之以化下。此先云上以風化下者，以其教從君來。上下俱用，故先尊後卑。[29]

The primary and original function of *feng*, then, is as a form of criticism of those in power. An inherent property of this form of criticism, according to the "Great Preface," is the ability to shield the speaker from culpability while still retaining the cogency of the critique. Meng Qi, using the term "admonition," alludes to these precepts.[30] The entries in *Storied Poems* provide fascinating examples of the change in scope of these precepts and how they hold up or break down within the realm of anecdotal narratives reflecting Tang poetic practice.

A strong note of immediacy prevails in the examples I have given of early usage of the terms for "lyricism" and "admonition." The phrases "plead my case," "unleash my ire," "he who speaks," and "he who hears" all suggest an oral performance, whether it is personally or politically motivated. By attaching these terms to phrases such as "exquisite composition" and "elegant words," Meng Qi has trans-

---

29. Ruan Yuan, *Shisan jing*, vol. 1, p. 271c.

30. Meng's use of the compound *fengci* 諷刺 condenses the verbal phrase of the "Great Preface," *xia yi feng ci shang* 下以風刺上, into a two-character nominal phrase, indicating its entrenchment as a fundamental concept. The addition of the speech radical (言) to *feng* 風 distinguishes the verbal denotation from the primary denotation of "wind."

ferred the oral performance onto the written page. And this is pre-
cisely what he has collected: a series of *written* texts that depict
performances of poetry in speech and writing; many performances
have only a secondary oral component or none at all. By referring to
the concreteness of the text, Meng has displaced us from a world
where poetry simply happens immediately to one where poetic
performance is captured and preserved through writing. The poem,
the one who speaks it, and the one who hears it now exist apart
from us as literary creations on the pages of "myriad books filling up
shelves and overflowing cabinets." Their world may threaten to
overflow the confines of our own, but it is forever separate.

Or is it? Faced with such a plethora of "exquisite" and "elegant"
texts, one needs a criterion to choose what is worthy of attention.
Meng Qi offers that "instances in them of being moved to intone a
poem by encountering events are what really cause one's feelings to
well up." Here we find two levels of emotional reaction, encom-
passing both production and reception. The concept summed up in
the phrase "being moved to intone a poem by encountering events"
觸事興詠 is yet another version of the ancient stimulus-response
model outlined in the "Great Preface." The external world stirs the
feelings, which then find expression in the form of a poem. The
primary sense of "things" (*wu* 物) as concrete objects rather than as
"events" (*shi* 事) providing stimulus for poetry is prominent in na-
ture poetry. In his preface to the *Collection of Emperor Wu* 武帝集,
Shen Yue 沈約 (441–513) writes, "The brilliance of sunshine and
moonbeams, the southern breeze—this is what moves one to intone
a poem" 日月光華。南風。所以興詠.[31] But, as the "Great Preface"
asserts (and the "Lesser Prefaces" demonstrate), events can also
move one to poetic production. Meng's use of the word "event"
rather than "thing" shifts the emphasis from a spatial to a temporal
extension. As *The Great Learning* 大學 states: "Things have a root
and extremity, while events have a beginning and end" 物有本末。
事有終始.[32] These poems are not in response to inanimate objects,

31. Yan, *Quan shanggu*, vol. 3, p. 3123.
32. Ruan Yuan, *Shisan jing*, p. 1674.

but result from what *happens* to people in their encounters with other people.

Meng goes on to say that the cases in which an emotional reaction to the external world leads to poetic utterance "are what really cause one's feelings to well up." The expression "feelings welling up" 鍾情 is derived from the following anecdote in *Topical Tales*, found in the section entitled "Grieving for the Departed" 傷逝:

When Wang Rong lost his son, Wanzi, Shan Jian went to ask after him only to find Wang overcome with grief. Jian said to him, "He was just a little sprout, still a babe-in-arms. Why are you in such a state?" Wang replied, "A true sage may be able to forget his feelings, while the lowest creatures do not even have them. Where feelings truly well up is in people just like us." Jian took his words to heart and even lamented on his behalf. [17.4]

王戎喪兒萬子。山簡往省之。王悲不自勝。簡曰。孫抱中物。何至於此。王曰。聖人忘情。最下不及情。情之所鍾。正在我輩。簡服其言。為之慟。[33]

Behind the phrase "feelings welling up" lies the sense that it is a certain type of person, still of this world but with sensibilities more refined than those of the average person, that can truly feel emotion. It is this type of person that can appreciatively respond to poetry with his own emotional reaction.

In his preface, however, Meng Qi does not specify where this emotional reaction lies. Is he referring to the reception of poetic performance as it is portrayed in the anecdotes he has collected? There are many striking examples of this in *Storied Poems*. Or is he referring to our reception as readers of that very portrayal? It is this vacillation of location that reestablishes a connection between the world depicted by the written text and our world. For if we share an emotional reaction to a poem with the audience depicted in an anecdote, has not a sentimental connection been established between the worlds of the story and of the reader? The reader's sympathy creates continuity between the text and the world it inhabits.

---

33. Liu Yiqing, *Shishuo*, p. 637.

The continuity between the present and the past through literary heritage is a fundamental tenet of Chinese literary thought. Mencius articulates it in the following famous passage:

An upright gentleman of a single district will seek friends among other upright gentlemen of the district. An upright gentleman of the state will seek friends among other upright gentlemen of the state. An upright gentleman of the world will seek friends among other upright gentlemen of the world. Should befriending other upright gentlemen of the world be insufficient, then he will take the extra step of considering the ancients. But should he sing their poems and read their books without knowing them personally? Because of this, he will consider the age in which they lived. This is what is meant by "taking the extra step" to seek out friends. (5B.8)

一鄉之善士。斯友一鄉之善士。一國之善士。斯友一國之善士。天下之善士。斯友天下之善士。以友天下之善士爲未足。又尚論古之人。頌其詩。讀其書。不知其人可乎。是以論其世也。是尚友也。

The possibility that an emotional continuity might be established through texts is compelling. It can only be reliably established, however, by taking the context of those texts into consideration. Such a context is ascertained, of course, through other texts, which leads to a well-known circle in Mencius's reasoning. Meng Qi takes up this point later in his discussion of how narrative may provide a context for poems.

The latent emotional force in texts underlies the language Meng Qi uses in his next statement regarding his motivation for compiling *Storied Poems*: "If someone does not manifest these instances, then who will comprehend their significance?"

What I translate as "manifest" 發揮 is a phrase with ancient and powerful connotations. It first appears in the *Classic of Changes*, in the "Commentary on the Words" 文言 for the first hexagram, *Qian* 乾: "The six individual lines open up and unfold the thought, so that the character of the whole is explained through its different sides" 六爻發揮 旁通情也.[34] In a more recent translation, reflecting Wang Bi's 王弼 (226–249) understanding of the *Classic of Changes*, Richard Lynn renders this passage as: "The six lines emanate their

_____

34. Wilhelm, *I Ching*, p. 378.

power and exhaustively explore all innate tendencies."[35] The dis-
crepancy between the translations as well as their general ambiguity
results from the nebulous language of the *Classic of Changes.* Kong
Yingda tries to elucidate the passage by saying, "*Fa* 發 means to
'diffuse,' and *hui* 揮 means to 'disperse.' It says that the six lines
diffuse and disperse, permeating the conditions of the entire uni-
verse" 發謂發越也。揮謂揮散也。言六爻發越揮散。旁通萬物之
情也.[36] Through a parallax view based on these different interpre-
tations we gain a sense that the core meaning of *fahui* involves an
uncovering and subsequent manifestation of inner power, a conver-
sion of the potential into the kinetic. This power, once unleashed,
naturally moves out and *into* the world.

Certainly by Meng Qi's time *fahui* might have meant nothing
more than "elucidate," but in using this precise term he opens the
door to a powerful analogy between the operation of the hexagrams
of the *Classic of Changes* and the way that the poems of *Storied Poems*
interact with the world. As the lines of a hexagram contain a power
that permeates the "conditions" 情 of the universe, so too do the
lines of a poem contain a power that penetrates the "feelings" 情 of
the hearts and minds of those who hear (or read) them. The
graphical coincidence of the character for "conditions" and "feel-
ings" strengthens this analogy. By selectively bringing to our atten-
tion instances of truly affective poems from a morass of texts, Meng
Qi claims to be unleashing the inherent power of a poem to affect
both the audience depicted in the anecdotes and the reader of those
depictions. His stated critical goal of uncovering the emotional
power of poetry mirrors the process of poetic production itself, in
which the feelings of the interior are uncovered. The passive voice
of Meng's supposition—literally, "if there is not a manifestation
then . . ." 不有發揮—implies that his goal will be accomplished
naturally once the texts are placed in a proper setting. Meng Qi
addresses what constitutes a "proper" setting later in his preface.

Meng rounds out his supposition with "who will comprehend
their significance?" His usage of the term "to comprehend signifi-

35. Lynn, *Classic of Changes*, pp. 130–31.
36. Ruan Yuan, *Shisan jing*, vol. 1, p. 17a.

cance" 明義 reinforces the apparent truth of what he is saying through its very connotations, derived from its earliest usage in the "Martial Success" 武成 section of the *Classic of Documents*:

He [King Wu of Zhou] showed the reality of his truthfulness, and proved clearly his righteousness. He honored virtue and rewarded merit. Then he had only to let his robes fall down and fold his hands, and the empire was orderly ruled.[37]

惇信明義。崇德報功。垂拱而天下治。

Here, Meng plays on the semantic range of classical Chinese. He replaces the factitive sense of *ming* 明, "to prove clear," with its putative sense, "to consider clear." The moral sense of *yi* 義, "righteousness," is diminished in favor of its epistemological sense of "significance," "principle," or "truth." In this last modulation he may again be influenced by the "Great Preface," which ascribes "six principles" of poetry 六義 to the *Classic of Poetry*. The implication is that Meng has discerned a truth about poetry, a principle of its operation that will become clear to us when a range of examples is collected in one place with narratives outlining their production and reception.

In these few opening lines of his preface, Meng Qi has not only sketched out a model of poetic production and reception, but also has stated his motives for compiling *Storied Poems*. An examination of individual entries will show how his pristine general principles fare in the face of gritty detail. The tension between his theory and the practice depicted in the texts proves particularly fruitful because Meng Qi did not compose the pieces himself and was thus unable to fashion them to suit his own agenda. He did exert influence over his texts as an editor in making his initial selections and subsequent emendations, but it was impossible for him to completely efface the inherent characteristics of his source materials. Nor would he have wanted to; a statement of general principles in a preface is not binding. The nature of *Storied Poems* results less from any theoretical agenda Meng Qi may have had than it does from his compositional methods and source materials: the subject that he takes up next in his preface.

---

37. Legge, *Shoo King*, p. 316.

因采爲本事詩。凡七題。猶四始也。情感。事感。
高逸。怨憤。徵異。徵咎。嘲戲。各以其類聚之。

So I have gathered them together in a book called *Storied
Poems*. In all there are seven headings akin to the Four
Beginnings [of the *Classic of Poetry*]: (1) Moved by Feelings,
(2) Moved by Events, (3) Highly Unconventional, (4) Re-
sentment and Frustration, (5) Signs of the Strange, (6) Signs
of Ill Omens, and (7) Mocking and Jesting. I have assembled
every one according to its category.

In his simple use of the word "gather" 采, Meng Qi speaks
volumes about his method of composition. The idea of gathering
works has very specific connotations derived from an early theory
of how the *Classic of Poetry* was compiled, quoted here from the
"Bibliographic Treatise" 藝文志 of the *Han History*:

In ancient times there were officials who gathered poems; through them
the rulers could observe the customs of their people and know their suc-
cesses and failures so that they might examine and rectify themselves.
古有采詩之官。王者所以觀風俗。知得失。自考正也。[38]

The mechanics of this are explained in the "Economic Treatise"
食貨志 of the same history:

During the first month of spring, when the common folk were about to
disperse [to work the fields], runners would circulate throughout the
roadways, sounding wooden clappers to gather poems. They would then
submit them to the Music Masters who would regularize the keys and have
them played for the emperor. Thus the saying, "The king does not even
peek out his doors or windows, yet he is aware of everything in the world."
孟春之月。群居者將散。行人振木鐸徇於路。以采詩。獻之大師。比其
音律。以聞於天子。故曰。王者。不窺牖戶而知天下。[39]

---

38. Ban, *Han shu, juan* 30, p. 1708.

The doctrine of "gathering poems" 采詩 from the people in order to inform the emperor of the quality of his rule had a profound influence on concepts of poetry in the Chinese tradition. It is fascinating to see how this doctrine plays out against Meng Qi's methods. Instead of runners circulating throughout the streets in search of *oral* compositions by the common people, Meng has traveled the pages of books in search of written texts by and about the official class of which he was a member. Instead of Music Masters regularizing the compositions and having them performed for the emperor, Meng has edited and categorized the texts for our reading pleasure. Thus, we are able to observe the "customs" of the literate class to which he belonged.

The ancient practice of culling texts is found in other prefaces of the Tang period. Fan Shu, in his colophon to *Friendly Debates at Misty Brook*, states that "the Sages selected from among the sayings of village elders; and Confucius collected the airs and ditties of the myriad states" 野老之言。聖人采擇。孔子聚萬國風謠, saying of his sources that "I have a great many old books, and, if we go by their accounts, surely they can shine with an aura of grandeur even if they may not approach the level of ancient classics" 攄昔籍眾多。因所聞記。雖未近於丘墳。豈可昭於雅量。[40] In his colophon to *Miscellaneous Records of Cloud-Dwelling Immortals* 雲仙雜記, Feng Zhi 馮贄 claims to have drawn upon his vast library of over two hundred thousand *juan* in order to "fashion a separate book from their essence [literally, 'fat and marrow']" 其膏髓別爲一書.[41] Though the practice of compiling a collection of excerpts from other books was not new to the Tang, it does seem to have become a popular pastime for the literate class of the period.

For Tang collectors, the orally transmitted anecdote attracted more attention than the written anecdote, as can be seen from the following quotations from prefaces:

---

39. Ban, *Han shu, juan* 24a, p. 1123. Yan Shigu 顏師古 (581–645) glosses the term "gathering poems" as "to gather poems of resentful criticism" 采取怨刺之詩也, another indication of the strong association between dissatisfaction and poetry.

40. Huang, *Zhongguo lidai xiaoshuo*, p. 141.

41. Huang, *Zhongguo lidai xiaoshuo*, p. 142.

Since I was a young child, I have heard many stories about the past. They are not strictly canonical works; so I append them to the end of the *xiaoshuo* classification.

余自髫丱之年。便多聞往説。不足備之大典。故系之小説末。[42]

Now, I have drawn in great detail upon the conversations I had both night and day during that time and recorded them all in no particular order, entitling the collection *A Record of Fine Conversations with His Honor Liu.* I pass it on to fellow enthusiasts as an aid in conversation.

今悉依當時日夕所話而錄之。不復編次。號曰劉公嘉話錄。傳之好事以爲談柄也。[43]

In his free time he would drift in his boat, passing along things he had heard and writing them down. And thus the collection is called *Hearsay Noted.*

暇日瀧舟傳其所聞而載之。故曰傳載。[44]

I remember when I was a young boy repeatedly hearing the high officials tell stories of our dynasty amongst themselves. Then they would all talk at length about the particularly extraordinary parts. I have taken the vestiges of these stories that must be true and compiled them into a small scroll in my free time, entitling it *Miscellaneous Records of Pine View Studio.*

浚憶童兒時。即歷聞公卿間敘國朝故事。次兼多語其事特異者。取其必實之跡。暇日輒成一小軸。題曰松窗雜錄。[45]

In his preface to *Collecting Mr. Liu's Stories of the Past* 次柳氏舊聞, Li Deyu gives a fascinating glimpse into the oral transmission of these sorts of stories.[46] He states that the stories regarding the reign of Xuanzong in his collection were told to him by his father, Li Jifu 李吉甫, who heard them from his friend, Liu Mien 柳冕, who heard them from his father, Liu Fang 柳芳, who got them firsthand from

---

42. Liu Su 劉餗 (fl. 728), preface to *Amusing Stories of the Sui and Tang* 隋唐嘉話, in Huang, *Zhongguo lidai xiaoshuo*, p. 93.

43. Wei Xuan 韋絢 (fl. 840), preface to *A Record of Fine Conversations with Adviser to the Heir Apparent Liu* 劉賓客嘉話錄, in Huang, *Zhongguo lidai xiaoshuo*, p. 129.

44. Preface to *Hearsay Noted from the Great Tang Dynasty* 大唐傳載, in Huang, *Zhongguo lidai xiaoshuo*, p. 132.

45. Li Jun 李濬, preface to *Miscellaneous Records of Pine View Studio* 松窗雜錄, in Huang, *Zhongguo lidai xiaoshuo*, p. 139.

46. Huang, *Zhongguo lidai xiaoshuo*, p. 115.

the eunuch favorite of Xuanzong himself, Gao Lishi 高力士—truly a case of hearing something from "a friend of a friend of a friend."

These prefaces consistently depict members of the official class telling stories to each other as a form of amusement in their free time, constituting an oral literature that has received scant scholarly attention due to its ephemeral nature. Coupled with this is the practice of writing these stories down at one's leisure as a form of amusement in itself. Wei Xuan's preface makes explicit the expectation that the conversations he records will become fodder for further conversation: "I pass it on to fellow enthusiasts as an aid in conversation." It soon becomes clear that it is a misguided task to attempt to draw a clear distinction between the orally transmitted anecdote and the textually transmitted anecdote, since any given story likely existed in both forms at some point in time.

What does this mean for Meng Qi and *Storied Poems*? There is only one entry (1.8) in which Meng explicitly states that he is recording an eyewitness account that was *told* to him. There are many entries that seem to be derived from textual sources; there are others for which provenance remains unclear. The background for all of these entries, however, is a rich complex of *casual* storytelling and recording. When Meng Qi came to compile his collection, he surely drew on his memory of stories both read and heard. The complexity of his sources is mirrored within the text of the anecdotes themselves, which contain poems written and sung, read and heard.

Meng Qi names his collection *Benshi shi* 本事詩. The term *benshi* 本事 literally means "based in events" in its verbal form and "originative events" in its nominal form. Thus the collection might be called *Poems Born of Events*, connoting that each poem included in the collection has some sort of background story, a series of events that led up to a particular instance of poetic production/performance and its subsequent reception/appreciation. These events are related in the form of a story, and because many of the poems in the collection are quite well known, it seemed appropriate to render the title as *Storied Poems* in English. There is an early usage of the term *benshi* in a discussion of the *Zuo Tradition* in the "Bibliographic Treatise" of the *Han History*:

The disciples [of Confucius] each withdrew and spoke [of their Master's words] differently. [Zuo] Qiuming feared that they would become complacent in their own understanding and lose sight of the truth. So he examined the originative events [behind the Master's words] and composed the *Tradition* in order to show clearly that the Master did not use groundless words in uttering the Classic [of *Springs and Autumns*].

弟子退而異言。丘明恐弟子各安其意。以失其眞。故論本事而作傳。明夫子不以空言説經也。[47]

This passage is a reference to the belief that Zuo Qiuming (or Zuoqiu Ming) wrote the *Zuo Tradition* as a supplement to the *Springs and Autumns* by Confucius, providing background stories in narrative form to fill out the laconic words of the chronicle. In addition to its emphasis on the truth, this early usage is also important because it identifies the term *benshi* with historical narrative, the form underlying the anecdotes of *Storied Poems*. It also sets up the relationship between a core text (a classic or a poem) and a supplementary text (a historical narrative or an anecdote) that may be used to elucidate and stabilize the interpretation of the core text, which is in danger of being misunderstood or misrepresented. In essence, the *benshi* or "originative events" convey the material context of an utterance to provide a privileged mode of interpreting and fixing the meaning of that utterance.

Meng Qi then goes on to explain the division of his collection into "seven headings akin to the Four Beginnings," returning to his metatext, the "Great Preface," which closes by defining the four sections of the *Classic of Poetry* ("Airs" 風, "Greater Odes" 大雅, "Lesser Odes" 小雅, "Hymns" 頌) and terms them "the Four Beginnings; they are the apex of the *Poems*" 是謂四始。詩之至也。[48]

This concept of the Four Beginnings has absolutely nothing to do with Meng Qi's "seven headings," which describe the circumstances that prompted poetic production, the deportment of the poet, the emotional quality of the poem, the conditions under which the poem was produced or received, the poem's function, and so on. Furthermore, his headings are devoid of the overarching moral or

---

47. Ban, *Han shu, juan* 30, p. 1715.
48. Ruan Yuan, *Shisan jing*, vol. 1, p. 272c.

political connotations attributed to the Four Beginnings. Meng Qi is simply trying to pull the mantle of tradition over his work by forging another link (albeit a tenuous one) with the canonical "Great Preface." One must look elsewhere to discern the provenance of his headings.

Storied Poems belongs to a lineage, stretching back to the Western Han, of works that may be called "anecdotal collections" 故事集, and which often have categorized contents. The exemplars of such collections are *New Narratives* 新序 and *Garden of Stories* 説苑, both compiled by the great classical scholar and bibliographer Liu Xiang 劉向 (ca. 77–6 B.C.E.). The first of these works corrals notable historical anecdotes from the pre-Qin and Han periods under the headings "Miscellaneous Incidents" 雜事, "Criticisms of Extravagance" 刺奢, "Men of Integrity" 節士, and "Excellent Strategies" 善謀. The second work collects similar material, and employs a more ambitious classificatory scheme:

Kingly Way 君道	Excellent Persuasions 善説
Courtier's Skill 臣術	Executing Orders 奉使
Laying Foundations 建本	Stratagems 權謀
Establishing Integrity 立節	Perfect Fairness 至公
Cherishing Virtue 貴德	Martial Guidance 指武
Repaying Kindness 復恩	Erudition 談叢
Principles of Rule 政理	Miscellany 雜言
Esteeming Worthies 尊賢	Analysis of Things 辨物
Remonstrance of Rule 政諫	Refining Statutes 修文
Respectful and Prudent 敬慎	Returning to Substance 反質

Judging from the headings and contents of these collections, Liu Xiang intended them to be repositories of exemplary behavior (of both the ruler and the ruled) to be used for the moral edification of the reader. His most famous work of this type is *Biographies of Virtuous Women* 列女傳, which contains the stories of exemplary women in history, divided into seven categories pertaining to womanly virtue, such as "Maternal Conduct" 母儀 and "Chastity" 貞順. Such textbooks of proper conduct satisfied the ruler's need for criteria to "evaluate the personality" 人物品評 of his subjects.

The disintegration of the Han dynasty and mass migrations to the "uncivilized" southlands in the early fourth century loosened the hold that Confucian mores had on elite society and wrought great changes in Chinese culture, which was not without implications for the tradition of the anecdotal collection. Liu Xiang's examples of staid behavior based on Confucian precepts of morality were joined by relatively outlandish examples of strange and spontaneous conduct among reclusive members of the elite who devoted themselves to the "natural" 自然 and engaged in abstruse causerie known as "pure talk" 清談. The anecdotal collection that incorporates examples of this "new" type of behavior is Liu Yiqing's *Topical Tales: A New Edition* (discussed in the previous chapter). Not only is the content of this collection less orthodox, but its purpose is as well. As Richard Mather, who has translated the work in its entirety, says, "It was partly an aid to conversation, and certainly one of its aims was to provide enjoyable reading."[49] Many aspects of *Topical Tales* help explain how a collection such as *Storied Poems* took shape, so I will digress here to examine its organization in more detail.

In similar fashion to Liu Xiang's anecdotal collections of centuries earlier, *Topical Tales* is divided into 36 categories, which have been translated by Mather as follows:

Virtuous Conduct 德行
Speech and Conversation 言語
Affairs of State 政事
Letters and Scholarship 文學
The Square and the Proper 方正
Cultivated Tolerance 雅量
Insight and Judgment 識鑒
Appreciation and Praise 賞譽
Classification Acc. to Excellence 品藻
Admonitions and Warnings 規箴
Quick Perception 捷悟
Precocious Intelligence 夙惠

Virile Vigor 豪爽
Appearance and Behavior 容止

Worthy Beauties 賢媛
Technical Understanding 術解
Skill and Art 巧藝
Favors and Gifts 寵禮
The Free and Unrestrained 任誕
Rudeness and Contempt 簡傲
Taunting and Teasing 排調
Contempt and Insults 輕詆
Guile and Chicanery 假譎

Dismissal from Office 黜免
Stinginess and Meanness 儉嗇
Extravagance and Ostentation 汰侈
Anger and Irascibility 忿狷
Slander and Treachery 讒險

---

49. Mather, *Tales of the World*, p. xiv.

Self-renewal 自新	Blameworthiness and Remorse 尤悔
Admiration and Emulation 企羨	Crudities and Slips of the Tongue 紕漏
Grieving for the Departed 傷逝	Blind Infatuations 惑溺
Living in Retirement 棲逸	Hostility and Alienation 仇隙

There is a marked swerve away from Liu Xiang of the Han and his sober-minded categories of behavior beneficial in government; instead, we confront a wide range of categories encompassing all sorts of personal interaction, and characterized by a strong verbal component. *Topical Tales* was the forerunner of the host of anecdotal collections in the Tang that claimed no other purpose for themselves than the simple joy of relating stories about people.

As was demonstrated in the previous chapter, the common thread running through many of the anecdotes in *Topical Tales* is the verbal manifestation of talent, whether in conversation, scholarship, or raillery. *Topical Tales* collects striking examples of this discourse across a broad range of circumstances. In doing so, it shows that poetic utterance had become a facet of daily interactions between members of a certain class of people. It also shows that instances of poetic production are objects worthy of collection, regardless of their motivations.

Other collections that may have influenced Meng Qi in his compilation of *Storied Poems* are Han Ying's *Supplementary Commentary on the Han School Poems* of the Han dynasty and Wu Jing's 吳兢 (670–749) *Explanations of Ancient Topics in* Yuefu *Poetry* 樂府 古題要解 of the early Tang. The former collection demonstrates how to cite the *Poems* effectively during argumentation, recounting anecdotes in which various interlocutors freely adapt lines from the *Poems* to drive home their points. It treats the *Poems* as received texts and does not concern itself with explanations of their origin, and is innovative in showing that the *Poems* could be cited in humorous or frivolous situations in addition to the more solemn occasions prevalent in works such as the *Zuo Tradition*. Wu Jing's *Explanations* does concern itself with the origins and subsequent development of *yuefu* topics from Han and Wei times, but it does so in an expository rather than a narrative format, often providing nothing more than a list of attributions for a particular *yuefu* passage. Meng Qi's innovation in shaping the content and form of *Storied Poems* was to produce the earliest surviving collection that exclusively records narratives about poetic production and reception. *Storied Poems* is often cited as a precursor to the *shihua* 詩話 ("remarks on poetry") genre that became so popular in the Song dynasty, and, while those later collections often collected more expository or descriptive remarks on poetry rather than narratives depicting its practice, some measure of the credit is due to Meng Qi.

While *Storied Poems* may be indebted to *Topical Tales* and other anecdotal collections for its categorical scheme, the actual headings themselves seem to be derived from elsewhere. The headings used by Liu Xiang and Liu Yiqing focus on the conduct of the people portrayed in their collections, while Meng's headings focus on the nature of poetic utterance. The contents of each section can be summarized as follows:

Moved by Feelings 情感	Affective poems (in production *and* reception)
Moved by Events 事感	Poems to mark an event
Highly Unconventional 高逸	Eccentric poets Li Bai and Du Mu
Resentment and Frustration 怨憤	Expressions of dissatisfaction
Signs of the Strange 徵異	Poems of supernatural origin
Signs of Ill Omens 徵咎	Poems portending the author's death
Mocking and Jesting 嘲戲	Mockery and banter with and about poetry

The first two headings are reminiscent of phrases that often appear in the titles of poems and poem cycles: phrases such as "expressing my heart" 詠懷, "moved by encounters" 感遇, "moved by events" 事感. The third heading covers behavior similar to that of the eccentrics in *Topical Tales*. The fourth heading is derived from the doctrine of resentment in poetry that I discussed above. The last heading is reflected in the "Taunting and Teasing" heading of *Topical Tales*, but the terms "mocking" 嘲 and "jesting" 戲 also appear in titles of Tang poems. The sixth and seventh headings are derived remotely from astrological terminology and more immediately from the types of narratives that Meng used as source material.

With the possible exception of the "Highly Unconventional" category, *Storied Poems* is less concerned with the individuals who utter poetry than with the poems themselves. By contrast, the much larger *Recorded Stories of Tang Poetry* 唐詩紀事, compiled in the Song by Ji Yougong 計有功 (*jinshi* 1121), organizes its material (which overlaps somewhat with *Storied Poems*) by individual poet. Meng Qi's emphasis on types of poetry may help explain why his collection was ultimately classified as a work of literary criticism. His poetic types are not predicated solely on content, but are often a function of the circumstances of production and reception of a given poem. How he conveys those circumstances is the point he takes up next.

亦有獨掇其要。不全篇者。咸爲
小序以引之。貽諸好事。

In some cases, I have just selected the important part and not the whole poem. For each one I have fashioned a "Lesser Preface" to introduce it. I offer them to all fellow enthusiasts.

Until this point in his preface, Meng Qi has been dealing exclusively with the topic of poetry: what it is, how it comes about, which poems are worthy of notice, and how he has gathered and categorized them. Now he returns to his methods of composition to inform us of two important points. First, in some cases, he quotes only a few lines from a given poem. Second, he provides an introduction for each selection. Taken together, these two points provide great insight into the nature of *Storied Poems* as a collection.

In saying that he often "selected the important part and not the whole poem," Meng Qi signals to us that his primary purpose was not to compile an anthology of poems in their entirety. Nor was it simply to amass a collection of striking poem fragments—a practice known as "plucking lines" 摘句. His use of the term "important" 要 suggests that he is after something else. Han Yu 韓愈 (768–824), in his essay entitled *An Explication of Advancing in Studies* 進學解, states, "Those who would record events must bring out what is important in them, while those who would collect words must draw out what is profound in them" 記事者必提其要。纂言者必鉤其玄.[50] If we compare this maxim with Meng's stated goal of "manifesting" instances of "being moved to chant a poem by encountering events," then what he considers "important" becomes clear: it is how the poem (or a portion of the poem) relates to the circumstances that surround it. In order to manifest this importance, he must provide us with a narration of the events.

In claiming, "For each one [poem] I have fashioned a 'Lesser Preface' to introduce it," Meng Qi is likely just being modest in denigrating his own compositions with the adjective "lesser," but the label itself—regardless of Meng Qi's intentions in using it—returns us to the region of canon. The "Lesser Prefaces" provided the orthodox interpretation of each entry in the *Classic of Poetry* for two millennia, although they did meet with a healthy amount of skepticism, especially from Zhu Xi 朱熹 (1130–1200) in the Song. The role of the "Lesser Prefaces" as miniature narratives purporting to give the "originative events" behind the poems of the *Classic of Poetry* must be understood, for they cast a very large shadow over Meng Qi's own work.

First, consider an example of a "Lesser Preface." Following is the first stanza of "I pray you, Zhongzi" 將仲子:

> I pray you, Zhongzi,
> do not leap into my hamlet;
> do not break our planted willows;
> it is not that I dare regret them,
> but I fear my father and mother;
> you, Zhong, are worth loving,
> but the words of father and mother
> are also worth fearing.[51]

A "naïve" reading of this poem would see it as a love song, gently (and perhaps disingenuously) admonishing a lover not to attempt a

---

50. Han Yu, *Han Changli wenji*, p. 26.
51. Mao #76. After Karlgren, *Book of Odes*, p. 51.

clandestine visit for fear of discovery. Here is the "Lesser Preface" for this piece, which interprets it as a critique of the Zheng ruler, Duke Zhuang (r. 743–701 B.C.E.):

"Jiang Zhongzi" is a criticism of Duke Zhuang.

He was unable to control his mother and so caused harm to his younger brother. His younger brother strayed from the right path, but the duke did not constrain him. Zhai Zhong remonstrated, but the duke would not listen to him. Thus, he brought about a great calamity because he would not suppress it when it was still insignificant.

將仲子。刺莊公也。不勝其母以害其弟。弟叔失道。而公弗制。祭仲諫。而公弗聽。小不忍以致大亂焉。[52]

This preface refers to a famous story recounted in the entry for Duke Yin 1st Year in the *Zuo Tradition*. Zhai Zhong is a minister who advised Duke Zhuang of Zheng to act quickly against his upstart younger brother, who was relying on his mother's favoritism to make gradual incursions on the duke's sovereignty. Because of his dilatoriness, the duke was ultimately forced to suppress his brother through military means and drive him out of the state.

The only textual link between this story and the poem is the coincidence of the name "Zhong" 仲, a very common name that simply means "second-born." In order to reconcile the poem with the story, the *Commentary on the Mao Poems* goes through some exegetical acrobatics in asking the reader to take this poem as Duke Zhuang's misguided rebuttal to Zhai Zhong's remonstrance.[53] The plea not to enter the homestead and harm the willow is interpreted as the duke's request that Zhai Zhong not counsel action against his younger brother. It is not that the duke is particularly fond of his brother, but he fears what his mother might say, and so, even though he cherishes Zhai Zhong's counsel, he cannot bring himself to follow it. The "Lesser Preface" is a somewhat distorted version of the account in the *Zuo Tradition*, where the duke refuses to act not out of fear of his mother (whom he actually ends up imprisoning!),

---

52. Ruan Yuan, *Shisan jing*, vol. 1, p. 337a.
53. The "Lesser Preface" claims that the poem "criticizes Duke Zhuang" because, as the text of the duke's refusal to listen to wise counsel, it functions as a minatory example.

but because he believes that his brother will bring about his own downfall through his rash actions. A portion of Zhai Zhong's admonition in the *Zuo Tradition*, in which he advises the duke that "it is best to deal with this matter early on" 不如早為之, is echoed in the closing lines of the "Lesser Preface." It is probable that the compiler(s) of the "Lesser Prefaces" selectively drew upon the narratives of the *Zuo Tradition* (or a source common to both) to provide background stories for many pieces in the *Classic of Poetry* and used the *Commentary on the Mao Poems* to explicitly link the poem and story when their mutual relevance was not obvious.[54]

What is the motivation for the frequently improbable interpretations of the "Lesser Prefaces," and how did they become not only tenable, but entrenched in the tradition? Confucius proclaimed the moral perfection of the *Poems* (*Analects* 2.2), and Mencius expounded the importance of providing a historical context for them in order to better understand them (*Mencius* 5B.8; 5A.4). The Traditionalists of the Han dynasty sought to consolidate the Confucian tradition as transmitted by these two exemplars; the "Lesser Prefaces" help achieve this goal in several ways. They demonstrate the moral perfection of the *Poems* by casting them as instruments praising normative behavior and censuring deviancy. By historically contextualizing the poems, the "Lesser Prefaces" not only bring them in line with Mencius's hermeneutics, they also demonstrate that the Confucian values purportedly embodied in the *Poems* are immanent in the world itself. As Haun Saussy puts it, "the tradition reads the *Odes* as the description of a possible ethical world. It reads them in the performative mode, as narrating, in the form of history, the model actions that its own reading must second in order to make them actual."[55] This is reinforced because, as Pauline Yu asserts, "not only are individual poems read as historically referential, but entire groups of songs are interpreted as miniature chronicles of the states from which they were said to originate."[56] Finally, by drawing on canonical texts—such as the *Zuo Tradition*—the "Lesser

---

54. See Zhu Guanhua's article on this link: *Fengshi xu yu Zuo zhuan*.
55. Saussy, *Chinese Aesthetic*, p. 105.
56. Yu, *Reading of Imagery*, p. 70.

Prefaces" weave the *Poems* into the larger Confucian canon of classics that complement one another in embodying all that is exemplary in human action, experience, and thought.

The "Lesser Prefaces," in the words of Van Zoeren, ultimately "constructed for the Odes a kind of mythology in which each Ode found a place in the sweep of early Chinese history."[57] In so doing, they realize the maxims of the "Great Preface" by depicting the circumstances under which each poem could be viewed as a manifestation of the author's state of mind, occasioned by an outburst of emotion (usually frustration), and intended to influence and/or admonish. They also betray a deep anxiety that the poem is not sufficient in itself to be completely understood. Narrative must be called upon to show the reader that the poem is doing exactly what it is *supposed* to do. The irony—obvious yet inescapable—is that the narrative subverts its own purpose by virtue of its necessity.

Having unpacked some of the connotations carried by the term "Lesser Preface," it remains to be seen how many of them Meng Qi will pick up in his own renditions. In his preface he claims to make many of the same "moves" made by his canonical precursors, but with his own twists: the narrative anecdotes of *Storied Poems* are meant to provide a context that will manifest the "significance" of the poems, but this significance has shifted from ethical concerns to affective ones; the anecdotes are drawn from other source material, but the sources are no longer canonical (as Meng acknowledges in his preface). There has also been a shift in the scope of the narratives; the "mythology" or "miniature chronicles" constructed by the "Lesser Prefaces" have given way to a quotidian depiction of life among the official classes. Finally, there is a significant departure in terms of composition. In the *Classic of Poetry*, the accompanying "Lesser Prefaces" are juxtaposed with the poems but not integrated with them—they never depict the act of poetic utterance within the framework of their narratives, but comment on it after the fact. The anecdotes of *Storied Poems*, however, invariably depict the utterance of the poem and any response it might receive within the narrative, which provides a means of ascertaining how far depictions of poetic

---

57. Van Zoeren, *Poetry and Personality*, p. 95.

practice deviate from the canonical precepts cited by Meng Qi in his preface.

After telling us of his marriage of poems to narratives, Meng Qi states, "I offer them to all fellow enthusiasts." This is an indication of the type of audience Meng expected to reach as well as of his motivations for compiling his collection. His use of the term "fellow enthusiasts" 好事 is illuminated by a passage in the *Han History* about the famous man of letters, Yang Xiong 揚雄 (53 B.C.E.-18 C.E.), who had retired on account of illness: "His home was unadorned and frugal; he was fond of wine, but people rarely arrived at his gate. Occasionally, a fellow enthusiast would bring along some wine and tidbits to follow him in their studies" 家素貧。耆酒。人希至其門。時有好事者載酒肴從游學.[58] The connotation is one of mutual enjoyment of a pleasurable pastime rather than a serious pursuit.

The phrase crops up in other prefaces of the Tang. We might recall Wei Xun's statement regarding his collection: "I pass it on to fellow enthusiasts as an aid in conversation." Zheng Qi 鄭棨 (d. 899), in his preface to *A Record of Credible Accounts Transmitted from the Kaiyuan and Tianbao Eras* 開天傳信記, asks that "fellow enthusiasts will contemplate my intent, forgive my foolishness, and affirm my heart" 好事者觀其志。寬其愚。是其心也.[59] Meng's use of the phrase indicates that, with *Storied Poems*, he is engaging in a widespread pastime among the official class: compilation of a collection of somewhat unorthodox texts for no other reason than the enjoyment of doing so and the pleasure it might bring others of a like mind.

其有出諸異傳怪錄。疑非是實者。
則略之。拙俗鄙俚。亦所不取。

In the passages drawn from strange tales and bizarre records
I have omitted anything of doubtful veracity. I also did not
include anything of a rude or vulgar nature.

---

58. Ban, *Han shu*, vol. 11, p. 3585.
59. Huang, *Zhongguo lidai xiaoshuo*, p. 140.

The tone of the preface's preceding line, with its offer to "fellow enthusiasts," seems to bring the preface to a close, creating the impression that this final passage was tacked on almost as an afterthought. It proves to be a highly revealing afterthought. This is the only place where Meng Qi addresses the nature of his source material. Aside from general collections, the collected works of individuals, and miscellaneous histories and biographies, he also drew upon materials classified as *xiaoshuo* in the bibliographies of orthodox histories. When Meng says that he made use of "strange tales and bizarre records" 異傳怪錄, he is referring to a broad range of unorthodox *xiaoshuo* narratives now known as "bizarre accounts" 志怪 (literally, "describing the bizarre," a term often paired with "accounts of people" 志人) and "fantastic tales" 傳奇 (literally, "transmitting the fantastic"). These labels were originally titles of collections and did not constitute generic designations until after the Tang. These generic distinctions are not hard and fast. Something as mundane as a particularly witty bon mot might be the subject of a "bizarre account," and strange happenings often found their way into narratives classified as history. The term "bizarre accounts" is now used to retroactively encompass a large corpus of short narratives that took shape from the fall of the Han onward, while "fantastic tales" refers to a longer narrative form that reached maturity in the Tang and borrows many structural features from historical biography.[60]

The earliest clear-cut distinction between "accounts of the bizarre" and "fantastic tales" was made by Hu Yinglin 胡應麟 (1551–1602), in his *Collected Notes from the "Humble Abode" Mountain Retreat* 少室山房筆叢:

Stories about strange phenomena flourished in the Six Dynasties, but they were mostly due to the faulty transmission of records and were not necessarily complete fabrications. It was not until the Tang that people began to consciously pursue the fantastic and write their compositions in the *xiaoshuo* mode.

---

60. See DeWoskin, "Six Dynasties *Chih-kuai*"; Yim, "Tang *Ch'uan-chi*"; Campany, *Strange Writing*; Hou, *Zhongguo wenyan xiaoshuo*.

凡變異之談。盛於六朝。然多是傳錄舛訛。未必盡幻設語。至唐
人乃作意好奇。假小說以寄筆端。[61]

Hu bases his distinction on authorial intent: did the author intend to fictionalize or is a lack of veracity due to faulty source materials? Authorial intent is often unreliable and always difficult to ascertain, making it a poor criterion for distinguishing genres. It makes more sense to place the "accounts" and the "tales" on the same spectrum and move from one to the other in terms of increasing sophistication in narrative techniques.[62] The importance of Hu Yinglin's statement lies in the common element of untruth shared by both types of narrative.

Faced with an ever-increasing number of stories in the Tang (a situation captured in Meng Qi's image of overflowing bookshelves),[63] the possibility that some stories might not be true was of great concern to compilers. Meng betrays this insecurity when he claims, "I have omitted anything of doubtful veracity," a statement that triggers some suspicion due to the very fact that he felt he had to make it. He was not alone in his suspicions regarding his source material:

---

61. Hu, *Shaoshi shanfang, juan* 20, p. 20b.

62. This is what Hu Yinglin seems to be driving at elsewhere in his work when he says, "As for bizarre accounts and fantastic tales, they are particularly prone to interpenetration. Sometimes both kinds of story will be included in a single book. Even within a single story, both types of narrative can coexist. [In these cases,] one should just simply pick out which type is prominent" 至于志怪傳奇。尤易出入。或一書之中。二事並載。一事之内。兩端具存。姑舉且重而已 (*juan* 13, p. 7a).

63. Liu Su, in his "General Discussion on *A New Account of the Great Tang*" 大唐新語總論, writes: "Between the Zhenguan and Kaiyuan eras [627–741] was a flourishing age of composition, indeed more glorious then preceding ages" 貞觀。開元述作爲盛。蓋光於前代矣 (Huang, *Zhongguo lidai xiaoshuo*, p. 106). Gao Yanxiu 高彦休, in his preface to *Incomplete Histories* 闕史, says, "And so from the time of the Wude and Zhenguan eras [618–649] onward there was an ever increasing number of people taking up brushes to write *xiaoshuo*, minor records, popular histories, private histories, miscellaneous records, and miscellaneous accounts" 故自武德。貞觀而後。咣筆爲小説。小錄。稗史。野史。雜錄。雜紀者多矣 (Huang, *Zhongguo lidai xiaoshuo*, p. 135).

In my opinion, stories of our dynasty were never more numerous than in the Kaiyuan and Tianbao eras [713–756] . . . occasionally they have lacunae in them.

竊以國朝故事。莫盛於開元。天寶之際 . . . 或有闕焉。[64]

He witnessed it all firsthand and it is not derived from hearsay; it is credible and proved by evidence, so it may constitute a "veritable record."

彼皆目睹。非出傳聞。信而有徵。可爲實錄。[65]

The *Gongyang Commentary* says, "Words may differ in recording what was seen, they may differ in recording what was heard." Every illustrative anecdote is filled out using things seen and heard.

公羊傳曰。所見異辭。所聞異辭。未有不因見聞而備故實者。[66]

I have taken the vestiges of these stories that must be true and compiled them into a small scroll in my free time, entitling it *Miscellaneous Records of Pine View Studio.*

取其必實之跡。暇日輒成一小軸。題曰松窗雜錄。[67]

The possibility of factual error produces an acute anxiety that lurks in Meng Qi's prefaces, because he admittedly makes use of *xiaoshuo* source materials known to be inherently unreliable. Certainly there are many entries in *Storied Poems* that may strain the credence of the modern reader (especially in the sections devoted to strange occurrences), but that is not really the issue here. Standards of verisimilitude change with culture, time, audience, and a host of other factors. What is significant is Meng Qi's impulse to purify his anecdotes and rid them of untruths (however he may have measured them).

Meng must keep the anecdotes pure in order to maintain the integrity of the poems. A poem, by his definition, results when "feelings stirred within take on outward form in spoken words."

---

64. Zheng Qi, preface to *Credible Accounts Transmitted from the Kaiyuan and Tianbao Eras*, in Huang, *Zhongguo lidai xiaoshuo*, p. 140.

65. Li Deyu, preface to *Collecting Mr. Liu's Stories of the Past* 次柳氏舊聞, in Huang, *Zhongguo lidai xiaoshuo*, p. 115.

66. Li Zhao 李肇, *A Supplement to the History of the Tang Dynasty* 唐國史補, in Huang, *Zhongguo lidai xiaoshuo*, p. 112.

67. Li Jun, *Miscellaneous Records of Pine View Studio*, in Huang, *Zhongguo lidai xiaoshuo*, p. 139.

Thus, sincerity is the essence of a poem, for while one may make a false display of feelings, "feelings stirred" by external stimuli can never be false. If we are to fully appreciate the expressive power of the poem—that which "gave rise to the intoning" 興詠—then we must be privy to its impetus, whatever "situation was encountered" 觸事. We must know what stirred the feelings, or there is a danger that we may misinterpret the outward signs of the interior.

An awareness of this danger is inscribed in the *Classic of Poetry* itself:

> That glutinous millet hanging down;
> oh, the sprouts of that panicled millet!
> I am walking slowly,
> in the core of my heart I am shaken;
> those who know me
> say that my heart is grieved,
> those who do not know me
> ask what I am seeking;
> oh, you distant blue Heaven,
> what kind of man is he?[68]

The bowed figure in the poem is strolling across the overgrown ruins of the old Zhou capital, pondering the tragedy of its demise in the hands of ineffectual rulers. If we are not aware of this story, told to us by the "Lesser Preface," then the emotional impact of the poem is lost, just as the uninformed observer might mistake the poignant image of a man bowed under the weight of his cares for something as mundane as a man searching for a lost object. The story is necessary to let us become one of "those who know me" 知我者.

The poetic practice depicted in the entries of *Storied Poems* is always more complicated than the theoretical statements made by Meng Qi in his preface. His insistence on maintaining the integrity of the background story is an attempt to portray the poem as the genuine result of a simple process—that of external events impinging on the interior, leading to an external verbal manifestation. He does not openly acknowledge that a rupture may occur between the emotion and the expression, a rupture into which the individual

---

68. Mao #65. After Karlgren, *Book of Odes*, p. 45.

will insert himself in order to manipulate the form and deployment of his expression with poetic competence. The person who utters poetry is not simply a passive conduit transforming the world into words; the transformation is shaped by motivations and expectations. The entries of *Storied Poems*, verbal constructs in themselves, are a fascinating hybrid between theory and practice, often attempting to manifest the former, but always attached to the latter.

Meng Qi's concern for purity turns from truth to morality when he states, "I also did not include anything of a rude or vulgar nature." The very fact that there would be anything rude or vulgar to exclude says something about his source material: it is certainly less than canonical. His puritanical streak can be traced back to a statement attributed to Confucius regarding the *Classic of Poetry*: "There are three hundred *Poems*, but one phrase may be used to cover them all: 'No evil in their thoughts'" 詩三百。一言以蔽之。曰。思無邪 (*Analects* 2.2). "No evil in their thoughts" is a word-for-word translation of the phrase *si wu xie* 思無邪, which is from one of the *Poems* (Mao #297), referring to the ability of fine horses to stay on the right path—"Oh, without swerving"[69]—a figure which came to stand for moral rectitude. Whether Confucius was exploiting the phrase's word-for-word meaning or its figural significance (or, most likely, punning on both meanings), the intent is clear. Meng Qi's attempt to purify his texts of "evil thoughts" is yet another example of the ongoing tension present in his preface. His sources are noncanonical materials, yet he tries to deal with them according to canonical precepts.

聞見非博。事多闕漏。訪於通識。期復續之。

My learning is not wide-ranging and my stories have many lacunae, so I extend an invitation to those with more comprehensive knowledge in the hopes that they will continue with them.

---

69. In the poem, the character *sai* 思 is simply an expletive and does not denote "thoughts" (*si*).

The self-deprecating statement in closure is a ubiquitous feature of prefaces. When Meng Qi refers to his learning (literally, what he has "seen and heard" 聞見) as not being "wide-ranging" 博, he employs a term with an informative history. It appears in the context of learning early on, in a statement attributed to Confucius: "Wide-ranging study and a steadfast will, sincere inquisitiveness and self-reflection: humaneness resides in these" 博學而篤志。切問而近思。仁在其中矣 (*Analects* 19.6). Since " humaneness" 仁 was a basic Confucian virtue, this placed great importance on wide-ranging study. Yet Confucius also placed tacit restrictions on what topics were worthy of inquiry: "The master never spoke of bizarre phenomena, use of force, violence, or spirits" 子不語怪。力。亂。神 (*Analects* 7.20). The period of disunion that followed the Han dynasty, however, saw the rise of the "bizarre accounts" that focused exclusively on these forbidden topics. It was during this time that the connotation of the term "wide-ranging study" shifted and began to indicate topics of inquiry *beyond* the canon.[70] This connotation persisted into the Tang, when we find no fewer than six prefaces using the term "wide-ranging" to justify the collection of noncanonical materials.[71] Meng Qi suggests that his knowledge is more traditional than that of the specialists who collect anecdotes.

Meng moves from a discussion of his own deficiencies to those of his stories, extending an invitation to those "with more comprehensive knowledge" than he to fill in their lacunae. The phrase "comprehensive knowledge" 通識 is similar to "wide-ranging study" in its scope and literary connotations. It is applied to Chen Qi 陳奇 in his biography in the *Wei History* 魏書: "Gao Yun, who collated and reviewed old books with Qi, delighted in his quick intellect and acclaimed his comprehensive knowledge, which was not restricted to the scope of ordinary studies" 高允與奇讎溫古籍。嘉奇遠致。稱奇通識。非凡學所窺.[72] This passage also serves as an illuminating

---

70. Zhang Hua's 張華 (232–300) seminal collection of "bizarre accounts," entitled *An Account of Wide-Ranging Things* 博物志, is a representative example of this phenomenon.

71. See Huang, *Zhongguo lidai xiaoshuo*, pp. 94, 106, 115, 132, 134, 138.

72. Wei, *Wei Shu*, vol. 4, *juan* 84, p. 1847.

example of how the pastime of going over old texts might be shared between friends.

In calling on those with more extensive knowledge to come to his aid in compiling his collection, Meng Qi makes an unusual suggestion in asking "that they will continue it." The customary request in such situations is that readers will forgive any errors, or perhaps bring them to the author's attention, not to carry on the work itself. Meng apparently considered his collection a work-in-progress in which all "fellow enthusiasts" could freely partake. The heterogeneous nature of *Storied Poems* suggests that it is highly likely more than one reader took him up on his offer. One even went so far as to compile a sequel called *More Storied Poems* 續本事詩.[73] *Storied Poems* is best characterized as a fluid work, an ongoing project of collection initiated by one man but open to all. Meng Qi's generous offer may aggravate the scholar who longs for a stable text, but its spirit of inclusion is a fascinating extension of the physical community of the literati of his time into the virtual community of all readers to follow.

時光啓二年十一月。大駕在襃中。前尚書
司勳郎中賜紫金魚袋孟棨序。

Dated this eleventh month of the second year of the Guangqi reign [886] while the imperial chariot is in Baozhong. Signed, the former Director of the Bureau of Merit Titles in the Department of State Affairs, recipient of permission to wear purple and to carry a gold insignia pouch, Meng Qi.

Even Meng Qi's mandatory citation of the date and his official title in closing hold some insight into his collection, particularly his circumstances when he compiled it. He mentions the seemingly irrelevant fact that "the imperial chariot is in Baozhong." From the

---

73. This is a partially preserved Five Dynasties (907–960) work in seven sections, signed by the "Master of Dwelling in Constancy" 處常子.

date, we know that this was a time of great chaos during the twilight
years of a once glorious dynasty. Meng wrote this preface shortly
after Emperor Xizong, in the face of rebel forces, fled the capital
region a second time under the influence of the powerful eunuch
Tian Lingzi 田令孜. Tian took the emperor across the treacherous
Qinling mountain range into Baocheng (also called Baozhong), in
the southwest corner of modern-day Shanxi. All of the officials had
deserted the capital as well, leaving it to be plundered by the rebel
armies. By mentioning the location of the emperor, Meng is indi-
rectly referring to this state of affairs and indicating that the em-
peror is in his thoughts. We might surmise that the emperor looked
upon Meng Qi with some favor since he was the "recipient of a
purple and gold insignia pouch" normally reserved for officials of
higher rank than his.

By using the qualifier "former" 前 in citing his official title, Meng
Qi lets us know that he too has left his post and fled the capital re-
gion. To withdraw from service in times of chaos is a traditional
response (that Meng probably had no choice in the matter is beside
the point). And the traditional activity to undertake when in re-
clusion is the study of books. In his colophon to *Miscellaneous Rec-
ords of Cloud-Dwelling Immortals*, Feng Zhi describes the circum-
stances under which he compiled his collection: "In the first year of
the Tianyou era [904], I retired to my home village and built myself
a 'book compiling' studio where I might dwell in seclusion and
draw upon my ancient works to fashion a separate book from their
essence" 天祐元年。退歸故里。築選書室以自居。取典籍其膏髓
別爲一書.[74]

With the dynasty crumbling around him and his own future
uncertain, Meng Qi also retreats into his books in search of moving
poetry. Perhaps he felt a sense of control in gathering and arranging
these texts when it was beyond his power to affect larger issues. In
this preface, he certainly attempts to shape our reading of his
specimens. Ultimately, however, these too slip out of his grasp in
most interesting fashion, as the practice of poetic competence asserts
itself in each miniature narrative.

----

74. Huang, *Zhongguo lidai xiaoshuo*, p. 142.

CR FIVE SO

Placing the Poem

I

Poetic competence was highly prized during Tang times as a means of advancement in political, social, and even romantic affairs. A survey of the titles of the thousands of poems included in the *Complete Tang Poems* 全唐詩 suggests that the production of poetry penetrated every facet of the elite lifestyle in Tang China. This catholicity of poetry is well represented in *Storied Poems*, in which poetic practice occurs in three main overlapping arenas: (1) politics, (2) literature, and (3) love. These arenas are defined by physical location, the status of the participants, and the nature of the relationships negotiated there. Elements of each arena can be found in the others, but one is clearly dominant in each anecdote.

The arena of politics comprises locations such as the imperial court, government offices, military grounds, and other official locations. The participants are invariably in a superior-inferior relationship carefully prescribed by an explicit hierarchy. In all cases, the inferior is trying to obtain something from the superior through his or her poetizing—perhaps a monetary reward, advancement in position, or rectification of an injustice. This is the most ancient and enduring form of demonstrating poetic competence, which can be clearly discerned in texts as early as the *Zuo Tradition*. Its prominent position in the Tang should come as no surprise. However, such competence finds fertile ground in areas of social interaction that cannot be defined as strictly political.

The arena of literature distinguishes itself from those of love and politics in that the advantage sought through poetic competence is nothing more than recognition of that very competence. It overlaps with the political arena as inferiors at court often seek recognition of their literary talents from superiors, but in the literary arena they do so purely for enhancement of their literary reputation rather than for the "political" reasons enumerated above. The line between politics and literature at court is fuzzy at best and will gain some measure of definition in the close readings of particular anecdotes to follow. More often, the literary arena is found away from court, wherever members of the elite class meet to enjoy each other's company—at home, at taverns, at temples, at inns—usually over drinks and food. The status of the participants in these situations is usually that of peers on a roughly equal footing. The relationships in these cases are more about mutual admiration, raillery, or simple camaraderie than any calculated pursuit of gain. This sort of poetic competence is already familiar from its repeated demonstration in *Topical Tales*.

The arena of love—or, more precisely, sexual love—is perhaps the most variable in terms of the location and status of the participants, but it does consistently involve poetic exchanges taking place predominantly between men *and* women. Another constant is the presence of a superior political figure—often the emperor, a high official, or a military man—who directly or indirectly causes the separation of the lovers, giving rise to the emotions that they express through poems. What is at stake for the man in each of these anecdotes is possession of the woman, whether bodily or in the form of a clear claim to the loyalty of her heart. What is at stake for the woman is her choice to pledge that loyalty to whomever she pleases. Poetic competence serves to preserve the romantic ideal that true love is chosen freely. The arena of love, as it is portrayed in *Storied Poems*, is the site where these two Tang cultures of poetry and romance converge, producing a richly textured, affective style

of narrative. This style of narrative, and the type of poetic compe-
tence depicted therein, reached its fruition during the Tang and will
receive extended treatment at the end of this chapter.

By most accounts in *Storied Poems*, the reception of poetry is not
a passive affair. Twenty-five of the forty-one entries depict poetry
leading to a definite change in the situation of the protagonist. In
fifteen cases these changes are positive; the remaining ten are de-
cidedly negative. For each positive outcome, the change for the
better stems from an authority figure's sympathetic reception of a
poem; the negative outcomes are a result of a hostile response or a
lack of response altogether.

In order to effect change through transmission, the poems cited in
these anecdotes are often written down. There are thirty instances in
which the narrative depicts a poem as inscribed in writing at the
moment of composition. The objectification of the poem in written
form allows it to become a "prop" in the story, making many of the
narrated events possible. There is a recurring pattern in which a
poem composed in private circumstances is subsequently disclosed
and gravitates toward the center of authority; such a pattern is con-
tingent upon a poem's transmissible form in writing. So too is its
ability to traverse boundaries of space, time, and even planes of ex-
istence, which is demonstrated by numerous anecdotes in the col-
lection. *Storied Poems* deals very much in a world where the written
word has power. The deferral of performance into a text that can be
reactivated in a subsequent performance or reading allows poetry to
do things. If a poem is to do anything at all, however, it must be
handled with competence in its production, performance, and re-
ception, whether it be in the arena of love, literature, or politics.

II

As was the case with the pre-Qin, Han, and Six Dynasties, the court
continues to be an important site of poetic production, reception,
and evaluation in the Tang. It is certainly not the only site, but
the court does form the center of a vast web of poetic discourse
that stretches across the empire. Poems that are produced in the
capital, the provinces, and even on the frontier or in barbarian lands
have an uncanny ability to make their way back to the center oc-

cupied by the emperor and other members of the royal family. Members of royalty continue in their role as the center of discourse, judging the poetic competence of others and occasionally being the objects of judgments expressed through poetry. Such judgments are an important element in gaining, maintaining, and losing status at court.

The court under the reign of Emperor Taizong 太宗 (627–649) is the earliest Tang court depicted in *Storied Poems*. In the following anecdote, Zhangsun Wuji 張孫無忌 (d. 659), the emperor's most powerful and trusted advisor, mocks the physical appearance of Ouyang Xun 歐陽詢 (557–641), an academician in the Institute of the Advancement for Learning and compiler of the imperially sponsored anthology, *A Categorized Collection of Literary Works* 藝文類聚.[1]

Near the beginning of this dynasty, Defender-in-Chief Zhangsun Wuji granted an audience to the Director of the Watches, Ouyang Xun, who was of a stumpy, homely appearance.[2] Wuji mocked him by saying,

> His shoulders hunch up into a mountain graph 山,[3]
> He buries his head between them, afraid to poke it out.
> Who would claim that in Qilin Hall[4]
> They would paint a portrait of this macaque?

---

1. I have based the following translations on the edition of *Storied Poems* found in *Gushi wenfang xiaoshuo* 顧氏文房小說 (hereafter *Gushi*) compiled by Gu Yuanqing 顧元慶 (1487–1565). The entry number following each translation corresponds to that edition. I have indicated in the notes where I have followed significant variants from other editions. See the Appendix for a finding list of the entries in other editions (Table 2). For poems, I have followed the versions that were circulated with the anecdotes rather than those found in poetry collections.

2. The official title cited for a person in *Storied Poems* is the highest reached by that person in his entire career; it is not necessarily the title held at the time in which the anecdote is set. Before becoming defender-in-chief at the beginning of Gaozong's reign (650–683), Zhangsun Wuji was grand preceptor of the heir apparent during Taizong's reign (627–649). This placed him on the same staff as Ou-yang Xun, who supervised the water clocks and ritual duties in the household of the heir apparent. Zhangsun, as a brother-in-law and longtime supporter of Taizong's, was entrusted with great power and latitude in his court.

3. *Taiping guangji* 太平廣記 (hereafter *Taiping*) reads 聳 for 聲.

4. The Qilin Hall was where portraits of officials of exceptional merit were displayed.

Xun retorted with:

> He draws in his head to warm it against his back,[5]
> He has ample drawers, afraid of getting his belly cold.[6]
> It is only because his mind is so muddled,
> That his face is so fat and round.

When Emperor Taizong heard of this he smiled and said, "Doesn't Xun fear the empress in making this mockery?"[7] (7.2)

國初。長孫太尉見歐陽率更。姿形么陋。嘲之曰。

> 聳膊成山字
> 埋肩畏出頭
> 誰言麟閣上
> 畫此一獼猴

詢亦酬之曰。

> 索頭連背暖
> 漫襠畏肚寒
> 祇緣心混混
> 所以面團團

太宗聞之而笑曰。詢此嘲。曾不爲皇后邪。

In his cruel quatrain, Zhangsun Wuji makes the mistake of confusing a man's outward appearance with his inner worth. The Qilin Hall was meant to house the portraits of meritorious officials, who would not be barred for bearing a simian resemblance. Zhangsun certainly must have realized his mistake when Ouyang retaliates with an even more insulting poem that demonstrates that he has formidable poetic competence despite his unimpressive exterior. This exchange is depicted as taking place when both Zhangsun and Ouyang were employed in the household of the heir apparent to Emperor Taizong, where Zhangsun occupied the superior position of grand preceptor of the heir apparent and Ouyang an inferior

---

5. *Taiping* and *Shihua zonggui qianji* 詩話總龜前集 (hereafter *Shihua*) read 縮 for 索.

6. *Taiping* reads a character consisting of the 衣 radical and 完 for 漫, and 當 for 襠. Wang Meng'ou suspects that the 衣 radical was transposed from the second character to the first and that it should read 完襠.

7. *Taiping* reads 豈不畏皇后邪. Zhangsun Wuji was the older brother of the principal imperial consort, who was known as Empress Wende.

custodial position supervising the water clocks and ritual duties of the household. Even though the poetic exchange is not set at the main court, it still finds its way to the ears of the emperor, who would certainly be privy to the circulation of gossip among members of royalty and the official class. The emperor thus becomes the ultimate audience and arbiter of the exchange between Zhangsun and Ouyang even though it was not originally uttered in his presence. His smile in response to hearing the poem is a tacit approval of Ouyang's rebuttal, but his question regarding the "empress" (Zhangsun's younger sister was the principal imperial consort at the time) is an acknowledgment that while Ouyang may have scored a verbal victory with his poetic competence, it could have dangerous ramifications in the nonpoetic arena of political and family factions. Zhangsun's relationship through marriage to the emperor, the trust he enjoys from the emperor, and his superior position in the household of the heir apparent (a result of his family connections) are the source of his arrogance. Ouyang may have been foolhardy in retaliating against such a powerful man, but he seems to have been saved from the ire of Zhangsun by the smile of Emperor Taizong; the narrative does not mention that he suffered any retribution for his poem. It made its own way to the only source of power that could trump that behind Zhangsun: the emperor himself.

Behind this brief story of an insulting poetic exchange lies the anxiety surely felt by all meritorious officials, who rose through the ranks on the basis of their performance in service, when faced with arrogant officials in positions of power because of their family connections. Zhangsun was not only a brother-in-law of the emperor but also a scion of a Northern Wei noble family and a lauded military hero. Ouyang, an academician and compiler of literary anthologies, was a scholar through and through. Their encounter is a classic confrontation between the "martial" (*wu* 武) and the "civil" (*wen* 文). Poetic discourse provides an arena that is easily misrecognized in these stories as transcending political, military, monetary, or familial influence, an arena in which literary talent is appreciated and rewarded, a place where the man of culture can get his own back against the crassly powerful. Even this story tacitly acknowledges, however, that such an arena has its limits, that whoever hears a poem shapes the ramifications of what is said through it. It is nice to think that poetry can be an effective weapon in the hands of the cultured against the oppression of the coarsely powerful. That desire is discernible even in the most playful of poetic exchanges found in *Storied Poems*, but it is always tempered by a cognizance of the importance of the variables of poetic performance. True competence lies not just in fashioning the words of a poem, but also in how, when, and where one places those words in the world. In this case, it seems that Ouyang Xun was competent more by accident than by design, for his words found their way of their own accord to a sympathetic and powerful audience.

As was the case in the *Zuo Tradition* and *Topical Tales*, the competence of one's audience to fully appreciate poetic discourse cannot always be assumed. It is no accident that Empress Wu Zetian 武則天 (r. 690–705), reviled by scholar-officials as a female usurper of the Tang throne, is portrayed in the following anecdote as lacking in the most basic skills of comprehension.

In the court of Empress Wu Zetian, Bureau Director of the Left Office Zhang Yuanyi was a comical sort good at making jokes. At this time, the barbarians to the west were menacing the borders.[8] Zetian intended to grant fiefs and titles to all officers of military distinction, so she ordered her nephew Wu Yizong to marshal forces in order to protect the borders. Before the invaders had even breached the frontier defenses, Yizong, who had only just crossed the outskirts of Bin,[9] grew cowardly and retreated. Yizong was short and ugly, so Yuanyi mocked him by saying,

> He may have a long bow, but his arrow is too short,
> He barely reaches the lofty knees of his tiny Shu horse.[10]
> Seven hundred leagues away from the enemy,
> He hid in a corner and fought with himself.
> Suddenly a tumbleweed became the enemy,
> And southward he fled, riding a pig.

At first when Zetian heard this she did not understand. "Did Yizong not have a horse?" she asked. "Why did he have to ride a pig?" Yuanyi ex-

---

8. Historically, it was the Khitan 契丹 to the north who were threatening the empire at this time.

9. Bin lay northwest of the capital.

10. Shu horses were known for their diminutive stature.

plained it for her by saying, "'Pig riding' is to run away while squeezing
'hog' between the legs."[11] Zetian laughed heartily, but Yizong was furious.
"Yuanyi had this all planned out," he said. "He relishes humiliating me."
Zetian bid Yizong compose a poem in return and he asked to do so using
the word "tousled" for his rhyme. Immediately, Yuanyi mocked him by
saying,

> He keeps his hair in an awful mess,[12]
> But he combs his sideburns so they are not tousled.
> Before you can notice his peach blossom complexion,
> He first makes his eyes like dainty apricots.[13]

Zetian was so delighted with this that Yizong was unable to make any
move to harm Yuanyi. (7.3)

則天朝。左司郎中張元一。滑稽善謔。時西戎犯邊。則天欲諸武立
功。因行封爵。命武懿宗統兵以禦之。寇未入塞。懿宗始逾幽郊。畏懦
而遁。懿宗短陋。元一嘲之曰。

> 長弓短度箭
> 蜀馬臨高蹁
> 去賊七百里
> 隈牆獨自戰
> 忽然蓬著賊
> 騎豬向南竄

則天聞之。初未悟。曰。懿宗無馬邪。何故騎豬。元一解之曰。騎豬
者。是夾豕走也。則天乃大笑。懿宗怒曰。元一鳳搆。貴欲辱臣。則天
命賦詩與之。懿宗請賦葦字。元一立嘲曰。

> 裡頭極草草
> 掠鬢不菶菶
> 未見桃花面皮
> 先作杏子眼孔

則天大歡。故懿宗不能侵傷。

---

11. The word *shi* 豕 "hog" is a homophone for *shi* 屎 "shit." The pun evokes the
comical image of Yizong fleeing in a state of extreme distress. It could also refer to
the region of Bin 豳 since its graph looks like two *shi* 豕 characters squeezed to-
gether.

12. I read *li* 理 for *li* 裡 in this line.

13. Both apricot-shaped eyes and a peach blossom complexion are clichés of
female beauty.

In this story, Zhang Yuanyi, who is known as a "comical sort good at making jokes," takes advantage of a correspondence between Wu Yizong's lack of courage and lack of impressive stature in fashioning his insulting poem. Unlike Zhangsun in the previous anecdote, who simply attacked Ouyang's looks gratuitously, Zhang Yuanyi paints a hilarious picture of a little man with a little arrow, dwarfed by his tiny pony, making a show of bravery in a mock fight until he is scared off by a passing tumbleweed. It is the last line about fleeing on a pig that poses a problem for Empress Wu. Zhang must assume the role of exegete in explaining to the empress (and ultimately to us as readers) what turns out to be a rather crude pun. The scene becomes a sort of parody of the familiar tableau found in the *Zuo Tradition*, where an erudite Traditionalist solemnly expounds to his ruler on the meaning of the *Poems*. All three personages in the anecdote are actually parodies: Zhang Yuanyi is a debased scholar, Wu Yizong a debased general, and Empress Wu a debased ruler. The anecdote is calculated to show how the rule of Empress Wu vitiated the solemnity of the Tang court. Instead of attending to important matters of the empire, she and her attendants engage in off-color insults that she has trouble grasping.

It is the nature of parody to carefully reproduce the fundamental form of that which it mocks, even as it subverts the expected content. In this case, the variables of poetic competence are maintained. Zhang's poem does not hit its mark until it has been fully explained to the empress. As the audience at the center of power, her appreciative guffaw once she "gets" the poem affords Zhang protection in the dangerous game of mocking the empress's own nephew, and is surely what enrages Wu Yizong himself. Wu Yizong's claim that Zhang "had this all planned out" is an attempt to question his poetic talent by suggesting his performance was calculated rather than improvised. By ascribing ulterior motives to Zhang's performance, Wu Yizong recasts this demonstration of poetic skill as a malicious bid to humiliate him. If the empress were not blinded by the humor of the poem, and could see it for the attack that it is, she might be indignant instead of amused. Unfortunately for Wu Yizong, his actions have proven that he *is* craven in addition to being short and ugly. Zhang's poem is not only funny; it is accurate. Empress Wu, in a somewhat disingenuous effort to be gracious, gives Wu Yizong the floor so that he may improvise a poetic retort to Zhang's insults. Wu Yizong would have done so already if he had the poetic competence, but lacking this, he tips his hand by announcing the character he will use to set the rhyme of his poem. This gives Zhang the chance to jump in and prove his verbal facility once again, as he appropriates Wu Yizong's own rhyme word and turns it against him—the true display of poetic competence in this anecdote. The empress's resultant delight renders Zhang impervious to any further attempts by Wu Yizong to retaliate.

The caricatures may be somewhat grotesque—the clownish scholar, the cowardly general, the dimwitted ruler—but the contours of poetic competence remain. The ancient desire that poetry may be used to "pierce" 刺 the inflated egos of the powerful and incompetent is still discernible in this farce of a regal court. This time it is a parody in which a cultured man (*wen*) wins out over a sham of a military one (*wu*).

If the in-laws of Taizong and blood relatives of Empress Wu are "fair game" for mockery through poetry in the preceding anecdotes, by the time of the court of Emperor Zhongzong's second reign (705–10), the sovereign himself comes under attack.

In the court of Emperor Zhongzong there was a censor-in-chief named Pei Yan who worshipped the Buddha. His wife was fiercely jealous, and Yan feared her as he would a strict father. He once declared that there were three things to be feared about his wife: (1) When she was young and pretty, he saw her as a Living Bodhisattva [and who wouldn't be afraid of a Living Bodhisattva?]. (2) With many children about her, he saw her as the Demon Brood Mother, and who wouldn't be afraid of the Demon Brood Mother?[14] (3) When she reached the age of fifty or sixty and would lightly apply her makeup—sometimes in a black shade—he saw her as Jiupancha the Soul Eater, and who wouldn't be afraid of

---

14. The Demon Brood Mother is the Chinese name for the Buddhist goddess Hariti. According to legend, she gave birth to five hundred sons and ate up all the other children in the village. After attaining enlightenment, however, she became the patron saint of child bearing.

Jiupancha?[15] At this time, Commoner Wei had taken on much of the influence of the Wu clan and Zhongzong gradually came to fear her. At a court banquet, people were singing lyrics to "Swirling Waves."[16] The lyrics by one performer said,

> In the swirling waves, there lies a basket,
> It is a fine thing to fear one's wife.
> Outside court only Pei Yan does so,
> But in here, no one surpasses Old Li.

Empress Wei assumed a self-satisfied expression and bestowed a bolt of silk upon the performer. (7.7)

中宗朝。御史大夫裴談。崇奉釋氏。妻悍妒。談畏如嚴君。嘗謂之妻有可畏者三。少妙之時。視之如生菩薩。及男女滿前。視之如九子魔母。安有人不畏九子魔母耶。及五十六十。薄施裝粉。或黑。視之如鳩盤茶。安有人不畏鳩盤茶。時韋庶人頗襲武氏之風軌。中宗漸畏之。內宴。唱回波詞。有優人詞曰。

> 回波爾時栲栳
> 怕婦也是大好
> 外邊祇有裴談
> 內裡無過李老

韋后意色自得以束帛賜之。

The performance proper in this anecdote begins with the line, "At a court banquet...."; preceding it is the background information necessary to successfully understand the performance—namely that Pei Yan is the epitome of a henpecked husband, and that the emperor lived in fear of his own wife, later derogatorily referred to by historians as "Commoner Wei" 韋庶人 because of her arrogation of power. Such information would be assumed knowledge of both the primary audience present at this performance and the secondary audience of contemporaries close to the court who may have heard about it, but the knowledge must be reconstructed for the extended audience comprising later readers of this anecdote. What the narra-

---

15. Jiupancha was a female demon in Buddhist folklore that sapped the vitality from human beings. According to an entry in *Taiping* (251), she had dark lips and blackened limbs.

16. This was a popular dancing melody during Zhongzong's reign. The opening line of the song would always begin, "When the waves were swirling . . . ."

tive does not mention here, but which was certainly known by all at the court of Zhongzong, was that Pei Yan was a vehement critic of the Wei clan's power in general and of the appointment of Empress Wei's own father as chief minister in particular. Factional politics is at the heart of this performance.

The performer is unnamed, but the Chinese term *youren* 優人 suggests that he or she was a member of the corps of royal performers that provided music and entertainment at banquets rather than an official in attendance. The poem is uttered as lyrics to a song for entertainment purposes, which places it in a playful context, providing the performer with some leeway in terms of propriety. But this particular poem transgresses any reasonable bounds of decorum, not only by flatly declaring that the emperor is henpecked but also by using the overly familiar appellation "Old Li." The performance is a bald-faced appeal to Empress Wei in that it elevates her status as a wife, insults Pei Yan (her most powerful critic), and subordinates her husband to her. This is no longer a world in which a concerned official uses poetry to gently admonish a wayward ruler for the good of the realm; this is a cynical attempt by a politically savvy performer to advance his or her position at court by currying favor with the de facto ruler. The poem does not rely on indirect language but goes out of its way to directly insult. Any protection afforded the performer stems not from patterned language but from the audience's approval, which is embodied in Empress Wei's smug expression and her material reward. To reward the performer with a bolt of silk is not only to clearly affirm the poem's sentiments, but is in itself a minor usurpation of the emperor's power, for it is he who should properly bestow such rewards. The narrative is obviously meant as an implicit critique of Emperor Zhongzong's weakness in the face of his wife, but in making this critique it must acknowledge that the production of poetic discourse can and does result from the most cynical of motivations.

In these anecdotes, one finds an express acknowledgment that any protection or advantage afforded by a poem is contingent upon the appreciation of an authority figure with enough power to provide that protection. One can only use a poem to admonish or insult a figure of authority with impunity when another figure of even higher authority appreciates that poem. If there is no such figure, and if the target of one's poem does not appreciate it, then no amount of "patterned language" will afford protection. It is the outward manifestation of appreciation in these last three anecdotes—the smile of Emperor Taizong, the laughter of Empress Wu, the gift of Empress Wei—that shields one from harm. But what is being appreciated in these cases? It is the "talent" or "wit" (*cai* 才) of the poet, as demonstrated not only in the poem itself but also in the competence with which the poet handles the circumstances of poetic production and reception. Despite Meng Qi's traditional reference in his preface to the Mao prefaces of the *Poems*, in the world depicted by the narratives of *Storied Poems*, *cai* 才 has replaced *wen* 文 as the characteristic of poetry that determines its efficacy. Here it is no longer the words themselves that hold power; rather, it is how one handles the words that is of prime importance.

Storied Poems also contains anecdotes set in the Early Tang court in which poetry serves to appeal, rather than attack—where one is not criticizing a figure of authority so much as complaining about circumstances that might be rectified by those in power. Both models of poetic performance—the criticism and the complaint—are at the core of ancient models of poetic production. Once again, however, the efficacy promised by ancient models is undermined by practice as it is depicted in these narratives.

In addition to being incompetent in comprehending poetry, Empress Wu is also portrayed as being unable (or unwilling) to appreciate a man's character as it is expressed through his poetry.

Song Zhiwen [ca. 656–712], the vice director of the Bureau of Evaluations, sought the position of academician of the North Gate in the court of Empress Wu Zetian.[17] He was not granted his wish, so he composed a piece entitled "The Milky Way" to manifest his feelings. The closing lines read:

---

17. Academicians of the North Gate were responsible for drafting imperial pronouncements and composing literary works under imperial sponsorship. They were the precursors to scholars of the Hanlin Academy.

I may gaze at the Milky Way but dare not draw near,
I long for a raft upon which to ride and ask of the ford.[18]
I would take the Weaving Girl's loom stone,
And return to visit the soothsayer of Chengdu.[19]

When Empress Wu Zetian saw his poem, she said to Cui Rong [651–705], "It is not that I am unaware of Zhiwen's literary talents; it is just that he has bad breath." In fact, Zhiwen did suffer from a dental malady and often had bad breath as a result. He felt humiliated by this until the end of his days. (4.1)

宋考功天后朝求爲北門學士。不許。作明河篇以見其意。末云。

> 明河可望不敢親
> 願得乘槎一問津
> 更將織女支機石
> 還訪成都賣卜人

則天見其詩。謂崔融曰。吾非不知之問有才調。但以其有口過。蓋以之問患齒疾。口常臭故也。之問終身慚憤。

---

18. The *Account of Wide-Ranging Matters* 博物志 (*juan* 10), by Zhang Hua 張華 (232–300), contains the story of a man who noticed in the ocean a raft that would float by during the eighth month of every year. One year, he got onto the raft and rode it for more than ten days before arriving at a magical place where he met a weaving girl and herd boy. He asked them where he was, but the weaving girl replied that he must go to Shu and inquire of the soothsayer Yan Junping 嚴君平. When he returned, the soothsayer informed him that a wandering star had traveled between the Weaving Girl and Herd Boy stars at the very time that he was on the raft. The *Huainan zi* 淮南子 tells us that these two stars are lovers, destined to be apart except for the seventh night of the seventh month 七夕 of every year, when a bridge of magpies allows them to cross the Milky Way to each other. The phrase "ask of the ford" is usually associated with an entry in the *Analects* 論語 (18.6) that tells of Confucius sending one of his disciples to ask directions of two recluses plowing a field. They reply that Confucius should know the way himself and that it is better to shun the world altogether than to lead the peripatetic life of Confucius. Confucius rejects this idea and says that he would rather associate with people and search for the Way in government.

19. The *Imperial Digest of the Taiping Reign Period* 太平御覽 (j. 8), completed in 982, recounts the journey of a man in search of the source of the Yellow River 黃河 (believed to be the earthly counterpart to the Milky Way 天河). He came upon a maiden washing silk, who informed him that he had reached the Milky Way and gave him a stone to take back with him. When he returned and made inquiries of Yan Junping, the soothsayer of Chengdu, he found out that it was the stone used to support the loom of the Weaving Girl.

The incongruous juxtaposition of Song's elegant use of a time-honored and highly allusive form of protest with the empress's crass reply highlights the debasement of an ideal model of poetic appreciation. Granted, the entire anecdote was likely fabricated to cast Empress Wu in a bad light, but the narrative insists upon its authenticity by noting, "In fact, Zhiwen did suffer from a dental malady and often had bad breath as a result." The *qi*, or "spirit," of Song's poem is tainted by the malodorous quality of his bodily *qi*, or "breath." A poem, no matter how exquisitely patterned, will lose its suasive power if the author's chanting of it physically repulses the audience. The term Empress Wu uses for "bad breath" (*kou guo*) literally means "a defect of the mouth," and while such a defect does not necessarily mean a defect in character or skill (the empress does acknowledge his "literary talents"), it does compromise any verbal manifestation of character or skill, and this is enough to disqualify Song Zhiwen from service in an academy of letters. This is no longer the world of the *Zuo Tradition* or *Topical Tales*, in which the narratives about poetic performance prove the efficacy of verbal facility. It is not the world of the *Han History*, where passionate poetic outbursts leave a noble posterity. This is a world with a cynical (some might say more realistic) outlook, where well-formed protests fall on deaf ears and merit is denied because of poor dental hygiene. In the *Zuo Tradition*, obtuseness in the royal listener was invariably punished. Song Zhiwen receives no such vindication, and "felt humiliated by this until the end of his days."

Another entry set during Emperor Zhongzong's second reign, when he regained the throne after Empress Wu's death, comprises two examples of poetic protest at court. The first part is about Shen Quanqi 沈佺期 (ca. 656–713).

Shen Quanqi, who had been exiled for an offence, was returned to his post by the grace of the emperor, but did not have his crimson robes restored to him. Once, at a court banquet, the assembled officials were all singing to the melody "Swirling Waves," composing lyrics to it and rising to dance to it—many of them sought to advance themselves in this way. Quanqi's lyric read:

> From the swirling waves, I, Quanqi,
> Returned alive from my exile beyond the Ling mountains.

My person and name have been granted employment,
But my gown and tablet are no longer crimson and ivory.

Emperor Zhongzong bestowed crimson robes and an insignia pouch upon him forthwith. (7.6a)

沈佺期曾以罪謫。遇恩官還秩。朱紱未復。嘗內晏。群臣皆歌回波樂。
撰詞起舞。因是多求遷擢。佺期詞曰。

> 回波爾時佺期
> 流向嶺外生歸
> 身名已蒙齒錄
> 袍笏未復牙緋

中宗即以緋魚賜之。

The substitution of verbal facility instead of virtuous action as the main criterion for judging the worthiness of a man, especially via the imperial examinations, was regularly decried but never remedied throughout the Tang.[20] In this case, Shen Quanqi's request seems somewhat petty and self-interested when compared with the lofty concerns of state that are the topic of poetry in canonical works such as the *Zuo Tradition* or with the outbursts occasioned by suffering and sorrow in the *Han History*. The representation of Shen's complaint in the form of a poem resulting in the emperor's immediate rectification of his grievance exemplifies the maxim found in the "Great Preface": "When patterned language is paramount in making a veiled admonishment, then he who speaks it is without culpability and he who hears it will take sufficient warning." The exemplification is an unsatisfying one, however. The moral seriousness attached to the theory of poetic protest articulated in the "Great Preface" is debased in this instance of practice by the pettiness of Shen's protest and the mediocrity of his poem.

The entry's initial scenario is repeated in its second part, with some significant variations.

Cui Riyong, who was vice censor-in-chief, had been granted permission to wear purple. At that time, it was necessary to enjoy exceptional imperial

---

20. For copious documentation of this phenomenon, see McMullen, *State and Scholars.*

favor in order to wear an insignia pouch. At a court banquet, Zhongzong commanded the assembled officials to compose lyrics. Riyong's lyric read:

> The rats within the palace should know it well,
> Trusting their feet to leap from beams up to niches
>   in the wall.
> They upset the lamp oil, soiling Zhang the Fifth,
> Returning, they repay Han the Third by gnawing
>   through his sash.
> Let us not speak rashly here,
> But they are fit to be princes or ministers.
> If every one must be granted a golden insignia pouch,
> Then just sell the cat to reward them.

Zhongzong bestowed a golden insignia pouch upon him. (7.6b)

崔日用爲御史中丞。賜紫。是時。佩魚須有特恩。內宴。中宗命群臣撰詞。曰。

> 臺中鼠子直須諳
> 信足跳梁上壁龕
> 倚翻燈暗污張五
> 還來齧帶報韓三
> 莫浪語
> 直王相
> 大家必若賜金龜
> 賣卻貓兒相報上

中宗亦以金魚賜之。

The narrative, in stating that at the time "it was necessary to enjoy exceptional imperial favor in order to wear an insignia pouch," establishes the stakes of poetic production in this anecdote. Cui's reaction to these conditions is paradoxical: he uses a poem to chastise the emperor for setting so trivial a task as improvising a poem to win imperial favor. The emperor then rewards him with a golden insignia pouch for engaging in the very activity that he has condemned. His remonstrance is framed in appropriately indirect language, figuring slanderous officials as rats in the palace and the emperor as the cat who keeps them in line. One may view this poem as a sly and subversive use by Cui of a protected form of discourse to reflexively criticize the practice of using this form of discourse as a criterion for judging merit in officials. If everyone—even a "rat"—is to receive imperial favor for poetic skill, then Cui attempts to preserve some measure of his scruples by making his contribution a condemnation of the whole process. In making the protest directly to the emperor, Cui is demonstrating the very quality of character that actually does deserve reward. His poem—with regard to itself and to the golden insignia pouch—is an attempt to restore value to that which is in danger of becoming mere empty utterance. The dangerous paradox that results is that in pointing out the debasement of poetic discourse, he threatens the cogency of the very medium through which he expresses his argument. It is only recuperated by his instance of practicing it under a particular set of circumstances before a particular audience.

In these narratives, the reigns of Empress Wu and her son Emperor Zhongzong are depicted as problematic for the proper operation of poetic discourse. The empress does not appreciate poetry as she should, and the emperor is too facile both in calling for it and in responding to it. These characteristics correspond with historical evaluations of the empress (as a woman who flouted proper rules of succession to arrogate power) and the emperor (as a weak man who fell under the undue influence of his mother). How a ruler handles poetic discourse becomes an index of the quality of his or her rule. When poetry becomes the vehicle of crude jokes at court, when its serious expression is denied, when its frivolous expression is rewarded—these are the symptoms of a court that has let the morally suasive power of poetry slip its grasp.

The court of Emperor Xuanzong 玄宗 (r. 712–756) provides a clear counterpoint to the reigns of Wu Zetian and Zhongzong. It should come as no surprise that in this golden era, poetry operates just as it should.

During the Kaiyuan era there was a general of the guards in Youzhou by the name of Zhang.[21] His wife was from the Kong clan and had given him five children when, unfortunately, she passed away. He took another wife, a woman from the Li clan, who had a fierce temper and was brutally violent. She treated the five children cruelly, flogging them every day. The children could not bear their suffering; so they went to lament before their

---

21. Youzhou is modern-day Beijing.

mother's grave.[22] The mother suddenly rose up from her tomb to soothe her children. She grieved for a time then wrote out a poem on her white calico scarf to be given to Zhang. It read:

> I cannot bear becoming a deceased wife,[23]
> I hide my face and weep endlessly into my scarf.
> Now that we are separated in life and death,
> There will never be a way to see each other again.
> In my powder box some makeup remains,
> Keep it to give to the one who follows me.
> I have no use for it in the Yellow Springs,
> How I hate being dust in a grave.
> With love I cherish my boys and girls,
> But I charge you with being heartless.
> If you wish to know where my heart breaks,
> The bright moon shines upon my lonely tomb.

The children took the poem and showed it to their father. Their father lamented in grief and reported it to the aggregate commander, who then submitted it to the emperor. He decreed that the Li woman receive one hundred floggings[24] and be banished to Lingnan.[25] Zhang was suspended from his official duties. (5.1)

開元中。有幽州衙將姓張者。妻孔氏。生五子。不幸去世。復娶妻李氏。悍怒狼戾。虐遇五子。日鞭箠之。五子不堪其苦。哭於其葬。母忽於冢中出。撫其子。悲慟久之。因以白布巾題詩贈張。曰。

不忿成故人
掩涕每盈巾
死生今有隔
相見永無因
匣裡殘妝粉
留將與後人
黃泉無用處
恨作冢中塵
有意懷男女
無情亦任君

---

22. *Taiping* reads 其母墓前.

23. *Taiping* and *Shihua* read 分 for 忿. I suspect it is a corruption of 忍 and have taken it as such here.

24. *Jindai mishu* 津逮秘書 (hereafter *Jindai*) reads 杖 for 决.

25. Lingnan is modern-day Guangzhou.

欲知腸斷處
明月照孤墳

五子得詩。以呈其父。其父慟哭訴於連帥。帥上聞。敕李氏決一百。流
嶺南。張停所職。

In this story, an emotional chain reaction is formed. It begins with
the fierce stepmother who mistreats the distraught children, who
move their mother to write a poem, which in turn moves the father,
then the commander, and, finally, the emperor, who ultimately acts
to rectify the situation that initially produced the emotions in the
children. The poem is both a result of disequilibrium and a catalyst
for regaining equilibrium—it recalls Han Yu's maxim that "all
things cry out when they cannot maintain tranquility" 凡物不得其
平則鳴. The poem is a symptom that has the power to command a
cure, but only if it falls into the right hands. Knowledge of the
children's suffering would never have reached the emperor without
the vehicle of their mother's poem. The anecdote shows the literal
extension of a maxim attributed to Confucius in the *Zuo Tradition*
(Xiang 25): "If one does not speak, then who will know the intent in
one's mind? But if one speaks of it without patterned language, it
will not travel far" 不言。誰知其志。言之無文。行而不遠. In this
case, the patterned language of the poem is able to traverse the
boundary between the world of the living and the world of the dead,
to traverse the social distance between the wife of a general and the
emperor, and to traverse the physical distance between Youzhou
(modern Beijing) and Chang'an (modern Xi'an). The poem also lives
up to the promise made in the "Great Preface" that "those below
may criticize those above," as the ghost of the children's mother
(who dwells in the underworld below) calls her husband to task for
not protecting her children. There is an interesting inversion in this
anecdote of another statement made in the "Great Preface": that
there is nothing better than poetry for "moving ghosts and spirits"
感鬼神. In this instance, a ghost is moved *to* poetry rather than *by*
poetry. "When emotions are stirred within, they will find outward
form in spoken words" is a principle that holds true in the spirit
world as well as the human one.

There is a small but telling discrepancy in the anecdote. The
mother's poem does not mention the abuse of the children at the

hands of their stepmother (who is only referred to indirectly, as "the one who follows me"). It only blames the father in general terms for heartlessness. Yet the emperor demotes the father and subjects the stepmother to the severe punishment of one hundred floggings and banishment. We might assume that the commander made a full report of the details of the case when submitting the poem to the emperor, but this is not mentioned in the anecdote. As it stands, the narrative creates the impression that the poem itself is sufficient evidence for the emperor to act to rectify the situation. As a good reader, he is able to "use his thoughts to get back to the intent" 以意 逆志 (*Mencius* 9A) in order to uncover the situation that produced the poem's emotional content and to see that justice is done.

Here, poetic discourse operates as it should. The one who produces the poem is moved by passionate, sincere feeling; the poem itself is passed along the chain of command until it is received by its proper audience; the audience appreciates *and* responds to the poem in a meaningful fashion. The account is not completely naïve, however. Rather than simply singing her poem in an outburst of grief, the ghost of the mother chooses to inscribe the poem on her burial scarf and to explicitly address it to her husband, thus providing her children with physical evidence of the supernatural encounter. The poem does not serve simply to vent her emotion; she certainly intends to put her poem out into the world as an enduring physical artifact that will continue to speak for her from beyond the grave. The poem eventually ends up before the emperor not because of what it says—for abuse of stepchildren is not a singular occurrence—but because of the extraordinary circumstances of its production. Even under the reign of an "enlightened emperor" 明皇 such as Xuanzong, the anecdote that best exemplifies the ideal operation of poetic discourse turns out to be a ghost story.

When one's audience is not a wise emperor but a chief minister who rules as virtual dictator and is suspicious of everyone, the efficacy of poetic discourse is severely compromised. Two entries in *Storied Poems* concern officials making complaints against the notoriously ruthless Li Linfu 李林甫 (d. 752).

Near the end of the Kaiyuan era [713–741], Grand Councilor Li Shizhi [d. 747] was a carefree and serene man who enjoyed a wonderful reputation. Li Linfu despised him and arranged to have him slandered and dismissed. A court official arrived and interrogated Shizhi very intensely despite knowing that he was without fault. Shizhi felt indignant and took to freely drinking strong wine every day. Then he composed a poem that read:

> When the Yielding Worthy first gave up his grand
> councilor post,
> The Happy Sage took to drinking from his cup.
> I ask about the guests at my door,
> How many have come this morning?

Li Linfu grew even more furious, and, in the end, Shizhi was unable to escape his wrath. (4.3)

開元末。宰相李適之。疏直坦夷。時譽甚美。李林甫惡之。排誣罷免。朝客來。雖知無罪。謁問甚稀。適之意憤。日飲醇酎。且爲詩曰。

> 避賢初罷相
> 樂聖且啣盃
> 爲問門前客
> 今朝幾個來

李林甫愈怒。終遂不免。

Li Shizhi, a worthy man who has been unjustly maligned, responds to Li Linfu's attack in a time-honored manner: he withdraws from office and takes up drinking. In the first line of his poem, he casts himself as the "Yielding Worthy" who willingly gives up his post to a superior man for the good of the state. The locus classicus for this figure is mythical sage-king Yao's 堯 abdication of the throne to Shun 舜 in ancient times. In the context of a worthy man ousted from his post by a tyrant, the reference becomes bitterly ironic. The rest of the poem slips into the voice of the famous poet of reclusion Tao Qian 陶潛 (365–427), with Shizhi drinking at home and wondering if anyone has come to visit him. While Tao Qian would have us believe that he was able to cut himself off from officialdom completely, Li Shizhi is actually less successful. Though the narrative does not explain how, the poem inevitably gravitates toward the center of authority and is received by the object of its derision, who responds to it with lethal wrath.

This poem is a classic example of the "outburst poem," in which the poem is a means of "venting frustration" 發憤, to use Sima

Qian's phrase regarding the production of the *Poems*. This is an attitude that can be traced back to Confucius's statement in the *Analects* that the *Poems* can be used to "express resentment" 可以怨. Li Shizhi was careful enough to veil his frustrations in allusive language, but obviously not careful enough to prevent his poem from reaching Li Linfu. If Shizhi deliberately put his poem on a path to Linfu, it may be that he misjudged the fury of the paranoid chief minister, or it may be that he simply felt he had to make his feelings known regardless of the consequences.

Another official who raises the ire of Li Linfu tries to use poetry to preempt an attack.

Zhang Jiuling [673–740] was ranked equal with Li Linfu at court. Because Jiuling had a keen knowledge of letters, Emperor Xuanzong had great confidence in his abilities. Linfu begrudged him this as though he were his mortal enemy. Jiuling considered Li's guile and worried that ultimately he could not escape it. He composed a poem called "Ocean Swallow" to convey his feelings. It read:

> The ocean swallows are so very small,
> They arrive with spring for a short while.
> How can they know of the meanness of dirt and filth,
> When they only behold jade halls open wide?
> Now and then they swoop in pairs through filigreed shutters,
> Day by day a few return to the painted balconies.
> They do not have a mind to struggle with other creatures,
> Let the falcon not be suspicious of them.

In the end he was forced to retire. (4.4)

張曲江與李林甫同列。玄宗以文學精識。深器之。林甫嫉之若讎。曲江度其巧譖。慮終不免。爲海燕詩以致意。曰。

> 海燕何微眇
> 乘春亦暫來
> 豈知泥滓濺
> 秪見玉堂開
> 繡戶時雙入
> 華軒日幾迴
> 無心與物競
> 鷹隼莫相猜

亦終退斥。

Zhang Jiuling uses poetry as a form of mild remonstration. His poem may "convey his feelings" 致意, but it is also a carefully constructed avian argument for harmonious collegiality. He shows some strategic sense in deciding to use a poem to defuse Linfu's anger, but the attempt is ultimately doomed to failure, for Linfu has already made up his mind to "begrudge him this as though he were his mortal enemy." Though Linfu would not be a receptive reader of Jiuling's poem under any circumstances, the latter compounds the problem by poetizing his plaint, for it is precisely his "keen knowledge of letters" that arouses such envy in Linfu.

These two anecdotes show the complete negation of poetry as a protected form of discourse that can shield the speaker from culpability. Indeed, the poems exacerbate the mistreatment of the protagonists at the hands of Li Linfu. This is stark evidence that poetic talent alone is insufficient to control a situation; success is contingent upon the sympathies of the audience. Li Linfu is an able enough reader—his ire is raised precisely because he correctly interprets Li Shizhi's irony and Zhang Jiuling's imagery—but he is ignorant (perhaps willfully so) of how he should respond according to the tradition of protest poetry. This "ignorance" is perceived only in the context of a narrative predicated upon canonical precepts of poetry. In reality, a petulant authority figure would have no reason to feel constrained by literary principles. But a significant pattern emerges in the anecdotes of *Storied Poems*: the "villains" (Wu Zetian, Li Linfu, and others) fail to appreciate poetic talent, while the "heroes" (Xuanzong, the wise ministers and generals) are highly responsive to it. Appreciation of poetry becomes a cultural litmus test to determine an authority figure's moral status.

Such a litmus test need not apply only to figures at court. In the Tang, even military figures can be adept at appreciating poetry.

When Zhu Tao was conscripting soldiers, he did not except members of elite families, but ordered all alike into the army and reviewed them himself on the polo fields. Once there was a scholar of handsome bearing who moved with a refined air. Tao summoned him and asked, "What is your vocation?" "I am a student of composing poetry," replied the scholar. "Do you have a wife?" asked Tao. "I do," answered the scholar. Tao ordered him to compose a poem to his wife right then and there. The scholar picked up a brush and was finished at once. The words read:

To hold a brush and write a poem is easy,
To shoulder a spear and march to the frontier
    is hard.
I am used to pursuing the warmth of our covers,
And afraid of heading for the cold of Yanmen pass.[26]
You waste away, your gown and sash hang loose,
With many sobs you soak the sandalwood of
    your headrest.
Try to leave some mascara to put on,
When I return, you will watch as I paint
    your eyebrows.[27]

Then Tao ordered the scholar to put himself in his wife's place and compose a poem in reply. It read:

Even with tangled hair and thorn pins, I am a rare
    beauty in this age,
My coarse skirt is still this one I was married in.
The sesame is ready for planting, but there is no
    one to do it,
Now he should be coming back, why has he
    not returned?

Tao gave him a bolt of silk and sent him home. (1.5)

朱滔括兵。不擇士族。悉令赴軍。自閱於毬場。有士子。容止可觀。進趨淹雅。滔召問之。所業者何。曰。學爲詩。問。有妻否。曰。有。即令作寄内詩。援筆立成。詞曰。

握筆題詩易
荷戈征戍難
慣從鴛被暖
怯向鴈門寒
瘦盡寬衣帶
啼多漬枕檀
試留青黛著
迴日畫眉看

又令代妻作詩答。曰。

---

26. Yanmen pass (in modern Shanxi province) marked the passage into the northern frontier.

27. The *Han History* (*juan 76*) relates the story of a governor named Zhang Chang 張敞 so devoted to his wife that he even painted her eyebrows for her.

蓬鬢荊釵世所稀
布裙猶是嫁時衣
胡麻好種無人種
合是歸時底不歸

滔遺以束帛。放歸。

Zhu Tao makes a point of enlisting members of elite families into the army, but there is something about the "handsome bearing" and "refined air" of the anonymous scholar that catches his attention. Thus Zhu demonstrates his ability to read a man's character based on his external features. He finds out, as he likely suspected, that the man is a "student of composing poetry," and then tests him to see if his internal assets measure up to his physical ones. Zhu Tao fashions the test's variables by specifying to whom the scholar should write his poem. This creates a strange scenario whereby the composition of the scholar's poem is not an impromptu reaction to circumstances—a communication from one person to another—but rather a contrived expression performed for the judgment of a third party. Matters become even stranger when Zhu Tao orders the scholar to "put himself in his wife's place" and compose her reply, thus producing a contrived response to a contrived missive. The scholar performs this odd poetic drama while standing before a general on military training grounds. The sharp contrast between his literary (*wen*) activity and the martial (*wu*) setting forms the basis of his first couplet, which contrasts the brush of a scholar with the spear of a soldier. The scholar's poem is replete with the imagery of tender affection between husband and wife, while his simulation of his wife's poem casts her in the ancient role of the farmer's wife waiting for her husband to return from military service.[28] Both poems envision a possible future in which military duty would force the husband and wife to be separated. Not only is the composition of these poems contrived, their very subject matter concerns events that have not yet taken place. The facility with which Zhu Tao and the scholar manipulate these poetic variables demonstrates how de-

---

28. The earliest exemplar of this theme is "My Husband Is Away on Duty" 君子于役 (Mao #66) from the *Poems*.

liberate poetic production has become by this time. The scholar originally claims it as his object of study; what he demonstrates here is not a sincere expression of irrepressible passion but an acquired skill that can be used to manufacture the *appearance* of sincere passion in poetic form.

When Zhu Tao rewards the scholar and excuses him from duty, he demonstrates that he is a good reader of both poetry *and* poetic skill. The whole exchange reflects as well on him as a receiver of poetry as it does on the scholar as a producer of it. Zhu certainly could be sympathizing with the feelings of longing expressed in the poems, even if they are hypothetical. The poems' expression of potential sorrow moves the authority figure to prevent that sorrow from arising; they are prophylactic rather than remedial. However, Zhu Tao's notice of the scholar's appearance, his question regarding his vocation, and his material reward in the form of a bolt of silk all suggest that he is recognizing the scholar for what he is—a man of letters—rather than reacting to a specific instance of poetic production. The poems simply serve to confirm what Zhu Tao already suspected, that the scholar is a man of the brush, not the spear, and that he belongs in the "field of letters" 文場 rather than the "polo fields." Zhu Tao's test serves as a miniature version of the imperial examination, which uses skill in poetic composition as one criterion to select men from the field of letters for service in the civil bureaucracy. The difference here is that passing the test means avoiding a post instead of obtaining one. Poetic competence, when recognized, can serve to remove one from the realm of physical violence and return one to the relative safety of the realm of literary expression.

There is another anecdote (2.5) in which poetry is used to avoid an examination altogether. Li Zhangwu 李章武 (fl. 827–835), vice governor of Chengdu, who "favored the ancient in his studies and had quite a reputation in his time" 學識好古有名於時, pens a poem for an old monk who fears he will not pass the newly instated mandatory examinations on the Buddhist scriptures. When the examination supervisor sees the poem (which opens: "The Southern Sect has always allowed all expedient means, / Where in the heart are the scriptures to be found?" 南宗尚許通方便／何處心中更有經), he excuses the monk from the examination. This is a case of poetic competence by proxy. Li Zhangwu understands that there is more than one path to enlightenment and that wisdom does not lie in texts alone; it is his text that excuses the monk from having to demonstrate knowledge of the scriptures. Of course, the examination supervisor is probably more impressed by *who* wrote the poem than what it says. The monk demonstrates his own form of competence in seeking out the help of a man whose words carry some weight.

Poetic competence alone does not guarantee success in the imperial examinations—even Du Fu 杜甫 (712–770) failed them twice—and *Storied Poems* contains an anecdote suggesting that poetic talent could even hinder success in the examination system.

When Jia Dao [779–843] first became famous for his poetry, he was wild and dissolute and was unable to pass the examinations for a long time. The Duke of Jin, Pei Du [765–839], excavated a pond in Xing-hua village, planted bamboo, and constructed raised gazebos.[29] Dao had just failed the imperial examinations when someone told him that the executive official [Pei Du] despised him and that was why he was not among those selected. Dao became extremely indignant and inscribed a poem inside Pei Du's pavilion. It read:

> You have smashed a thousand homes to make
>   a pond,
> And planted roses instead of peaches and pears.
> When the rose blossoms have fallen in the
>   autumn breeze,
> You shall at last realize that your courtyard is
>   filled with thorns.

Because of this, everyone scorned Dao's effrontery and lack of respect. As a result, he died without ever passing the examinations and regretted it to the end of his life. (4.5)

賈島初有詩名狂狷薄行久不中第裴晉公興]化里鑿池種竹。起臺榭。方下第。或謂執政惡之。故不在選。怨憤尤極。遂於內題詩曰。

> 破卻千家作一池
> 不栽桃李種薔薇

薔薇花落秋風後
荆棘滿庭君始知

由是人皆惡其侮慢不避。故卒不得第。憾而終。

Pei Du was a notoriously strict examiner (he even failed Han Yu), but Jia Dao's poetic venting of his indignation only made matters worse for him. The line about planting thorny roses instead of peaches and pears is particularly biting, as "peaches and pears" or "peaches and plums" were often used as a figure for students and disciples gathered around the supporting "trunk" of a kind and worthy teacher. As Jia Dao surely intended in prominently inscribing his poem inside Pei's pavilion, the poem leaks out to a wider audience—simply denoted in this case as "everyone."[30] This "everyone" must include influential officials, for Jia Dao is unable to pass the examinations for the rest of his life. Thus, the normal role of poetry as a means to official employment is inverted and becomes an impediment. The "effrontery" so despised by everyone seems to be just as much a matter of Jia's audacity in inscribing the poem in Pei Du's pavilion as it is any pointed criticism in the poem itself. Jia Dao may have a "reputation for poetry" 詩名, but in this case he lacks competence in deploying his poetic discourse—unless never being able to pass the examinations was his intent.

Poetry is associated with criticism of authority to such an extent that, in some cases, it becomes a dangerous form of discourse even when its motivations are innocent.

Minister Liu Yuxi [772–842] was demoted from his position as vice director of the State Farms Bureau to that of an assistant prefect of Langzhou.[31] After a total of ten years he was finally summoned back to the capital. It had just turned spring, so Liu composed a poem, entitled "Given to All the Fine Gentlemen Viewing Flowers," that read:[32]

---

30. This is not the only example of protest graffiti in *Storied Poems*. In entry 4.2, Wu Wuling (fl. 806–827) inscribes a protest poem on a roadside shrine as a public complaint against government investigation into his misconduct.

31. Langzhou is modern-day Jingde in Hunan province.

32. In the *Collected Works of Liu Mengde* 劉夢得文集 (j. 4), this poem is entitled "Playfully Presented to the Gentlemen Viewing Flowers upon my Return to the Capital from Langzhou in Response to an Imperial Summons in the Tenth Year of

On the purple paths I arrive brushing red dust
    from my face,[33]
Everyone told me that I should return to view
    the flowers.
Within Xuandu temple there are a thousand
    peach trees,[34]
But all of them were planted after Gentleman
    Liu had gone.

Once his poem got out, it was circulated throughout the capital. There was someone who had always been jealous of his fame who informed the executive official of the poem and slandered Liu by saying that he bore a grudge for being demoted. Later, Liu met the man who was the executive official at the time and was seated with him at a banquet. He comforted Liu and asked after him with great concern. After Liu left, he immediately said to himself, "My new poem of late has surely made trouble for me. What am I to do?" It had not been more than a few days when he was sent back to become prefect of Lianzhou.[35] In his own explanation of the poem, he wrote, "In the spring of the twenty-first year of the Zhenyuan era [805], when I was vice director of the State Farms Bureau, this [Xuandu] temple had no flowers as yet. That same year I was dispatched to be prefect of Lianzhou. Upon arriving in Jingnan, I was demoted again to assistant prefect of Langzhou.[36] I remained there for ten years before I was summoned back to the capital. Everyone said that the temple grounds were filled with 'Immortal Peach Trees' planted by the Daoist priests with their own hands and that, in full bloom, they resembled rosy clouds.[37] And so the preceding piece was a record of this transitory phenomenon. Then I

---

the Yuanhe Reign" 元和十年自朗州承召至京戲贈看花諸君子, which would place its date of composition in 815. The custom of "viewing flowers" was practiced by those who passed the spring examinations in the capital.

33. The "purple paths" refer to roads of the capital. "Red dust" often connotes a place of great activity, but is also used figuratively by Buddhists to refer to the mundane cares of the everyday world.

34. Xuandu temple was a Daoist monastery in Chang'an.

35. Lianzhou is modern-day Lianxian in Guangdong province.

36. Jingnan is modern-day Jiangling in Hubei province.

37. The term "Immortal Peach Trees" usually refers to the peach trees grown in the Imperial Gardens. There is a legend that recounts the story of the Queen Mother of the West bringing "Immortal Peaches" to Han Emperor Wu, each one of which would add three thousand years to one's life. (See *The Inside Story of Emperor Wu of the Han* 漢武帝內傳.)

was dispatched yet again, and now, after fourteen years, I have finally become the director of the Bureau of Receptions. I returned to stroll in Xuandu and it was desolate, lacking even a single tree. Only mallow and wild oats rustled in the spring breeze. And so I wrote another poem in 28 characters to await a future outing there. Written this third month of the second year of the Taihe era [828]." The poem reads:

> The expansive courtyard is half-covered with moss,
> The peach blossoms silently perish as the bean
>   flowers open.
> Where now are the priests who planted the peach trees?
> Gentleman Liu from once before now arrives alone. (2.2)

劉尚書自屯田員外。左遷朗州司馬。凡十年。始徵還。方春。作贈看花諸君子詩曰。

> 紫陌紅塵拂面來
> 無人不道看花回
> 玄都觀裡桃千樹
> 盡是劉郎去後栽

其詩一出。傳於都下。有素嫉其名者。白於執政。又誣其有怨憤。他日見時宰。與坐。慰問甚厚。既辭。即曰。近者新詩未免爲累。奈何。不數日。出爲連州刺史。其自敘云。眞元二十一年春。余爲屯田員外時。此觀未有花。是歲出牧連州。至荊南。又貶朗州司馬。居十年。詔至京師。人人皆言。有道士手植仙桃滿觀。盛如紅霞。遂有前篇。以記一時之事。旋又出牧。於今十四年。始爲主客朗中。重遊玄都。蕩然無復一樹。唯兔葵燕麥。動搖於春風耳。因再題二十八字。以俟後再遊。時大和二年三月也。詩曰。

> 百畝庭中半是苔
> 桃花靜盡菜花開
> 種桃道士今何在
> 前度劉郎今獨來

Liu's quatrain in honor of the recent graduates of the spring examinations, who by custom go to view the flowers in the city temples, contains a seemingly innocent reference in the last line to his extended absence from the capital region. The narrative resumes by telling us: "Once his poem got out, it was circulated throughout the capital." This is an explicit reference to a principle manifested repeatedly in the anecdotes of *Storied Poems*: poetry always seeks a wider audience. The corollary, that poetry always seeks a higher audience, is demonstrated when the poem is reported to the execu-

tive official by a jealous rival as evidence of Liu's defiant state of
mind. That a poem could be used as reliable evidence to substantiate
such a claim shows that expectations of protest sentiments in poetry
were still vital.[38] After an interview with the executive official, Liu
is demoted once again and sent off to resume his previous position,
suggesting that his enemy's ruse was successful.

Storied Poems provides the "insider's story" by appending Liu
Yuxi's own explanation of this poem and its sequel. In his own
account, Liu mentions his repeated demotions in the course of
matter-of-factly outlining his official career, giving no hint of frus-
tration or dissatisfaction. He claims that he wrote his poem about
the peach blossoms as "a record of this transitory phenomenon" and
nothing more. A poem may be defined as "emotions stirred within
that take on outward form in words," but the interpretation of this
outward form is contingent upon a number of factors external to
the poem, including audience and context.

The anecdotes of *Storied Poems* usually provide us with an indi-
cation of both audience and context. This particular narrative pre-
sents two different scenarios. In the first scenario, as told in the
voice of the anonymous "historian," the audience consists of the of-
ficial class in general and the executive official in particular; the con-
text is the return of Liu to the capital and his subsequent demotion
on charges, substantiated by his poem, of being a malcontent. In this
context, the audience takes his closing couplet as a protest against his
extended absence from the capital. Liu Yuxi shows that he is fully
aware of this reading when he laments, "My new poem of late has
surely made trouble for me. What am I to do?" In the second sce-
nario, told in Liu Yuxi's own voice, the audience is made up of both
the "Fine Gentlemen Viewing Flowers" to whom the poem is ini-
tially addressed, and the readership of the *Collected Works of Liu
Mengde* [Yuxi] 劉夢得文集, from which this excerpt is drawn; the
context is Liu's return to the capital and his viewing of remarkable
peach blossoms on the advice of his acquaintances. Read in this

---

38. They remained vital long after the Tang. The famous "Crow Terrace" 烏臺
trial of the Northern Song saw Su Shi's poems entered in evidence against him as
proof of his seditious thoughts.

light, the closing couplet marks the rise of the ephemeral peach blossoms along the timeline of Liu's life.

The second scenario, from the mouth of the author himself, corrects the misinterpretation forced upon Liu's poem by the slanderous intent of his foe. Liu's enemy cleverly tapped into the tradition of protest poetry to support his charge. By including both anecdotes, *Storied Poems* implicitly acknowledges the danger of a poem being misunderstood without proper contextualization—a concern that goes back to the Mao prefaces of the *Poems*. By using his absence from the capital to set the time frame in which the peach trees flourished, Liu *is* drawing attention to his demotion. The question lies in whether he intended this as a form of protest, as a simple means of marking the passage of time, or as a combination of the two; resolving this question requires knowing Liu's state of mind at the time of composition. According to canonical precepts, state of mind is precisely what a poem articulates. For the state of mind to be intelligible, however, a context is required; by providing two contexts—one of production and one of reception—the narrative renders Liu's state of mind ambiguous. The Chinese tradition provides a way of resolving the ambiguity: since the poem, by definition, is an expression of Liu's state of mind, then Liu's interpretation is naturally more reliable than that of any outsider, particularly one with a political ax to grind. In the end, however, it is the reception of the poem, regardless of the state of mind that produced it, that has the power to affect Liu Yuxi's life. He languished for another fourteen years in the south as a result of his poem, regardless of whether he meant it to be a form of protest.

In all of these "political" anecdotes, poetic discourse is used as an attempt to achieve an end: defense against verbal attack, criticism of incompetent authority figures, pursuit of material reward, elevation of status at court, restoration of justice for the wronged, release from military duty, exemption from examination, exposure of abuse of power, or promotion of peace. And, as was the case with Liu Yuxi, a poem can be taken as attempting to achieve a political end even when the author disavows that intention. What emerges as a common theme in all of these narratives is that the efficacy of poetic discourse in achieving its end is contingent upon how well it is deployed in its social and political context. This is a bound form of discourse, bound to its world—bound to succeed, or bound to fail, depending on how it negotiates those worldly binds.

III

There is more than one way of measuring status. All of the anecdotes discussed above concern poetry's impact in sociopolitical realms: determining positions at court or in the civil bureaucracy, establishing the parameters of military and religious service, even influencing the treatment of children. And while the power of poetry often extends to these realms, it has its immediate impact in the realm of poetry itself. As the anecdotes of *Topical Tales* so clearly show for a previous era, competence in poetry can be demonstrated simply to enhance one's reputation for poetic competence.

The express admiration of the emperor is held up as the ultimate recognition of poetic competence. This attitude can already be discerned in the *Zuo Tradition*, it underlies the performance of poetic expositions (*fu* 賦) at the Han courts, and it continues right into the Tang. The anecdotes in *Storied Poems* that demonstrate this principle stretch back to the Six Dynasties.

Emperor Xiao Wu [r. 454–464] of the Liu Song dynasty [420–79] once intoned Xie Zhuang's [421–466] "Poetic Exposition on the Moon" and sighed in admiration for a long while. He declared to Yan Yanzhi [384–456], "Now that Xie Zhuang has composed this, I can say that I will no longer hold much regard for the ancients nor those who are to come in the future. Is old Prince of Chen worthy of veneration any longer?"[39] Yanzhi replied, "It truly is as your majesty thinks. But, when he says,

> My beauty is far off and news of her is scarce,[40]
> She may be a thousand leagues distant but we share
>   the bright moonlight.

---

39. This is a reference to Cao Zhi 曹植 (192–232), who was enfeoffed as Prince of Chen. He wrote one of the most famous *fu* in Chinese literature, "Poetic Exposition on the Spirit of the Luo River" 洛神賦, and was widely acclaimed as a "literary genius."

40. *Jindai* reads 邁兮 for 兮邁.

Is it not a little late in the day to be realizing this?" The emperor truly thought this to be so. He granted an audience to Xie Zhuang, who responded by saying, "Yanzhi has a poem that goes something like:

> If you live, we always yearn for one another,
> If you die, you shall never return.

Is not this even worse than what I said?" The emperor clapped his hands over this for the rest of the day. (7.1)

宋武帝嘗吟謝莊月賦。稱歎良久。謂顏延之曰。希逸此作。可謂前不見古人。後不見來者。昔陳王何足尚邪。延之對曰。誠如聖旨。然其曰。

> 美人兮邁音信闊
> 隔千里兮共明月

知之不亦晚乎。帝深以為然。及見希逸。希逸對曰。延之詩云。

> 生為長相思
> 歿為長不歸

豈不更加於臣邪。帝拊掌竟日。

The narrative opens with the emperor himself intoning "Poetic Exposition on Snow" by Xie Zhuang, thus granting the work prestige because it has found its way into the personal repertoire of the emperor and because he takes the time to perform and savor the work for himself at court. With his comments to Yan Yanzhi, the emperor moves from an appreciation expressed physically through his chanting and subsequent sighing to an appreciation expressed in the evaluative terms of literary genealogy. In his hyperbolic judgment, the emperor claims that Xie Zhuang's literary talent transcends the temporal limits of past and future, rivaling that paragon of literary talent, Cao Zhi. Emperor Wu has anointed Xie Zhuang's composition with a tripartite appreciation, consisting of a performance by his own person at court, a heartfelt reaction expressed through his sighs, and a highly favorable evaluation of Xie's talent.

Despite its effusiveness, the emperor's judgment is by no means absolute. He was likely seeking confirmation of his judgment from Yan Yanzhi, who quickly gives it with a pat phrase—"It truly is as your majesty thinks"—but then just as quickly proceeds to question the royal judgment. Yan Yanzhi, who seems to be somewhat piqued by the emperor's hyperbole, bases his criticism of Xie's composition on a witty turn of phrase, suggesting that while one may realize that one shares the moonlight with one's lover, it does not do much good if the lover is a thousand miles away. The emperor is swayed by Yan's logic and "truly thought this to be so." The narrative then immediately proceeds to an audience with Xie Zhuang, during which he diffuses the criticism by pointing out a line in Yan's poetry that seems even more futile than his own. The emperor, "clapping his hands for the rest of the day," indicates that Xie has won out in this battle of literary wits.

While the emperor may be the ultimate arbiter in the contest between Xie Zhuang and Yan Yanzhi, he is a curiously insubstantial sort of judge. His original evaluation of Xie is facile and overstated, and despite his initial fervor, he abandons his opinion after a minor objection by his underling. He then just as quickly reverses himself again in the face of Xie's equally minor rebuttal. He seems to lack any sound principle on which to base his literary judgments. In short, the emperor is poetically incompetent. He exists merely as a foil, enabling the true protagonists of this anecdote, the "literary" men Xie Zhuang and Yan Yanzhi, to show forth their talents. In fact, judging by this narrative, it would seem that the emperor has nothing better to do than engage in witty banter with literary men at court, thus converting what should be a site for political negotiation over imperial administration into an arena for polite verbal sparring. In fact, the entire anecdote is not about poetic performance at all, but about debating the merits of poetic compositions. The debate here is not about how verbal expression can demonstrate which man's character is of a higher quality or which man is better suited to serve. The debate is closed off to any concern that might be characterized as political or moral, engaging instead in fancifully contrived analyses of a poetic discourse that is really about nothing but itself. This was a common criticism lodged by later critics against the literary compositions of the Six Dynasties era: that they suffered from a morally dangerous absence of any substantive meaning. In this anecdote, the literature's moral vacuum seems to have infected the very center of political power, by bending the discourse found there toward its own pointless ends.

The figure in the Tang that embodies this principle of poetry for poetry's sake is, of course, Li Bai 李白 (701–762), who liked to portray himself as the quintessential, free-spirited, drunken Poet. His efforts at self-representation were highly effective, as is attested by three different anecdotes about him collected together under one entry in *Storied Poems* (3.1). The entry appears under the "Highly Unconventional" category and does not concern any type of poetry so much as it does Li Bai's behavior as "The Poet." The first anecdote narrates Li Bai's arrival in the capital and the early recognition of his talent by He Zhizhang 賀知章 (659–744), who tags him with the famous epithet, "Banished Immortal" 摘仙. The second anecdote establishes Li Bai's disdain for rules of prosody when he teases Du Fu for exerting so much effort over them: "Why has he grown so thin since last we parted? / It must be how hard he has struggled with his poems" 借問別來太瘦生 / 總爲從前作詩苦. This sets the stage for the third and primary anecdote.

Emperor Xuanzong heard of Li Bai and summoned him to be a member of the Hanlin Academy.[41] Because his literary aptitude surpassed that of everyone else and his ability and experience were both superb, the emperor immediately placed him in a top position, and, as a result, he was never ordered to perform official duties. Once, the emperor was amusing himself with the palace women, when he said to Gao Lishi [his eunuch attendant], "Faced with this lovely sight at this fine hour, should we be the only ones to take delight in these singing girls? What if we were to have a literary man of extraordinary talent make them known through his words so that we may vaunt them to later ages?" And so the emperor ordered Li Bai to be summoned. Meanwhile, the Prince of Ning had invited Li Bai to a drinking party at which he had already become intoxicated.[42] He arrived at court and made his obeisance respectfully. The emperor, knowing that Li Bai disdained tonal regulations and claimed that it was not his strong point, commanded him to compose ten pentasyllabic regulated verses on the theme of "Merrymaking in the Palace." Li Bai kowtowed and said, "The Prince of Ning has been offering me drink, and I am already quite intoxi-

---

41. Li Bai was offered the post of academician in attendance 翰林供奉, a nominal post in the Institute of Academicians 學士院, also known as the Hanlin Academy 翰林.

42. The Prince of Ning (680–741) was the eldest son of Emperor Ruizong (r. 710–712). He was originally the crown prince but abdicated his position to the Prince of Chu, who later became Emperor Xuanzong.

cated. If Your Majesty were to assure me that I have nothing to fear, then I should exert my meager talents to the utmost." The emperor agreed to this. He then sent two eunuchs over to hold Li Bai up by his armpits and commanded that ink should be ground and that a brush should be moistened in it and given to him. Then the emperor ordered two more people to roll out a piece of ruled vermilion silk in front of Li Bai. Li Bai picked up the brush to pour out his thoughts and without a single pause he completed ten verses in an instant, requiring no revision whatsoever. The brush-strokes were powerful and sharp, like a phoenix rising and a dragon clawing; the prosody was well balanced. There was not a single verse lacking in peerless elegance. The first one read:

> The hue of willow: paleness of yellow gold,
> Pear blossoms: fragrance of white snow.
> The jade tower nests the halcyon,
> The pearl palace houses the duck and drake.
> The chosen girls attend the emperor's engraved chariot,
> The summoned singers emerge from the inner chambers.
> Who is the paragon of the palace?
> Soaring Swallow in Zhaoyang hall.[43]

All of the verses are not recorded here. Li Bai was constantly in and out of the palace and enjoyed great favor from the emperor. In the end, he was expelled due to his carelessness, and the emperor even made a special proclamation dismissing him because of his lack of administrative competence. (3.1c)

玄宗聞之。召入翰林。以其才藻絕人。器識兼茂。便以上位處之。故未命以官。嘗因宮人行樂。謂高力士曰。對此良辰美景。豈可獨以聲伎為娛。倘時得逸才詞人。詠出之。可以誇耀於後。遂命召白。時寧王邀白飲酒。已醉。既至拜舞頹然。上知其薄聲律。謂非所長。命為宮中行樂五言律詩十首。白頓首曰。寧王賜臣酒。今已醉。倘陛下賜臣無畏。始可盡臣薄技。上曰。可。即遣二內臣腋扶之。命研墨濡筆以授之。又令二人張朱絲欄於其前。白取筆抒思。暑不停綴。十篇立就。更無加點。筆跡遒利。鳳跱龍拏。律度對屬。無不精絕。其首篇曰。

> 柳色黃金嫩
> 梨花白雪香
> 玉樓巢翡翠
> 珠殿宿鴛鴦

---

43. Han Emperor Wu's favorite dancer, Zhao Feiyan (Flying Swallow), lived in Zhaoyang hall, one of the eight halls of the rear palace.

選妓隨雕輦
徵歌出洞房
宮中誰第一
飛燕在昭陽

文不盡錄。常出入宮中。恩禮殊厚。竟以疏縱。乞歸。上亦以非廊廟
器。優詔罷遣之。

Li Bai's poem has no political or moral overtones, but is simply an
appreciation of the beauty of the emperor's palace ladies, comparing
the lead singer to the legendary Han beauty, Zhao Feiyan. The em-
phasis in the anecdote is not on the motivation for the poems (a
simple command) or any reaction to them (none is mentioned), but
on the performance of composing and inscribing the poems. Li Bai
first asks for immunity from the emperor should he fail, an ac-
knowledgment that there is something at stake in his performance.
One senses that he makes this request out of deference to the em-
peror, and perhaps to generate some suspense in his audience, know-
ing full well that he is capable of meeting the challenge. The narra-
tive describes the preparation for the performance in vivid detail:
eunuchs supporting Li Bai in his drunken state, the grinding of the
ink, the moistening of the brush, the unfurling of the silk. The
performance itself is described in temporal terms: the speed and
certitude with which it is executed are indicators of Li Bai's prodi-
gious talent. Even the bold quality of the resulting brushstrokes is
mentioned—as the consummate showman, Li Bai excels in every
aspect of his art. He is "collected" by the emperor as a showpiece for
his court; in the end, Li Bai's poetic competence is about nothing
more than itself. Such self-referential competence cannot maintain
the poet's status at court for long. It fails to compensate for his
"carelessness" and his lack of "administrative competence" because it
is not properly deployed to win and maintain political advantage. Li
Bai craves a stage at the center of power upon which he can display
his talent, but when the powerful are no longer dazzled by his tal-
ent, they soon realize that he has nothing else to offer. The story of
Li Bai shows that poetic talent alone is not enough to maintain a
position in the political hierarchy, but the very fact that there *is* a
story of Li Bai shows that poetic talent may constitute itself as
something worthy of record outside the political hierarchy.

Li Bai's immediate performance before the emperor during the High Tang is transmuted into a deferred "performance" through writing, in an anecdote about the Mid-Tang poet Bai Juyi 白居易 (772–846).

Minister Bai Juyi had a concubine named Fansu, who was expert at singing, and a singing girl named Xiaoman, who was expert at dancing. Once he composed a poem, which read in part:

> Cherries: Fansu's mouth,
> Willows: Xiaoman's waist.

He was already quite old when Xiaoman was just at the height of her attractiveness. So he composed lyrics to the melody of "Willow Branch" as a figurative expression of his thoughts.[44] They read:

> Myriad branches on a single tree in the spring breeze,
> Are paler than a golden hue, softer than silk.
> In the southeast corner of Yongfeng ward,[45]
> Not a soul all day: to whom shall it entrust itself?

When Xuanzong [r. 847–860] was in power, the imperial musicians sang this song. The emperor asked who it was by and where Yongfeng was located. Those in attendance answered all of his questions. As a result, he commanded the east commissioner to retrieve two willow branches from Yongfeng and to plant them within the imperial palace. Bai was moved that the emperor knew of his reputation and, moreover, that he esteemed his elegant style. He composed another stanza; its last lines read:

> From now on, I surely know that within the constellations,
> A pair of stars has been added to the glow of Willow House.[46] (2.4)

---

44. The song "Willow Branch" 楊柳枝 was originally a *yuefu* piece of the Han dynasty entitled "Breaking a Willow Branch" 折楊枝. It became a palace-style song 宮詞 in the Sui dynasty, but it was Bai Juyi who refurbished it as a popular piece of music for the quatrain form. His concubine, Fansu, was famous for her performance of it.

45. Yongfeng was the name of a ward in Chang'an.

46. *Taiping* reads 星 for 枝. This reading matches the rhyme set in the first two lines of the poem (found in *juan* 37 of *Baishi Changqing ji* 白氏長慶集): 一樹衰殘委泥土，雙枝榮耀植天庭. "Willow House" refers to the twenty-fourth of the twenty-eight Chinese constellations. It includes eight of the stars in the Hydra constellation.

白尚書姬人樊素善歌。妓人小蠻善舞。嘗爲詩曰。

　　櫻桃樊素口
　　楊柳小蠻腰

年既高邁。而小蠻方豐艷。因爲楊柳之詞以託意。曰。

　　一樹春風萬萬枝
　　嫩於金色軟於絲
　　永豐坊裡東南角
　　盡日無人屬阿誰

及宣宗朝。國樂唱是詞。上問誰詞。永豐在何處。左右具以對之。遂因
東使。命取永豐柳兩枝。植於禁中。白感上知其名。且好尚風雅。又爲
詩一章。其末句云。

　　定知此後天文裡
　　柳宿光中添兩枝

All of the personages in this anecdote may be real, and Bai may have actually penned the lines attributed to him, but a glaring discrepancy remains. Bai Juyi died one year before the reign of Xuanzong 宣宗 began. This discrepancy could be attributable to scribal error; perhaps Emperor Wuzong 武宗 (r. 841–846) was meant instead. It is more likely that it points to the nature of the anecdote itself: it was cobbled together from "known facts" about these poems with no particular care paid to historical accuracy. The emphasis is not on producing a reliable account of the events, but on telling a story about the interaction between Bai Juyi and the emperor—whoever that might be—through the medium of poetry.

The narrative portion of the anecdote predisposes us to read the text of Bai's "Willow Branch" song "as a figurative expression of his thoughts." These thoughts are summed up succinctly in the preceding line: "He was already quite old when Xiaoman was just at the height of her attractiveness." They are given further shading by the initial couplet quoted in the anecdote, in which Bai compares Xiaoman's supple waist to willows. Thus, the stage is set for a song that figures Xiaoman as a solitary willow in the entertainment quarters of Chang'an, pining away for a companion who would be Bai Juyi himself were he not so old. The emperor, appreciating the figurative aspect of the poem, converts the abstract sentiment into a concrete symbol by having two branches from a Yongfeng willow transplanted to the palace gardens, representing the union of the would-be lovers. Bai, to show his appreciation for this gallant gesture, responds with a poem that transports these concrete symbols to the celestial plane—the heavenly reflection of the imperial court.

Bai Juyi was famous in the entertainment quarters for his popular songs. Here, one of his songs finds its way into the repertoire of the imperial musicians—an example of the cross-fertilization that took place between court music and "popular" music. As we have already noted, this inward movement of poetry to the center of power is a common theme in *Storied Poems*. The imperial musicians' gathering of poems from outside the court to play for the emperor on the inside mirrors the ancient practice of "gathering poems" touched on in Meng Qi's preface, whereby the music master would play poems to the king that reflected the grievances and delights of the people. The shape of the transaction has been preserved here, but the content is entirely different.

We are no longer dealing with the king as the ultimate audience for works reflecting the state of mind of the undifferentiated mass of people. This is a more personal relationship between the emperor and a member of the elite official class who also happens to be a famous poet. Such a relationship has already been seen in the anecdote about Li Bai; the difference in this case is that Bai Juyi is not actually *in* the emperor's entourage. It is his poem alone that has reached the emperor. Bai is not rewarded for his deft performance of the poem, but purely for the affective power of the poem—its ability to move the emperor to respond emotionally. It is a personal expression of his emotions in "an exquisite composition of lyricism," to employ Meng Qi's phrase. The first two sections of *Storied Poems*—"Moved by Emotions" and "Moved by Events"—constitute half of the bulk of the collection and are filled exclusively with this type of poetry.

When Meng Qi claims in his own preface to be providing "Lesser Prefaces" for these types of poems, he may simply be deprecating his short narratives, but the label strongly evokes the ancient mode of exegesis found in the Mao prefaces to the *Poems*. Meng Qi in his own "Lesser Prefaces" does not mimic the form of his exemplars (the terse first line followed by a fuller narrative). The form of narrative he employs in his anecdotes owes more to his source materials than it does to ancient canonical prefaces. Meng's narratives *do* portray the poet as being engaged with society, but on different terms than those found in the "Lesser Prefaces." The paradigm of the disgruntled "masses" criticizing or praising their lofty ruler has been replaced by the figure of the individual literatus negotiating his relationship with another individual (whether it be a concubine or the emperor himself) through the vehicle of poetry. In this case, the negotiation of that relationship—Bai Juyi's poetic acknowledgment of the emperor's appreciation—becomes part of the very poem that caught the emperor's ear in the first place. The reception of the poem is woven back into its production.

It is no surprise that the court—with its explicit, often formalized, emphasis on the importance of discourse—is a likely site for the demonstration of talent through poetic competence, either immediate or deferred. *Storied Poems* shows that such demonstrations were conducted in private conversation as well. In such circumstances, well away from the arena of authority, wit in poetry is used as an instrument to build and strengthen bonds of friendship.

Su Weidao 蘇味道 (648–705) and Zhang Changling 張昌齡, "both famous for their poetry," engage in some friendly banter during their holidays, when they can relax and leave their official roles behind them.

During the Kaiyuan era, Grand Councilor Su Weidao and Zhang Changling were both famous for their poetry.[47] They met once while on their holidays and began teasing each other good-naturedly. Changling said: "The reason my poems are not as good as yours, Sir, is because they lack the phrase 'silver blossoms close.'" Su had a poem called "Viewing Lanterns" that read:

On trees of fire silver blossoms close,[48]
The starry bridge unfurls its iron chains.[49]

---

47. This seems to be the wrong era title since both Su Weidao and Zhang Changling lived before the Kaiyuan era. *Shihua* reads 俱有詩名.

48. The image of silver blossoms on trees of fire is a metaphor for the dazzling display of lanterns festooning city streets during a festival.

49. The "starry bridge" refers to the mythical bridge that forms every year on the seventh day of the seventh lunar month in order to allow the Weaving Girl and the Herd Boy to visit one another across the Milky Way.

Murky dust whisks off with the horses,
A luminous moon follows from behind.

"Your poems may lack 'silver blossoms close,'" said Weidao. "But they do have 'brass nails' (*jintong ding*)." Changling had given a poem to [his older brother] Zhang Changzong that read:

On a day off I am Fu Qiubo,[50]
Today I'm just like Ding Lingwei (*jin
    tong* Ding Lingwei).[51]

They both clapped their hands and laughed together. (7.4)

開元中。宰相蘇味道與張昌齡俱有名。暇日相遇。互相誇誚。昌齡曰。
某詩所以不及相公者。為無銀花合故也。蘇有觀燈詩曰。

火樹銀花合
星橋鐵鎖開
暗塵隨馬去
明月逐人來

味道云。子詩雖無銀花合。還有金銅釘。昌齡贈張昌宗詩曰。

息日浮丘伯
今同丁令威

遂相與拊掌而笑。

The pun here is found in poetry already composed and hinges on aurally discerning a coincidence in the pronunciation of three characters. This is evidence that in the Tang poems continued to be first and foremost for the ear rather than the eye. The whole exchange is contingent upon each man's intimate familiarity with the other's corpus of poetry. The narrative must pause to quote the relevant lines so that the reader may share in the joke. The entire anecdote suggests that knowing a man well includes knowing his

---

50. Fu Qiubo was the name of the immortal who led Wangzi Qiao up a lofty mountain by his sleeve.

51. The first three characters of this line (*jin tong ding* 今同丁) are homophonous with the characters for "brass nails" (*jin tong ding* 金銅釘). In folklore, Ding Lingwei is a Han figure who went to study the occult on Lingxu mountain. He succeeded in becoming an immortal and returned to his hometown in the form of a crane. When a young boy tried to shoot him down, he flew off, chanting a poem lamenting the changes that had taken place in the people during his absence.

poetry well, and that poetic wit can be demonstrated in fanciful "reading" of poetry and not just in the production of it.

A similar interaction based on fanciful readings occurs when Zhang Hu 張祜 meets Bai Juyi for the first time.

The poet Zhang Hu had never made the acquaintance of Bai Juyi. When the Honorable Bai was prefect of Suzhou, Hu came to visit him for the first time, and upon meeting him Bai said, "I've been a great admirer of yours for a long time. I remember the poem you wrote for your examination."[52] Hu was amazed and asked, "What does Secretary Bai mean?" Bai replied,

> Where has the mandarin duck filigreed sash
> been cast aside?
> To whom has the peacock silken gown
> been entrusted?

"Is this not your examination poem?" Zhang lowered his head[53] and smiled, then looked up and replied, "I too remember the Secretary's 'Song of Mulian.'" Bai asked, "What is it?" Hu said,

> Above, the endless Blue Vault; below, the
> Yellow Springs,[54]
> Both planes vast and boundless, in neither
> was she seen.

"Is this not the 'Song of Mulian'?"[55] And so the two of them drank together joyfully the whole day through. (7.5)

詩人張祜。未嘗識白公。白公刺蘇州。祜始來謁。才見白。白曰。久欽籍。嘗記得君款頭詩。祜愕然曰。舍人何所謂。白曰。

> 鴛鴦鈿帶拋何處
> 孔雀羅衫付阿誰

非疑頭何邪。張頓首微笑。仰而答曰。祜亦嘗記得舍人目連變。白曰。何也。祜曰。

---

52. *Taiping* adds 甚 before 欽. *Shihua* reads 問頭詩 instead of 款頭詩. This was a Tang term for poems written for the civil service examinations.

53. *Taiping* reads 張頻.

54. The "Blue Vault" is a Taoist term for the sky. The "Yellow Springs" refer to the underworld.

55. Mulian is the abbreviated Chinese transcription of Sanskrit for Maudgalyayana, the hero of Buddhist folklore who went to the underworld to rescue his mother.

上窮碧落下黃泉
兩處茫茫皆不見

非目連變何邪。遂與歡晏竟日。

In this case, the fanciful reading takes the form of willful misattribution. The lines that Bai Juyi quotes actually come from a poem of Zhang Hu's titled "Moved by the Death of General Wang's 'Thorn Branch' Dancer" 感王將軍柘枝妓歿, a sensual evocation of the absent beloved. Bai seems to be having some fun at Zhang's expense by suggesting he would write such a sensual poem on his examination. This is why Zhang bashfully lowers his head and smiles. But he soon turns the tables on Bai Juyi and demonstrates his own wit by willfully misattributing a line from Bai's "Song of Everlasting Sorrow" 長恨歌 to his "Song of Mulian," taking a description of the emperor's longing for his absent beloved and "rereading" it as a description of Mulian's search for his mother in the underworld. There may be more subtle overtones to the exchange, but it is clear that these playful misattributions produce an instant rapport between the two men, who "drank joyfully the whole day through." Zhang Hu and Bai Juyi already knew one another through poetry even though they had never met in person. The intimacy of their virtual relationship is concretized when each demonstrates an easy familiarity with the poems of the other. Their playful demonstrations of poetic competence identify the two "players" as being two of a kind: educated officials with a sophisticated attitude toward poetic production and appreciation.

The two previous anecdotes depict talking about poetry as a pastime. This practice is depicted repeatedly in *Storied Poems* as an activity closely related to poetic production itself, and the two activities inevitably converge in the production of poetry *on* the production of poetry. The three anecdotes about Li Bai mentioned above include a narrative about an encounter he supposedly had with Du Fu.

Li Bai's talent was superior and his bearing aloof; his reputation rivaled that of Reminder Chen Ziang [661–702], and the two of them coincided in their aims. In his discussion of poetry, Li said: "Ever since the Liang and Chen dynasties [502–589] poetry has been sensual and frivolous in the extreme; moreover, Shen Yue [441–513] even regulated it on the basis of tones![56] Who is there but me to revive the ancient style?" Therefore, there is very little regulated poetry in the collections of Li and Chen. Once, Li said: "To lodge one's initial impulse in something profoundly subtle, the five-character line is not as good as the four-character line, and the seven-character line is even worse; let alone getting bogged down by tonal antics!" Therefore, Li made fun of Du Fu by saying,

> I came across Du Fu on top of Fanke hill,[57]
> He wore a bamboo hat in the noonday sun.
> Why has he grown so thin since last we parted?
> It must be how hard he has struggled with his poems.

In fact, this mocks Du Fu for being constrained by tonal regulations. (3.1b)

白才逸氣高。與陳拾遺齊名。先後合德。其論詩云。梁陳以來。艷薄斯極。沈休文又尚以聲律。將復古道。非我而誰與。故陳李二集。律詩殊少。嘗言興寄深微。五言不如四言。七言又其靡也。況使束於聲調俳優哉。故戲杜曰。

> 飯顆山頭逢杜甫
> 頭戴笠子日卓午
> 借問別來太瘦生
> 總爲從前作詩苦

蓋譏其拘束也。

The anecdote opens by establishing Li Bai's poetic credentials, comparing his reputation to a poet of the previous generation who would eventually be surpassed by Li Bai in the estimation of posterity. When Li "discourses on poetry" 論詩, he is portrayed as inveighing against the poetry of the Southern Dynasties: it is obsessed with surface detail, lacks substance, and is overly concerned with tonal regulation. He sets himself up as the only poet of his generation who can "revive the ancient style" 復古 that avoids these pitfalls. Li Bai is also depicted as criticizing the longer lines, particularly the seven-character line that was popular in the Tang. The entire speech is included to set up the irony of Li Bai fashioning a tonally regulated poem in seven-character lines to mock Du Fu,

---

56. Shen Yue was a Liang dynasty historian and literary scholar who is credited with developing explicit rules governing the euphony of poetry.

57. Fanke hill was said to be in the capital region.

one of his contemporaries famous for his meticulously crafted regulated poems.

The other two anecdotes in the entry on Li Bai depict him as the poet par excellence in terms of both the texts he produces and his execution of them. This anecdote concerns his competence as a critic. The basic features of poetic competence—being able to utter, understand, and evaluate poems—certainly persist in the Tang, but as is shown by this anecdote and others in *Storied Poems*, these basic features are complemented by increasing playfulness and sophistication. Part of that sophistication arises from an increasing tolerance of differences of opinion with regard to what constitutes good poetry. Poetic competence necessarily involves staking out the parameters of what will be admitted as competence. When Li Bai gently mocks Du Fu, it is not to point out that he is a bad poet, but to chide him for exerting so much effort on a form of poetry that does not lend itself to demonstrating competence. For Li Bai, true poetic talent is best discerned in the clarity of "old style" poetry, not in slavish adherence to complex rules of prosody. And in making this assertion through a poem in the very form he disdains, he demonstrates a playfully self-referential type of poetic competence, fusing production and evaluation in one discursive instance.

As is the case in *Topical Tales*, playful displays of poetic competence not only take place between individuals in their meetings, but also are very common at group gatherings, where poetic performance provides entertainment over shared food and drink in a pleasant natural setting. Some of these gatherings—often in the form of outings or excursions—were led by the emperor himself in the tradition of the literary salons at the courts of the Southern Dynasties, but members of the official class would also engage in such entertainments on their own initiative whenever they happened to get together. *Storied Poems* contains several anecdotes that put unusual twists on such literary gatherings.

Minister Yuan Zhen [779–831] was going to hear cases as a censor in Zitong. At this time, Bai Juyi was in the capital going on an outing to Cien temple with some notable associates. They stopped for a drink beneath the blossoms, and Bai composed a poem to send to Yuan, which read:

When the flowers bloom, we get drunk together to
    dispel cares of spring,[58]
Tipsy, we break off sprigs of blossoms to use as our
    wine tallies.
Suddenly I think of my old friend off to the ends of
    the earth,
And reckon that he must have reached Liangzhou
    by today.[59]

At that time, Yuan Zhen had actually reached the city of Baocheng in Liangzhou. He in turn had sent a poem to Bai called "Dream Journey":

I dream of you and your brothers at the head
    of Serpentine,[60]
And of you heading for a stroll in the yards of Cien.[61]
The stationmaster calls someone to take our horses away,
Suddenly, I am startled to find myself in old Liangzhou.

Their spirits communicated over a thousand *li*, joining just as two pieces of a tally fit together. Is this not the way of friendship: coinciding without planning to? (5.4)

元相公稹。爲御史。鞠獄梓潼。時白尚書在京。與名輩遊慈恩。小酌花下。爲詩寄元曰。

> 花時同醉破新愁
> 醉折花枝作酒籌
> 忽憶故人天際去
> 計程今日到梁州

時元果及褒城。亦寄夢遊詩曰。

> 夢君兄弟曲江頭
> 也向慈恩院院遊
> 驛吏喚人排馬去
> 忽驚身在古梁州

千里神交。合若符契。友朋之道。不期至歟。

---

58. *Jindai*, *Taiping*, and *Lei shuo* read 春 for 新.

59. Liangzhou was a region southwest of Chang'an on the way to Zitong (in modern-day Sichuan).

60. Serpentine was the river that ran by Cien temple southwest of Chang'an.

61. *Jindai*, *Taiping*, and *Lei shuo* read 裡 for the second 院.

The two friends are united in their thoughts and reverie, but it is their poems that give their feelings for each other a transmissible concrete form, thereby allowing them to complete their connection in the corporeal world. It is the narrative context that renders these two poems remarkable, for without it there would be no way to know that the poems were composed simultaneously. The poetic competence in this case has slipped into the realm of the strange, for it is not manifested by any purposeful deployment of poetic discourse. In fact, just the opposite: in their moments of poetic production they "coincided without planning to."

Gatherings of literary men often featured a drinking game called "linked verses" 聯句 in which a topic and rhyme scheme would be chosen for poetizing and each person present would have to improvise a couplet using the theme and rhyme or else be forced to drink a penalty draught.[62] The importance of poetic competence is easily discernible in such a context, but there is such a thing as being *too* competent.

Vice Minister of Personnel Han Yu [768–824] composed "The Tale of Xuanyuan Miming," in which he recounts once spending a night with several literary companions. There was an elderly Taoist priest of fantastic appearance who told them his name and asked for lodging. His conversation was quite extraordinary. Once they had started drinking, everyone thought that he certainly would not be inclined to poetizing. They were chanting linked verses about a stone tripod in the cooking fire when they got stuck.[63] The first verse read:

> A marvelous craftsman chiseled the mountain bone,
> Hollowed out its innards to simmer and boil.

When it came to Miming's turn, he said of himself, "I am not good at common calligraphy; when I write people rarely understand it." Then he told someone else to take the writing brush in hand as he intoned,

> The dragon's head recoils into a stubby nub,
> The pig's stomach swells into a fat belly.

---

62. This game is the descendant of "word chain," which appears frequently in *Topical Tales*.

63. *Shihua* reads 石鼎 for 石翠.

All the guests sighed in amazement. The group exerted their mental faculties to the utmost, but they could not carry on, so Miming proceeded to finish it off. Someone else was chanting softly in pathetic tones, so Miming mocked him in the midst of his own chanting by saying,

> While still in the earthworm's hole,
> You make the buzzing of a fly.

His lines on the shape of the tripod already seemed sharp, but when his mockery of the soft chanter also kept to the topic and rhyme everyone was shocked into submission. After a short while he leaned up against a wall and fell fast asleep. From his nose emerged a great snoring that sounded like thunder. The guests were amazed and fearful of him; so they all scurried off to bed. In the morning he was missing, and no one knew where he was. (5.3)

韓吏部作軒轅彌明傳。言嘗與文友數人會宿。有老道士形貌瑰異。自通姓名求宿。言論甚奇。既及飲酒。眾度其必不留情於詩。因聯句詠爐中石鼎。將已困之。其首唱曰。

> 妙匠琢山骨
> 刳中事調烹

至彌明。自云。不善俗書。書則人多不識。遣人執筆。吟曰。

> 龍頭縮菌蠢
> 豕腹漲膨脝

座客無不歡異。會人思竭。不能復續。彌明連足成之。有微吟者。其聲淒苦。彌明詠中譏侮之曰。

> 仍於蚯蚓竅
> 更作蒼蠅聲

狀鼎之聲既已酷似。譏微吟者亦復著題。皆大驚伏。須臾。倚壁而睡。鼻中大鼾。其聲如雷。座人異且畏之。咸避就寢。既明。失之。莫知所在。

The monk is so exceptional in his appearance and conversation that none of the "literary companions" think he would be interested in the frivolous drinking game of composing linked verses. Even his calligraphy is beyond the ken of ordinary people. It is only fitting then that the monk comes up with a couplet so wonderful that it renders the ordinary men unable to even continue the game. As the monk finishes off the poem, one of the lesser talents mumbles to himself in the corner. This provides a striking juxtaposition between the incompetent and the supremely competent, as the monk is able to lampoon the mumbler without departing from the topic or rhyme scheme. Such a forceful display of competence "shocks everyone into submission"; the monk then removes himself from the realm of social intercourse altogether by falling into a deep sleep, his massive snores filling the silence left by his decisive demonstration of talent. The literary companions, their talents quashed, simply leave.

The monk can be read as a figure for Han Yu, who thought his own style of writing to surpass the normal writing of his age—not in degree, but in kind. This is not a contest of evenly matched opponents. When faced with such extraordinary poetic competence, mundane talents are forced to flee the arena altogether. It is not that the monk seeks to scare off his partners in the exchange; he cannot help being so talented. He is not displaying his competence in a calculated manner; it simply shows itself forth.

An unconventional poetic competence could also be deliberately fashioned and displayed. The Later Tang poetic figure Du Mu 杜牧 (803–852) is a prime example of a man who would represent himself as an extraordinary poet in spite of occupying the mundane job of government official.

Du Mu was a censor stationed in Luoyang. At this time, Minister of Education Li Yuan had quit his post of Defense Command and was living in leisure. Li's singing girls were gorgeous, paragons of their time. All the notable gentlemen of Luoyang paid him visits to see them. Li held a grand banquet, and all of the most prominent officials of the day attended. Because of Du's authority, Li did not dare to invite him to the banquet. Du sent a guest to make it known that he wished to be included in the party. Li had no choice but to rush him an invitation. Du was drinking alone before the flowers and was already quite tipsy when he heard the request and hurried to attend. Meanwhile, they had already begun drinking at the party and were being waited on by more than a hundred slave girls, all of them superbly skilled and extremely beautiful. Du sat down alone in the southern row and stared with wide open eyes, helping himself to three full drafts. "I have heard that you have one called Purple Cloud," he said to Li. "Which one is she?" Li pointed her out and Du fixed his gaze upon her for a long time before saying, "She deserves her reputation. I should think it fitting if she were to receive special favor." Li looked down and laughed.

All of the slave girls turned their heads and broke into smiles. Du drank another three goblets,[64] rose to his feet and intoned in a clear voice:

> In the radiant hall today the elegant mats
>> are unfurled,
> Who asked that Head Censor to come?
> Suddenly he blurts out something crazy to
>> shock all the guests,
> Two rows of red powdered cheeks turn at once.

Du Mu had a very relaxed demeanor and acted as if there were no one else around. (3.3a)

杜爲御史。分務洛陽。時李司徒罷鎮閒居。聲伎豪華。爲當時第一。洛中名士。咸謁見之。李乃大開筵席。當時朝客高流。無不臻赴。以杜持憲。不敢邀置。杜遣坐客達意。願與斯會。李不得已馳書。方對花獨酌。亦已酣暢。聞命遽來。時會中已飲酒。女奴百餘人。皆絕藝殊色。杜獨坐南行。瞪目注視。引滿三巵。問李云。聞有紫雲者孰是。李指示之。杜凝睇良久曰。名不虛得。宜以見惠。李俯而笑。諸奴亦皆回首破顏。杜又自飲三嚼。朗吟而起。曰。

華堂今日綺筵開
誰喚分司御史來
忽發狂言驚滿座
兩行紅粉一時迴

意氣閒逸。傍若無人。

Even as the narrative carefully indicates Du Mu's position and power in the political hierarchy, it casts him in the role of the drunken poet "drinking alone before the flowers" when the invitation to the banquet arrives. His excessive drinking and ogling of the singing girls at the party already push the bounds of decorum, but when he makes a blatant request for Li's prized girl, the impropriety is enough to make Li look sheepish and to turn the heads of the singing girls.

It is at this point—when things threaten to become uncomfortably embarrassing—that Du Mu rescues the evening with his masterful display of poetic competence. In four lines, he skillfully sums up the evening: the elegant setting of a banquet is disrupted by the arrival of a high official who invited himself and then proceeds to so

---

64. *Taiping* reads 爵 for 嚼.

unsettle everyone with his impertinent behavior that even the performers take notice. Because Du Mu performs this summation by rising to intone it with a clear voice, he successfully transmutes his boorish behavior into the stuff of poetry. The host and other guests can excuse Du Mu's impertinence because he is playing a role: the flamboyant drunken poet who ignores social conventions. The closing line—"Du Mu had a very relaxed demeanor and acted as if there were no one else around"—indicates that he has successfully occupied the role. The impetus for the poem is deeply rooted in the effect of his behavior on other people in a social setting, but his performance of the poem puts him in a state of mind that transcends that setting. The role of the carefree drunken poet has its roots in Tao Qian and was perfected by Li Bai. Tao Qian asserts the role with such insistence that it undermines his claims of successfully occupying it. Li Bai often seems to have forgotten that he was playing a role. Du Mu is in complete control of it, stepping in and out of the role as it suits him. The competent deployment of poetic discourse is the main vehicle by which Du Mu plays the role of the hedonistic poet and is the means by which he displays it to others.

In all of these anecdotes that unfold in what may be called the "literary" arena, poetic discourse is used to achieve ends less tangible than in the political arena: attracting the recognition of the emperor or satisfying his wishes, expressing gratitude for appreciation, establishing camaraderie, engaging in raillery, winning a game, playing a role. Poetry of the political arena is necessarily outward-looking, as the one who utters it attempts to maximize its efficacy by taking the circumstances of production and reception into account. Such poetry carries expectations attendant upon poetic discourse into a preexisting situation and lives or dies by the parameters of that situation. Poetry of the literary arena is more inward-looking. It emerges from circumstances arranged expressly for the production and reception of poetry—literary debates, command performances, polite correspondence, informal gatherings of friends and colleagues—and is more self-referential as a result. Under these sorts of conditions, poetry easily slips from a mode of discourse to an object of discourse—many of the anecdotes cited above narrate instances of talking about poetry rather than performing it (and, in one case, doing both). Poetic production in the literary arena is concerned less with responding to a set of preexisting circumstances than with constituting its own circumstances: forging a literary moment that is set apart from political concerns. Failure or success in such a moment does not depend on obtaining an ensuing outcome or tangible reward. Rather, it hinges on displaying the competence required to seize the moment and master it. The immediate outcome, the intangible reward, is the respect and solidarity of your peers; and it is won or lost in the moment.

IV

Tang anecdotes about poetry are rife with a theme that is all but effaced in pre-Tang narratives on poetry: love. It is only natural that the Tang would witness an explosion of poems about love, and, consequently, of narratives about those poems. At the time, poetic discourse was increasingly used to negotiate social relationships among members of the official class; meanwhile, metropolitan centers experienced a proliferation of entertainment quarters that made a business of selling the illusion of romance to these same officials. When the first activity is brought into the second locale, an endless stream of poetic and narrative discourse on the romantic ideal results. The elements of the love story are surprisingly consistent: the man is a low to mid-level official in government service; the woman is a singing girl or concubine; they are kept apart by an authority figure superior to the man; poetic discourse is used to express the pain of the lovers' separation; finally, the resulting poem finds its way to the authority figure, who may or may not react favorably to it. The variations on this standard story stake out possibilities as they were desired by men who would employ poetry to negotiate affairs of the heart.

Even though the culture of romance grew out of the entertainment quarters of Chang'an and other metropolitan centers, the values formed there were constantly read back into the court and palace—the center of political power in the immediate vicinity of the emperor. The palace was home to hosts of wives and concubines, a large portion of whom rarely enjoyed the "favors" of the emperor and thus provided the perfect vessels for the poetry of romantic longing.

During the Kaiyuan era, the padded clothing that was sent to the armies on the frontier was made by the women in the palace. There was a soldier who found a poem in his coat that read:

> The frontier soldier guarding the sandy wastes,
> Suffering the cold, how can you sleep?
> This war coat passed through my hands in the making,
> I wonder at whose side it has fallen?
> From my secret thoughts I have added extra threads,[65]
> From my hidden feelings I have given it more padding.[66]
> In this life it is already too late,
> We will fulfill our fate in the next.[67]

The soldier showed the poem to his commander, who then submitted it to the capital. Emperor Xuanzong ordered the poem to be circulated among the Six Palaces of the harem and said, "If one of you should be the author, do not conceal yourself and I will not hold you guilty of a crime." One of the palace women came forward and said that she deserved ten thousand deaths. Xuanzong pitied her deeply; so he gave her in marriage to the man who had found the poem. She then said to him, "You and I have fulfilled our fate in this life."[68] All those in attendance were moved to tears. (1.4)

開元中。頒賜邊軍纊衣。製於宮中。有兵士於短袍中得詩曰。

> 沙場征戍客
> 寒苦若為眠
> 戰袍經手作
> 知落阿誰邊
> 畜意多添線
> 含情更著綿
> 今生已過也
> 重結後身緣

---

65. "Thread" calls to mind "silken thread" (*si* 絲), which is a pun for thoughts of "longing" (*si* 思).

66. "Padding" (*mian* 綿) evokes the reduplicative term *mianmian* 綿綿, with its sense of endless yearning.

67. *Shihua* and *Tangshi jishi* (hereafter *Tangshi*) read 重結後生緣.

68. *Tangshi* reads 吾與汝結今生緣.

兵士以詩白於帥。帥進之。玄宗命以詩遍示六宮曰。有作者勿隱。吾不
罪汝。有一宮人。自言萬死。玄宗深憫之。遂以嫁得詩人。仍謂之曰。
我與汝結今身緣。邊人皆感泣。

As with the ghost-mother's poem cited earlier, the poem in this
anecdote behaves as a literal extension of Confucius's maxim "An
utterance without patterned language will not travel far." The pal-
ace woman's poem in written form traverses not only the great
physical distance between the center of the realm and its furthest
edge, but it also crosses the formidable social barriers between a lady
of the palace and a frontier soldier. The poem leaves the palace as a
secret utterance of private thoughts and returns to it as a publicly
circulated document, resulting in an openly sanctioned marriage at
which all those in attendance weep. It also travels far in terms of
making a deep impression on the emperor; a palace lady could never
have made a direct appeal to the emperor to leave the harem and
wed a soldier. If Emperor Xuanzong is to be portrayed in this nar-
rative as competent in his reception of poetry, however, he must be
moved by the patterned language of a heartfelt poem.

The poetry of *Storied Poems* often operates in this fashion. It be-
gins as a disclosure of private thoughts, but once it becomes known
to a figure with enough power to alter the circumstances of the
author, change rapidly ensues—sometimes for the better, sometimes
for the worse. In this case, the poem had to circulate back along a
chain of military command before it found an audience equipped
with both the literary sensibilities to appreciate it and the power to
effectively respond to it. The extremes in this particular story—
between the social status of the palace lady, the soldier, and the
emperor, and between the intensely private utterance and its public
result—coupled with its lack of specific detail, suggest that it is pure
fabrication. This is the perfect anecdote, either found or fashioned
by Meng Qi, to demonstrate the principles of poetry he outlines in
his preface. It is a passionate appeal with lyrical force that touches
the emotions of its audience. The affective power of the poem is
unleashed when it is literally uncovered and allowed to move out
into the world. There is a danger that the poem could be seen as an
exploitation of literary talent for gain rather than as a spontaneous
expression of the heart, but this view is countered by the conceal-

ment of the missive in a jacket and the palace woman's complete indifference as to who might receive it. She does place her poem out into the world, but not in a calculated fashion. This entry constitutes the purest example of the literary imagination envisioning poetry as it was meant to operate.

Sometimes communion between hearts and minds can constitute a love affair in the absence of a physical union.

Gu Kuang [ca. 726–ca. 808] was enjoying some free time[69] in Luoyang by strolling in the gardens with a few fellow poets.[70] They found a large *wutong* leaf floating in a stream.[71] It had a poem inscribed upon it that read:[72]

> Ever since I entered deep within the palace,
> I have not seen spring for many a year.
> I will just write upon this single leaf,
> And send it off to someone with feeling.

The next day Kuang strolled upstream where he, in turn, wrote upon a leaf and dropped it amidst the ripples. The poem read:

> Blossoms fall, deep within the palace even the oriole is sad,[73]
> This is when the hearts of Shangyang palace ladies break.[74]
> Imperial walls do not forbid the stream's eastward course,
> I write a poem on a leaf, but to whom am I sending it?

Just over ten days later, a guest of Kuang's had come to enjoy the spring scenery in the gardens when he found yet another poem on a leaf, which he showed to Kuang. The poem read:

> A single poem written upon a leaf left this Forbidden City,
> Who answered it with such singular hidden feelings?
> I sigh to myself for I can never be a leaf upon the ripples,
> Tossing and twirling, going wherever spring takes me. (1.6)

---

69. *Taiping* and *Shihua* read 閒 for 門.

70. *Taiping* reads 一二 instead of 三.

71. *Taiping* omits the 坐 character, which is probably an interpolation, according to Wang Meng-ou. *Shihua* omits 坐流.

72. *Taiping* reads 上題詩曰. *Shihua* reads 有詩曰.

73. The oriole was known for its joyful music and was a common figure for courtesans and singing girls.

74. Shangyang palace was built in Luoyang during the reign of Gaozong (r. 650–683). It lay southwest of the imperial palace and east of the gardens.

顧況在洛乘門。與三詩友遊於苑中。坐流水上。得大梧葉。題詩上曰。

> 一入深宮裡
> 年年不見春
> 聊題一片葉
> 寄與有人情

況明日於上游亦題葉上。放於波中。詩曰。

> 花落深宮鶯亦悲
> 上陽宮女斷腸時
> 帝城不禁東流水
> 葉上題詩欲寄誰

後十餘日。有客來苑中尋春。又於葉上得詩以示況。詩曰。

> 一葉題詩出禁城
> 誰人酬和獨含情
> 自嗟不及波中葉
> 蕩漾乘春取次行

In this anecdote, an intimate emotional bond is formed between strangers through an exchange of their interior feelings expressed in a concrete form, a form that is able to transcend physical and social barriers. Variations of this anecdote appear in *Friendly Discussions at Misty Brook* 雲溪友議 by Fan Shu 範攄 of the Tang and *Lofty Discussions Under the Green Window* 青瑣高議 by Liu Fu 劉斧 of the Song, a testament to the enduring popularity of this story. Just as with the previous anecdote about the palace woman and the soldier, this seems to be another fabricated account demonstrating the ideal operation of poetry. In this case, however, instead of a person arriving at the palace in response to a poem, it is another poem that arrives. The poems, even as they accentuate their anonymity, serve to capture a sympathetic state of mind in both parties. The palace woman laments that she is not a leaf that can float beyond the walls as her poem did, but there is some compensatory value in having her poem answered by "someone with feeling." As the fifth of the "Nineteen Old Poems" says, "I do not regret that the singer is in pain, / I am only hurt that few understand her music" 不惜歌者苦 / 但傷知音希. In both of these anecdotes, the palace women are portrayed as taking the initiative in sending out their poetic missives to see what might happen. They are the speaking subjects of poetic discourse on love rather than its objects, enjoying a freedom of expression if not of movement.

Most of the remaining narratives about love fall into a category that can be termed "stolen love." In these stories, an established relationship between a man and a woman is torn asunder by a more powerful figure, who then becomes the audience for the poetry expressing the suffering that he has wrought. In these stories, the women are more likely to appear as objects: first as physical objects that are stolen by other men, and then as the figurative objects of love poetry.

The very first entry of *Storied Poems* provides the template for the "stolen love" story.

During the Chen dynasty [557–589], the wife of Xu Deyan, secretary to the heir apparent, was the younger sister of the last ruler, Shubao [r. 583–589], and was enfeoffed as Princess of Lechang. Her talent and beauty were unparalleled. At this time, the Chen government was in disarray, and Deyan knew that they would not be able to preserve themselves. He told his wife, "Because of your talent and beauty you will certainly end up in the household of some tyrant when the dynasty collapses, and we will be separated forever. If our ties of love are to remain unbroken and we hope to see each other again, we should have some proof of it." Then he broke a mirror[75] in two, and each of them[76] took half. He pledged, "In the days to come you must offer your half for sale in the marketplace of the capital on the full moon of the first month. If I am still living, I will be looking for it on that day." When the Chen dynasty collapsed, Deyan's wife indeed ended up in the household of Yang Su, Duke of Yue, where she was favored very highly.[77] Deyan drifted about in dire straits and was barely able to make it to the capital. Then, on the full moon of the first month, he visited the marketplace. There was an old servant asking a greatly inflated price for half a mirror at whom everyone was laughing. Deyan led him directly back to his lodgings where he set out a meal for him and explained

---

75. *Taiping, Shihua,* and *Lei shuo* all read 鏡 for 照 throughout this entry.

76. *Taiping* reads 各 for 人.

77. During the Chen dynasty, Yue was the name of a region in modern-day Guangxi province. Yang Su 楊素 (d. 606) was a ruthless general instrumental in the founding of the Sui dynasty (581–618). He served as head of the Censorate under the first Sui ruler, Emperor Wendi (r. 581–604), who rewarded him for his success in defeating the Chen dynasty with women from its royal household.

everything. He brought out the other half of the mirror, fit them together then inscribed a poem upon it that read:

> The mirror and she both departed together,
> The mirror has returned, but she has not.
> No more does it reflect Chang'e's image,[78]
> All that remains is the bright moonlight.

When Princess Chen received the poem, she wept and refused to eat. When Yang Su found out, he was anguished, and there was a change in his countenance. He summoned Deyan at once, returned his wife to him and presented them with generous gifts. Everyone that heard about it was moved to sigh. Then he drank together with Deyan and Princess Chen and bid her compose a poem. It read:

> How bewildered I am today,[79]
> When my new and old master come face to face.
> I dare neither laugh nor cry,
> For now I feel the pain of being human.

Thereupon she returned with Deyan to the Southlands where they lived out their old age together. (1.1)

陳。太子舍人徐德言之妻。後主叔寶之妹。封樂昌公主。才色冠絕。時。陳政方亂。德言知不相保。謂其妻曰。以君之才容。國亡必入權豪之家。斯永絕矣。儻情緣未斷。猶冀相見。宜有以信之。乃破一照。人執其半。約曰。他日必以正月望日。賣於都市。我當在。即以是日訪之。及陳亡。其妻果入越公楊素之家。寵嬖殊厚。德言流離辛苦。僅能至京。遂以正月望日。訪於都市。有蒼頭賣半照者。大高其價。人皆笑之。德言直引至其居。設食。具言其故。出半照以合之。仍題詩曰。

> 照與人俱去
> 照歸人不歸
> 無復嫦娥影
> 空留明月輝

陳氏得詩。涕泣不食。素知之。愴然改容。即召德言。還其妻。仍厚遺之。聞者無不感歎。仍與德言陳氏偕飲。令陳氏爲詩。曰。

---

78. Legend has it that the Queen Mother of the West 西王母 gave an elixir of immortality to the great archer, Hou Yi 后羿. When Hou Yi's wife, Chang'e, stole the elixir and consumed it, she flew up to the moon where she was transformed into a goddess whose silhouette is said to be visible on the moon's surface.

79. *Lei shuo* reads 造 for 遷.

今日何遷次
新官對舊官
笑啼俱不敢
方驗作人難

遂與德言歸江南。竟以終老。

The key to the reunification of the separated couple is, of course, the poem. Though Princess Chen herself may have been touched by the return of the mirror with its missing piece restored, the ruthless Yang Su would surely not have been moved by the mute object. By inscribing the mirror with a poem, Xu allows it to speak his interior. The imagery in the closing couplet—"No more does it reflect Chang'e's image, / All that remains is the bright moonlight"— imbues the emptiness of the mirror's reflection with the pain of the goddess/wife's absence, made more acute by the traces of moonbeam left behind. The concrete object is thus given a voice to communicate the void that Xu Deyan feels in his heart. Yang Su, while he may be ruthless, is sensitive to the feelings expressed in the poem and moves to correct the "loss of equilibrium" felt by Xu by restoring his wife to him. Yang Su's behavior in this anecdote is supported by accounts of traditional historians who invariably note his "barbarian" background but concede that he was accomplished in his literary studies—an indication that he was capable of interpreting and appreciating a poem. The events of this narrative may never have taken place in this form, but they are plausible nonetheless.

Before Yang allows Princess Chen to go home with her husband, he drinks to the health of the couple and commands her to compose one last poem. In doing this, he is treating her as though she were still one of his concubines, whose duties include singing for their master's enjoyment. Yet, even as he exerts his power over her, Yang creates an opportunity for Princess Chen to give expression to her interior. The princess finds herself in the difficult position of "playing" to an audience that includes her old husband and her new master, both of whom have been on intimate terms with her. Her poem reflects the turmoil that this situation must create inside her; she has suffered a double loss of equilibrium in leaving her old and new husbands. Her closing couplet, "I dare neither laugh nor cry, /

For now I feel the pain of being human," captures the ambivalent feelings produced by her situation. In taking up her new role as Yang Su's concubine, she violated her role as a faithful wife to Xu Deyan, which required her to commit suicide or at least to refuse to speak to her new master. In fact, the narrative states that she was "favored very highly" in Yang Su's household. When her husband returns, she is forced to face the difficult knowledge that she can no longer comfortably occupy the role of concubine or wife. Instead, she must "feel the pain of being human," of being a fallible person who is more than a role to be played. In her poem, she is a speaking subject emerging from the point of tension between the two roles that would objectify her.

The events of this story are narrated in order to confirm the canonical model of poetry. Care is taken to show that Xu Deyan's utterance is a heartfelt and spontaneous reaction to external events, and that Yang Su's reception is equally genuine ("there was a change in his countenance"). The story reflects the desire for poetry to have an inherent power to make things right in this world, that it be a cry born of disequilibrium that can work to restore the lost balance. It is perhaps no coincidence that this story is set before the beginning of the Tang dynasty. One sign of its pre-Tang context is that the true lovers are man and wife rather than man and singing girl or concubine. Once the "stolen love" story enters the Tang, the naïve power of the poem seen here mutates into something more complicated and conditional.

During the Zaichu era [689–690] of Empress Wu's reign in the Tang dynasty, Bureau Director of the Left Office Qiao Zhizhi had a servant girl named Yaoniang, who was unparalleled in skill and beauty in her time. Zhizhi doted on her and remained unmarried for her sake. Wu Chengsi[80] heard about her and sought to bring her for an audience. His power could not be resisted, and once he saw Yaoniang, he held onto her with no intention of ever returning her. Zhizhi suffered from such vexation that he fell ill. He then composed a poem, wrote it out onto white silk, and got it

---

80. *Lei shuo* and *Tangshi* read 武承嗣 in this and ensuing instances. I have followed this variant since there is no record of 武延嗣. Wu Chengsi was the eldest nephew of Empress Wu and bore the title Emperor Expectant 皇嗣.

through to Yaoniang[81] by bribing the gatekeeper handsomely. Yaoniang was sorely grieved upon receiving the poem. She tied it to her sash and threw herself into a well, where she perished. When Chengsi saw the poem he dispatched a cruel henchman to slander Zhizhi and destroy his household. The poem read:

> The Shi house liked the latest songs in its "Golden Valley,"[82]
> Ten bushels of shining pearls went to buy graceful elegance.
> In former days you took pity and promised yourself to me,
> At that time my singing and dancing captured your heart.
> The boudoirs of your household were never locked up,[83]
> For you loved to let others watch my singing and dancing.
> A rich and highborn tyrant overstepped his bounds,
> Haughty with power he took a perverse interest in me.
> To be apart from you, to leave you, this I could never bear,
> Vainly struggling to hide behind my sleeve, I mar my makeup.
> Parting for life occurs here on this tower,
> For you my rouged cheeks are suddenly no more.

This occurred in the third month of the Zaichu era's first year [689]. In the fourth month, Zhizhi was imprisoned. By the eighth month, he had died. (1.2)

唐武后載初中。左司郎中喬知之。有婢名窈娘。藝色爲當時第一。知之寵待。爲之不婚。武延嗣聞之。求一見。勢不可抑。既見。即留無復還理。知之痛憤成疾。因爲詩。寫以縑素。厚賂閽守以達。窈娘得詩悲惋。結於裙帶。赴井而死。延嗣見詩。遣酷吏誣陷知之。破其家。詩曰。

> 石家金谷重新聲
> 明珠十斛買娉婷
> 昔日可憐君自許
> 此時歌舞得人情
> 君家閨閣不曾難

---

81. *Shihua* and *Taiping* both add 窈娘 here.

82. *Topical Tales* (36.1) relates the story of a certain wealthy man of the Jin dynasty named Shi Chong 石崇 who enjoyed entertaining his friends in his "Golden Valley" garden. He had a favorite singing girl, named Green Pearl 綠珠, who was coveted by a corrupt and powerful official named Sun Xiu 孫秀. Sun Xiu had Shi Chong arrested on trumped-up charges when he refused to give up his singing girl. When Green Pearl found out, she threw herself to her death from atop a tower in the garden to prevent Sun from having her.

83. *Shihua* and *Tangshi* read 關 for 難.

好將歌舞借人看
富貴雄豪非分理
驕奢勢力橫相干
別君去君終不忍
徒勞掩袂傷紅粉
百年離別在高樓
一旦紅顏爲君盡

時載初元年三月也。四月下獄。八月死。

The circumstances of this story are very similar to those recounted in the story of Xu Deyan and his stolen wife, yet the poem in this case results in the destruction of the lovers rather than their reunification. The contrast in the events of the stories is due at least in part to the type of poem that Qiao sends to Yaoniang. Xu Deyan composes a short, lyrical poem expressing his longing for his absent wife through the figure of their troth mirror. He inscribes the poem on the mirror itself, a token of their undying love. Qiao Zhizhi, in the voice of a servant girl named Green Pearl 綠珠, writes a longer, narrative poem recounting her famous story, told in *Topical Tales*, of being snatched away from her loving master and choosing to throw herself to her death from atop a tower rather than be possessed by a tyrant "haughty with power." Qiao inscribes the poem on the white silk of a funeral scarf (similar to the ghost-mother's scarf in entry 5.1), a concrete reminder of the duty to which he alludes in the poem. Qiao's poem—an unsubtle yet powerful suggestion that his servant girl play the role of the faithful lover in committing suicide—is cruel by any standard. In appropriating Yaoniang's own voice, he attempts to convert his singing girl into a "literary" object, a thing that will be governed by patterns of behavior set down in received narratives. He is grimly successful: the body fished from the well is just as much an object as the poem tied to its sash. Yaoniang's wearing of this poem to her death inscribes her act of suicide with significance; it is a move calculated to ensure that the meaning of her final performance is not lost on her audience. There is some "poetic justice" in Qiao's lethal poem surviving to double back on him and bring about his own death. Thus his poem reaches a primary audience in Yaoniang and a secondary one in Wu Chengsi, resulting in violence in both cases. The power of a poem to change the course of events—its directional aspect—is framed in deeply negative terms in this narrative, a stark contrast to the happy ending that Xu Deyan and his wife enjoy. In both cases, the audiences must take the poems seriously, as heartfelt expressions of sorrow, for them to have an effect. But even this sacred notion is subject to compromise in the Tang.

A gathering of "literary men" in the mansion of a prince provides a natural setting for the game of "intoning poems on objects" 詠物. The object at this particular gathering, however, is not the usual incense burner or stone tripod.

Prince Xian of Ning,[84] who was highborn and wealthy, kept several tens of singing girls of the utmost skill and beauty. To the left of his mansion there was a cake seller whose wife was delicate and pale with glowing features. Once the prince laid eyes upon her, he bestowed lavish gifts upon her husband and seized her for himself. He doted on her excessively. After a full year he asked her, "Do you still think of your cake seller?" She remained silent and would not answer. The prince summoned the cake seller and brought him to see her. His wife gazed at him fixedly with tears streaming down her cheeks and seemed overcome with emotion. Just then, the prince had about a dozen guests with him who were all literary men of the time; every one of them was struck with sorrow and amazement. He commanded them to offer poems on this topic and Right Aide Wang Wei completed his first:

> Never for the favor she receives now,
> Would she forget her former love.
> See the blossom with eyes full of tears,
> She will not speak with the King of Chu.[85] (1.3)

寧王曼貴盛。寵妓數十人。皆絕藝上色。宅左有賣餅者。妻纖白明媚。
王一見屬目。厚遺其夫。取之。寵惜逾等。環歲。因問之。汝復憶餅師
否。默然不對。王召餅師。使見之。其妻注視。雙淚垂頰。若不勝情。

---

84. *Shihua* and *Tangshi* both read 寧王憲. This refers to Li Xian 李憲, who was enfeoffed as prince of Ning (northwest of Chang'an, in modern-day Gansu province).

85. The *Zuo Tradition* relates the story of Xi Gui 息嬀 (the wife of the Marquis of Xi), who was abducted by the King of Chu. She bore her new husband two children but refused to speak for years. She eventually broke her silence to inform him that her refusal to speak was out of loyalty to her former husband.

時。王座客十餘人。皆當時文士。無不悽異。王命賦詩。王右丞維。詩
先成。

莫以今時寵
寧忘舊日恩
看花滿目淚
不共楚王言

The pitiful sight of the woman struggling with her emotions and weeping moves everyone present. It is precisely at this point that the prince commands them all to compete in composing poems, treating the pathetic scene as though it were nothing more than a still life to be quickly rendered in poetry. Wang Wei 王維 (701-761) is the first to finish his poem, a vivid encapsulation of the couple's plight. He manages to capture the woman's tender display of feelings with an image of her as a blossom in tears. The cake seller's wife, who declines to answer Prince Xian's question, is able to maintain her virtuous silence because Wang Wei has given her a voice. His poem lends significance to her refusal to speak, and, in doing so, it becomes a touching gesture on his part. The prince attempts to convert the mute stolen wife into an aesthetic object to be appreciated by the "literary men" in attendance. Wang Wei, in turn, converts the woman into a literary object by couching her refusal to speak in a received narrative, from the *Zuo Tradition*, of another stolen wife who refuses to speak to her captor, the King of Chu. His choice of narrative, unlike Qiao's in the previous anecdote, does not end in suicide. It allows the woman to maintain her virtuous silence by endowing that silence with significance. In the final analysis, however, she too is forced to play a role with no escape. Unlike the liberating influence of the poems in the story of Xu Deyan and his wife (who is able to speak for herself), these examples of poetry serve to trap the "stolen love" in repeatable, recognizable patterns—one resulting in death, the other in muteness.

The cake seller's wife is not the only "thing" that is objectified at the prince's banquet. The prince arranges the meeting between her and her husband so that their feelings for one another—their love—can be used as the "object" 物 about which poetry may be chanted. In this spectacle, poetry's own canonical function—that of giving exterior verbal articulation to the interior—is objectified through contrivance and surrogacy. Even the expression of the most poignant and sincere feelings can become the stuff of games.

This anecdote neatly combines aspects of poetic competence explained at length in preceding chapters. The prince's command to produce poetry recalls the courts of the *Zuo Tradition*; the passion captured in the poem by Wang Wei echoes the historians of the Han who use poetry to capture the angst of their subjects; the notion of a poetic contest among a gathering of literary men is familiar from the pages of *Topical Tales*. By the time of the Tang, all of these aspects of poetic competence can be absorbed and handled deftly by a poet of Wang Wei's caliber. Such adeptness in handling the variables of poetic production and reception can even be used strategically to achieve specific objectives in the arena of love.

Han Huang, the Duke of Jin, commanded the Zhexi circuit.[86] Rong Yu was a prefect in his administration, but the name of his prefecture has been lost. There was a tavern singing girl in the prefecture who excelled at singing and whose looks were also quite exquisite.[87] Yu was deeply attached to her. The music director of the region heard of her abilities and informed the Duke of Jin, summoning her to be registered on the roll of singers.[88] Yu did not dare to keep her. He arranged a farewell meal by the lake and composed song lyrics as a gift for her. He said, "When you arrive there and he tells you to sing, you must first sing these lyrics." After she arrived, Han put on a banquet at which he personally lifted a flagon and told her to sing a song for passing it around. So she sang Rong's lyrics. As soon as the tune was finished, Han inquired of her, "Does Lord Rong still have feelings for you?" She stood up timidly and answered, "Yes." Tears streamed down following her words. Han told her to change her gown and await his orders. Everyone at the banquet was anxious for her. Han summoned the music director and berated him: "Lord Rong is a notable gentleman who still cares for this local singing girl. How is it you did not know this and summoned her to register? You have placed me in the

---

86. According to the *Old Tang History* 舊唐書 (*juan* 129), Han Huang (723–787) served under Emperor Dezong 德宗 (r. 780–805) and was appointed Duke of Jin in 786. Zhexi was in modern-day western Zhejiang province.

87. *Taiping* reads 閑妙 for 爛妙. *Tang Song congshu* 唐宋叢書 reads 嫻妙. Wang Meng'ou believes 爛 is a corruption of 嫻, and I follow his suggestion here.

88. The government maintained a class of "official singing girls" 官妓 who were employed as companions for officials stationed around the empire.

wrong." Then he had him flogged ten times. Han ordered that one hundred rolls of fine silk be given to the singing girl and that she be returned forthwith. The lyrics [of Rong Yu's song] read:

> Farewell spring breeze at the lakeside pavilion,
> Willow branches and palm vines fasten our hearts.
> The oriole long lingers for she knows me so well,
> Upon parting she calls urgently again and again. (1.7)

韓晉公鎮浙西。戎昱爲部內刺史。失州名。郡有酒妓。善歌。色亦爛妙。昱情屬甚厚。浙西樂將聞其能。白晉公。召置籍中。昱不敢留。餞於湖上。爲歌詞以贈之。且曰。至彼令歌。必首唱是詞。既至。韓爲開筵。自持盂命歌送之。遂唱戎詞。曲既終。韓問曰。戎使君於汝寄情邪。悚然起立曰。然。淚下隨言。韓令更衣待命。席上爲之憂危。韓召樂將責曰。戎使君名士。留情郡妓。何故不知而召置之。成余之過。乃十笞之。命妓。與百縑。即時歸之。其詞曰。

> 好去春風湖上亭
> 柳條藤蔓繫人情
> 黃鶯久住渾相識
> 欲別頻啼四五聲

All of these events, including the happy outcome, are very similar to those recounted in the story of Xu Deyan and his wife (1.1). The transmission of the poem to the source of authority, Han Huang, is markedly different, however. The mirror in the earlier story provides a tangible link that allows the transmission of the poem between lovers and its eventual disclosure to Yang Su; the white scarf performs the same function in the story of Qiao Zhizhi and Yaoniang (1.2). In this story, however, the singing girl herself acts as the vessel for the poem, the performance of which leads to the restoration of her true love. She smuggles in the means of her own escape. The poem is so effective because it simultaneously speaks in the voice of the woman singing it and in the voice of her absent lover, Rong Yu. The "willow branches and palm vines" of the second line fasten both of their hearts together. The oriole that "calls urgently again and again" in the last couplet could be a figure for either lover at the point of separation, but is a particularly apposite image for a singing girl. The poem attests to their love by speaking both their hearts.

The hierarchy of power in this story, which takes place during the reign of Emperor Dezong (r. 780–805), is quite different from the

chaos that accompanied the fall of the Chen dynasty in the story of
Xu Deyan and his wife. Han Huang, as the commissioner of the
Zhexi circuit, is virtual governor of the region and acts as liaison
between the center of power in the capital and a cluster of prefec-
tures, one of which is administered by Rong Yu. The relationship of
superior to inferior here is objectively constituted in the bureau-
cratic institutions in which they both consent to play a role. This
objectification of power relations is what allows Han Huang to
appropriate Rong Yu's beloved singing girl simply by having her
registered on his official roll of singers. Unlike the "barbarian" Yang
Su, who receives his women through military means, Han Huang
does not need to resort to the brutality of physical violence to get
what he wants; he can exercise symbolic violence through the
power that accompanies his politically and socially sanctioned po-
sition as a superior. Han Huang's actions do not constitute a per-
sonal attack on Rong Yu (indeed, he was unaware of Rong's at-
tachment to the singing girl)—he is simply taking that to which he is
entitled. In his inferior position, Rong Yu does not have the po-
litical authority to directly address the perceived wrong done to him
without incurring severe recriminations. He naturally resorts to the
only option left to the "civil" man in such situations: the production
of poetry. But he does so in a most calculated way.

In arranging a farewell banquet by the lake, Rong Yu stages the
situation out of which he fashions his poem. After composing it, he
gives the singing girl careful instructions to sing it only after she has
arrived at Han Huang's and is asked to perform at his banquet.
Rong Yu remains in complete control of the circumstances of
composition and performance, using the singing girl to smuggle the
poem into the banquet, where it will be performed at a specified
time to produce the desired result of securing her return. His mas-
terstroke is to have anticipated Han Huang's command for her to
sing at his banquet, which grants the singing girl the opportunity to
utter the poem that challenges his authority.

The poem constitutes an effective challenge because Rong Yu has
successfully played out a strategy, manipulating the variables of
what the poem is about, *who* utters it, and, most important, *when* it
is performed. By placing the poem (a poignant evocation of the pain

of separation) in the mouth of the singing girl (the victim) and postponing its performance until a banquet (attended by many important guests), Rong Yu publicly calls Han Huang's honor into question, putting him in a situation where he could potentially suffer a loss of face. Rong is successful in doing this because he incorporates into his strategy the interval of time between the production of his poem and its subsequent performance. The prime example of such a temporal strategy is in the practice of gift giving: a gift requited too hastily is seen as an uncouth attempt to erase a debt; too much of a delay, however, leads to the appearance of ingratitude and exposes the gift-giver to the danger of being "condemned by 'what people say,' which decides the meaning of his actions."[89] Rong Yu knows that "what people say" about Han Huang is important to him and times the performance accordingly.

If Rong Yu is adept in the strategy of poetic production, Han Huang's strategy of reception is equally adept. First, he makes a show of asking the singing girl whether Rong Yu still has feelings for her, demonstrating to his "public" that he has successfully interpreted the significance of the poem. He then tells her to change her clothes and await his orders. This fine piece of showmanship leaves Han's audience wondering whether he is stripping her of her costume because he plans to punish her, or because he plans to return her to Rong Yu—a choice that will prove his sensitivity to the poem's testimonial aspect. The emotional investment of the audience in the situation is tangible in the statement "Everyone at the banquet was anxious for her." Han Huang then summons his music director and, in the fine tradition of embarrassed leadership, passes the buck. But in doing so, he is careful to refer to Rong Yu by the honorific "Lord" and to call him a "notable gentleman," thus building him up as a figure worthy of the magnanimity that Han is about to bestow. Finally, in punishing the music master and rewarding the singing girl with fine silks, he shows his willingness to make generous restitution for any wrongdoing. Through all of this, Han Huang must appear as though he believes in the poem as a genuine expression of emotion, even though he may be fully aware of Rong

---

89. Bourdieu, *Logic of Practice*, 106.

Yu's ploy. Far from allowing the poem to subvert his power, Han Huang skillfully turns the challenge to his advantage. He uses his reception of the poem to prove his image as a worthy leader and thus makes himself appear as though he deserves to wield power by virtue of his character rather than because of the position he happens to hold in the political hierarchy.

And so, through the exercise of judicious strategy in the production, performance, and reception of a poem, Rong Yu recovers his loved one and Han Huang is able to appear as a wise and generous leader. But has not something been lost in this transaction? Is it not the essence of the poem itself, according to the canonical model? How can Rong Yu's poem be seen as a spontaneous and sincere expression of his emotions when the circumstances of its composition and utterance have been staged? How can Han Huang's equally staged reception of it be seen as a genuine response to its affective power? Here, the power no longer inheres in the words of poem; it is the circumstances under which they are produced and received that determine their efficacy. This story, in effect, forges a compromise between theory and practice. It is true that the story's outcome satisfies the desire that poetry be a force for positive change. But the satisfaction of this desire is tempered by an anxiety, which acknowledges that poetry, as a socially engaged form of discourse, is not powerful enough to do the job alone.

As surely as an effective poetic strategy will achieve success, an ineffective strategy will result in failure.

At the beginning of the Taihe era [827–835] there was a censor stationed in the capital at Luoyang whose descendants are illustrious in officialdom; so his name will be concealed here. He had a singing girl who excelled at her art and was acclaimed a rare beauty of the age. At this time, Defender-in-Chief Li Fengji, who was acting as regent, heard of her and invited her to an audience. Since he had expressly requested her presence, she did not dare to decline; she adorned herself splendidly and went. When Li saw her, he ordered her to line up with all of his concubines face to face. Li had over 40 singing girls, but all ranked inferior to her. Having retired with her, he did not come out again. After a short while, Li excused himself on the pretense of illness and dismissed everyone in attendance. For two nights there was absolutely no knowledge of them. The nameless censor was racked with unending rancor; so he composed two poems and submitted them to the throne. The next day he was given an audience with Li, who simply smirked at him and said, "These are very good poems," and then concluded the audience. The first poem read:

> Have you not seen the Three Mountains in the
>   fathomless sea?[90]
> Are there footprints of the immortals that can yet
>   be followed?
> When the bluebird leaves, the road to the clouds is
>   cut off,[91]
> Chang'e has returned to her place deep in the
>   lunar palace.
> Behind the window screen she reflects on their
>   spring memories,
> Behind the study curtains who pities the one chanting
>   alone at night?
> I expect that at this very moment the moon up in
>   the sky,
> Responds merely by shining upon both our hearts. (1.11)

大和初。有為御史分務洛京者。子孫官顯。隱其姓名。有妓善歌。時稱
尤物。時太尉李逢吉留守。聞之。請一見。特説延之。不敢辭。盛妝而
往。李見之。命與眾姬相面。李妓且四十餘人。皆處其下。既入。不復
出。頃之。李以疾辭。遂罷坐。信宿。絕不復知。怨歎不能已。為詩兩
篇投獻。明日見李。但含笑曰。大好詩。遂絕。詩曰。

> 三山不見海沉沉
> 豈有仙蹤尚可尋
> 青鳥去時雲路斷
> 嫦娥歸處月宮深
> 紗窗暗想春相憶
> 書幌誰憐夜獨吟
> 料得此時天上月
> 祇應偏照兩人心

---

90. The legendary Three Divine Mountains 三神山, Penglai, Fangzhang, and Yingzhou, were reputed to be the dwelling place of immortals in the Eastern Sea 東海.

91. Orioles with blue wings acted as messengers of the Queen Mother of the West 西王母. In *Stories of Emperor Wu of the Han* 漢武故事, when the Queen Mother was about to visit Emperor Wu, two birds flew in from the west. The birds are evoked as messengers between lovers. The "road to the clouds" means the path to heaven; the phrase is also used as an expression for advancement in officialdom.

As this story belongs to the category of "stolen love," one expects some sort of reaction to the poems, whether it is positive or negative. This anecdote stands out in *Storied Poems* for the peculiar lack of efficacy of the poem cited in it. The poems that appear in every other "stolen love" story are initially communicated between the lovers themselves as a vehicle for expression of their feelings for one another. Here, the nameless censor composes a love poem expressing the pain of separation, but instead of smuggling it to his lover he submits it directly to the throne, an act that marks his composition as a protest poem rather than a love poem. Because it is openly submitted, the poem does not carry the weight of authentic feeling guaranteed by secrecy; it cannot be inevitably disclosed to Li Fengji and so sway him through its revelation of genuine sentiments. Since the piece is addressed to him directly, Li can read it as a rhetorical appeal made by an inferior to a superior. While he may appreciate its aesthetic qualities, he can reject its import out of hand simply because he has the power to do so. It is tempting to attribute this rejection to faulty reading skills on Li Fengji's part, but his smirk tells another story.

The hapless censor has failed to effectively strategize his deployment of poetic discourse. His poem may genuinely testify to his suffering, but it lacks power because he has not successfully manipulated the contexts of poetic production or reception. In fact, given the difference in political and social status between a censor and a regent, there was probably very little the censor could have done by way of strategy. For Li Fengji to even *acknowledge* the challenge of someone so far beneath him (let alone acquiesce to it) would result in a loss of face. Li's awareness of this results in his "smirk" (literally: "restrained laugh" 含笑), within which lies the duplicity of knowing how he is expected to act and knowing that he is not compelled to act at all. In his appraisal of the poems as "very good," he appreciates them on an aesthetic level while pointedly ignoring any suasive power they are meant to have.

With this story, we have strayed very far from the canonical model of poetry and the official accounts that seek to confirm it. We have arrived at a depiction of poetry as a form of socially engaged discourse that is just as likely to fall flat as it is to succeed, depending on the circumstances in which it is produced, performed, and received. Poetry has been ignored before in the tradition, but always at the listener's peril. In the entries of the *Zuo Tradition*, when a ruler is deaf to protest cast in poetry, the narrative continues in order to show us that he will live to regret it. This narrative ends with two graphs literally meaning "then it was over" 遂絕. No regrets. No repercussions. The poem has simply failed.

These "stolen love" stories, extending from the fall of the Chen dynasty in the late sixth century to the middle of the ninth century in the Tang, form a larger story arc about the devolution of faith in the power of poetic discourse to effect positive change in the world. From the optimism found in the portrayal of Yang Su's genuine "anguish" and "change in countenance," to the pragmatism of Han Huang's staged response, to the cynicism of Li Fengji's smirk, a distinct anxiety finds its way to the surface of these narratives. The anxiety is born of a suspicion that gradually allows itself to be spoken: poetic discourse has no inherent suasive power; it all depends on the who, where, and when of its production, performance, and reception: on how competently it is deployed and received. This truth is effaced from canonical writings on poetry—particularly the "Great Preface" and the ensuing critical writings that reiterate the principles found there. It is only in the practice of poetry as it is depicted in narrative that the unspoken truth may be revealed.

The static nature of critical discourse on poetry is a result of the expectations governing what one says in that genre of writing. These expectations are formed by the desire to find ancient ideals inherent in the object at hand or to show that a certain age has strayed from those ideals. That same desire informs the effort of the preface to *Storied Poems*, to carve out for that work an acceptable niche in the tradition.

The narrative anecdote is less beholden to these desires. As a reflection of practice rather than theory (no matter how murky that reflection may be), narrative discourse is more susceptible to desires regarding what people might *do* with poetry—or to anxieties about what they cannot do with it—rather than what poetry is supposed to *be*. The narrative form of the anecdotes in *Storied Poems* creates a space in which to portray poetry as a socially engaged form of discourse, a space in which canonical precepts can be questioned or even subverted. Examining these narratives gives us a different eye with which to see this thing called "poetry" (*shi* 詩).

By the end of the Tang, the *shi* poem has emerged as a highly malleable form of discourse. For the self that utters a poem, it appears as a powerful means of manipulating the behavior and impressions of others—but only if handled with competence, only when the words are well put on the page *and* in the surrounding world. The enduring lesson that the narratives of *Storied Poems* teach is that the full maturity of poetic competence in the Chinese tradition meant the death of poetry's innocence, in practice if not in principle. In order to retain its suasive power, the poem has to be *viewed* as a genuine and spontaneous expression of the heart, even though both the person who produces it and the person who receives it surely know—in their heart of hearts—that this is a fiction.

Conclusion

At this point, it may be possible to step back and make a tentative generalization regarding the development of the concept of poetic competence over the fifteen hundred years that separate the earliest narratives of the *Zuo Tradition* from the latest narratives of *Storied Poems*. With each successive age, the notion of poetic competence spreads to a larger group of people using a larger repertoire of words for poetic performance. And yet, with each successive age, the concerns addressed by those people with that repertoire diminish in scope.

The *Zuo Tradition* depicts a group of specialists, the Traditionalists, who attempt to monopolize the correct performance, use, and interpretation of the *Poems*, a limited corpus of texts for offering and citation. They do so with (in their minds at least) nothing less than the fate of domains hanging in the balance. Poetic performance always takes place on a public stage, usually before a figure of authority. Even the most minor of exchanges between individuals reflects on the status of an entire state. Poetic competence in the pre-Qin emerges as a highly politicized concept, with a restricted repertoire of words and limited field of application. It truly is a matter of diplomacy, which sees the individual striving to produce an apt offering or citation to ensure that his state stays on the right side of the Tradition.

In the final analysis, the aggregate of the narratives that constitute the *Zuo Tradition* is about more than any single state or group of states. It is about the Tradition itself and about its power to make the conduct and speech of individuals, courts, states, and the world morally intelligible. In such a context, poetic competence emerges as an important strand of cultural competence. It allows the speaking subject to weave his discourse into the strongest fibers of the larger Tradition while still pursuing the more limited goals of state and person. The *Zuo Tradition* sets the basic premise required for poetic competence to emerge; it portrays the poetic utterance as an instance of discourse able to shape events in a world that is shaped by and understood through discourse.

The *Han History* widens the net of poetic performance to include words produced in song form as the result of a passionate outburst. Poetic competence may now be enacted on a potentially limitless repertoire of words by anyone with the ability to put words into song form. Competence in this case does not require the knowledge and skill of a specialist in the Tradition, but the ability to stage the outburst in such a way that the sincerity of its words will not be questioned. Under this model, competence in poetry shifts from adeptly using old words to fashioning sincere expression of heartfelt new words. A secondary competence is found in the subsequent inscription of these words by the officials who made it their task to collect and record them as part of historical biographies. This largely ineffectual poetry recasts competence as the ability to maximize the appearance of authenticity in order to secure a place in the eyes of posterity, rather than to effect immediate change in the present.

The narratives that depict song performance in the *Han History* create a space in which the utterance of noncanonical words is legitimate if not entirely suasive. The lack of traditional sanction for these words means they remain largely powerless to effect change in the world. The stage for poetic performance during the Han remains politically charged, but a tension emerges between the discourse of politics, which deals with the legitimization and maintenance of imperial power, and the discourse of the heart, which deals with the frustrations that arise from political anxiety and failure. It is the discourse of politics that eventually triumphs in shaping the world, although the discourse of the heart is given a voice in the subsequent representation of that world in historical writing.

Topical Tales shrinks the stage of poetic competence to encompass daily verbal interaction between members of the elite ruling class during the Southern dynasties. Appreciation of poetic competence, which itself includes the notion of appreciation, becomes a means of evaluating the individual apart from the destiny of states or dynastic houses. A man, woman, or child may succeed or fail in the moment of his or her poetic utterance and reception. The prize is the right to be considered by one's peers as "one who knows," as a connoisseur who is able to properly handle poetic discourse, whether it be the received text of the *Poems*, a text drawn from another source, or an original composition. Competence in such a context is not a matter of achieving an external goal through the deployment of poetic discourse so much as owning and displaying one's competence as an end in itself.

Poetic competence during the Tang dynasty emerges as a multivalent notion, informed on the one hand by received notions and narratives, and on the other hand by the realities of poetic practice during an age in which the ability to produce and evaluate poetry became de rigueur among the literate class as a means of social and political advancement. The ability to successfully produce, perform, and receive poetic discourse begins to yield a benefit for the individual in a broadening sphere of experience, including the political, social, and romantic realms. The political savvy and erudition of the *Zuo Tradition*, the apparent sincerity of the *Han History*, and the polished wit and talent of *Topical Tales* come together to produce a powerful mode of discourse that can yield great benefits for those who have the competence to deploy it at the right time and place before the right person. Those who lack such competence are doomed to fail.

As the manipulation of the variables of poetic production and reception rises to the surface of narratives in the Tang, it spells the end of any remaining faith in the power of poetry as an *inherently* suasive form of discourse. As the *shi* poem becomes an increasingly self-conscious form of self-representation, clues as to the nature of the speaking subject behind the words are legible less in the words themselves than in *how* those words are put into the world. There are two hearts or minds (*er xin* 二心) at work in each person: one that is inscribed in the poem and one that frames that inscription for the reception of others. One must look to the uttering rather than the utterance to discover the person behind it.[1]

Over time, as more people develop facility with the tools of poetic competence and gain a voice in recording performances of competence in narrative form, the importance of poetic competence is inevitably diffused. The more discourse there is, the less any one instance of discourse seems to matter. Poetry, as a special form of language that is marked as distinct from mundane conversation, will always carry the promise of extraordinary power. The explicit depiction of the betrayal of that promise by the time of the Mid-Tang dynasty is both a symptom of and a catalyst for the maturation of China's entire literary tradition.

---

1. The most celebrated narrative of the Tang that deftly captures this duplicitous quality of discourse is "The Story of Yingying" 鶯鶯傳 by Yuan Zhen 元稹 (779–831), in which the young maiden, Yingying, sends an erotic verse beckoning her would-be seducer, Zhang, only to harshly upbraid him for his impertinence with a carefully prepared speech upon his arrival. The next night, she initiates a sexual liaison with him on her own terms, thus calling the consistency of her motives into question. Stephen Owen says of this: "A large space is opened here for interpretation. . . . But whatever interpretation we make, discourse no longer directly represents the feelings, motives, and intentions of the human subject. Once initiated, such destabilization of the authority of discourse is infectious" (*The End of the Chinese "Middle Ages*," p. 159).

Appendix

Appendix

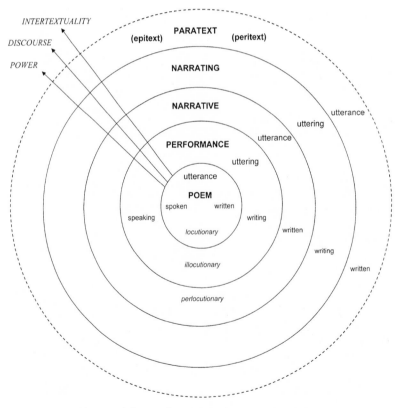

Figure 1   The poetic utterance in a narrative context

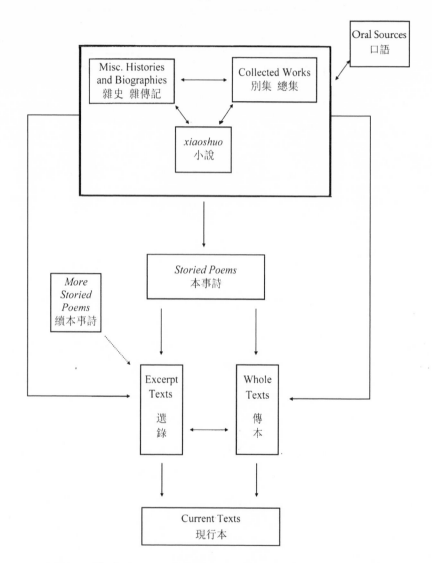

Figure 2   The formation, transmission, and emendation of *Storied Poems*

Table 1
Sources for *Storied Poems*

No.	Title of collection	Completion date	Compiler	Official position of compiler	Location of compiler at time of completion	Previous position of compiler	Intertextual links between collections	Classification in *Xin Tang shu*	Comments
I	朝野僉載	~714	張鷟	刺史	冀州	監察御史		雜傳記	also wrote 游仙窟
2	隋唐嘉話	~750	劉餗	右補闕	京	修國史		小説	son of 劉知幾
3	大唐新語	807	劉肅	登士郎	京	主簿		雜史	imitates 世説新語
4	國史補	~822	李肇	刺史	澧州	右補闕	#2	雜史	
5	次柳氏舊聞	834	李德裕	節度使	淮南	翰林學士	#2	雜史	knew 段成式, 韋絢
6	逸史	847	盧肇	從事官	鄂岳		#4	小説	friend of 李德裕
7	明皇雜錄	855	鄭處晦	校書郎	京		#5	雜史	
8	摭異志	~870	李伉	前刺史	明州		#2, 3, 7	小説	
9	松窗雜錄	~877	李濬	校書郎	京	史館		小説	son of 李紳
10	雲溪友議	~882	范攄	處士	越州			小説	paired with 本事詩
11	闕史	884	高彦休	從事官	淮南			小説	

SOURCE: *Zhongguo gudai xiaoshuo baike quanshu* 中國古代小説百科全書.

Table 2
Finding List for Translations of Entries from *Storied Poems*

Entry	Page	Entry	Page	Entry	Page
1.1	262	2.3	n/a	5.3	252
1.2	265	2.4	242	5.4	250
1.3	268	2.5	249	5.5	n/a
1.4	258	2.6	n/a	6.1	n/a
1.5	226	3.1b,c	239, 248	6.2	n/a
1.6	260	3.2	n/a	6.3	n/a
1.7	270	3.3a	254	7.1	236
1.8	163	4.1	215	7.2	206
1.9	n/a	4.2	n/a	7.3	209
1.10	n/a	4.3	223	7.4	245
1.11	274	4.4	225	7.5	247
1.12	n/a	4.5	230	7.6a,b	217, 218
2.1	n/a	5.1	220	7.7	212
2.2	231	5.2	n/a		

Table 3

Finding List for Entries of *Storied Poems* in Other Sources

Entry	Page	Entry	Page	Entry	Page
1.1	A166; B23; C51	2.3	A496; D37; B25	5.3	A55; B36
1.2	A274; B29; C51; D6	2.4	A198; C51; B23	5.4	A282; C51
1.3	D16; B25; C51	2.5	A496; C51; D59	5.5	A138; C51; D51; B48
1.4	A274; C51; D78; B23	2.6	A70; C51; D56; B33	6.1	A143; C51; D13
1.5	D80; C51; B23	3.1b,c	A201; D18; B4, 6; C51	6.2	A143; D20; B31
1.6	A198; D78; B23	3.2	C51; B30	6.3	A144; B33
1.7	A274; B23	3.3a	A273; C51; B3, 35	7.1	B6
1.8	A48, 198; C28, 51; D30; B23	4.1	A493; C51; D11	7.2	A248; C51; B35
1.9	A177, 251; C51, 52; B23, 42; D40	4.2	A497; D43; B35	7.3	A254; D13; B38
1.10	A177; C51	4.3	A362; C51; D20; B24	7.4	A250; C51; B38
1.11	A273; C51; D80; B23	4.4	A188; D15; B17	7.5	A251; B38
1.12	A274; C51; D40; B5	4.5	D40; C51; B37	7.6a,b	A249; C51; D9, 11
2.1	D10	5.1	A330; C51; B48	7.7	A249; C51
2.2	A498; D35; B29	5.2	A91; C51; D7; B13		

SOURCES: (A) Li Fang, *Taiping guangji*. (B) Ruan Yue, *Shihua zonggui*. (C) Zeng Zao, *Leishuo* 類説. (D) Ji Yougong, *Tangshi jishi juaojian*.

Reference Matter

Works Cited

Austin, J. L. [1962] 1975. *How to Do Things with Words*. Edited by J. O. Urmson and Marina Sbisà. 2d ed. Cambridge, Mass.: Harvard University Press.

Bai Juyi 白居易 (772–846). 1988. *Bai Juyi ji jianjiao* 白居易集箋校 (A critical annotated edition of the collected works of Bai Juyi). Annotated by Zhu Jincheng 朱金城. 6 vols. Shanghai: Shanghai guji.

Ban Gu 班固 (32–92 C.E.). 1970. *Han shu* 漢書 (History of the Former Han). Annotated by Yan Shigu 顏師古 (581–645). 12 vols. Hong Kong: Zhonghua.

Benveniste, Emile. 1966 [1971]. *Problems in General Linguistics*. Translated by Mary Elizabeth Meek. Coral Gables: University of Miami Press.

———. 1974. Problèmes de linguistique générale II. Paris: Gallimard.

Bourdieu, Pierre. [1972] 1977. *Outline of a Theory of Practice*. Translated by Richard Nice. Cambridge: Cambridge University Press.

———. [1980] 1990. *The Logic of Practice*. Translated by Richard Nice. Stanford: Stanford University Press.

———. [1982] 1991. *Language and Symbolic Power*. Edited by John B. Thompson. Translated by Gino Raymond and Matthew Adamson. Oxford: Polity Press.

———. 1984. *Distinction: A Social Critique of the Judgement of Taste*. Translated by Richard Nice. Cambridge, Mass.: Harvard University Press.

———. *In Other Words: Essays Toward a Reflexive Sociology*. Translated by Matthew Adamson. Stanford: Stanford University Press.

Campany, Robert. 1988. "Chinese Accounts of the Strange: A Study in the History of Religions." 2 vols. Ph.D. dissertation, University of Chicago. Photocopy of typescript. Ann Arbor: University Microfilms.

———. 1996. *Strange Writing: Anomaly Accounts in Early Medieval China*. Albany: SUNY Press.

Chao Gongwu 晁公武 (d. 1171). 1895. *Junzhai dushu zhi* 郡齋讀書志 (A record of books read in the Prefect Studio). 20 *juan*. Changsha: Wangshi.

Chen Zhensun 陳振孫 (fl. 1234–1236). 1975. *Zhizhai shulu jieti* 直齋書錄解題 (An annotated register of the books of Upright Studio). 22 *juan* in 12 vols. Taipei: Shangwu.

Dawkins, Richard. 1976. *The Selfish Gene*. New York: Oxford University Press.

DeWoskin, Kenneth J. 1975. "The Six Dynasties *Chih-kuai* and the Birth of Fiction." In *Chinese Narrative: Critical and Theoretical Approaches*, edited by Andrew H. Plaks, pp. 21–52. Princeton: Princeton University Press.

———. 1986. "*Hsiao-shuo*." In *The Indiana Companion to Traditional Chinese Literature*, edited by William H. Nienhauser, Jr., pp. 423–26. Bloomington: Indiana University Press.

Durrant, Stephen W. 1995. *The Cloudy Mirror: Tension and Conflict in the Writings of Sima Qian*. Albany: State University of New York Press.

Fan Shu 范攄 (fl. 870). 1934. *Yunxi youyi* 雲溪友議 (Friendly debates at Misty Brook). Shanghai: Shangwu.

Genette, Gérard. [1972] 1980. *Narrative Discourse: An Essay in Method*. Translated by Jane E. Lewin. Ithaca: Cornell University Press.

———. 1982. *Palimpsestes: La littérature au second degré*. Paris: Editions du Seuil.

———. [1983] 1988. *Narrative Discourse Revisited*. Translated by Jane E. Lewin. Ithaca: Cornell University Press.

———. 1987. *Seuils*. Paris: Editions du Seuil.

Gu Yuanqing 顧元慶 (1487–1565), comp. 1925. *Gushi wenfang xiaoshuo* 顧氏文房小説 (*Xiaoshuo* of Mr. Gu's study). Shanghai: Shanghai hanfang lou.

Guo Shaoyu 郭紹虞. 1980. *Zhongguo lidai wenlun xuan* 中國歷代文論選 (Selections of Chinese literary criticism through the ages). 4 vols. Shanghai: Shanghai guji.

Han Ying 韓嬰 (fl. 150 B.C.E.). 1996. *Hanshi waizhuan jishi* 韓詩外傳集釋 (A variorum edition of the *Supplementary Commentary on the Han School Poems*). Edited by Xu Weiyu 許維遹. Beijing: Zhonghua.

Han Yu 韓愈 (768–824). 1972. *Han Changli wenji jiaozhu* 韓昌黎文集校注 (An annotated critical edition of the *Collected Works of Han Changli* [Han Yu]). Annotated by Ma Tongbo 馬通伯. Kowloon: Zhonghua.

Hanyu da cidian 漢語大詞典 (The great dictionary of the Chinese language). 1988–94. 12 vols. Shanghai: Hanyu da cidian chuban she.

Hawkes, David, trans. 1985. *The Songs of the South: An Ancient Chinese Anthology of Poems by Qu Yuan and Other Poets*. New York: Penguin Books.

Hightower, James Robert. 1948. "The *Han-shi wai-chuan* and the *San chia shi*." *Harvard Journal of Asiatic Studies* 11: 241–310.

———, trans. 1952. *Han-shi wai-chuan, Han Ying's Illustrations of the Didactic Applications of the "Classic of Songs."* Cambridge, Mass.: Harvard University Press.

Holcombe, Charles. 1994. *In the Shadow of the Han: Literati Thought and Society at the Beginning of the Southern Dynasties*. Honolulu: University of Hawaii Press.

Hou Zhongyi 侯忠義. 1990. *Zhongguo wenyan xiaoshuo shi gao* 中國文言小説史稿 (A draft history of Chinese classical *xiaoshuo*). Beijing: Beijing daxue.

Hu Yinglin 胡應麟 (1551–1602). 1632. *Shaoshi shanfang bicong* 少室山房筆叢 (Collected notes from the Humble Abode mountain retreat). 17 vols. Wu Guoqi edition.

Huang Qingquan 黃清泉. 1989. *Zhongguo lidai xiaoshuo xuba jilu* 中國歷代小説序跋輯錄 (A compilation of prefaces and colophons of Chinese *xiaoshuo* through the ages). Hubei: Huazhong shifan daxue.

Hucker, Charles O. 1985. *A Dictionary of Official Titles in Imperial China*. Stanford: Stanford University Press.

Ji Yougong 計有功 (fl. 1121–61), comp. 1989. *Tangshi jishi jiaojian* 唐詩紀事校箋 (A critical annotated edition of *Recorded Stories of Tang Poetry*). Chengdu: Bashu.

Ji Yun 紀昀 (1724–1805), ed. N.d. *Siku quanshu zongmu tiyao* 四庫全書總目提要 (An annotated full list of the complete library of four branches of books). Shanghai: Shangwu.

Kamata Tadashi 鎌田正. 1971–77. *Shunju Sashi den* 春秋左氏傳 (The *Springs and Autumns* and *Zuo Tradition*). 4 vols. Tokyo: Meiji shoin.

Karlgren, Bernhard. 1950. *The Book of Odes: Chinese Text, Transcription and Translation*. Stockholm: Museum of Far Eastern Antiquities.

Lao Xiaoyu (fl. 1736). 1936. *Chunqiu shihua* 春秋詩話 (Poetic remarks on the *Springs and Autumns*). Shanghai: Shanghai wu yin.

Legge, James. [1893–1895] 1991. *The Shoo King or The Book of Historical Documents* 尚書. The Chinese Classics, vol. 3. Reprint. Taipei: SMC Publishing.

Lewis, Mark Edward. 1999. *Writing and Authority in Early China*. Albany: SUNY Press.

Li Fang 李昉 (925–996), comp. 1960. *Taiping yu lan* 太平御覽 (Imperial digest of the Taiping era). Beijing: Zhonghua.

———. 1986. *Taiping guangji* 太平廣記 (Vast gleanings of the Taiping era). Beijing: Zhonghua.

Liu Fu 劉斧 (11th century). 1987. *Qingsuo gaoyi* 青瑣高議 (Lofty debates under the green window). Beijing: Zhongguo shudian.

Liu Yiqing 劉義慶 (403–444). 1993. *Shishuo xinyu jianshu* 世説新語箋疏 (*Topical Tales: A New Edition* with notes and commentary). Annotated by Liu Jun 劉峻 (462–521) and Yu Jiaxi 余嘉錫. Shanghai: Shanghai guji.

———. 2002. *Shih-shuo hsin-yü: A New Account of Tales of the World*. Second edition. Translated by Richard B. Mather. Ann Arbor: Center for Chinese Studies.

Liu Yuxi 劉禹錫 (772–842). 1994. *Liu Mengde wenji* 劉夢得文集 (Collected works of Liu Mengde [Yuxi]). Shanghai: Shanghai guji.

Lu Ji 陸機 (261–303). 1984. *Wen fu* 文賦 (Poetic exposition on literature). Annotated by Zhang Shaokang 張少康. Shanghai: Shanghai guji.

Lu Qinli 逯欽立. 1983. *Xian Qin Han Wei Jin Nanbei chao shi* 先秦漢魏晉南北朝詩 (Poems of the Pre-Qin, Han, Wei, Jin, and Northern and Southern Dynasties). Beijing: Zhonghua.

Lynn, Richard John, trans. 1994. *The Classic of Changes: A New Translation of the* I Ching *as Interpreted by Wang Pi*. New York: Columbia University Press.

Makaryk, Irena R. 1993. *Encyclopedia of Contemporary Literary Theory: Approaches, Scholars, Terms*. Toronto: University of Toronto Press.

Mao Jin 毛晉 (1599–1659), comp. 1628–1644. *Jindai mishu* 津逮秘書 (Secret book of Jindai). 748 *juan* in 71 vols. Mao shi Ji gu ge.

McMullen, David. 1988. *State and Scholars in T'ang China*. New York: Cambridge University Press.

Nietzsche, Friedrich. 1969. *On the Genealogy of Morals*. Translated by W. Kaufmann and R. J. Hollingdale. New York: Vintage Books.

Ouyang Xiu 歐陽修 (1007–1072), comp. 1975. *Xin Tang shu* 新唐書 (A new history of the Tang). 20 vols. Beijing: Zhonghua.

Owen, Stephen. 1977. *Poetry of the Early T'ang*. New Haven: Yale University Press.

———. 1992. *Readings in Chinese Literary Thought*. Cambridge, Mass.: Harvard University Press.

———. 1996. *An Anthology of Chinese Literature: Beginnings to 1911*. New York: Norton.

———. 1996. *End of the Chinese "Middle Ages": Essays in Mid-Tang Literary Culture*. Stanford: Stanford University Press.

Plaks, Andrew H. 1977. "Towards a Critical Theory of Chinese Narrative." In *Chinese Narrative: Critical and Theoretical Essays*, edited by Andrew H. Plaks, pp. 309–52. Princeton: Princeton University Press.

Qian Nanxiu. 2001. *Spirit and Self in Medieval China: The* Shih-Shuo Hsin-Yü *and Its Legacy*. Honolulu: University of Hawai'i Press.

Qu Yuan 屈原 (340–278 B.C.E.) et al. 1980. *Chu ci xin zhu* 楚辭新注 (A new annotation of *Lyrics of Chu*). Annotated by Nie Shiqiao 聶石樵. Shanghai: Shanghai guji.

Peng Dingqiu 彭定求 (1645–1719) et al., eds. [1707] 1960. *Quan Tang shi* 全唐詩 (Complete Tang poems). Beijing: Zhonghua.

Récanati, François. 1979. *La Transparence et l'énonciation*. Paris: Seuil.

Rouzer, Paul. 2001. *Articulated Ladies: Gender and the Male Community in Early Chinese Texts*. Cambridge, Mass.: Harvard University Asia Center.

Ruan Yuan 阮元 (1764–1849), comp. 1980. *Shisan jing zhushu* 十三經注疏 (Annotations and commentaries on the Thirteen Classics). 2 vols. Beijing: Zhonghua.

Ruan Yue 阮閱 (fl. 1085), comp. 1987. *Shihua zonggui* 詩話總龜 (Complete compendium of remarks on poetry). Beijing: Renmin wenxue.

Sargent, Stuart H., trans. 1982. "Understanding History: The Narration of Events, by Liu Chih-chi." In *The Translation of Things Past: Chinese History and Historiography*, edited by George Kai, pp. 27–33. Hong Kong: Chinese University Press.

Saussy, Haun. 1993. *The Problem of a Chinese Aesthetic*. Stanford: Stanford University Press.

Schaberg, David. 2001. *A Patterned Past: Form and Thought in Early Chinese Historiography*. Cambridge, Mass.: Harvard University Asia Center.

Sima Guang 司馬光 (1019–86). 1997. *Zizhi tongjian fu kaoyi* 資治通鑑附考異 (*Comprehensive Mirror for Aid in Government* with variants attached). Compiled by Wu Guoyi 鄔國義. Shanghai: Shanghai guji.

Sima Qian 司馬遷 (c. 145–86 B.C.E.). 1964. *Shi ji* 史記 (Historical records). 10 vols. Annotated by Pei Yin 裴駰 (fl. 438). Beijing: Zhonghua.

Suzuki Shūji 鈴木修次. 1967. *Kan Gi shi no kenkyū* 漢魏詩の研究 (A study of Han and Wei poetry). Tokyo: n.p.

Tam, Koo-yin. 1975. "The Use of Poetry in *Tso Chuan*: An Analysis of the 'fu-shih' Practice." Ph.D. dissertation, University of Washington. Photocopy of typescript. Ann Arbor: University Microfilms.

Tōdō Akiyasu 藤堂明保, comp., and Takeda Akira 竹田晃, trans. 1983–84. *Sesetsu shingo* 世説新語 (*Topical Tales: A New Edition*). 2 vols. Tokyo: Gakushu Kenkyusha.

Tuotuo 脱脱 (1313–1355) et al. 1985. *Song shi* 宋史 (A history of the Song). 40 vols. Beijing: Zhonghua.

Tyler, Royall, ed. and trans. 1987. *Japanese Tales*. New York: Pantheon Books.

Uchiyama Chinari 内山知也. 1977. *Zui Tō shōsetsu kenkyū* 隋唐小説研究 (A study of Sui and Tang fiction). Tokyo: Mokujisha.

Van Zoeren, Steven. 1991. *Poetry and Personality: Reading, Exegesis, and Hermeneutics in Traditional China*. Stanford: Stanford University Press.

Waley, Arthur, trans. [1937] 1988. *The Book of Songs: The Ancient Chinese Classic of Poetry*. Reprint, with foreword by Stephen Owen. New York: Grove Weidenfeld.

Wang Dingbao 王定保 (870–ca. 954). 1922. *Tang zhiyan* 唐摭言 (Gleanings from the Tang). Shanghai: Shangwu.

Wang Meng'ou 王夢鷗. 1974. *Tangren xiaoshuo yanjiu san ji* 唐人小説研究三集 (Studies on the *xiaoshuo* of the Tang people, vol. 3). Taipei: Yiwen.

Wang Shizhen 王士禛 (1634–1711). 1988. *Gufu yu ting zalu* 古夫于亭雜錄 (Various notes by an antiquated man in his pavilion). Annotated by Zhao Botao 趙伯陶. Beijing: Zhonghua.

Wang Xianqian 王先謙, ed. 1987. *Zhuangzi jijie* 莊子集解 (Variorum edition of *Zhuangzi*). Beijing: Zhonghua.

Watson, Burton. 1958. *Ssu-ma Ch'ien: Historian of China*. New York: Columbia University Press.

——, trans. 1989. *The* Tso Chuan: *Selections from China's Oldest Narrative History*. New York: Columbia University Press.

Wei Shou 魏收 (506–572). 1974. *Wei shu* 魏書 (History of the Wei). 5 vols. Beijing: Zhonghua.

Wilhelm, Hellmut, trans. 1967. *The I Ching or Book of Changes*. 3d ed. Rendered into English by Cary F. Baynes. Princeton: Princeton University Press.

Wu, Laura Hua. 1995. "From *Xiaoshuo* to Fiction: Hu Yinglin's Genre Study of *Xiaoshuo*." *Harvard Journal of Asiatic Studies* 55, no. 2, pp. 339–71.

Yan Kejun 嚴可均 (1762–1843). 1958. *Quan shanggu san dai Qin Han Sanguo Liuchao wen* 全上古三代秦漢三國六朝文 (Complete prose of high antiquity, the Three Dynasties, Qin, Han, Three Kingdoms, and Six Dynasties). Beijing: Zhonghua.

Yang Bojun 楊伯峻, ed. 1990. *Chunqiu Zuozhuan zhu* 春秋左傳注 (Commentary on the *Springs and Autumns* and *Zuo Tradition*). Rev. ed. Beijing: Zhonghua.

Yang Shuda 楊樹達. 1984. *Han shu kuiguan* 漢書窺管 (A limited view of the *Han History*). Reprint. Shanghai.

Yang Xiangshi 楊向時. 1972. *Zuo zhuan fushi yinshi kao* 左傳賦詩引詩考 (A study of poetry offering and poetry citation in the *Zuo Tradition*). Taipei: Zhonghua.

Yim, Sarah M. 1979. "Structure, Theme, and Narrator in Tang *Ch'uan-ch'i*." Ph.D. dissertation, Yale University. Photocopy of typescript. Ann Arbor: University Microfilms.

Yoshikawa Kōjirō 吉川幸次郎. 1954. "Kō Yu no 'Gaikako' ni tsuite" 項羽 の垓下歌について (On Xiang Yu's "Song of Gaixia"). *Chūgoku bungaku hō* 中國文學報 1: 1–18.

———. 1955. "Kan no Kōzo no Taifūko ni tsuite" 漢の高祖の大風歌につい て (On Han emperor Gaozu's "The Great Wind" song). *Chūgoku bungaku hō* 中國文學報 2: 28–44.

Yu, Pauline. 1987. *The Reading of Imagery in the Chinese Poetic Tradition*. Princeton: Princeton University Press.

Zeng Qinliang 曾勤良. 1993. *Zuo zhuan yinshi fushi zhi shijiao yanjiu* 左傳引 詩賦詩之詩教研究 (A study of the poetics of poetry citation and poetry offering in the *Zuo Tradition*). Taipei: Wenjin.

Zeng Yongyi 曾永義. 1980. *Shuo su wenxue* 説俗文學 (A discussion of popular literature). Taipei: Lianjing.

Zeng Zao 曾慥 (1091–1155), comp. 1996. *Leishuo* 類説 (Classified works). Fuzhou: Fujian renmin.

Zhang Hua 張華 (232–300). 1939. *Bowu zhi* 博物志 (Account of wide-ranging matters). Changsha: Shangwu.

Zheng Xuan 鄭玄 (127–200). *Mao shi Zheng jian* 毛詩鄭箋 (Zheng's annotation of the Mao *Poems*). Included in Ruan Yuan.

Zhongguo congshu zonglu 中國叢書總錄 (General catalogue of Chinese collectanea). 1959–1962. 3 vols. Shanghai: Zhonghua.

Zhongguo gudai xiaoshuo baike quanshu 中國古代小説百科全書. 1993. Beijing.

Zhu Guanhua 朱冠華. 1992. *Fengshi xu yu Zuo zhuan shishi guanxi zhi yanjiu* 風詩序與左傳史實關係之研究 (A study of the relationship between the prefaces to the "Airs [of the States]" and the historical data of the *Zuo Tradition*). Taipei: Wenshizhe.

Zhu Ziqing 朱自清. 1956. *Shi yan zhi bian* 詩言志辨 (An analysis of [the precept] "poetry articulates intent"). Beijing: Guji.

Žižek, Slavoj. 1989. *The Sublime Object of Ideology*. London: Verso.

Index

admonition (*feng*), 173–74, 190–91, 218. *See also* remonstration
aestheticization, 98, 99, 276
aesthetic sense, 147, 153, 155; Xie An and, 136, 141, 143
Amusing Stories of the Sui and Tang (Sui Tang jiahua), 161
Analects (Confucius), 171, 172–73, 192, 199, 200, 225; on poetic incompetence, 33; Traditionalists and, 22*n*6, 24–26, 151
anecdotal collections, *see Storied Poems*
Anthology of Literature (Wen xuan), 169
appreciation, 143–44, 146, 148, 153, 237
Aristotelian literary theory, 80
audience, 106, 144, 178, 213, 264; competence of, 209; emotional investment of, 259, 273; emperor as, 101–2, 208, 211, 223, 236–38, 245; judgment of, 155; power

figure as, 262; reception of, 44, 85; ritual reenactment and, 30, 31, 54; stand-up comedy and, 50; in *Storied Poems*, 194, 233–34; sympathy of, 89, 93, 101–2, 176, 226; Traditionalists and, 22, 24
authority, 50, 58, 66, 69, 272–73. *See also* power
authority figure, 205, 226, 229; protection of, 214–15; romance poetry and, 257, 259, 262, 271. *See also* emperor

Bai Juyi, 242–44, 245, 247–48; "Willow Branch," 242–43; Yuan Zhen and, 250–52
Ban Gu, 73, 106, 166; *Poetic Expositions on the Two Capitals*, 147. *See also Han History*
banquet songs, 32, 33, 43
Bao Xi (Fu Xi), 165
barbarians, campaigns against, 123, 124–25

benshi (based on events), 183–84
Benshi shi, see *Storied Poems*
biography, 106, 107, 109
bizarre accounts (*zhiguai*), 164, 166, 194–97, 200
Bourdieu, Pierre, 139
"Bo zhou," 129–31
Buddhists, 212, 229

cai, see talent
Campany, Robert, 162
canonical texts, 141, 199
Cao Cao, 117, 133–34; "I May Be Old," 133–34
Cao Pi, 113–19, 132, 144; *Authoritative Discourses,* 114; "Grand," 118n12
Cao Zhi, 113–21, 132, 237; literary genius of, 115, 117; "Seven Steps Poem," 114, 115–16, 117, 119–21, 134
categories, in anthologies, 185–89
Categorized Collection of Literary Works, A (*Yiwen leiju*, Ouyang Xun), 206
Ceremonies and Rituals (*Yili*), 32
Chang'e (moon goddess), 263, 264, 275
Chao Gongwu: *A Record of Books Read in Prefect Studio,* 158
Chen, Princess, 262–65
Chen dynasty, fall of, 13
Chen Qi, 200
children, 121–23, 140–41; ill treatment of, 220–22; word play and, 136–37
Chong'er, Prince of Jin, story of, 34–49, 53; cultural incompetence in, 35, 36–38, 43–44; poetic exchange in, 37–45; ritual protocol

in, 31–33, 41, 42–43; Zhao Cui's role in, 34–38, 42–45, 48
Chu ci, 83, 143, 171, 173
Chu Mei, 56, 66
Chunqiu, 16, 21, 72, 165–66, 184
Chusheng meter, 83–84, 99
Chu song, of Liu Bang, 82–84, 86
Ci Liushi jiuwen, 182
citation, irony in, 123, 125, 131. *See also under* Poems
civil man (*wenren*), *see* cultured man
civil service exams, *see* examination system
clans, competition among, 111, 112
Classic of Changes (*Yi jing*), 28, 30, 139, 166, 177–78
Classic of Documents (*Shu jing*), 16, 31n20, 78, 108, 165, 179; "Canon of Shun," 70–71; citation of, 30; encoded guidelines in, 28–29
Classic of Poetry (*Shi jing*): *Storied Poems* and, 180, 190, 192, 193, 198, 199. *See also Commentary on the Mao Poems*; "Great Preface"; *Poems*
closure, sense of, 50, 87, 154
Collected Works of Liu Mengde (*Liu Mengde wenji*), 234
Collecting Mr. Liu's Stories of the Past (*Ci Liushi jiuwen*), 182
Collection of Emperor Wu (*Wudi ji*), 175
commentary, 13, 49–50
Commentary on the Mao Poems (*Maoshi jian*), 191, 192
competence, 22, 52. *See also* cultural competence; poetic competence
Complete Tang Poems (*Quan Tang shi*), 203

composition of poetry, 69, 107, 134–35, 144, 252; merit in, 238; written, 16, 29*n*17, 93, 205. *See also* poetic production

composition-performance disjunction, 93–94

comprehensive knowledge, 200–201

concubines, *see* palace concubines

Confucian mores, 186, 199. *See also* moral didacticism

Confucius, 45*n*39, 81, 166, 181; *Spring and Autumn Annals,* 16, 21, 72, 165–66, 184; on patterned language, 222, 259; as Traditionalist, 15–16*n*1, 27. *See also* *Analects* (Confucius)

connoisseur, 149, 150, 281

context, 177, 234, 235; social, 3, 6, 9; trancontextual forces and, 8–9; of utterance, 2–3, 5, 8–10

conversation, art of, 135, 144, 183, 186

court, 220; cultural competence at, 26–27; hierarchy at, 18–19, 20, 52; manners at, 36; music of, 244; performance at, 29–31, 52; poetic competence at, 204, 205–6, 245; poetic protest at, 217–19; speechmaking at, 51–52. *See also* emperor; palace concubines/ ladies

Cui Riyong, 218–20

cultural competence, 11, 44, 72, 135, 136, 144–47; citation and, 67–68; moral worth and, 119; performance and, 144, 146, 155–56; power of, 112, 120–21, 132; in Prince Chong'er story, 35, 36–38,

43–44; of Traditionalists, 19, 23–27, 29, 125, 133, 280. *See also* poetic competence

cultural context, 3, 10

cultured man (*wenren*), 12, 21, 132, 142, 144, 208–9; military (*wu*) and, 19, 208, 212, 228. *See also* Traditionalists

"Cypress-Wood Boat" ("Bo zhou"), 129–31

"Dafeng ge," *see* "The Great Wind"

Dai Kui, 151, 153, 155

Dan, Prince of Yan, 102–4

Daoist parable, 27

Daoist priests, 232

Da Tang chuanzai, 182

"Da xu," *see* "Great Preface"

Da xue, 175

death and despair, 104–5. *See also* suicide

Dezong (Tang emperor), 271

Ding Lingwei, 246

diplomacy, 19, 31–33, 46, 50, 279

discourse, 54, 276, 282; literary talent in, 208; marked, 30; object of, 256; power of, 277; proper operation of, 220; as transcontextual force, 8; utterance and, 2, 3, 7

Documents, see Classic of Documents

dramatic unity, 80

dream, 4

drunken poet, 239, 241, 255–56

Du Fu, 230, 239, 248–50

Du Mu, 254–56

Duan Chengshi, 161, 166

Eastern Zhou, 10, 11, 14, 32, 46, 111; Traditionalists in, 15, 19, 20, 28, 37

"elegant words," 172, 174–75

elite (ruling) class, 112, 158, 159, 203, 244; art of conversation and, 135, 186; émigré aristocracy, 113; improvisational skills of, 135, 136–37, 140; literary talent and, 204; Traditionalist, 19, 20. *See also* literate class; official class

elite knowledge, 125, 136, 137, 140. *See also* Traditional knowledge

emotion/feelings, 13, 79, 103, 143, 145, 167–70; audience and, 259, 273; chain reaction of, 222–23; impulse (*xing*), 41, 151, 152–54, 155; intent and, 168–69, 197–98; outburst song and, 98–99, 101, 171–72; in performance, 74, 75, 76–77, 85; poetic offering and, 33; poetic power and, 178; poetry as response to, 234, 244, 261; state of mind and, 107, 108; stimulus-response model and, 175–76; stolen love and, 269. *See also specific emotions*

emperor, 244; as audience, 101–2, 208, 211, 223, 236–38, 245. *See also* court; imperial power; *and specific emperors by name*

examination system, 157, 168, 218, 229–31, 247, 248

explicit comment, 49–50

"exquisite lines," 141, 172, 174–75

fahui (manifestation of power), 177–78

family ties, 147–48, 208

Fan Shu, 165–66; *Friendly Debates at Misty Brook*, 161, 181, 261; *Xunxi*, 166

feelings, *see* emotion/feelings

feng, see admonition

Feng Zhi, 181, 202

folk song (*yuefu*), 133–34, 187–88

Forest of Conversations (*Yu lin*), 145

frustration, venting of, 87, 89, 119, 193; outburst song and, 11, 81, 84, 92, 98, 224–25

"Gaixia ge," *see* "Song of Gaixia"

Gao Lishi, 183

Gao Yun: *Wei History*, 200

"gathering poems" doctrine, 180–81

gentlemanly conduct, 22. *See also* cultured man

ghost-mother's poem, 221–23, 259

gift giving, 273

Golden Age, 20, 22, 23

Gongyang Commentary (*Gongyang zhuan*), 197

"Great Preface" ("Da xu," to *Classic of Poetry*), 13, 72, 158, 193, 218, 222, 277; cited in *Storied Poems*, 167–75 *passim*, 179, 184–85

Great Learning (*Da xue*), 175

"Great Wind, The" ("Dafeng ge," Liu Bang), 75–78, 85, 86, 93–94

Green Pearl (servant girl), 266n82, 267

Gu Kaizhi, 135, 138, 150

Gu Kuang, 260

Guo Pu, 145, 146

Guo Zhaojun, 104, 105

"Gushi shijiu shou," 261

Han dynasty, 11, 14, 108, 192, 270; disunion following, 109, 112, 185, 200

Han History (Han shu), 10, 12, 98, 166, 194; clan competition in, 111, 112; Empress Lü's cruelty and, 91, 92; "gathering poems" doctrine in, 180; imperial power in, 120; narrative frame and, 106, 109; performance in, 280–81; on ruling class, 113; on Xiang Yu and Liu Bang, 73, 78, 82; *Zuo Tradition* in, 183–84. *See also under* outburst song

Han Huang, Duke of Jin, 161, 270–74, 277

Hanlin Academy, 161, 239

Han shu, see *Han History*

Han Ying: *Supplementary Commentary on the Han School Poems,* 187

Han Yu, 189, 222; *An Explication of Advancing in Studies,* 190; "The Tale of Xuanyuan Miming," 252–54

He Zhizhang, 239

Hearsay Noted from the Great Tang Dynasty (Da Tang chuanzai), 182

heart, discourse of, 131, 281. *See also* romance

hermeneutic skills, 136, 192. *See also* Traditional knowledge

heterogeneity, 160, 201

hierarchy, 132, 138, 157; at court, 18–19, 20, 52; political, 37, 203, 241, 255; of power, 41, 271–72

historical context, 3, 10

historical fact, 164

historical narrative, 92, 106–8, 184

Historical Records (Shi ji), 11, 80–81, 154

historiography, 16, 162, 163

Hu Yan, 34–35, 36–37, 42–43, 44, 48

Hu Yinglin, 159, 195–96; *Collected Notes from the "Humble Abode" Mountain Retreat,* 195

Huai Ying, 35, 36

Huan Wen, 135

Huan Xuan, 133, 138

Huan Yin, 145

Huangfu Mi, 146, 147, 148, 149

Huarong, Lady, 102, 104

Hui (Han emperor), 87, 88

Hui, King of Liang, 133

Hui, Prince of Zhao, 92–93, 94

Huizi, 39–40*n*35

human swine, Lady Qi as, 88, 89–90

humiliation, 211, 216, 217

humility, 43, 44–45, 58

humor, 126, 127, 138, 150; puns, 211, 246; stand-up comedy, 50. *See also* wit

imperial power, 111, 112, 114, 116–19, 281; symbolic power and, 116, 117–18, 120. *See also* court; emperor

impotence, 81, 109, 149. *See also* powerlessness

improvisation, 26, 27*n*12, 115, 118, 139–40; "word chain" game, 135–38. *See also* spontaneous performance

impulse (*xing*), 41, 151, 152–54, 155

incest taboo, 59–60

innovation, 120, 160, 188

inscribed objects, 3

instrumental accompaniment, 84

intent, 71–72, 108, 196; feeling and, 168–69, 197–98
interiority, 47, 130–31, 198, 269; outburst song and, 11–12, 79
interpretation, 54, 69–70
intertextuality, 8, 59, 162
interval (*jian*), 9. *See also* time frane
irony, 193, 226; in citations, 123, 125, 127, 131

Ji Yougong: *Recorded Stories of Tang Poetry,* 189
Ji Yun, 160
Jia Dao, 230–31
jian, see interval; time frame
Jifu, 45, 48
Jin dynasty, 41, 43, 62, 112
jokes, *see* humor; wit
judgment, imperial, 237–38

Kang Sengyuan, 138–39, 144
Kong Yingda, 167–69, 174, 178; *Standard Meaning of the Mao Poems,* 167
Kui (music director), 70–71

Lao Xiaoyu, 69
"Lesser Preface(s)" ("Xiao xu"), 48, 158, 189, 190–93, 198, 215, 235, 244–45
Li Bai, 238–44, 248–50, 256
Li Deyu, 161–62, 163–64, 182; *Notes on Traveling in Zhou and Qin,* 169
Li Fengji, 274–77
Li Jun, 163–64; *Miscellaneous Records of Pine View Studio,* 162, 182, 197
Li Kang, 161

Li Linfu, 223–26
Li Shizhi, 223–26
Li Yuan, 254–56
Li Zhangwu, 229–30
lianju, see "linked verses"
Ling, Duke of Jin, 55–59, 62, 63, 65–67
"linked verses" (game), 252–54
Li sao, 83
literary arena, 256–57
literary gatherings, 250, 252, 268, 270
literary heritage, 177
literary judgment, 237–38
literary production, 114–15, 203; talent in, 120, 137; theory of, 80–81. *See also* poetry production
literary reputation, 12, 144, 146, 148, 149, 204, 229
literary talent, *see* talent
literate class, 13, 181, 201, 281
Liu Bang, 73, 81–87, 89, 112, 118n13; "The Great Wind," 75–78, 85, 86, 93–94; "The Wild Swan," 82–85, 86
Liu clan, 83, 182
Liu Fu: *Lofty Discussions Under the Green Willow,* 261
Liu Gong jiahua lu, 182
Liu Jun, 112, 126, 145, 153
Liu Mengde wenji, 234
Liu Su, 161, 196n63
Liu Xiang, 186, 187, 188; *Biographies of Virtuous Women,* 185
Liu Yiqing, 12, 112. *See also Topical Tales*
"Liu yue," *see* "Sixth Month"
Liu Yuxi, 231–35; "Given to All the Fine Gentlemen Viewing

Flowers," 231–32, 234; "Immortal Peach Trees," 232–35
Liu Zhiji, 161
locutionary act, 7–8
"Look at the Rat" ("Xiang shu"), 51
loss of face, 273. *See also* humiliation
love stories, 203, 243–44. *See also* "stolen love" stories
Lu Ji, 144, 169
Lu Zhao, 162
Lü, Han Empress, 82, 84, 86–93; Prince You and, 90–92; torture of Lady Qi by, 87–90
Lü clan, 90, 91–92
Lunyu, see *Analects*
Lupu Gui, 59–60
Lynn, Richard, 177
lyricism, 173
Lyrics of Chu (*Chu ci*), 83, 143, 171, 173

manifestation, 190, 193, 198, 215; of power (*fahui*), 177–78
Mao prefaces ("Maoshi xu"), to *Poems*, 27n13, 28, 125, 140, 215, 235, 244
Maoshi jian, 191, 192
"Maoshi xu," *see* Mao prefaces
martial (*wu*) and civil (*wen*) men, 19, 208, 212, 228
master-slave relations, 127–31, 132
Mather, Richard, 134, 186
mediocrità, 26
Mencius, 19, 21, 45n39, 177
Mencius, 21, 169, 223
Meng Qi, 13, 187. *See also Storied Poems*
Mengzi, see *Mencius*
meter, 83–84

military tactics, 22–23. *See also* martial; warfare
mind, theory of, 39–40, 43. *See also* state of mind
Miscellaneous Offerings from Youyang (*Youyang zazu*), 161–62, 166
Miscellaneous Records of Cloud-Dwelling Immortals (*Yunxian zaji*), 181, 202
moral didacticism, 142–43, 149
moral worth, 119, 131, 226
morality, 185–86, 199, 238; Confucian, 186, 192, 199
Mu, Duke of Qin, 35–40 *passim*, 43–48 *passim*, 53. *See also* Chong'er, Prince of Jin
"Mulian bian" (Song of Mulian), 247, 248
"Multitudes," 63–65
musical performance, 69, 70–71, 84, 169, 244; ritual and, 32–33. *See also* performance

narrative, 7, 85, 110, 148, 154–55; as context for poems, 77–78, 177, 193–94; historical, 92, 106–8, 184; performance and, 6–7, 78, 86, 102, 103, 104, 217; poem-bearing, 5, 9; repetition in, 17–18; veracity of, 164, 196
"Nineteen Old Poems" ("Gushi shijiu shou"), 261
Niu Sengru: *Record of the Mysterious and Weird*, 162

official class, 181, 183, 193, 232, 244; anecdotal collections by, 161–62, 181, 194; as audience, 234; authenticity and, 280; court hierarchy and, 18–19; judging merit in, 219; poetic competence and, 157, 254; romance poetry and, 257; speechmaking by, 51–52, 65. *See also* Traditionalists

oral performance, 175. *See also* performance

oral transmission, 1, 154, 182–83

outburst song, 224–25; in *Han History*, 79–81, 112, 217, 280; of Lady Qi, 88–89, 101; of Liu Bang, 84, 86; passion and, 171–72; Prince Qu's perversion of, 98–99; of Prince You, 90–92, 101; of Princess Xijun, 99–102; sorrow and, 77, 93, 96, 102, 104, 106; suffering and, 81, 98, 99, 101, 218; tripartite form of, 100–101; venting of frustration in, 11, 81, 84, 92, 98, 119, 224–25; of Wang Huizi, 151, 152. *See also* Liu Bang; Xiang Yu

Ouyang Xiu: *New Tang History*, 159, 164

Ouyang Xun, 206–9

Owen, Stephen, 169

ownership, 156

palace concubines/ladies, 101, 102–3, 104; singing girls, 239–41, 242, 254–55, 257, 265–67, 270–73; stolen love and, 262–67, 270–73, 274; torture and death of, 94–99

"Pan shui," 123

Pan Yue, 144

passionate feeling, 171–72, 229; in performance, 74, 75, 76–77, 85, 172. *See also* emotion/feelings; romance

past-present perspective, 20, 21, 67–68

patterned culture, 21, 27. *See also* cultural competence

patterned language, 168, 169, 214, 215, 218; Confucius on, 222, 259

Pei Du, 230–31

Pei Yan, 212–14

performance, 107, 109, 111, 140, 213; appreciation of, 143–44, 146, 237; audience and, 85, 89, 93, 101–2, 106, 144; captured in writing, 175; composition and, 93–94; context of, 2; mode of, 52, 84; musical, 32–33, 69, 70–71, 84, 169, 244; narrative frame and, 6–7, 78, 86, 102, 103, 104, 217; ownership of, 156; passion in, 74, 75, 76–77, 85, 172; poetic competence and, 13, 49, 157–58, 209, 211, 279, 282; politics and, 213–14, 280–81; of Prince Dan, 102–4; of Prince Qu's concubines, 95–99; public, 155; repertoire and, 279; as source of power, 120; spontaneous, 14, 49, 76–77, 84, 85, 107, 119, 265; staged, 76–77, 85, 274; strategy of, 86, 94, 101, 102, 108, 274; suasive effect of, 108–9; Traditionalists and, 19, 24, 27; variables of, 209. *See also* musical performance

perlocutionary act, 7–8

person, unity of, 80, 94

Ping, King of Zhou, 170, 171

play, 126, 155

poem fragments, 189

Poems, 11, 21, 28, 78, 184; citation from, 26, 111, 119–20, 121, 130, 140–42; Confucian tradition and,

33, 151–52, 192, 193, 199; cultural
competence and, 24–26; intent
in, 72, 108; interpretation of,
69–70; Mao prefaces to, 27*n*13,
28, 125, 140, 215, 235, 244; mean-
ing of, 211; "No Use," 128;
original meanings of, 69–70; on
outburst song, 79–80, 81; re-
monstrance from, 55–56, 58–59,
60, 67, 68; Sima Qian on, 171,
225; in speechmaking, 30, 52–54;
"Swelling Waters," 37–38, 41, 43;
tetrasyllabic forms in, 24, 52,
83–84; Traditionalists and, 47, 49,
126, 131, 279. *See also Classic of
Poetry*
"Poems of My Heart" ("Yong huai
shi"), 133
poetic competence, 53, 72, 113,
119–43, 156, 238; aesthetic sense
and, 136, 141, 143; Confucius on,
33; at court, 29–31, 204, 205–6,
245; display of, 158, 212, 248–50,
254–55, 281; elite knowledge and,
125, 136, 137; examinations for,
229–30, 231; explicit comment
and, 49–50; flexibility in, 142;
improvisation and, 135, 139–40;
intent and, 71–72; master-slave
relations and, 127–31, 132; narra-
tive and, 6, 12; performance and,
13, 49, 157–58, 209, 211, 279, 282;
in Prince Chong'er story, 35,
36–38, 42–44, 46; self-referential,
241, 250, 256–57; simultaneous
composition and, 252; in
speechmaking, 62; in *Storied
Poems*, 10, 13–14, 164, 172, 199,
203, 278; in *Topical Tales*, 10, 12,
113, 121–23, 126–27, 132, 133, 137,

204, 236, 250, 281; in utterance,
14, 16, 42, 47; word-chain game,
135–38; *Zuo Tradition* and, 10, 11,
16, 24, 33, 203–4, 236, 270, 279,
280. *See also* talent
poetic exchange/offering, 47–49,
50, 53, 59; at court, 206–8;
male-female, 204; in Prince
Chong'er story, 37–44; ritual
protocol in, 31–33, 41, 42–43, 46,
49
*Poetic Exposition on Literature
(Wen fu)*, 169
poetic performance, *see* perform-
ance
poetic praxis, 72, 164
poetic production, 6, 13, 119, 170,
229, 248; in literary arena,
256–57; strategy of, 273; theory
of, 109–10. *See also* composition
poetic utterance, *see* utterance
poetry: definition of, 78, 167;
power of, 265, 267–68, 281, 282;
shi poetry, 4–5, 165, 166, 278, 282
poetry for poetry's sake, 238
political factions, 112, 214
political hierarchy, 37, 203, 241, 255
political power, 28, 149, 154, 238, 257,
272. *See also* imperial power
political sphere, 157, 256. *See also*
court; official class
politics, 203–4, 235–36, 280–81. *See
also* diplomacy
popular taste, 146
power: competition for, 111–12, 123;
at court, 18, 19, 37, 208; in cul-
tural capital, 72; expressive, 198;
hierarchy of, 41, 271–72; mani-
festation of (*fahui*), 177–78; in
master-slave relations, 128; of

poetry, 265, 267–68, 281, 282; political, 28, 149, 154, 238, 257, 272; symbolic, 43, 116, 117–18, 120–21, 128, 132, 272; in written word, 205; of *Zuo Tradition*, 16. *See also* imperial power; suasive power

power figures, 259, 262. *See also* authority figures

powerlessness, 11, 87, 92. *See also* impotence

practical sense, 140

production, *see* composition; poetic production

propaganda, 92, 115

protest poems, 217–18, 235, 276. *See also* remonstration

public discourse, 151, 154

Qi, Lady, 82, 84–90 *passim*; as human swine, 88, 89–90; outburst song of, 88–89

Qiao Zhizhi, 265–67, 271

Qilin Hall, 207

Qin dynasty, 41, 48, 68, 73

Qing Feng, 50–51, 126

Qu, Prince of Guangchuan, 94–99, 101

Quan Tang shi, 203

reader, 178. *See also* audience

Recording the Events of Tang Poems (*Tangshi jishi*), 159

Record of Fine Conversations with His Honor Liu, A (*Liu Gong jiahua lu*) 182

"remarks on poetry," 159, 188

remonstration (*jian*), 54–67, 218–19; admonition (*feng*), 173–74, 190–91, 218; of Duke Ling, 55–59,

62, 63, 65–67; "Grand" cited in, 59, 60–62; "Multitudes" cited in, 63–65; by Shi Ji, 55–56, 57–59, 60–67; by Zhang Jiuling, 225–26

reputation, 12, 156, 231. *See also* literary reputation

resentment, 170–71

rhetorical gesture, 13, 65

rhetorical resource, 28, 31, 54, 68, 108. *See also* speechmaking

ritual: offering, 59–60; protocol in, 27, 31–33, 41, 42–43, 49; reenactment, 29–31, 43, 46, 53–54, 68; in song performance, 106

romance, 204, 257. *See also* "stolen love" stories

Rong Ai, 95–96, 99

Rong Yu, 270–74

Ruan Fu, 145

Ruan Ji, 133

Rujia, see Traditionalists

rulers: officials and, 18–19, 37; remonstration of, 54–59. *See also* court; *specific rulers by name*

ruling class, *See* elite (ruling) class; official class

Ruyi, Prince of Zhao, 88, 89

sadness: separation and, 171

Saussy, Haun, 27n13, 192

scholars (*oratores*), 19. *See also* Traditionalists

self-consciousness, 107

self-deprecation, 36

self-pity, 94

self-presentation, 85. *See also* performance

self-referentiality, 241, 250, 256–57

self-representation, 239, 282

"Semicircular Waters" ("Pan shui"), 123

sexual love, 204, 282*n1*. *See also* romance

shamanistic ritual, 144

shame, 116, 119. *See also* humiliation

Shang-Yin dynasty, 60–61, 62

Shen Quanqi, 217–18

Shen Yue, 175, 248

Shi, see *Classic of Poetry; Poems*

Shi ji. see *Historical Records*

Shi Ji, remonstration by, 55–56, 57–59, 60–67

Shi jing, see *Classic of Poetry*

shi poetry, 4–5, 165, 166, 278, 282

shi yan zhi, 70, 71

shihua, see "remarks on poetry"

shihua genre, 159, 188

Shishuo xinyu, see *Topical Tales: A New Edition*

Shu jing, see *Classic of Documents*

Shun (emperor), 70

Sima Daozi, 124, 125–26

Sima Guang: *Comprehensive Mirror for Aid in Government*, 161

Sima Qian, 106, 109, 224–25; "Grand Historian's Account of Himself," 80, 171; *Historical Records*, 11, 80–81, 154; "Letter in Reply to Ren An," 80

Sima Zhenzhi, Prince of Liang, 133

singing girls, 239–41, 242, 254–55, 257; stolen love and, 265–67, 270–73, 274

Six Dynasties era, 10, 12, 112, 162, 195, 236, 238

"Sixth Month" ("Liu yue"), 38–39, 44, 48

slave girls, 254–55

slave-master relationship, 127–31, 132

"Small Carriages" ("Xiao rong"), 124

snow imagery, 136–37, 141, 152, 153

social competence, 140, 204

social context, 3, 6, 9

social engagement, 14

social status, 259. *See also* hierarchy

"Son of Heaven," 45, 48, 65

song, canonical definition of, 78. *See also* outburst song

Song, Duke of, 22

Song dynasty, 159

"Song of Gaixia" ("Gaixia ge"), 73–78, 84–85, 101, 103–4

"Song of Mulian" ("Mulian bian"), 247, 248

song performance, *see* performance

Song Zhiwen: "The Milky Way," 215–17

sorrow, 145, 229, 268; song and, 77, 96, 102, 104, 106

Southern Dynasties, 14, 112, 157, 249, 281

speaking subject, 3, 4, 7, 8. *See also* narrative

speech, 17, 19

speechmaking, citation in, 29–30, 51–68; remonstration, 54–67, 190–91

spirit (*qi*), 217

spontaneous performance, 14, 84, 107, 265; staged performance compared, 76–77, 85; suasive power in, 49, 119. *See also* outburst song

sprezzatura, 26, 135. *See also* spontaneous performance

Spring and Autumn Annals
(*Chunqiu*), 16, 21, 72, 165–66, 184
stand-up comedy, 50
state of mind, 41–42, 102, 104, 235,
261; of audience, 244; emotion
and, 107, 108, 169; theory of
mind and, 39–40, 43
"stolen love" stories, 262–77; loss
of equilibrium and, 264–65;
palace ladies and, 262–67,
270–73, 274; Rong Yu, 270–74;
separation of lovers, 204, 227–28,
248, 257–61, 268–70; woman as
"literary" object in, 267, 269; Xu
Deyan, 262–65, 267, 268;
Yaoniang, 265–67, 271
Storied Poems (*Benshi shi*), 158–202,
236, 244; audience in, 194, 233–34;
bizarre tales (*zhiguai*) in, 164,
166, 194–97, 200; categories in,
158–59, 185–89; examination
story in, 230–31; gathering doc-
trine, 180–81; "Great Preface"
cited in, 167–68, 170, 171, 173–75,
179, 184–85; innovation in, 160,
188; on intent, 167–69, 196,
197–98; "Lesser Prefaces" and, 48,
158, 189, 190–93, 198, 215, 235,
244–45; Li Bai anecdotes in,
238–44, 248–50, 256; Li Linfu
anecdotes in, 223–26; literary
criticism in, 165, 189; oral lit-
erature and, 181–83; poetic
competence in, 10, 13, 164, 172,
199, 203, 277, 279; poetic ex-
changes in, 209; preface to, 12–13,
14, 160, 164–65, 179, 198–202, 244,
277; protest poems in, 235; ro-
mance in, 204, 259, 262; search
for truth in, 163–64, 179, 184, 196;

Tang court and, 205–6; wider
audience for, 233–34; wit in, 245,
250; as work-in-progress, 201
strange tales, *see* bizarre accounts
(*zhiguai*)
Su Weidao, 245–46
suasive power, 9, 11, 152, 220, 277,
278; of music, 70; in perform-
ance, 108–9; spontaneity and, 49,
119
suffering, 262; outburst song and,
81, 98, 99, 101, 218
Sui Tang jiahua, 161
suicide, 75, 93, 265; of Chu Mei, 56,
66; of Green Pearl, 266n82, 267;
of Prince Xu, 104, 105, 106
Sun Chuo, 144
Sun Fang, 121–23, 132
symbolic code, 19
symbolic power, 43, 117–18, 128, 132;
physical violence and, 116,
120–21, 272
sympathetic response, 89, 93, 101–2,
148, 176, 226

Taiping guangji, 158
Taizong (Tang emperor), 206,
207–8, 215
talent (*cai*), 187, 204, 208, 215, 230;
acknowledgment of, 217; ap-
preciation of, 237; audience
sympathy and, 226; display of,
245, 254; political hierarchy and,
241; self-referential competence
and, 250; wit and, 238, 281. *See
also* poetic competence
Tang dynasty, 14, 157, 162, 174, 181,
204; court of, 205–6, 211, 215;
elite literati of, 13, 158, 203, 281;
love narratives, 257; poetic

power in, 282. *See also Storied Poems*

Tangshi jishi, 159

Tao Qian, 224, 256

Tao Wangqing, 94–95, 98

tetrasyllabic meter, 24, 52, 83–84

texts, 1–2, 3

time frame, 104; interval (*jian*), 9; unity of, 80, 94

Topical Tales: A New Edition (Shishuo xinyu), 152, 155, 270; audience in, 209; Cao Zhi anecdote in, 113–21; categories in, 186–87, 188; compilers of, 148; cultural competence in, 112–13, 132, 144–45, 147, 156; performance in, 217; poetic competence in, 10, 12, 113, 121–23, 126–27, 132, 133, 137, 204, 236, 250, 281; preface to, 165; "Speech and Conversation," 135–36; stolen love in, 266n82, 267; "Taunting and Teasing," 138–39, 188; welling up of feelings in, 176

Traditionalists, 11, 15–72, 16, 210, 280; *Analects* and, 22n6, 24–26, 151; Confucius as, 15–16n1, 27; cultural competence of, 19, 23–27, 29, 125, 133; *Poems* and, 279; remonstration and, 54–67; ritual reenactment and, 29–31. *See also Zuo Tradition*

Traditional knowledge, 18, 28, 126, 131, 152; cultural competence and, 35, 37, 280; Golden Age and, 20–21; speechmaking and, 29, 30, 31, 52

trancontextual forces, 8–9

transcendent ecstasy, 144

transtextuality, 4

"Treatise on Literature" ("Yiwen zhi"), 78, 81

truth, search for, 163–64, 179, 184, 196

urban myth, 164

utterance, 2–10, 107, 187, 282; context of, 2–3, 5, 8–10; as locutionary act, 7–8; musical quality of, 167; narrative framework and, 17, 193; performance and, 6–7; poetic competence and, 14, 16, 42, 47; reception and, 281; speaking subject and, 3, 4, 7, 8

values, 20–21. *See also* morality

Van Zoeren, Steven, 24n8, 193

Vast Gleanings of the Taiping Era (Taiping guangji), 158

veracity, 163–64, 196. *See also* truth, search for

violence, 114, 119, 132; in clan competition, 111, 112; symbolic *vs.* physical, 116, 120–21, 272. *See also* suicide; warfare

voice, 67–68; as aesthetic object, 98; in speechmaking, 62; unity of, 80, 94

Wang Bi, 177

Wang Dao, 138–39

Wang Dun, 133–34

Wang Gong, 145

Wang Huizhi, 143–44, 150–51, 152–56

Wang Ji, 145

Wang Rong, 176

Wang Wei, 268–70

Wang Xianqian: *Zhuangzi jijie*, 3–4, 27, 39–40n35

warfare, 22–23, 84–85; martial and
    civil men, 19, 208, 212, 228
Wei, Tang empress, 213, 214, 215
Wei clan, 214
Wei dynasty, 112, 200
Wei Xuan, 161; *A Record of Fine
    Conversations with Adviser to
    the Heir Apparent Liu*, 162
Wei Xun, 194
wen, see cultured men
Wen, King of Zhou, 55, 60–62
Wen (Wei emperor), 113–19
Wen fu, 169
Wen xuan, 169
Western Han, 10
Western Zhou, 16, 20–21, 28, 41, 46
wise counsel, 18
wit, 14, 126, 139, 156, 195; friendship
    and, 245–47, 248, 250, 251–52;
    talent and, 238, 281. *See also*
    humor
women: as "literary" object, 267,
    269; slave-master relations,
    127–31; stories of exemplary, 185.
    See also palace concubines/ladies
"word chain" (*yuci*), 135–38
written composition, 16, 29n17, 93,
    205. *See also* composition of
    poetry
Wu, Duke of Wei, 142
Wu, King of Zhou, 179
Wu Chengsi, 265–66, 267
Wu (emperor), 81, 175
Wu Ying: *Explanation of Ancient
    Topics in Yuefu Poetry*, 187
Wu Yizong, 209–12
Wu Zetian (Tang empress), 209–12,
    215–17, 220
Wudi ji, 175

Wusun barbarians, 99–100, 101
Wuzong (Tang emperor), 243

Xi, Marquis of Lu, 123
Xi Gui, 268n85
Xian, Prince of Ning, 268–69
Xiang, Duke of Qin, 59, 124, 125
"Xiang shu," 51
Xiang Yu, 112, 118n13; "Song of
    Gaixia," 73–78, 84–85, 101, 103–4
"Xiao rong," 124
Xiao Tong, 169
Xiao Wu (Liu Song emperor),
    236–38
"Xiao xu," *see* "Lesser Preface(s)"
Xiaoman (singing girl), 242, 243
Xie An, 140, 141–43, 147, 148, 149;
    word chain game and, 136–37
Xie Lang, 136
Xie Lingyun, 123–24
Xie Xuan, 140, 141–43
Xie Zhan, 150
Xie Zhong, 124–26, 132
Xie Zhuang, 236–38
Xijun, imperial princess, 99–102
xing, *see* impulse
Xu, Prince of Guangling, 104–6
Xu Deyan, 262–65, 267, 268
Xuan, Duke, 55
Xuan, King, 41, 45, 48, 65
Xuanyuan Miming, 252–54
Xuanzong (Tang emperor), 163,
    183–84, 220–23, 225, 239–43;
    separated lovers and, 258–59

Yan Yanzhi, 236–38
Yang Fu: "Ode to Snow," 145
Yang Su, Duke of Yue, 262–65, 272,
    277

Yang Xiong, 194
Yao, sage-king, 224
Yaoniang, 265–67, 271
Yi jing, see *Classic of Changes*
Yin Zhongkan, 138
Yiwen leiju, 206
"Yiwen zhi," 78, 81
"Yong huai shi," 133
You, Prince of Zhao: "Captivity Song," 90–92, 101
Youyang zazu, 161–62, 166
Yu, Pauline, 192
Yu Chan, 147, 148
Yu Liang, 121–23, 147–48, 149
Yuan Zhen, 250–52; "Story of Yingying," 282*n*1
yuci, see "word chain"
yuefu (folk song), 133–34, 187–88
Yu lin, 145
Yunxian zaji, 181, 202

Zhai Zhong, 192; "I pray you, Zhongzi," 190–91
Zhang (Tang general), 220–22
Zhang Changling: "Viewing Lanterns," 245–46
Zhang Hu, 247–48
Zhang Hua, 146, 147, 149; *Account of Wide-Ranging Matters,* 216*n*18
Zhang Jiuling: "Ocean Swallow," 225–26
Zhang Liang, 82
Zhang Yuanyi, 209–12
Zhangsun Wuji, 206–8
Zhao Cui, 34–38, 42–45, 48
Zhao Dun, 55, 56, 57, 66
Zhao Feiyan, 240*n*43, 241
Zhao Meng, 71–72
Zhao Wei, 163

Zhaoxin, 94–99
"Zheng min," 63–65
Zheng Qi: *A Record of Credible Accounts . . . ,* 194
Zheng Xuan, 125, 126; master-slave relations and, 127–29, 130–31; *Zheng's Annotation of the Mao Poems,* 125, 126
zhiguai, see bizarre accounts
Zhong Shanfu, 63–65
Zhongzong (Tang emperor), 212–14, 217–19, 220
Zhou Chang, 88
Zhou dynasty, 68, 108, 111, 123. *See also* Eastern Zhou; Western Zhou
Zhu Tao, 226–29
Zhu Xi, 190
Zhuang, Duke of Zheng, 191
Zhuangzi, 3–4, 27, 39–40*n*35
Zigong, 25–26
Zixia, 166
Zuo Qiuming, 184
Zuo Si, 148, 149; *Poetic Expositions on the Three Capitals,* 146, 147; "Summoning the Recluse," 151, 152–53, 155
Zuo Tradition (Zuo zhuan), 12, 31–68, 113, 152, 268*n*85, 281; admonition poems in, 67, 191–92, 218; audience competence in, 209; citations from *Poems* in, 59, 69, 108, 111, 119, 126; Confucius in, 222; cultural competence and, 24, 27, 36–37, 280; in *Han History,* 183–84; parody in, 211; performance in, 217; poetic competence and, 10, 11, 16, 24, 33, 119–20, 203–4, 236, 270, 279, 280;

poetic intent in, 71–72, 168–69; Prince Chong'er story, 34–49; protest poetry in, 277; protocol offerings in, 27, 31–33, 41, 42–43, 49; ritual reenactment in, 29–31, 43, 46, 53–54, 68; speechmaking in, 51–68; *Storied Poems* and, 165; "Taunting and Teasing," 123–24. *See also* Traditionalists

Harvard-Yenching Institute Monograph Series
(titles now in print)

11. Han shi wai chuan: *Han Ying's Illustrations of the Didactic Application of the* Classic of Songs, translated and annotated by James Robert Hightower

21. *The Chinese Short Story: Studies in Dating, Authorship, and Composition,* by Patrick Hanan

22. *Songs of Flying Dragons: A Critical Reading,* by Peter H. Lee

24. *Population, Disease, and Land in Early Japan, 645–900,* by William Wayne Farris

25. *Shikitei Sanba and the Comic Tradition in Edo Fiction,* by Robert W. Leutner

26. *Washing Silk: The Life and Selected Poetry of Wei Chuang (834?–910),* by Robin D. S. Yates

27. *National Polity and Local Power: The Transformation of Late Imperial China,* by Min Tu-ki

28. *Tang Transformation Texts: A Study of the Buddhist Contribution to the Rise of Vernacular Fiction and Drama in China,* by Victor H. Mair

29. *Mongolian Rule in China: Local Administration in the Yuan Dynasty,* by Elizabeth Endicott-West

30. *Readings in Chinese Literary Thought,* by Stephen Owen

31. *Remembering Paradise: Nativism and Nostalgia in Eighteenth-Century Japan,* by Peter Nosco

32. *Taxing Heaven's Storehouse: Horses, Bureaucrats, and the Destruction of the Sichuan Tea Industry, 1074–1224,* by Paul J. Smith

33. *Escape from the Wasteland: Romanticism and Realism in the Fiction of Mishima Yukio and Oe Kenzaburo,* by Susan J. Napier

34. *Inside a Service Trade: Studies in Contemporary Chinese Prose,* by Rudolf G. Wagner

35. *The Willow in Autumn: Ryūtei Tanehiko, 1783–1842,* by Andrew Lawrence Markus

36. *The Confucian Transformation of Korea: A Study of Society and Ideology,* by Martina Deuchler

37. *The Korean Singer of Tales,* by Marshall R. Pihl

38. *Praying for Power: Buddhism and the Formation of Gentry Society in Late-Ming China,* by Timothy Brook

39. *Word, Image, and Deed in the Life of Su Shi*, by Ronald C. Egan

40. *The Chinese Virago: A Literary Theme*, by Yenna Wu

41. *Studies in the Comic Spirit in Modern Japanese Fiction*, by Joel R. Cohn

42. *Wind Against the Mountain: The Crisis of Politics and Culture in Thirteenth-Century China*, by Richard L. Davis

43. *Powerful Relations: Kinship, Status, and the State in Sung China (960–1279)*, by Beverly Bossler

44. *Limited Views: Essays on Ideas and Letters*, by Qian Zhongshu; selected and translated by Ronald Egan

45. *Sugar and Society in China: Peasants, Technology, and the World Market*, by Sucheta Mazumdar

46. *Chinese History: A Manual*, by Endymion Wilkinson

47. *Studies in Chinese Poetry*, by James R. Hightower and Florence Chia-Ying Yeh

48. *Crazy Ji: Chinese Religion and Popular Literature*, by Meir Shahar

49. *Precious Volumes: An Introduction to Chinese Sectarian Scriptures from the Sixteenth and Seventeenth Centuries*, by Daniel L. Overmyer

50. *Poetry and Painting in Song China: The Subtle Art of Dissent*, by Alfreda Murck

51. *Evil and/or/as the Good: Omnicentrism, Intersubjectivity, and Value Paradox in Tiantai Buddhist Thought*, by Brook Ziporyn

52. *Chinese History: A Manual, Revised and Enlarged Edition*, by Endymion Wilkinson

53. *Articulated Ladies: Gender and the Male Community in Early Chinese Texts*, by Paul Rouzer

55. *Allegories of Desire: Esoteric Literary Commentaries of Medieval Japan*, by Susan Blakeley Klein

56. *Printing for Profit: The Commercial Publishers of Jianyang, Fujian (11th–17th Centuries)*, by Lucille Chia

57. *To Become a God: Cosmology, Sacrifice, and Self-Divinization in Early China*, by Michael J. Puett

58. *Writing and Materiality in China: Essays in Honor of Patrick Hanan*, edited by Judith T. Zeitlin and Lydia H. Liu

59. *Rulin waishi and Cultural Transformation in Late Imperial China*, by Shang Wei

60. *Words Well Put: Visions of Poetic Competence in the Chinese Tradition*, by Graham Sanders